Fletcher's Essays on Criminal Law

Fletcher's Essays on Criminal Law

EDITED BY RUSSELL L. CHRISTOPHER

OXFORD
UNIVERSITY PRESS

OXFORD

UNIVERSITY PRESS

Oxford University Press is a department of the University of Oxford.
It furthers the University's objective of excellence in research, scholarship,
and education by publishing worldwide.

Oxford   New York
Auckland   Cape Town   Dar es Salaam   Hong Kong   Karachi
Kuala Lumpur   Madrid   Melbourne   Mexico City   Nairobi
New Delhi   Shanghai   Taipei   Toronto

With offices in
Argentina   Austria   Brazil   Chile   Czech Republic   France   Greece
Guatemala   Hungary   Italy   Japan   Poland   Portugal   Singapore
South Korea   Switzerland   Thailand   Turkey   Ukraine   Vietnam

Oxford is a registered trademark of Oxford University Press
in the UK and certain other countries.

Published in the United States of America by
Oxford University Press
198 Madison Avenue, New York, NY 10016

Library of Congress Cataloging-in-Publication Data
Fletcher, George P.
Fletcher's essays on criminal law / edited by Russell L. Christopher.
    p. cm.
Includes bibliographical references and index.
ISBN 978-0-19-994123-0
1. Criminal law.   2. Criminal justice, Administration of.   I. Christopher, Russell L.   II. Title.
III. Title: Essays on criminal law.
K5018.F55 2013
345—dc23
2012010471

ISBN 978-0-19-994123-0

9 8 7 6 5 4 3 2 1
Printed in the United States of America
on acid-free paper

In memory of my father, Dr. Albert Christopher, who passed away on April 3, 2012. His zest for life and learning has been my abiding inspiration.

ACKNOWLEDGMENTS

The following essays that appear in this volume were previously published: George P. Fletcher, *The Nature and Function of Criminal Theory*, 88 CALIFORNIA LAW REVIEW 687 (2000); George P. Fletcher, *What Is Punishment Imposed For?* 5 JOURNAL OF CONTEMPORARY LEGAL ISSUES 101 (1994); George P. Fletcher, *Punishment and Compensation*, 14 CREIGHTON LAW REVIEW 691 (1982); George P. Fletcher, *The Fault of Not Knowing*, 3 THEORETICAL INQUIRIES IN LAW 265 (2002); George P. Fletcher, *Mistake in the Model Penal Code: A False False Problem*, 19 RUTGERS-CAMDEN LAW REVIEW 649 (1987–88); George P. Fletcher, *Individualization of Excusing Conditions*, 47 SOUTHERN CALIFORNIA LAW REVIEW 1269 (1974); George P. Fletcher, *The Right and the Reasonable*, 98 HARVARD LAW REVIEW 949 (1985); George P. Fletcher, *The Nature of Justification*, in ACTION AND VALUE IN CRIMINAL LAW (S. Shute, J. Gardner, and J. Horder eds., Oxford University Press 1993); George P. Fletcher, *The Psychotic Aggressor—A Generation Later*, 27 ISRAEL LAW REVIEW 227 (1993); George P. Fletcher, *Domination in the Theory of Justification and Excuse*, 57 UNIVERSITY OF PITTSBURGH LAW REVIEW 553 (1996); George P. Fletcher, *Blackmail: The Paradigmatic Crime*, 141 UNIVERSITY OF PENNSYLVANIA LAW REVIEW 1617 (1993); George P. Fletcher, *Justice and Fairness in the Protection of Crime Victims*, 9 LEWIS & CLARK LAW REVIEW 547 (2005).

I gratefully thank the numerous people without whom this volume would not have been completed. Cyndee Jones, Sharon Miller, and Barbette Veit supplied expert administrative assistance in preparing the manuscript. Caroline Lukaszewski provided superb proofreading of an early version of the entire manuscript. The project received generous support from a University of Tulsa College of Law Research Grant. The editorial team at Oxford University Press—Caelyn Cobb, Susan Ecklund, David McBride, Peter Mavrikis, Cynthia Read, and Amy Whitmer—greatly improved the volume and made it the best that it could be. (Any errors are, of course, my own.)

CONTENTS

PART II   ■   **MENS REA AND MISTAKE**

PART III   ■   **JUSTIFICATION AND EXCUSE**

LIST OF CONTRIBUTORS

Larry Alexander is Warren Distinguished Professor of Law, University of San Diego School of Law.

Russell L. Christopher is Professor of Law, The University of Tulsa College of Law.

Joshua Dressler is Frank R. Strong Chair in Law, Michael E. Moritz College of Law, The Ohio State University.

Susan R. Estrich is Robert Kingsley Professor of Law and Political Science, University of Southern California Law School.

Kimberly Kessler Ferzan is Professor of Law, Rutgers University School of Law, Camden.

George P. Fletcher is Cardozo Professor of Jurisprudence, Columbia University School of Law.

John Gardner is Professor of Jurisprudence and Fellow of University College, University of Oxford.

Alon Harel is Philip P. Mizock and Estelle Mizock Chair in administrative and criminal law, Hebrew University Law Faculty, Jerusalem, Israel.

Kyron Huigens is Professor of Law, Yeshiva University, Benjamin N. Cardozo School of Law.

Heidi M. Hurd is David C. Baum Professor of Law and Philosophy, University of Illinois.

Douglas Husak is Distinguished Professor of Law and Philosophy, Rutgers University.

Judge John T. Noonan Jr. is Judge, U.S. Court of Appeals, Ninth Circuit; Professor Emeritus, University of California, Berkeley School of Law.

Victoria Nourse is Professor of Law, Georgetown University Law Center.

Stephen J. Schulhofer is Robert B. McKay Professor of Law, New York University.

Alan Wertheimer is Senior Research Scholar, Department of Bioethics, National Institutes of Health.

Peter Westen is Professor Emeritus, University of Michigan School of Law.

Fletcher's Essays on Criminal Law

INTRODUCTION AND OVERVIEW

CHAPTER 1

Introduction

◼

Russell L. Christopher*

Had George Fletcher never penned a single word beyond his magisterial *Rethinking Criminal Law* in 1978, his reputation as perhaps the foremost criminal law scholar in the world would be assured. Hailed as "the most important book in the English language about the philosophy of criminal law written in the past century,"[1] *Rethinking* is still the most cited book on criminal law and one of the most cited books on law, period. *Rethinking* has been the focus of several symposia and countless analyses.

Equally important, but comparatively overlooked, are Fletcher's essays on criminal law. Though Fletcher has written more than fifty major articles on criminal law spanning more than six decades, they have neither been the focus of a symposia nor been collected in a volume—until now. It is in these essays, all but one written after the publication of *Rethinking*, that Fletcher hones and polishes the themes of *Rethinking* as well as advances new arguments and breaks new ground. They are critical in understanding the evolution of his views on criminal law.

This volume is the first to focus exclusively on Fletcher's essays on criminal law. Though not a comprehensive collection, it includes twelve selected essays. The essays selected include many of Fletcher's most famous and important articles as well as some that are less well known but equally rich and interesting. The topics of the essays range widely: punishment, mens rea, mistake, justification, excuse, self-defense, necessity, duress, construing criminal conduct as a form of domination, the specific crime of blackmail, the protection of crime victims, as well as the very status and purpose of theoretical criminal law scholarship. Reflecting this diversity, there are essays from each of the last four decades. The essays were originally published in leading student-edited law reviews, peer-reviewed journals, and foreign journals and as book chapters. They appear much as they originally did, with only two of the essays edited for length.

* Professor of Law, The University of Tulsa College of Law.

This volume is unusual in three respects. First, it contains not only Fletcher's essays but also critical commentaries by leading criminal law scholars, philosophers, and an appellate judge. Each of Fletcher's twelve essays is followed by a critical assessment of its current relevance. Second, though the selected essays are representative of Fletcher's singularly distinguished career, the selection process is atypical. Neither Fletcher nor the editor nor the publisher selected the essays. Selection was done by the scholars critiquing the essays. As a result, the selection itself provides an interesting comment on the breadth, scope, and continuing vitality of Fletcher's corpus of work in the theory of criminal law. It supplies insight into the aspects of Fletcher's scholarship that still inspire, motivate, challenge, draw admiration, and induce sharp disagreement. Third, concluding the volume is a new essay by Fletcher in which he replies to the critical commentaries and reflects on his career as a criminal theorist.

Not surprisingly, the area occupying the bulk of the commentators' attention is the justification/excuse distinction. Five of the twelve essays address aspects of the distinction. These essays are presented in chronological order of original publication so as to afford a view of the evolution in Fletcher's thought. Fletcher has long been credited, and these commentators continue to extend that credit, with resurrecting the justification/excuse distinction. Lauded for prophetically "crying in the wilderness,"[2] Fletcher, in essay after essay, demonstrated the significance and importance of the distinction. He showed us the analytical richness of a criminal law embracing the distinction and the impoverishment of a criminal law denying it. But while Fletcher enjoys near-universal acclaim for focusing our attention on it, the details and contours of the distinction have wrought near-universal disagreement. Scholars, including those in this volume, find no shortage of aspects of the distinction with which to disagree with Fletcher as well as with each other. And even to the extent that Fletcher's critics agree with him, they often find that he is right for the wrong reason.

But Fletcher's true legacy might well be that even when his specific doctrinal conclusion is wrong, he is wrong for the right methodological reason. That is, Fletcher's lasting influence might not be his specific positions on doctrinal issues but the methods and modes of argumentation by which he has transformed criminal law scholarship. Fletcher favors the philosophical over the empirical and psychological, the normative over the positive, the deontological over the teleological, and principle over policy. By favoring cosmopolitanism over provincialism, Fletcher is credited with practically inventing the field of comparative criminal law. Not content to stand pat with this new field of comparative criminal law, Fletcher upped the ante by fusing it with the linguistic analysis of Wittgenstein and H. L. A. Hart. Blessed with fluency in innumerable languages, Fletcher not only critically compares the substantive doctrines of disparate legal cultures but also plumbs, for insight and understanding, the very words that different languages use to express those doctrines. In the opening words of one of his most famous articles, "The Right and the Reasonable," Fletcher lays down the challenge: "We lawyers should listen to the way we talk [in different languages]."

Fletcher also favors argument from reason over argument from authority. In one of his essays in this volume he declares that philosophy is about great ideas, not great philosophers. In his concluding essay to this volume, Fletcher reminisces that at the start of his career he was the rebel outsider railing against the establishment figures of criminal law. It cannot be understated that this is no longer the case. Now that Fletcher has ascended to the status of an authority, one might expect that he might feel conflicted about his original views on reason over authority, great ideas over great thinkers. But, if anything, one senses in Fletcher that the conflict runs the other way. One senses his nostalgia for an earlier time when *only* reason was his ally.

In his Nobel Prize acceptance speech, William Faulkner remarked that the only thing worth writing about was "the human heart in conflict with itself." Such internal conflict may be at the heart of criminal theory. As Fletcher's first essay in this volume notes, criminal theory truly came alive in the conflict between Jeremy Bentham's utilitarianism and Immanuel Kant's and Georg W. F. Hegel's retributivism. If the true spirit and function of this enterprise of criminal theory is dialectical—thesis and antithesis clashing to reach a synthesis—the form of this volume follows suit. Each of Fletcher's twelve essays is followed by a critical comment. And following each of these twelve pairs of contrasting views is Fletcher's critical reply to his critics. Whether Fletcher's reply essay reaches a true and lasting synthesis is open to question. Perhaps the most that can be hoped for is a tentative and transitory reflective equilibrium at which only the reader and future generations of criminal theoreticians will arrive.

Bertrand Russell once said of Ludwig Wittgenstein, after Wittgenstein supplied a particularly withering critique of Russell's argument: "I couldn't understand his objection—in fact he was very inarticulate—but I feel in my bones that he must be right." In contrast, neither Fletcher nor any of his critics is inarticulate; and clearly, neither feels in his or her bones that the other is right. Each pair of essay and corresponding critical reply suggests a quarrel. But while there are pointed words and sharp disagreement, there is no Wittgenstein chasing Karl Popper with a fireplace implement. This volume spawns no mythic tale of Fletcher's Poker. If each pair of essay and corresponding critical reply suggests a quarrel, it is, as many of the critical replies attest, a lover's quarrel.

What follows is a brief summary of the twelve selected articles and their critical replies, followed by a brief comment on Fletcher's closing essay replying to his critics.

Introduction and Overview

In his aptly named essay "The Nature and Function of Criminal Theory," Fletcher seeks to describe and explain the curious enterprise of theoretical criminal law. He situates it in the intersection of positivist law and philosophy.

Though Fletcher dates the philosophical roots of this enterprise as far back as Aquinas and Aristotle, philosophical methodology truly bears fruit for criminal law in the clash between Kantian retributivism and Benthamite utilitarianism. Why philosophy? Fletcher answers that criminal theory is more a humanist inquiry than a social science; it is not an empirical endeavor.

The task of the criminal theoretician is both to articulate the intuitions that underlie widely accepted features or doctrines of criminal law and to support them with convincing argument. Likening the criminal theoretician to a religious scholar, both must interpret authoritative, but parochial or indigenous, sources or texts and by applying reason draw out universal principles that might have persuasive force to all.

But what if source, text, or practice conflicts with theory and reason? This occurs in two different ways. First, the authoritative sources, traditional doctrines, or widespread practices may be seriously wrong or violate other principles of criminal law. For example, the felony murder rule is deeply entrenched in America, despite its violation of both the culpability requirement and the presumption of innocence. Second, a widely accepted theoretical position may be seriously wrong in its opposition to a nearly universal feature of criminal law systems. For example, perhaps a substantial majority of scholars wrongly opposes the widely accepted doctrine of punishing completed offenses more severely than attempts.

In addressing these conflicts, the criminal theoretician faces a crisis of method. First, the use of intuitions to resolve the conflicts is problematic because we are unsure as to whose intuitions should be dispositive—the average person on the street or lawyers/judges or a scholar such as Michael Moore. Additionally, one's intuitions might conflict. For example, Fletcher suggests that one might hold both of the following seemingly conflicting intuitions: (1) the consequences of an actor's conduct should be irrelevant as to the punishment of an actor, and (2) punishing as felony murder the robber who accidentally kills. Second, a comparative law analysis that a doctrine or practice is not merely embedded in one legal system but many or most legal systems worldwide may provide some support. But this method is flawed because worldwide trends or widespread practices may be as wrong as they are right. For Fletcher, the parochial view of the United States favoring felony murder and capital punishment in the face of worldwide opposition suggests that the U.S. position is wrong. But impossible attempt liability is wrong despite the widespread support it enjoys throughout the world's legal systems. Third, in addition to legal authority, the philosophical authority of, for example, a Kant or Aristotle might be invoked. But "philosophy is not the history of philosophy." While we may grant Kant or Aristotle the honor of the first word in the debate, we should not grant them the last. In addition, philosophical argument may be misused by lawyers. For example, Fletcher demonstrates how Kant's views have been misread as supporting the irrelevance of the consequences of our actions in determining our punishment. Fourth, "strict logical argument" might be utilized, but "strict logical arguments are rare in the literature." Fletcher concludes that the criminal theoretician's methods are a hodgepodge of intuition, case law, philosophical references, and policy arguments.

In addition to the competing, contributing perspectives of law and philosophy, criminal theory also "defines an intersection between moral and political philosophy." Individual guilt and punishment is the domain of moral philosophy while collective guilt and state punishment is the domain of political philosophy. While considerable attention has been paid to the debate between retributivism and deterrence as the preferable justification for punishment, the logically prior question of political philosophy—"What makes it legitimate for the state to make people suffer?" under either or any justification of punishment—receives comparatively short shrift. Fletcher defends two propositions emanating from his political theory. First, the criminal law should be act-based not actor-based. But liability for impossible attempts and enhanced punishment under "three strikes and you're out" legislation punish not for conduct but rather because of the dangerousness of the actor. Second, the criminal law should serve as the remedy of last resort for wrongful harms. But this principle conflicts with retributivism's view that the state has an absolute duty to punish all those who deserve it.

For Fletcher, the function of criminal theory "is to probe the basic concepts that bear on legal analysis, order these concepts in some kind of structure, and elaborate the values and principles that lie behind the structure of liability. That is, the theorist takes the details of the criminal law as more or less given and tries to elicit from these details some synthetic principles." An example is the maxim formulated by Lord Coke that "'the act is not criminal unless the mind is criminal.'" This is not a philosophical truth of reason but rather has become a recognized truth about the law that has become a constituent element of law as authoritative as any case or legislation. Fletcher himself offers ten such synthetic claims of criminal law. These principles differ from Ronald Dworkin's famous ethical maxims like "'no one should profit from his own wrong.'" Rather, they derive "from theoretical reflection and generalization from the concrete instantiations of the principle." Fletcher stresses that Americans should join Europeans and Asians as recognizing that such principles derived from theoretical reflection may enjoy the same binding status as case law and legislation. Theoretical commentary should be a primary source of law.

But even Fletcher questions what it might mean for these principles to be sources of law. What happens if these principles conflict with the conventional sources of primary authority? Fletcher answers that they are not refuted because "their appeal and their binding force are a function both of the extent to which they are realized in practice and of their intrinsic moral and logical appeal." But then, on that basis, are cases and statutes invalidated by a conflict with these principles?

In Kyron Huigens's reply, "On 'The Nature and Function of Criminal Theory,'" Huigens addresses the precise nature of the criminal law's obligation to conform to these principles. Huigens expresses surprise that Fletcher does not helpfully invoke Kant's account of the law which stresses that law has a necessary and universal content based on "inherent, universal features of human reasoning." Moreover, Huigens finds that Fletcher describes the normativity of criminal theory in terms inconsistent with Kant. Whereas Fletcher explains that criminal theory involves generalization from particulars, a Kantian account would proceed from the universal to the particular. Huigens concludes that after reading Fletcher's essay, "one is virtually certain to be at a loss to know what the nature and function of criminal law theory might be." Huigens attributes this loss to Fletcher not invoking "the legal theory that most clearly satisfies the need he describes."

Punishment

In "What Is Punishment Imposed For?" Fletcher poses a deceptively simple but rarely asked question. Fletcher interprets it as posing neither of the traditional questions of punishment: What qualifies as punishment and what is the justification of punishment? In tort law it is clear for what compensation is paid—for the injury suffered by the victim. Although the answer is less clear for punishment than it is for compensation, both are only for something that has already happened. While compensation may be paid or punishment inflicted "for the sake of" some forward-looking goal like deterrence, compensation may be paid and punishment inflicted only "for" some "untoward state of affairs" that has already happened. The preposition "for" presupposes a backward perspective because both compensation and punishment are remedies. But while it is clear that compensation is meant to remedy the injury, it is not so clear what punishment is meant to remedy.

Fletcher considers four possibilities. First, punishment is imposed as compensation for the crime victim's injury just as tort law affords compensation for the tort victim's injury. But if both are compensation then a victim should not be able to be compensated twice—once in criminal law and once in tort—for the same injury (as the law does allow). Another difference is that in tort law the degree of liability does not determine the degree of damages; in criminal law the degree of liability is a factor in the degree of punishment. Second, punishment is imposed for the act of wrongdoing—"the unjustified violation of a statutory norm." This view finds support in one of H. L. A. Hart's elements of the definition of punishment: "'punishment must be for an offense against legal rules.'" Third, punishment is imposed for culpability alone. The view finds support in the punishment of impossible attempts. The difficulty of both the second and third possible views, however, is that each ignores the other: inflicting punishment for wrongdoing ignores the role of culpability, and inflicting punishment for culpability alone ignores the role of wrongdoing. Robert Nozick's formula of deserved punishment (deserved punishment = wrongdoing multiplied by the actor's responsibility) suggests that neither factor alone can be what punishment is imposed for. And fourth, punishment is imposed for "the dominance the criminal acquires over his victim." Fletcher rejects the fourth possibility because the criminal deserves punishment based on what he or she has done, not on the advantages acquired, and because this fourth possibility cannot generate the fine gradations of deserved punishment that Nozick's formula affords. So, influenced by Nozick's formula of deserved punishment, Fletcher seemingly concludes that punishment is imposed "for wrongdoing as reduced by the extent to which culpability is diminished."

In Douglas Husak's reply, "The Importance of Asking the Right Question: What Is Punishment Imposed For?" Husak observes that Fletcher's question is as provocative as it is infrequently raised. Husak notes that while the question seems straightforward, it admits of three possibilities. First, the question supplies an alternative framing of the much-discussed issue of what justifies punishment. Husak believes that the question, interpreted this way, can be answered either retributively or consequentially. Second, the question asks, "What is it about crime that allows us to punish it?" Of the three core components of criminality—wrongdoing, culpability, and harm—Husak concludes that wrongdoing is the most significant. Strict liability and inchoate crimes demonstrate that culpability and harm, respectively, are dispensable. Husak rejects the possibility that *mala prohibita* offenses reveal wrongdoing to be dispensable. Still unanswered, according to Husak, is "what it is *about* wrongdoing that merits punishment." Third, the question may address the debate between choice and character models of criminal responsibility.

Husak finds Fletcher's question to be most fruitful in its second interpretation, which suggests the primacy of wrongdoing. "An account of why some wrongs concern the state, and why this concern should take the form of punishing those who perpetrate these wrongs, may reveal whether and why consequences are relevant to the justification of penal sanctions." By reframing our basic questions about punishment in a novel way, Fletcher's question "may help us to gain insights about some of the fundamental issues in criminal theory that have bedeviled philosophers for centuries."

In "Punishment and Compensation," Fletcher illuminatingly compares and contrasts punishment and compensation through the vehicle of providing a conceptual account of compensation in the same mode as philosophical accounts of punishment. Fletcher's inquiry is not the purpose of punishment and compensation. That results in making an explicit moral choice between deontological and utilitarian theories. Rather, by inquiring into the conceptual nature of punishment and compensation, their intrinsic deontological component is revealed. Fletcher distinguishes between intrinsic and extrinsic perspectives. The intrinsic perspective focuses on whether the punishment "rectif[ies] the public imbalance generated by the defendant's wrongdoing" and whether the compensation "rectif[ies] the private imbalance generated by the defendant's causing harm." The extrinsic perspective focuses on the impact that punishment or compensation has, if any, on future behavior. Fletcher criticizes the extrinsic perspective for blurring important distinctions between sanctions that may have the same impact. For example, from the extrinsic perspective it is difficult to distinguish the following: punishment versus civil commitment; the defendant's payment of compensation to the victim versus payment of a fine to the state; and the plaintiff's receipt of compensation versus receipt of incentive payments, welfare, or relief.

Fletcher explores two parallels between punishment and compensation. First, what is the requisite relationship between the person or entity performing the punishing and the wrongdoer being punished? Not all suffering inflicted against a wrongdoer qualifies as punishment. For example, when consumers stage an economic boycott of a corporation's products or one country boycotts another country's Olympic Games as a way of protesting their practices, an extrinsic perspective would view these as punishments. But from an intrinsic perspective, these boycotts do not qualify as punishment because the punishing person stands as an equal to the punished person. "Equals cannot punish each other. Punishment presupposes a superior authority [inflicting it on an inferior.]" Similarly, compensation is limited to a payment by a party responsible for the harm to the party harmed. An equivalent payment—in the form of relief funds, welfare, and so on—by a party not causally responsible for the injury fails to qualify as compensation. For example, payment by an insurance company for the loss is not compensation because the insurance company, while contractually obliged to pay, is not causally responsible for the harm.

Second, what are the reasons for requiring the wrongdoer to suffer? While impeachment, deportation, and disbarment may all qualify as punishment from an external perspective, none is punishment. Where the purpose of inflicting these sanctions is to separate dangerous wrongdoers from society, the purpose is not punitive. But expatriation is properly punishment because its sole purpose is to stigmatize, not to protect. Similarly, the purposes or reasons for making payment may help to distinguish between compensation and redistribution. For example, if the comparative wealth of the parties is a factor in assessing damages, the payment is likely a redistribution. But if the focus is limited to the harm-causing transaction, the payment is more likely compensation.

Fletcher concludes by urging the adoption of conceptual analyses of punishment and compensation that eschew particular goals or purposes. But such a seemingly neutral account nonetheless comparatively favors the intrinsic, deontological perspective over the extrinsic, utilitarian perspective.

John Gardner's reply, "'Punishment and Compensation': A Comment," observes that "Fletcher's essay remains important as one of very few philosophical works that compare and contrast the compensatory and the punitive." Gardner offers to augment and refine Fletcher's account. He argues that, rather than compensation, Fletcher is really concerned with reparation—a subset of compensation where it is paid by the party causally responsible for the injury. Gardner further offers a number of asymmetries between reparative compensation and punishment. First, the pains of reparation are incidental whereas the pain of punishment is intentional. Second, consumer boycotts may well be punitive. Third, rectification of imbalance may well be part of the very idea or concept of reparation but it is not of punishment. Fourth, and most significantly, Gardner conceives of reparation as the fallback duty owed to the victim for his failure to perform the original duty. In contrast, "punishment is not something that the wrongdoer owes. For it is not something that he can give. It is something that is inflicted upon him by others."

Mens Rea and Mistake

In "The Fault of Not Knowing," Fletcher attacks the orthodox view that objective negligence, or inadvertent negligence, is an insufficient basis for blaming someone for causing harm. Fletcher argues that objective negligence is a test for fault or culpability in the same way that subjective standards are. After discussing how the conventional reading of Oliver Wendell Holmes's views on negligence is misleading, Fletcher explains the importance of the connection between negligence and omissions. In both, one is neither negligent nor liable for an omission unless one was under a duty to act to prevent harm and one breached that duty. "As the law of negligence evolved, however, the failure to exercise due care—an omission—came to be seen as part of affirmative risks to others.... The fault was not the passivity of an omission, but the affirmative wrong of creating an unreasonable risk." A remnant of this older view of negligence as an omission survives today in the doctrine of unforeseeability. The doctrine underscores the aspect of fault involved in not knowing: "When the risk is too bizarre and the outcome so unexpected that no one can be faulted for running it, the appropriate way of talking about fault is to focus on the difficulty of knowing the unforeseeable." Fletcher then applies this concept to ideological offenders—such as Timothy McVeigh and Ted Kaczynski—who believed that their homicidal conduct was necessary. Their fault of not knowing that their conduct was wrong was the result of separating themselves "from the potential self-correction one receives from being embedded in a community of opinion." Fletcher concludes that "having the opportunity to correct one's belief and failing to exercise that capacity lie at the foundation of the fault of not knowing."

In Larry Alexander and Kimberly Kessler Ferzan's reply, "Fletcher on 'The Fault of Not Knowing,'" Alexander and Ferzan disagree with Fletcher and argue that objective or inadvertent negligence is not blameworthy. Objective negligence depends on the hypothetical reasonable person in the actor's situation (RPAS), which they argue cannot be articulated in a principled way. There are two possible boundaries for such an articulation: (1) an RPAS that knows all the relevant facts, and (2) an RPAS that has the same beliefs as the actor. Under the first articulation, a defendant would always be found negligent; under the second articulation, a defendant would never be found negligent. Where between these boundaries should the RPAS be located? Alexander and Ferzan maintain that any location between these boundaries will be "morally arbitrary." And at either boundary itself, the RPAS collapses into either strict liability or recklessness. As a result, there is no satisfactory possible way to articulate the RPAS standard upon which inadvertent or objective negligence depends.

In "Mistake in the Model Penal Code: A False False Problem," Fletcher critiques the Model Penal Code's (MPC) approach to mistakes that treats all types of mistakes (regarding substantive, not procedural, matters) the same—they are relevant if and only if they negate the requisite culpability. In contrast, under the common law the rules differ depending on whether the mistake is reasonable or unreasonable, is about fact or law, offense or defense, or justification or excuse. Fletcher demonstrates that the MPC's approach leads to superfluity, inconsistency, and absurdity. While the MPC mistake provisions may apply well to core elements of offenses, problems arise when they are applied to justifications and excuses as negative elements of offenses. The Code's general mistake provision renders the specific rules on mistaken justification to be superfluous. Fletcher further demonstrates that treating mistakes of law about justifications and excuses, and mistakes of fact about excuses, the same as mistakes of fact regarding core elements of the offense not only produces unfortunate results but is problematic under the Code itself. Fletcher concludes that the MPC's attempt to make the problem of mistakes a false problem by treating all mistakes under a one-size-fits-all approach is significantly mistaken. Different types of mistakes pertaining to different inculpatory or exculpatory elements should be treated differently. Mistake is not a false problem. But under the MPC, mistake is a false false problem.

In Heidi M. Hurd's reply, "The Model Penal Code's Mistakes About Mistakes: An Analysis of George Fletcher's 'Mistake in the Model Penal Code: A False False Problem,'" Hurd observes that Fletcher's essay "well illustrates why Fletcher became and has remained a defining figure in criminal law jurisprudence." While Hurd agrees with Fletcher's critique of the MPC's general mistake approach applying to justifications and excuses, she raises several questions/points supporting an alternative theory of mistake that would have the virtue of avoiding Fletcher's criticisms of the MPC. First, if justifications had no mens rea requirements, mistakes about justifications would be irrelevant. Second, if excuses lacked objective requirements, then mistakes about excuses would also be irrelevant. Third, if the relevant mental states could not be so easily negated "by factual inaccuracies within our beliefs," mistakes about core elements of the offense would be minimized. Hurd's alternative approach to mistakes seeks to render the issue of mistakes largely irrelevant. Hurd concludes that "while Fletcher successfully proves that mistakes are not a false problem for the MPC, they may, in the end, prove to be a false problem for the criminal law."

Justification and Excuse

"The Individualization of Excusing Conditions" explores the distinction between justification and excuse defenses, particularly focusing on four different excuses—necessity, duress, insanity, and mistake of law. Fletcher traces the common law's "abuse and transformation" of these excuses in an attempt to explain the common law's "aversion" to a robust recognition of these defenses. Contrasting the common law with German and civil law approaches, Fletcher locates the source of the common law's posture toward excuses in its position "about the indispensability of rules"—that the law consists "of rules and nothing but rules." While justifications are amenable to this approach, assessing whether an individual defendant may be fairly blamed for wrongdoing because of an asserted excuse is not. Every defendant and each defendant's situation is, according to Fletcher, unique. But the common law employs "rules that suppress the differences among persons and situations." After considering and rejecting two possible arguments against the individualization of excuses, Fletcher maintains that we should reject the common law's limited concession to and expression of individualization—prosecutorial discretion and executive mercy. Individualizing excuses, Fletcher concludes, "complements rather than detracts from the rule of law."

In Susan R. Estrich's reply, "George Fletcher, Critical Feminist: Comment on Fletcher, 'The Individualization of Excusing Conditions,'" Estrich finds that Fletcher's 1974 article is "still famous," its "sheer intellectual vigor has met the test of time," and it has sparked a still continuing debate that has "produced some of the most important books and articles in the criminal law literature." Estrich traces the influence of Fletcher's "seminal" article in presaging the important critiques of orthodox criminal law doctrine on spousal abuse and rape. Building on Fletcher's attack of the nonindividualized reasonable man rule of the common law, scholars demonstrated that the reasonable man standard required individualization to accommodate the assessment of whether a female defendant's conduct was reasonable. While Estrich declares that Fletcher's efforts (as well as those of others) to rigorously distinguish justifications from excuses are "not entirely successful," more important in her view is Fletcher's powerful case for relinquishing the grip the objective, reasonable man rule has had on the law. Estrich agrees wholeheartedly that the rule must be subjectified, but she parts company with Fletcher on the extent of that subjectification—"individualization in a diverse society must be limited." Individualization based on an almost infinite range of sources leads to the "plethora of 'abuse excuses.'" But Estrich admits that there is no "inevitable answer" as to where to appropriately draw the line between "lawlessness and blatant unfairness, between anarchy and injustice."

"The Right and the Reasonable" compares the common law's focus on reasonableness with the German and civil law's focus on what Fletcher terms the Right. Each approach's focus leads to or reflects different styles of legal reasoning. Fletcher links reasonableness/common law with flat and the Right/civil law with structured legal thinking. A flat style packs all the relevant criteria as to whether a defense will prevail into a single standard—for example, whether the defendant's conduct was reasonable. A structured style proceeds in multiple stages—"first an absolute norm is asserted; and second, qualifications enter to restrict the scope of the supposedly dispositive norm." This opposition is then used to explain the differing positions that the common and civil laws have adopted with respect to the justification/excuse distinction in general and, more specifically, the special issue of what Fletcher terms putative self-defense. The issue of putative self-defense arises when an actor employs force against another when she reasonably, but mistakenly, believes she is facing unlawful aggression. Fletcher argues that the flat style, as exemplified by the reasonableness standard, has the effect of suppressing the distinctions between both justification and excuse as well as actual and putative self-defense. But the structured style allows the distinctions to become clear. The flat style simply assesses whether the actor's conduct was reasonable and thereby determines that the actor's force is justified and actual self-defense. The structured style yields, in Fletcher's view, the superior result of the actor being unjustified in self-defense but excused for her faultless mistake. The actor's mere belief, however reasonable, cannot rise to the level of actual, justified self-defense.

In Victoria Nourse's reply, "The Right and the Reasonable: Analyzing the Basic Idioms of American Criminal Law," Nourse observes that "[t]here is no more important concept in the criminal law than that of the 'reasonable man.'" She lauds Fletcher's essay as "one of the most erudite and penetrating analyses of 'reasonableness' ever written." Nourse makes three central points. First, Fletcher's identification of the common law's reliance on flat discourse both correctly predicts and explains why "American criminal law evades direct analytic engagement with its most important concept"—reasonableness. The very style of discourse giving rise to the primacy of reasonableness suppresses inquiry and assessment of it. Second, while there may be deterrence benefits to flat/reasonableness discourse, the costs of diminished guidance to actors and due process to defendants may outweigh them. Third, reliance on flat/reasonable discourse contributes to conflation of "'descriptive reasonableness'" and "'prescriptive reasonableness.'" That is, what is empirically reasonable will dispositively inform legal and moral assessments of blameworthiness.

"The Nature of Justification" explores whether justifications are merely negative elements of offenses—that is, whether a justification, on a conceptual level, may equivalently be situated either as a positive defense or as a negative element of an offense. Fletcher contrasts what he terms the ideal theory and the unity theory. The ideal theory holds that justifications conceptually belong to the category of defenses and may not equivalently be considered as negative elements of an offense. The unity theory argues that justifications may be equivalently considered either way. This opposition is yet another way of considering whether justification should be purely objective (the unity theory) or partially subjective (the ideal theory). Fletcher frames his argument in favor of the ideal theory in light of a prosecution, after the unification of Germany, of preunification conduct by East German border guards who shot and killed East German citizens trying to escape into West Germany under an East German statute authorizing or justifying such force. Fletcher marshals seven differing consequences for the criminal law depending on whether the ideal or unity theory applies. These seven consequences, Fletcher concludes, support the ideal theory of justification. And this informs the border guard case. As a defense—as opposed to a negative element of the offense—the East German statutory justification can be retroactively disregarded by the unified German state and not provide a basis for acquittal. Conceiving of the statutory justification as a defense—as opposed to a negative element of the offense—affords the conviction of the East German border guards without violating the principle of legality or any legitimate right of reliance on the statutory justification.

In Peter Westen's reply, "Fletcher on Subjective Justification," Westen declares that "Fletcher has done more than any other American scholar to clarify the norms of criminal law." And his "most influential contribution…[is] the distinction between justification and excuse." Westen regards "The Nature of Justification" as "Fletcher's most extended effort" to defend a partially subjective theory of justification against the purely objective theory of justification espoused by Paul Robinson. After comparing Fletcher's and Robinson's positions, Westen directly disputes four of Fletcher's claimed seven adverse consequences of the unity/purely objective theory (the other three Westen dismisses as either already included or as features, not adverse consequences). Westen concludes that the unity/purely objective theory of justification is preferable to Fletcher's ideal/partially subjective theory. Westen also disputes Fletcher's conclusions as to the fairness and justice of the border guard case.

"The Psychotic Aggressor—A Generation Later" takes a second look at a canonical problem of criminal theory that Fletcher first presented more than twenty years earlier. The enduring example is this: if a psychotic attacks an innocent person in an elevator, is the innocent person justified, excused, or ineligible to use defensive force against the psychotic aggressor? While ordinarily an innocent victim of aggression would be justified in self-defense against the aggressor, the uncertain status of the psychotic makes the nature of the innocent's defensive response uncertain. Is the psychotic's attack wrongful, but excused or outside of the reach of the criminal law altogether? In analyzing this problem, Fletcher probes the contours of the justification/excuse distinction. Fletcher argues that the psychotic aggressor is wrongful, but excused, and implies that the innocent is justified in self-defense against the psychotic. Fletcher defends his view of the justification/excuse distinction against the so-called subjective theory of justification, espoused by the MPC and Kent Greenawalt, treating putative justification as actual justification. Fletcher observes that the strongest case for the subjective theory stems from the employment of force under situations of epistemic uncertainty, where there is no truth of the matter, and where force ultimately proves to be unnecessary. Such cases might well be, Fletcher concedes, justified. But the subjective theory is less persuasive in the more typical case of the actor mistakenly using force where there was a fact of the matter at the time of acting. There, the subjective theory, Fletcher concludes, incorrectly grants the actor a justification when the actor should only be excused.

In Alon Harel's reply, "A View of the Psychotic Aggressor: Two Generations Later," Harel notes at the outset that "[t]here is too much with which I agree with George Fletcher to justify writing this comment." But Harel does muster two points of disagreement. First, Fletcher's "one right" thesis that rejects the possibility of conflicting justifications is incorrect. Harel disagrees that conflicting justifications would be logically inconsistent. Two parties, each using force against the other, might well each be justified. There is no logical inconsistency in conflicting justifications. Second, Harel objects to Fletcher's use of the justification/excuse distinction as a means of clarifying the message a jury's acquittal sends to the public. The distinction's importance is in legal reasoning undertaken by actors in the criminal justice system, but not in educating or mollifying the public.

"Domination in the Theory of Justification and Excuse" addresses the feminist challenge to the traditional requirement of self-defense that the aggressor's threat be imminent. Fletcher considers the imminence requirement in light of battered women killing their battering spouses in so-called nonconfrontational circumstances—when the batterer is asleep. Particular focus is given to perhaps the most notorious such case—Judy Norman killing her sleeping husband after twenty years of horrible abuse and degradation. After explaining the five principal requirements for justified self-defense, Fletcher advances two fundamental theses. First, an actor's mistaken, albeit reasonable, belief in the imminence of aggression or the necessity of defensive force is insufficient for justified self-defense but may be the basis for an excuse. Second, "past relationships of domination should not affect the analysis of justification" but do "bear, at most, on the reasonableness of the mistaken belief in the necessity of defensive force." As a result, Fletcher concludes that battered spouses, even those in a plight similar to Judy Norman's, should not be justified in self-defense in killing their sleeping or nonaggressing abusers. Fletcher explains that the imminence requirement falls into the domain of political rather than moral theory. It is the subject of the proper allocation of authority between the state and the citizen. The imminence of the aggression, understood to be actual and public, signals to the community that the force is defensive and a legitimate infringement on the state's virtual monopoly on force.

In Joshua Dressler's reply, "Battered Women, Sleeping Abusers, and Political and Moral Theory," Dressler observes that "Fletcher almost single-handedly inspired attention to the distinction between justificatory and excusatory defenses" and inspired "many of the greatest legal minds to reflect on and write about substantive criminal law." And he admires Fletcher's defense of the traditional imminence requirement as a provocative "swim against the intellectual and political currents." While agreeing with Fletcher's conclusion that nonconfrontational self-defense cannot be justified (but can be excused), Dressler disagrees with Fletcher's premise that putative justification cannot be actual justification. Rather, Dressler maintains that it cannot be reasonable to believe that a sleeping abuser represents an imminent threat. To find otherwise, Dressler argues, results in "the oxymoron of a 'reasonable irrational person.'" For Dressler, the traditional imminence requirement assures that even a monster like John Norman cannot justifiably be killed unless his death is necessary. By requiring that an attack be "under way or imminent, the risk of factual error is reduced to virtually nil."

Domination and Protection of Victims

In "Blackmail: The Paradigmatic Crime," Fletcher offers a justification of the criminalization of one of the criminal law's most elusive crimes—blackmail. While nearly everyone agrees that it should be criminalized, no one has been quite able to explain why. The paradox of the offense of blackmail is that it criminalizes conditionally threatening to do that which one has a right to both unconditionally threaten to do and actually do. Under Fletcher's account, however, "blackmail is not an anomalous crime but rather a paradigm for understanding both criminal wrongdoing and punishment." After considering ten cases of unlawful blackmail and lawful, near blackmail, Fletcher demonstrates that no extant account of blackmail satisfactorily analyzes the cases. He then demonstrates how his own novel justification of blackmail's criminalization does satisfactorily sort the cases. Blackmail is criminalized because the blackmailer effects a relationship with her victim of "dominance and subordination." After successfully obtaining payment from the victim, the blackmailer can demand payment from the victim again and again. "Living with that knowledge puts the victim of blackmail in a permanently subordinate position." Blackmail is properly criminalized because counteracting dominance-submission relationships is precisely what punishment accomplishes. Punishment of the blackmailer not only negates the blackmailer's dominance of the victim but also restores the dignity of the victim. This understanding of blackmail's criminalization is not unique but rather is representative of the core of criminal law—crimes of rape, burglary, robbery, and even nonviolent theft "carry in their train a relationship of dominance and subordination." The victim feels exposed and vulnerable and fears repetition of the crime. Punishment of the offender breaks this relationship and restores the victim to his pre-crime dignity.

In Judge John T. Noonan Jr.'s reply, "The Crime of Trying to Dominate," Noonan describes an extraordinary case that came before him on appeal. He notes that his view of the case was strikingly consistent with Fletcher's view of blackmail as effecting a relationship of dominance and submission. The case involved a "psychosexual game" in which two persons "were engaged in alternate attempts to dominate each other." Precisely because each actor was trying to dominate the other, neither was entirely subordinate. Because what occurred was a "consensual game" of mutual attempted domination, the crime of blackmail did not actually occur. While finding that Fletcher's account of blackmail as domination is apt, Noonan nonetheless finds that blackmail is not the paradigmatic crime for three reasons. First, federal tax evasion is a fairly common crime, but in no way is the defendant trying to dominate the federal government. Second, effecting a relationship of domination is not always immoral, let alone a crime. And third, there is simply too great a variety of crimes for one crime to serve as the paradigm.

In Alan Wertheimer's reply, "George Fletcher on Blackmail," Wertheimer raises the following four questions: (1) Is Fletcher's account of the ten cases correct? (2) Does it render the law's treatment of the cases coherent? (3) Does it explain why blackmail should be criminalized? (4) Does it help explain the justification of punishment? Although Wertheimer finds that Fletcher's account largely gets the ten cases right, he is less convinced that Fletcher's test of whether the transaction effects a dominance and subordination relationship provides the best explanation of which cases are and are not unlawful blackmail. On Wertheimer's preferred test, unlawful blackmail might be sorted from lawful conduct by the distinction between coercive threats and noncoercive offers. Furthermore, Wertheimer argues that Fletcher's dominance test is neither a necessary nor a sufficient condition to establish the criminality of blackmail. While Wertheimer agrees that blackmail may be a paradigmatic crime, it is not for the reasons Fletcher asserts. Instead, the criminalization of blackmail, like attempts and other crimes, involves not private harms done to the victim but harms to society as a whole. And finally, Wertheimer argues that Fletcher's justification of punishment—that it negates the blackmailer's (or any criminal's) dominance of the victim—is plausible but no more persuasive than asserting that the threat of punishment reduces the incidence of blackmailers dominating their victims.

In "Justice and Fairness in the Protection of Crime Victims," Fletcher continues his interest in exploring the protection of crime victims. Where his blackmail article concerned protecting crime victims from being dominated by crime perpetrators (specifically blackmailers), this article concerns the protection of crime victims from prosecutors and criminal justice systems that might refuse to prosecute clear cases of wrongdoing. After comparing the rights of defendants and victims in American criminal law and discussing issues that arise in determining who qualifies as a victim, Fletcher explains the considerably greater recognition of victims' rights outside America. In a number of cases, the European Court of Human Rights has explicitly recognized that the state has an affirmative obligation to protect its citizens. States' failure to prosecute the rape of a mentally handicapped woman, the battery of a child by his stepfather, and the failure to enact laws defining rape in the absence of force were all held to be violations of the European Convention of Human Rights. In addition, Fletcher asserts that the very purpose of the Rome Statute establishing the International Criminal Court "is to vindicate the interests of victims." The preamble particularly focuses on the special injustice of the impunity of offenders. Fletcher explains that the particularly acute injustice of impunity is that "when the state tolerates criminality that it has the capacity to punish, it becomes complicit in the crime. The state, which derives its legitimacy in part from its mission to protect its citizens against crime, becomes an agent of criminality by failing to prosecute." Fletcher grounds the state's obligation to victims to prosecute wrongdoers as an aspect of retributivism—punishment as an end in itself.

In Stephen J. Schulhofer's reply, "Justice for Victims and Justice for Society," Schulhofer notes that American crime victims have won a variety of minor procedural rights but still lack the more substantial right that is enjoyed in some parts of Europe—the right that a prosecution be commenced. Schulhofer compares two conceptions—the modest and the ambitious—of victims' rights as to prosecution. Under the modest conception, the prosecutor retains the discretion of whether to prosecute; the victim only has the right that this discretion be exercised on permissible grounds. The more ambitious conception is based on the retributivist principle that justice requires that crime must always be punished. Here, the victim has a right to insist that a guilty defendant be prosecuted and punished. Schulhofer questions whether this transformation in Europe—from the modest to the more ambitious conception—is desirable. "Do the goals of ending a cycle of violence and achieving social repair, reconciliation, and a peaceful future ever justify amnesty or forgiveness for the low-level foot soldiers who may, nonetheless, have perpetrated unspeakable crimes?" Or is it permissible to forgo prosecution and punishment of the leaders to bring an otherwise unending war to a close? Schulhofer answers that "[t]he choices are all bad" and the path is unclear "in the proper pursuit of justice and fairness for the victims of crime."

Underlying much of Fletcher's work has been the conflict, in matters of both law and faith, between reason and authority. Referring to this conflict, it is sometimes said that the pope's word is final because he is infallible and the Supreme Court's word is infallible only because it is final. While Fletcher's critics assert—strongly, unreservedly, and repeatedly—that Fletcher is far from infallible, Fletcher's views (like those of the preceding institutional authorities) are important both in their own right and because, simply, they are his. The once rebel outsider railing against the establishment figures of the criminal law has now become the establishment, the Man. The figure imbued with near authority over criminal law jurisprudence has supplanted the angry young man armed with mere reason. Martin Luther has become the imposing edifice of ecclesiastical authority against which new theses are tacked and tested. David has become Goliath. As a result, it is only fitting for this volume to grant to Fletcher the final word. Even if his critics deny him infallibility, this volume will not deny him finality.

Concluding the volume is an original essay by George Fletcher, "Remembrance of Articles Past," which is part reminiscence and part critical reply to his critics. Looking back over his scholarly career, Fletcher finds it apt to compare himself with perhaps the greatest philosopher of the twentieth century, Wittgenstein. (Surely, Fletcher's critics are kicking themselves for missing their Lloyd Bentsen v. Dan Quayle moment.) But, surprisingly, the comparison is negative. Fletcher notes that while Wittgenstein famously reversed course in midcareer and repudiated his earlier work, he has stayed the course: "The first thing that impresses me about scholarly work is the high probability of consistency over a scholarly career of forty years or more....I have not changed my mind often, whether this is to my credit or discredit." Fletcher's critics in this volume might find the more apt comparison to be to Ralph Waldo Emerson's foolish consistency as a hobgoblin rather than Wittgenstein. Spoiler alert: Fletcher does not undergo a Wittgensteinian transformation in the face of his critics' cogent arguments. There is no Galileoesque recanting for his heresies committed against criminal law orthodoxy.

But, to his credit, Fletcher does give some ground—perhaps more ground than he ever has in his career. True, the ground ceded is not large swaths but small patches; not large themes, but only small details. But even this is quite significant. As many frustrated criminal law scholars can attest, getting Fletcher to admit he is wrong and another is right is a quixotic mission. As I can personally attest, many a misspent scholarly career has waited in vain for such a reversal. But perhaps because of its sword in the stone quality, effecting such an admission from Fletcher has become the gold standard of vindication.

While typically publication of a volume of one's essays is a glorious triumph marking the crowning achievement in a scholar's career, there is a touch of sadness to this volume. There are reports that this is George's swan song in pure criminal theory. He is abdicating his crown to pursue his claimed newfound true love of writing novels. His first is already out—*The Bond*, published by Hart in the United Kingdom, and he is working on a second called *The Bible Lesson*. Perhaps this is only a brief dalliance—like Michael Jordan's flirtation with minor-league baseball. Hopefully these reports, as Samuel Clemens once said of his death, are greatly exaggerated. The philosopher-king George of criminal theory is dead? Say it ain't so. Long live the king!

CHAPTER 2

The Nature and Function of Criminal Theory

George P. Fletcher

Introduction

The practice of teaching and writing in the field of criminal law has changed dramatically in the last half-century. In the United States and England, and to a lesser extent in other English-speaking countries, we have witnessed a turn toward theoretical inquires of a greater depth and variety than had existed previously in the history of Anglo-American law. The subjects of this new literature include the nature and rationale of punishment;[1] the theory of justification and of excuse, that is, of wrongdoing and responsibility;[2] the relevance of consequences to the gravity of offenses (the problem of moral luck);[3] and the proper structuring of specific fields of law, notably the law of homicide, particularly at the beginning and the end of life,[4] of rape,[5] and of victimless offenses that result in no material harm to other persons.[6] As far as the United States goes, the roots of this flowering lie in the classic article by Jerome Michael and Herbert Wechsler, "A Rationale of the Law of Homicide."[7] The casebook by the same authors provided the first serious teaching tool for a reflective and systematic approach to American criminal law.[8] The Model Penal Code, a project initiated by Herbert Wechsler and the American Law Institute in the 1950s, brought together many of the most serious legal minds of the generation to work out, for the first time, the rules and principles that would constitute the general part of American criminal law, namely the rules and principles that would be applicable to all offenses.[9] And significantly, the 1962 publication of the first edition of the novel, theoretically-minded casebook by Sanford Kadish and Monrad Paulsen[10] helped to create a community of scholars who read the same cases and followed up on the same set of citations to the journals and law reviews.

There were certainly historical precursors to this burst of theoretical inquiry. Stephen,[11] Mill,[12] Bentham,[13] and Blackstone[14] come readily to mind. One of the most famous maxims of the theoretical criminal law—*actus not facit reus nisi mens sit rea*[15]—dates back to Edward Coke's formulation in the early seventeenth century.[16] Yet this earlier legal literature consists largely in apodictic statements about how the criminal law should be formulated. It lacks the reflective attention to issues that we have come to associate with philosophical inquiry.

In trying to understand the nature and function of this theoretical work, the term "philosophy" is the first descriptive word to come to mind. Indeed, without the devoted interest of a group of philosophers in the 1950s and 1960s, it is doubtful that the field would have taken off. The philosophical analogue to Herbert Wechsler was H.L.A. Hart, who, as teacher and scholar, brought the methods of analytic philosophy to bear on the study of criminal law. Herbert Morris,[17] Joel Feinberg,[18] Robert Nozick,[19] Judith Jarvis Thomson,[20] and many others deepened this interdependency of law and philosophy. These philosophers were building on a long tradition dating back, on some issues, to Aquinas and even to Aristotle. Yet the major debates in the philosophical reflection on the criminal law have a distinctively modern ring to them. Established authorities have been punishing criminals from the beginning of organized society, but it is not until the late eighteenth century that we find serious engagement and disagreement about the purposes of inflicting this harm on those who have transgressed the norms of the community. Today, we take the debate between Kant's retributivism and Bentham's utilitarianism to be paradigmatic of the style of intellectual confrontation that has induced philosophical reflection on every factor bearing on the question whether we should punish a particular individual on a particular occasion.

At this juncture, on this occasion honoring one of the founders of the field (Sanford Kadish), it might be appropriate to pause and reflect on the nature and the function of this shared inquiry into the foundations of the substantive criminal law. Criminal theory has clearly come of age, and therefore it can endure this Essay, written as a critical assessment both of its promise and its shortcomings.

I. What Kind of Inquiry Is Criminal Theory?

The field of criminal theory should be thought of more as a humanist inquiry than as a social science. The questions that concern us are not empirical. The task is not to explain how the system actually works. Of course, it is important to know, for example, how the police function, how juries decide, how the system affects minorities, and so on. So far as other researchers can inform us of these facts of life, we should take note. This is not, however, the essence of the theoretical enterprise.

To say that the field is a humanist inquiry underscores the great mystery of the human condition that comes into focus in criminal trials. How is it that human beings can commit heinous acts, and how can we justify blaming and punishing them for having committed them? The first part of this question stresses the issues of individual guilt and punishment and connects readily to moral philosophy. The second part, regarding collective blaming and state punishment, raises a question of political philosophy: When should the state be able to act in the common good by imposing sanctions against particular individuals? As criminal theory lies at the union of law and philosophy, it also defines an intersection between moral and political philosophy.

These two points of intersection require further reflection. First, how do law and philosophy impose competing perspectives on theoretical work in criminal law? And second, how do moral and political philosophy differ in their concerns and procedures?

A. THE DIFFERING DEMANDS OF LAW AND PHILOSOPHY

Law and philosophy are in fact two entirely different kinds of inquiry, and the difference between them is captured in the word "authority." Legal studies proceed by reflecting on the meaning and extension of certain authoritative texts—constitutions, statutes, regulations, and case holdings. This deference to authoritative rules and prescriptions runs contrary to the philosophical method, which involves searching for the best reasons to defend a particular position. Law tends toward the parochial, for authority is always limited to a particular time and place. If you are thinking about self-defense and the duty to retreat in the United States, you pay attention to American authorities. If you are thinking about self-defense in Germany, you heed the local statutory and case law and scholarly prescriptions about self-defense. By contrast, philosophy represents a universal inquiry independent of time and place. No one is constituted as the authority to prescribe certain sources as the ones you must read and think about.[21] In doing legal theory, it is a mistake to ignore the local criminal code; but if you do not find Hegel illuminating, it is not a "mistake" in a philosophical inquiry simply to ignore him.

Admittedly, in the United States, we enjoy a certain tendency toward universalist thinking that is not shared by our colleagues in Germany, France, and Italy. If you live and teach in California, you are not limited in your horizons to the California Criminal Code and the California cases. Indeed, these materials have no privileged position in any of the great casebooks, such as the book by Kadish and Paulsen, now transformed into Kadish and Schulhofer.[22] Cases from New Zealand are just as important as those from the court down the street, and

Stephen's draft code for India carries weight, as does the Model Penal Code. The degree of parochial thinking outside the English-speaking world is much stronger. French writing on criminal law reveals little knowledge about legal sources outside of France, and the Germans, who know more about law abroad, still write and teach as though the authoritative German materials define their universe of inquiry.

In the end, however, the difference between the English-speaking world, or "common law system," and the rest of the world is simply a matter of degree. A large number of Anglophone countries share the same language and take cognizance of each other's legal sources, but the boundaries of parochial thinking become clear sooner or later. English-speaking lawyers do not recognize the relevance of legal authorities written in other languages. They might be curious about odd things done in one country or another, but they do not take "foreign" statutes or cases seriously as authorities that constrain their thinking.

This parochial thinking runs afoul of the philosophical temper. There is nothing about philosophy written in English that makes it intrinsically more appealing than works originally published in Greek, Latin, or German. Indeed, it is not clear why in philosophical inquiries one cares at all about what philosophers in the past have said. Philosophy is not the history of philosophy, as my teacher Norman Malcolm used to preach. Yet teachers of philosophy do in fact concentrate on reading and explicating the "greats" as though their work commanded some authority on the problems they raise. Perhaps there is a need to start somewhere, and those who have brought wisdom to bear in the past warrant the honor of having the first, if not necessarily the last, word in the discussion.

The danger in legal studies is to treat jurists of the past, who were often rather pedestrian thinkers, as having the last word in determining what the law is. We read their constitutions, statutes, and case opinions as though they actually solved the problem they were addressing. We do this for various reasons. Their words acquire authority by virtue of the political system that we are willing to live by or, in the case of constitutions, because they lived and wrote at particularly poignant moments in history, such as the concluding hours of a political revolution.

One is tempted to draw an analogy between the reliance of lawyers on their parochial sources of law and the invocation of God's recorded word in a religious community. The culture of the law is, in fact, much like the culture of religious belief. Both start with the text. But a sophisticated practitioner of either law or religion will always seek to go beyond the text and bring to bear the insights of reason on the ultimate issues at hand. Theology, when it is done well, resembles the informed groping of legal theorists trying to bring diverse sources to bear on the ineffable problems of action, responsibility, guilt, and justified punishment. Great religious thinkers like Maimonides and Aquinas never limited themselves to the sources of revelation. Great legal minds proceed in a similar way: They take their traditions seriously (the analogue to revelation) and move beyond them in the direction of universal answers based on the kinds of reasoning that could appeal to thinking people everywhere.

The appeal of the analogy between theology and legal thought is that it accounts for the parochial nature of legal studies. The loyalty that lawyers show to their local constitutions, statutes, and cases is quite remarkable and can only be understood as the expression of a culture of faith. At some level Americans must believe that those fifty-five white men who met in Philadelphia in the sweltering summer of 1787 really got it right. At least they believe it in a way that Europeans and Chinese hardly share. These commitments to belief resemble the socialized instincts of members of religious communities. They take their own holy texts seriously and totally ignore, if not attack, the texts of neighboring cultures.

Scholars who seek to work on the philosophical foundations of criminal responsibility, then, are caught between the forces of competing disciplines. The customs of legal scholarship drive theorists toward taking the indigenous "sources of law" seriously, treating them as the authoritative basis for solving problems. The traditions of philosophy generate an impulse toward universalist arguments based on sources available to all. This conflict comes to the fore in assessing the relevance of particular decisions by the courts or legislatures. Suppose that the local law givers have decided that strict liability is acceptable in rape cases, that consequences matter in assessing the gravity of punishment, that felony-murder is a permissible doctrine, or that the insanity defense is indispensable in a proper assessment of criminal responsibility. Why should the theorist care about these purely parochial decisions? Of course, they should matter if the theorist has sound reasons for thinking that the decisions are right. But the fact that some judge somewhere made a certain decision hardly generates a sound reason in itself for taking the decision to be authoritative.

The problem becomes more difficult if we can detect a pattern of decisions and principles that cuts across legal systems and constitutes a nearly universal practice. A good example is the relevance of consequences to determining the gravity of an offense and the severity of punishment. Virtually all legal systems in the world punish completed offenses more severely than they punish attempts. Harm matters—at least in the way the vast majority of lawyers and judges think about things. Yet a considerable body of theory has developed to the effect that under a proper analysis of culpability, consequences should be regarded as purely arbitrary and therefore irrelevant to the actor's criminal responsibility.[23] An actor, malicious to his core, may shoot to kill, but for purely physical reasons the bullet may not strike home. The argument is that this blameworthy actor is just as culpable as one who succeeds in his intentions. This argument is sufficient to turn some distinguished minds, including Joel Feinberg and Sandy Kadish, to the view that last-step attempts (where there is nothing more the actor can do) should be punished just as severely as actions that actually succeed and result in irreversible harm.[24]

Here is an example of practice in conflict with theory, and the question is how to proceed. Is there a rule of thumb telling us whether to favor theory over practice? Alas, no. It all depends on the practice and on the theory. In this particular case, I happen to think the theoretical arguments are wrongly conceived and developed (as I will show later), and the practice should constitute the basis of our philosophical inquiry. The question should not be whether the nearly universal practice is right, but why it is right. Here I rely on a point of philosophical psychology that I learned from my mentor Herbert Morris: When an intuition is deeply held, the task of theory should be to generate convincing arguments that those who hold the intuition may not be able to articulate themselves.

The problem with this view is that some widespread practices are clearly wrong, or at least inconsistent with other basic principles of the criminal law. Perhaps there are many people who would claim that the felony-murder rule represents a deeply held intuition. Yet the general theory of culpability holds that actors should be held responsible for the consequences of their actions only to the extent that they are culpable in generating those consequences. Culpability is determined by considerations such as whether the actor intended the consequences; whether she acted knowingly, recklessly, or negligently with respect to the risk of the consequence; and whether she is excused or partially excused for her actions. An offender who accidentally kills someone in the course of a robbery is not, without further proof, culpable for the homicide. Yet the felony-murder rule in effect presumes culpability with respect to the result, in violation both of the requirement of culpability and the presumption of innocence. Again, there is conflict between practice and theory. Should the theorist apply the Morris maxim and seek to defend the felony-murder rule as a deeply held intuition of common people, just like the judgment about the relevance of consequences to punishment?

My answer is: clearly not. But now we face a serious problem of methodology. How do we decide when to take the practices of the legal system seriously and when not? Here are a few suggestions about how to proceed in thinking through this matter.

First we have to clarify whose intuitions we are talking about. Do we mean the intuitions of the man, woman, and child on the street? Do we follow the results of the interesting study by Robinson and Darley[25] on the intuitions of common people about the conundrums of the type we have been discussing? Or do we mean the educated intuitions of lawyers and judges—people trained and perhaps "corrupted" by the criteria of legal analysis? I would not be at all surprised if the guy in the street were to favor both (a) treating consequences as irrelevant to the punishment of the person who acted with evil intent and (b) blaming the robber for the homicide that his criminal action accidentally brings about. But so what? A refinement of our intuitions takes place when we work on the casuistic problems of legal analysis. It seems to be more sensible to rely upon the intuitions of actors in the actor culture. But then comes the response: They, like the guy in the street, seem to favor the felony-murder rule.

At this juncture in the argument, comparative law becomes acutely relevant. If a practice is widespread among legal systems, there is good reason to think that it reflects an intuition that we should credit and seek to justify. If, on the other hand, the United States is isolated in its practice, we should have second thoughts about taking our local and parochial judgments seriously. In the case of the felony-murder rule, it is difficult to find a jurisdiction outside the United States—even in the English-speaking world—that still applies the rule. Also relevant, it seems to me, is the strength of the opposition to the parochial position of the United States. The Canadian Supreme Court has declared various aspects of the felony-murder rule unconstitutional.[26] One could expect a similar decision in Germany and Italy; if they had the rule, their courts would probably find it to be in violation of their constitutional requirement of culpability as a condition for criminal responsibility.[27]

Of course, American politicians and policy makers are notoriously indifferent to the attitudes of jurists beyond our borders. Witness our persistent faith in capital punishment despite the deliberate killing of offenders having been discredited every other place in the civilized world. But politicians' parochial attitudes provide no excuse for scholars of criminal theory to remain indifferent to the patterns that have emerged in Western jurisprudence. Our perspective should reach wider than our language and deeper than our supposedly shared debt to the English common law.

I am not arguing that the theorist should submit to every worldwide trend. Sometimes trends are wrong. A good example, in my opinion, is the widespread tendency toward punishing impossible attempts, a trend that has become manifest in the last few decades in England, the United States, and Germany. The argument is that if the actor intends to commit a crime and engages in a serious effort to execute his intention, there is no reason to give him the benefit of the circumstances turning out to be different from what he expected. Yet there are also counterindications in the legal thought of the industrialized world. Japan and Italy have always held out against the intent-based, subjective theory.[28] Spain has recently joined the ranks of European countries favoring the countertrend.[29] When the nations of the world are so clearly divided, we have to probe the arguments for and against more deeply. The trend means very little if it is not in keeping with the best arguments available for and against criminal liability.

The problem is: How do we evaluate the arguments bearing on criminal responsibility? If we have a conflict between theory and practice, we should be very sure that our theoretical or philosophical arguments are well-grounded. If the arguments invoke the "authority" of Kant or Aristotle, then we should be sure that we have read these supposed authorities correctly. My favorite example of philosophical misreading is the attempt to invoke Kant's theory of the good will in morality to support a concentrated focus on criminal intention as the basis of criminal liability. Kant argued that a good will—as he understood that term—was essential to the claim that an act had moral value.[30] He never argued that a bad will rendered an action evil. Yet we find recurrent efforts in criminal theory to adapt Kant's thinking to support, for example, the view that consequences should not matter in assessing the gravity of the offense.[31] The argument—to the extent that it can be articulated—would run as follows:

A: A good will is necessary for an action to be good.

B: A good will implies a good intention. Therefore a good intention renders an action good.

C: A bad will implies a bad intention and a bad intention renders an action evil.

D: If the intention is sufficient to make an act good or evil, then the consequences are irrelevant to determining the good or evil represented by the action.

If these inferences, from A to B, B to C, and C to D, were correct, Kantian theory might provide some support for the view that the core of the criminal law consists in evil intentions and that consequences should be irrelevant to assessing just punishment. But apart from the first premise, all of these inferences are false. Here is a short explanation why:

A: This represents a correct reading of Kant's view as set out in the first few lines of *The Prolegomenon to the Metaphysics of Morals.*[32]

A to B: In the Kantian system, intention differs fundamentally from will. *Der Wille* is defined as the capacity to act without the influence of sensual stimuli from the external world; it is the capacity to reflect the dictates of the universal law of reason.[33] That is why an act can have a moral quality only if it is an expression of *der Wille*. It is not true that a good intention, which might be responsive to sensual stimuli in the world, renders an action good. There is no reason to think that an intentional act, just because it is intentional, is a product of *der Wille*.

B to C: This is probably the biggest fallacy of the set. Under the Kantian system, good acts and bad acts are asymmetrical; if a theory applies to the former, it does not necessarily apply to the latter. For an act to have moral worth it must be autonomous. Bad acts are, by definition, heteronomous.[34] They are not products of *der Wille*. One cannot autonomously choose to do evil, to commit a crime. Of course, under Kant's legal theory, we find a lengthy discussion of crime and punishment.[35] But Kant explicitly describes the seat of criminal conduct as *die Willkür* (heteronomous arbitrary choice) rather than *der Wille* (autonomous choice based on reason).[36]

C to D: In his extensive discussion of criminal actions, Kant ignores the problem of attempts and inchoate acts. All the examples given are those based on consummated actions. The conclusion that consequences are foreign to the Kantian way of thinking about crime and punishment represents a total perversion of Kantian thought.

Despite all of these errors, this misreading of Kant has won the loyalty of some sophisticated thinkers.[37] It is one of the primary props of the supposedly theoretical argument in favor of punishing attempted offenses at the same level as consummated offenses. Perhaps lawyers are naturally drawn to the citation of philosophical authority; it is a professional vice. But if the name of one of the great philosophers of modernity comes into play, one should at least get the reading right.

Writers of legal theory are drawn not only to Kant but to Aristotle. The *Nichomachean Ethics* is often cited to support analysis of the theory of excuses.[38] I think that, by and large, this tracing of excuses to Aristotle is correct, even though the philosopher was concerned not about criminal responsibility but about the problem of virtue and the flourishing of individuals. Though Aristotle has many insights to offer, we should be careful about relying on an exegesis of his text to decide, for example, whether negligence is a suitable ground for criminal liability. That was not a problem to which he addressed his energy.

Apart from relying on these historical "authorities," theorists are left with few convincing arguments in their arsenal. Michael Moore relies heavily on intuition,[39] but, as we have noted, we have a serious problem determining whose intuitions should matter and why. Strict logical arguments are rare in the literature. Recently Russell Christopher has pressed the avoidance of contradiction as an argument for structuring the theory of justification,[40] and his work may portend an effort to develop more rigorous arguments for particular outcomes in the theory of criminal responsibility.

As things stand now, our methods of argument are a hodgepodge of intuition, citations to case law, philosophical references (sometimes laced with misreading), and, of course, policy arguments about the behavior we seek to encourage and discourage. There has been and presumably always will be attention paid to the classic debate between retribution and deterrence as the rationale for punishment and, in general, between deontological and utilitarian approaches to moral problems. Yet there has not been enough attention paid to the difference between moral, political, and other kinds of arguments about the proper approach to criminal law.

B. THE DIFFERING PERSPECTIVES OF POLITICAL
AND MORAL PHILOSOPHY

Criminal law begins with punishment, and the kind of punishment with which we are concerned represents an intrusion of the state into the individual's freedom. Therefore the first question that must be asked is all too often ignored: What makes it legitimate for the state to make people suffer? The answer can hardly be, "The state must do justice," or "Criminals deserve punishment." The preliminary demand is to develop a theory of the state that legitimates action in pursuit of justice or authorizes state agents to decide what people deserve and to distribute suffering accordingly. The range of these theories includes libertarian, liberal, communitarian, utilitarian, and perfectionist theories of the state.

Given the centrality of political legitimacy in the criminal law, one can only be amazed at the extent to which the question is ignored both in the philosophical and legal literature. In Joel Feinberg's masterful study of the limits of the criminal law,[41] there is almost no attention paid to political theory. Our leading liberal philosophers—Rawls,[42] Dworkin,[43] Ackerman[44]—have almost nothing of value to add to our understanding of criminal law. Libertarians such as Nozick do address the problem of legitimating state action, and indeed punishment is one of their central concerns.[45] Communitarians in the former Soviet Union also had a distinctive take on the phenomenon of crime and the role of the state in educating "the new person" who would transcend the corruption of bourgeois society.[46] But apart from the libertarians and the Communists at the extremes, the vast majority of us are simply unreflective liberals. We are suspicious of common law crimes and accept at face value Mill's principle that the state should punish only to prevent harm,[47] and we take these two positions to be an adequate theoretical foundation for our work.

Perhaps the greatest theoretical tension in the literature derives from the simultaneous sympathy for certain liberal maxims and a commitment to retributive punishment. Liberals are supposed to believe that it is not the business of the state to try to formulate and act upon ultimate principles of justice; the state cannot purport to do God's work on earth. If that is true, it is hard to understand how the state can hold to a liberal epistemology and yet seek to right the "natural order" by punishing those who deserve it. Despite the great attention devoted to "desert" and retributive theory in recent years, no one has advanced a systematic argument about the political presuppositions of the state legitimately punishing offenders in the name of ultimate principles of justice. This, of course, has become a major problem in the international arena as well, for retributive impulses to punish war crimes and crimes against humanity—sometimes dressed up as an imaginary preventive policy—drive the formation of the new International Criminal Court.[48] I think it is fine for the international community to believe that it must punish in the name of justice, but at least we should have some argument about how a diverse community of nations can claim to know what justice requires, and why it is empowered to prosecute and punish those who "deserve" punishment.

As far as domestic policies are concerned, the formerly fascist powers of Europe—namely Germany, Spain, and Italy—seem to be more sensitive than are we Americans to the demands of liberal or libertarian theory in practice. Perhaps a society must have had some experience with political corruption of the criminal law in order to develop strong liberal sensitivities. The battle against fascistic criminal law has led to certain liberal slogans designed to limit the power of the state over the lives of individuals. It is worth paying attention to two of these.

1. Criminal Punishment Should Be Imposed for Acts Committed, Not for Being a Certain Kind of Person

This proposition is now taken for granted in most Western legal systems. It is expressed in the U.S. Supreme Court's aversion to status offenses.[49] The German literature has cultivated the point as the distinction between an act-based criminal law (*Tatstrafrecht*) and an actor-based criminal law (*Täterstrafrecht*).[50] Communitarian criminal law, taken to extremes in fascist and communist legal systems, has tended to focus on the whole person, on characteristics of social dangerousness, and on using the criminal sanction as a medium of social reeducation. Liberal regimes stress the limited focus of the criminal sanction; it must be imposed solely for acts, not for the crime of being different. It is worth noting that this limitation differs radically from some moral perspectives, particularly from an Aristotelian concern with virtue. Virtue theory focuses on character as it develops over time. Individual acts are important only so far as they reveal character and tend to develop a better or worse character in the future. We praise and condemn people for the kinds of character they have developed, but this perspective is not compatible with the deliberate limitation of criminal punishment to the condemnation of actions.

If American theories were more sensitive to the political dangers of an actor-based criminal law, we would be quick to criticize arguments based on the supposed dangerousness of certain types of offenders. We would have more trouble with increasing punishment for recidivists (and certainly with the policy of "three strikes and you're out") and with punishing impossible attempts on the ground that the mistaken actor is dangerous and likely to succeed next time. Yet it is very clear that American criminal theorists today are willing to accept certain actor-based arguments such as dangerousness inferred from past actions.[51] And despite their lip service to liberal principles, German scholars have virtually no qualms about imposing liability for impossible attempts.[52] This is fairly good proof that criminal theory seems to function today as a potpourri of political theory. Everyone seems to pick and choose from liberal, communitarian, utilitarian, and perfectionist assumptions as the choice suits their immediate purposes. But the task of the theorist should ideally be first to work out a political theory and then explore the implications of that political theory in the details of the criminal law.

2. The Criminal Law Should Serve as the Last Resort (Ultimo Ratio). It Should Be Invoked Only If All Other Sanctions Fail

This additional principle for restricting the power of the state flies in the face of those, like Moore, who take retributivism so seriously that they think that the state has an absolute duty to punish all those who deserve it.[53] A more restrictive theory of legitimate punishment would hold that the state must first seek to solve the problem of apparent crime by invoking less drastic remedies. For environmental offenses, corporate crime, embezzlement, and crimes of negligence, it might be sufficient to rely on the very effective American tort system. The fact that conduct is harmful and morally wrong hardly suffices to conclude that it must be treated as a punishable wrong under the criminal law. Tort liability, fueled by eager, contingency-fee-motivated private lawyers, might do the job just fine. However one comes out on this question, we cannot but recognize the issue at stake, namely: What is the general theory of the state, and how should it be applied to solve social problems?

My plea, then, is for criminal theorists to pay more attention to political as well as moral philosophy. The political theory we choose will invariably shape our answers to innumerable questions about what should be punished, when nominal violations are justified, and when wrongdoing should be excused.

II. What Is the Function of Criminal Theory?

Much of the work done in criminal theory is really not about issues that could be classified as philosophical in the traditional sense. The function of much "theoretical" work in law is to probe the basic concepts that bear on legal analysis, order these concepts in some kind of structure, and elaborate the values and principles that lie behind the structure of liability. That is, the theorist takes the details of the criminal law as more or less given and tries to elicit from these details some synthetic principles. Consider, for example, the famous maxim formulated by Lord Coke in the early seventeenth century: *Actus not facit reus nisi mens sit rea*.[54] Literally, this means that "the act is not criminal unless the mind is criminal." This is not a philosophical truth based on reason, but rather a synthetic claim about the criminal law as Coke observed it in practice. Every punishable act requires a union of *actus reus* and *mens rea*. Coke inferred the generality of his thesis from two primary cases. The first was the exemption provided in cases of theft for someone who acquired possession of an object and then decided later to keep it. Since the act was innocent at the time of acquisition, the subsequent criminal intent was insufficient to generate liability.[55] The second case was the excuse recognized in cases of insanity. If the mind was not culpable, then the act could not be criminally culpable.[56] In these two different applications of the principles of *actus reus* and *mens rea,* the terms mean different things, but I will not allow that point to detain us here. The fact is that Coke coined a maxim that, however ambiguous, has become a recognized truth about the criminal law.[57]

As an accepted truth, Coke's maxim definitely functions as a constituent element of the law and as a source for further legal development. It has as much authoritative status as any legislative declaration or case holding. The courts will interpret legislative prescriptions in line with Coke's maxim. They will seek to bring the details of the law into "reflective equilibrium" with this general maxim of the criminal law.

There are other maxims that express the same kind of synthetic truths of criminal justice. Consider these ten:

1. Every criminal offense presupposes a voluntary human act.
2. Every criminal offense includes a dimension of wrongdoing.
3. Claims of justification negate wrongdoing.
4. Every punishable act presupposes blameworthy commission of the elements of the offense.
5. Blameworthy commission requires at least negligent conduct with respect to every element of the offense.
6. Intentional, knowing, and reckless actions are worse than negligent conduct with respect to the elements of the offense.
7. Excused conduct is not blameworthy.
8. Reasonable mistakes are not blameworthy.
9. Subjective perceptions alone cannot justify conduct.
10. Self-defense is available only against unjustified attacks.

These are propositions that practitioners of criminal theory would, in varying degrees, hold to be true and binding as principle, at least to the same extent that Coke's maxim is binding on the criminal law. But few of them have ever been enacted by a legislature or written into a constitution, and most of them have never been clearly articulated in the Anglo-American case law. Nonetheless, they are just as binding as any principles implicit in our legal practices.

These ten propositions are grounded in the criminal law as it is routinely applied in most Western legal systems. And to the extent that they are grounded in the conventional behavior of the courts, their existence runs against the purely philosophical mode of inquiry I considered in the first half of this Essay. The authority for the principle is not reason alone, but reason as recognized in the practices of the community. The binding force of the propositions derives from the simple recognition by actors in the legal culture that we have felt bound by the underlying principle all along, whether we have articulated it or not.

By stressing the function of criminal theory as a source of binding principle, we have come to a more refined understanding of the nature of the discipline and the kind of philosophical work that enriches the effort. The starting point should not be the writings of the great philosophers but rather the humble, not-fully-understood work of lawyers, legislators, and courts. From the mundane we can derive deeper truths about the principles that drive the practice of punishing crime.

Yet the mundane is not enough. Neither Coke's maxim nor any of the ten principles that I have proposed find validation just in the language or decisions of the cases. The raw words and actions of practice require interpretation, and the interpretative framework must rest on a justification in political theory. Coke's maxim requiring the concurrence of *actus reus* and *mens rea* would hardly make sense if it did not stand for an important principle of legality. Yet it is not so clear why legality requires the temporal union of action and intent. What would be lost, say, by defining theft to permit a taking at one moment of time and the relevant intent at a later time? The answer is not obvious. Explaining the principle of concurrence requires that we ponder the foundations of the state's authority to punish and the nature of criminal responsibility.

Once principles are adequately grounded, they acquire normative force in our analysis of criminal liability. They become a source of law. But what precisely does this mean? Suppose the legislated law deviates from a principle in a particular case? Is the principle refuted? If they were purely synthetic or empirical propositions, of course, an empirical counter-example would count against their continuing validity. But their appeal and their binding force are a function both of the extent to which they are realized in practice and of their intrinsic moral and logical appeal. I recognize that some of these propositions are controversial, and though I hold all of them to be true, many contrary voices sound in the Anglo-American literature.

These principles differ from the kinds of principles that Dworkin analyzed in his classic essay, "The Model of Rules."[58] These have not come into the law as conventionally recognized ethical maxims—like the famous "no one should profit from his own wrong." They derive rather, as did Coke's maxim, from theoretical reflection and generalization from the concrete instantiations of the principle.

Americans are loath to recognize that theoretical work of this sort—characteristically the work of scholars and not of courts—generates maxims that have a binding effect upon the law. Europeans and Asians—particularly those in the German sphere of influence—recognize that "theory" or scholarly generalizations of principle can provide a source of law along with legislation and case law. In these systems, theoretical commentary is not a secondary but a primary source of law.

Americans fail to grasp the dynamic of the so-called civil law because they fail to understand the significance of theoretical work as a source of law. As I have attempted to show in this Essay, we also fail to understand the way our own system of criminal law works because we have yet to appreciate the important role of theoretical generalization as a source of American law.

CHAPTER 3

Reply: On "The Nature and Function of Criminal Theory"

Kyron Huigens[*]

George Fletcher's "The Nature and Function of Criminal Theory" attempts to present the theory of punishment as normative for the content of criminal law. Fletcher writes:

> Americans fail to grasp the dynamic of the so-called civil law because they fail to understand the significance of theoretical work as a source of law. As I have attempted to show in this Essay, we also fail to understand the way our own system of criminal law works because we have yet to appreciate the important role of theoretical generalization as a source of American law. (35)

Fletcher's question is how to understand this normativity: "Once principles are adequately grounded, they acquire normative force in our analysis of criminal liability. They become a source of law. But what precisely does this mean?" (34).

It is odd that Fletcher should say that English and American punishment theorists do not believe that their theorizing is normative for the content of criminal law doctrine, when they plainly *do* believe this. They routinely refer to their scholarship as work in "the normative theory of punishment." Here, for example, is Antony Duff describing his communicative retributive theory of punishment: "[I] have always insisted that what I offer (as any normative theory of punishment offers) is an account of what punishment *ought to be*, not a comforting justification of the penal status quo."[1] This kind of normative punishment theory is a theory of just punishment, exemplified by the scapegoating objection to consequentialist theories.

[*]Professor of Law, Yeshiva University, Benjamin N. Cardozo School of Law.

Fletcher, however, seems to be saying that legal theory is legally normative; that it is binding on perpetrators, prosecutors, courts, and even legislatures, just as a codified offense definition or a constitution is. He writes that "the theorist takes the details of the criminal law as more or less given and tries to elicit from these details some synthetic principles. Consider, for example, the famous maxim formulated by Lord Coke in the early seventeenth century: Actus not facit reus nisi mens sit rea" (32). Coke might have been describing the gist of extant cases in the common law of crime. Fletcher thinks that he was, instead, setting forth a principle that ought to be followed by judges. The question is, by virtue of what are we obligated to follow these principles? Coke's stature? The authority of common law itself? Fletcher suggests that criminal law ought to conform to these principles by virtue of the theorizing that produced them. The nature of this obligation is evidently the nature of criminal law theory.

Fletcher writes:

> Theology, when it is done well, resembles the informed groping of legal theorists trying to bring diverse sources to bear on the ineffable problems of action, responsibility, guilt, and justified punishment. Great religious thinkers like Maimonides and Aquinas never limited themselves to the sources of revelation. Great legal minds proceed in a similar way: They take their traditions seriously (the analogue to revelation) and move beyond them in the direction of universal answers based on the kinds of reasoning that could appeal to thinking people everywhere. (24–25)

The last sentence of this passage posits universal truths about law that are based on inherent, universal features of human reason. Kant's legal philosophy has been described in this way:

> [Law] has a necessary and universal content that lifts it above the emptiness of positivism, and yet this content is not fissured by the internal tensions considered inescapable by today's radical critics. Kant sees law as a coherent ordering of purely external relationships among moral persons, and he undoubtedly would agree that this ordering can be grasped without reference to any of the modes of analysis (economics, ethics, literary criticism, and so on) that dominate current legal writing.[2]

It is astonishing, then, that Fletcher does not invoke a Kantian account of legal validity.

Kant's theory of criminal law has been spelled out in three sentences:

> Acting out of duty is an internal quality of a good will and therefore is not part of the external ordering contained in the concept of right. Since the point of right is to hold the external aspect of action to the external demands

of practical reason, law must posit an external source capable of determining the actor's will, that is, capable of acting as a deterrent. The prospect of external coercion complements the prospectivity of legal duty, by giving potential violators notice of the consequences attending any violation.[3]

Now, this passage is admirably succinct. It is also intriguing, given that it addresses deterrence and not retribution. But it is also opaque to the uninitiated. Fortunately, this quotation (like the preceding one) appears in what is surely the best short explication of Kant's theory of law: Ernest Weinrib's "Law as a Kantian Idea of Reason." With Weinrib's guidance, unpacking this paragraph is easier than one might think.

Human beings have capacities for choice and self-determination. This means more than to say that we are not in the grip of instinct and appetite; it is to recognize that we determine our purposes by reflecting on multiple objectives before we choose among them and act.[4] Our freedom from determination by instinct and appetite is our free will (*freie Willkur*), and the positive capacity for reflective choice is practical reason (*Wille*).[5]

It is well known that, in Kant's ethics, a virtuous action is one done from duty. What is less often recognized is that this has nothing to do with Kant's conception of law. Kant describes the difference between ethics and law, between virtue and justice (*das Recht*) in terms of internal and external aspects of practical reason:[6]

> Both practical reason and the principle of right abstract the form of free choice from whatever content it happens to have, and make this form determine the operation of the free will. The principle of right is therefore the external aspect of practical reason, or practical reason as it pertains to interaction among free wills. Under its external aspect, practical reason or *Wille* becomes the general or universal will (*der allgemeine Wille*).[7]

As Weinrib says in the seemingly opaque description of criminal law that I quoted earlier, action from duty, as virtuous action, has to do with practical reason's internal aspect. Law, including its coercive devices and deterrent effects, is a matter of *das Recht*, or the external aspect of practical reason. In the public realm, practical reason determines our purposes and actions, not by the recognition of duty but by the threat of enforcement.

Our present concern, however, is not with Kant's legal theory but with his account of law's normativity. Practical reason determines choice and action. To say that it determines choice and action is to say that it tells us which choice we ought to make and which course of action we ought to pursue. Practical reason, from this perspective, is inherently normative:[8]

> [P]ractical reason does not impose any demands on free choice from without, but merely makes explicit the normativity implicit in purposiveness

as a spontaneous causality of concepts. The meaning of normativity is precisely the determination of free choice in accordance with its own nature. Therefore one cannot intelligibly ask what additional consideration gives the demands of practical reason a normative significance: they are normative inasmuch as they are the requirements of practical reason.[9]

If *das Recht* is the external aspect of practical reason, then it determines what we do in the public square, including our choices in creating and enforcing legal rights and prohibitions. In other words, *das Recht* is inherently normative for the content of legal doctrine.

Regardless of the actual merits of Kant's theory of normativity, it suffices for present purposes to see that it is a realist theory. Weinrib describes Kantian legal realism when he contrasts it with the so-called legal realism of Holmes. Holmes claimed that the life of the law is not logic but experience. Weinrib writes:

> For Kant, activity and reason are fundamentally integrated in a way that eludes the Holmesian dichotomy. Practical reason is not something apart from—but is immanent to and constitutive of—free purposive activity. The conceptual structure of law that emerges from practical reason does not, therefore, waft down from above. In Kant's view our experience as purposive beings is literally inconceivable without the requirement that external action conform to the principle of right.[10]

Legal punishment is not just punishment if criminal law doctrine fails to conform to *das Recht*. Because *das Recht* is the external aspect of practical reason, just punishment is immanent in practical reason, which is in turn immanent in purposive human activity of any kind.

On the Kantian view, a correct account of legal punishment is an account of just punishment. On the safe assumption that we aspire to have legal punishment be just punishment, we ought to conform criminal law doctrine to a correct theoretical description of legal punishment.

Fletcher not only fails to use Kant's philosophical legal realism to explain the normativity of legal theory but also describes the normativity of legal theory in terms that are inconsistent with the Kantian account. Fletcher twice describes punishment theory's operations in terms of generalization from particulars:

> These principles differ from the kinds of principles that Dworkin analyzed in his classic essay, *The Model of Rules*. These have not come into the law as conventionally recognized ethical maxims—like the famous "no one should profit from his own wrong." They derive rather, as did Coke's maxim, from theoretical reflection and generalization from the concrete instantiations of the principle.

Americans are loath to recognize that theoretical work of this sort—characteristically the work of scholars and not of courts—generates maxims that have a binding effect upon the law. Europeans and Asians—particularly those in the German sphere of influence—recognize that "theory" or scholarly generalizations of principle can provide a source of law along with legislation and case law. In these systems, theoretical commentary is not a secondary but a primary source of law. (34)

A Kantian punishment theory, however, would proceed from universal to particular, because law has its genesis in the universal features of practical reason. For example, Kant describes *das Recht* as pertaining to choice, not to wishes or desires; and as pertaining to choice in the abstract, not to the substance of the choices made. Weinrib notes that this excludes beneficence as a source of obligation and frees the agent to choose any course of action that is consistent with others' exercise of free will.[11] One can infer from this that the criminal law does and ought to include only crimes of misfeasance, excluding crimes of nonfeasance.[12] One might arrive at a correct account of the law by working in the opposite direction—toward, instead of from, the universal sources of law—but, from the Kantian point of view, one's chances of success would seem to be radically diminished by doing so.

After reading "The Nature and Function of Criminal Theory," one is virtually certain to be at a loss to know what the nature and function of criminal law theory might be. I would prefer to report that this is because the piece has the evocative tentativeness of a good essay or because it adopts a well-considered agnosticism about whether criminal law theory has an identifiable nature at all. In the end, however, we are left at a loss because Fletcher does not invoke the legal theory that most clearly satisfies the need he describes.

PUNISHMENT

CHAPTER 4

What Is Punishment Imposed For?

George P. Fletcher

The institution of punishment invites a number of philosophical queries. Sometimes the question is: How do we know that inflicting discomfort and disadvantage is indeed punishment? This is a critical question, for example, in cases of deportation or disbarment proceedings.[1] Classifying the sanction as punishment triggers application of the Sixth Amendment and its procedural guarantees. In other situations the question might be: Why do we punish? What is the purpose of making people suffer? In this context, we encounter the familiar debates about the conflicting appeal of retribution, general deterrence, special deterrence, and rehabilitation.

In this article I wish to pose a different sort of question: What is punishment imposed for? When those convicted of crime are punished properly, I assume that they are being punished *for* something. Yet it is not clear what this "something" is. In tort cases, we ordinarily say that compensation is paid *for* the injury suffered by the plaintiff. Note that this connection between the injury and compensation holds regardless of the purpose one advocates for tort liability. Even those who subscribe to the programs for promoting efficient behavior would not say that compensation is paid *for* the efficient consequences of imposing liability. Compensation can be paid only for something that has already happened.

When x (compensation, punishment) is imposed for y, then y must be a state of affairs that has already occurred. Even if one believes, as I do, that punishment is an expression of solidarity for victims,[2] the expression of solidarity could not satisfy the requirements of the variable y. The grammar here is interesting. It would be correct to say that compensation is required "for the sake" of deterrence or that punishment is imposed "for the sake" of solidarity, but not correct to say that either form of liability is imposed simply for deterrence or solidarity. In this context the preposition "for" demands not a goal but an untoward state of affairs.

The reason that compensation and punishment are imposed for something that has happened is that both institutions function, at least in part, as remedies. They are responses to something that has happened. Damages remedy the injury, or at least they are supposed to. The scope of tort injuries sets the ambit of the damages. Now what does punishment remedy? Unfortunately, the answer is not readily at hand.

Perhaps we could reason backwards in the following way: if a certain factor conventionally increases punishment, then that factor should be included in that for which the offender is punished.[3] This inference obtains in the case of torts. The scope of the injuries determines the damage award, and damages are paid for the injury. Whatever determines the degree of punishment, then, should be that for which punishment is imposed. Unfortunately, the connection is less plausible in the case of criminal punishment than in tort law. There are many factors that aggravate punishment, with seeming legitimacy. Note the role of prior convictions, lack of remorse, and other factors that indicate that an offender is dangerous. The need for social protection may dictate a higher punishment in this situation even though the offender is not being punished for symptoms of likely recidivism. The question what the offender is punished for, therefore, remains a puzzle.

Let us consider some possible answers.

1. Injury

One might be tempted to draw an analogy from tort law and argue that as compensation is paid for injury, punishment is also inflicted for the injury that occurs to the victim of violent crime or property damage. This might be the thought underlying the claim that retributive punishment itself is a form of compensation.

Before resolving this suggestion, we should clarify a few terms. Compensation offers the party who deserves something in place of damage suffered or labor expended. It differs from restitution, which typically restores the status quo ante by returning to the injured party something that has been taken from her. There can be restitution, it seems, of money or things taken, but not of labor expended or of damage suffered. The fact of compensation recognizes that the clock cannot be turned back, that a surrogate for the loss is the only response possible. Restitution enjoys the illusion of erasing the loss, leaving as the only damage the period of time during which the aggrieved party properly claimed restitution.

Restitution comes closer than does compensation to Aristotle's ideal of corrective justice. Aristotle reasoned that wrongful acts created an imbalance in the equilibrium established under criteria of distributive justice.[4] The injurer causes a loss and as a result, a shift of resources occurs from the victim to the injurer.[5] Corrective justice requires that the injurer give half of the imbalance as a payment to the victim. This payment restores the status quo ante: the just distributive equilibrium is reinstated by eliminating loss to the victim and the corresponding gain to the injurer. What is "corrected" according to the view is neither the wrong nor the loss, but the imbalance that has occurred in the distributive scheme.

One could imagine a legal system in which punishment came close to the concept of compensation. This seems to have been the approach of ancient talmudic law, which conceived of all possible sanctions as points on a single scale of justice between the injurer and the injured. Suppose that A assaults B. Under the shared approached of modern legal systems, the following legal consequences ensue. B may repel the attack in self-defense. B may sue A in tort for the injuries suffered in the initial assault; and this is true regardless of whether he successfully repels the attack. In addition, A might be prosecuted for the crime of assault. All three of these responses are possible, and the use of one has no bearing on the others. But talmudic law espoused the principle that invoking the more severe sanction preempted the less severe.[6] If the victim sought punishment of the offender, he could not demand damages thereafter. This is a version of double jeopardy that makes sense in a system that ranks all sanctions on a single linear scale of severity. For good or for ill, we have come to see self-defense, punishment, and tort suits as parallel and non-exclusive responses to those who threaten and do harm to others. Our concept of punishment presupposes this structure of parallel remedies and responses.

It is hard to imagine a criminal injury to a person (as opposed to abstract entities such as "the administration of justice") that would not also be compensable in tort. If punishment were compensation, one would wonder why the victim should be compensated twice, once in tort and then again by putting the offender in jail or imposing some other sanction on him. Of course, in some situations the offender is judgment-proof in tort. But the principle of punishing crime is designed for rich and poor alike. True, the defendant's having made restitution may bear upon sentencing. Voluntary amends by the offender presumably provide evidence of good character to counterbalance, in part, the evidence provided by the crime itself. The rationale for a lighter sentence is not that the restitution takes the place of the justified punishment.

Of course, in tort the victim sues; in a criminal case, the state takes the lead. But the difference between punishment and compensation, or between crime and tort, lies not only in the identity of the suing party. The structure of liability also differs. The underlying principle of tort law is the separation of the criteria of liability from the criteria of damages. Once liability is established, the plaintiff recovers the full amount of her injuries, regardless of how tenuous the liability link might have been. This principle is expressed in the "eggshell skull" rule: even if the extent of the injury is unforeseeable and therefore beyond the injurer's fault, the victim recovers in full.[7]

The principle of reducing liability on the basis of contributory negligence as well as the principle of compensation according to "market shares" represent seeming exceptions to this principle. In these cases, the criteria of liability have a bearing on the degree of damages. In fact, both institutions are reconcilable with the general principle that the injuring party must pay for all the damage that he or she causes. Contributory negligence should be understood as a division of damages based on relative degrees of causation. The same with the principle of "market share" liability, which simply apportions causal responsibility over the class of injuries as a whole.[8]

Criminal law places a different emphasis on the occurrence of harm. So far as fault matters (and not strict liability), the degree of the defendant's fault (blameworthiness, or culpability) bears on the degree of liability. The difference between common law murder and manslaughter lies not in the damage done, but in whether the killer acts with malice. Tort damages do not depend on whether liability is based on negligent or intentional wrongdoing. Yet in tort cases, juries decide the issue of damages as well as of liability; this enables the jury informally to consider the degree of fault in setting the level of damages. In criminal law, the way in which the harm is done—negligently or intentionally, by act or omission—determines the level of liability as a matter of principle. Criminal juries are permitted to consider issues in assessing liability that tort juries raise covertly in setting the level of damages.

In view of all these differences between the two types of sanction, the interpretation of punishment as compensation enjoys particular tenacity. The root of "retribution," namely "retribuere," conveys the idea of "paying back." And there is indeed an analogy between the ideas of compensation and paying back, or returning to the offender that which he has done. Foucault's interpretation of punishment as reenacting the crime on the body of the offender, captures the same idea.[9] *Vergeltung* in German conveys the same point of applying to the offender that which he has imposed on the victim.

It is tempting to mischaracterize retribution as requiring that the same offense be committed on the offender. If the offender rapes, he should be raped in return. Admittedly, the unfortunate metaphors of the *lex talionis* support this reductio ad absurdum. It is not clear that Exodus chapter 22 really meant "eye for an eye, a tooth for a tooth." The rabbis of the Talmud understood the text to require a life for a life—under certain conditions of culpable killing. But they readily interpreted the rest of the bodily references to require compensation for injuries suffered by those physical harms short of death.

Kant developed a version of retribution that clearly had nothing to do with returning the crime in kind. The central message in Kant's teaching is that punishment should bring home the meaning of the crime to the criminal offender. Thus he proposes castration as the proper punishment for rape, and exile for other sex offenders who display what he took to be an inability to live in civilized society.[10]

The only sensible punishment for theft, he taught, was imprisonment as the functional equivalent of commitment to the "poor house." The thief should be treated as someone who displays contempt for the value of property and thus as someone who, himself, has no property.[11] This is not a matter of reenacting the crime on the body of the offender, but of forcing the offender to confront the meaning of his acts.

Thus we may conclude: In tort, compensation is paid and received for the injury, in criminal cases, the punishment is imposed not for the harm done, but, it seems, for some other aspect of the actor's conduct. What could that other aspect be?

2. Wrongdoing

If one inmate turns to another and asks, "What are you in for?" the response would normally include a reference to what the inmate did—some action that he or she performed. The answers would typically be the names of crimes themselves: drunk driving, selling crack, or "bumping someone off." The appropriate description of the action would include a reference to the norm implicitly violated. These conventional understandings of why men and women are imprisoned provides some guidance to what, as a conceptual matter, punishment is imposed *for.* It is imposed for the act of wrongdoing, the unjustified violation of a statutory norm.

H.L.A. Hart hints at the same point when he lists the following elements defining the concept of punishment:

[1] Punishment must involve pain or other consequences normally considered unpleasant.

[2] It must be for an offense against legal rules.

[3] It must be of an actual or supposed offender for his *offense.*

[4] It must be intentionally administered by human beings other than the offender.

[5] It must be imposed and administered by an authority constituted by a legal system against which the offense is committed.[12]

The point underscored in this list is that punishment is imposed for the offense committed by an actual or supposed offender. The offense is a violation of a prohibition against a specific action or a prescription requiring a particular action. I refer to this violation of the norm as wrongdoing. It might be worth adding a word on behalf of this usage if for no other reason than that in this symposium Michael Moore asserts the contrary: "wrongdoing" supposedly refers only to causing harm.[13] It follows for his purposes that attempts and other non-harmful inchoate offenses, such as possession offenses, are not wrongful; they are not instances of wrongdoing.

Consider the prohibited possession of a weapon. The mere act of possession causes no harm—though it may generate a risk of accidental discharge or of purposeful misuse. It is not clear why Moore balks at labelling the knowing violation of the statutory prohibition as an instance of wrongful behavior. Surely he would have to say that the knowing possession of the weapon violates the law: it is unlawful. Referring to an action as wrongful provides another description of the same state of affairs. The term "wrong" underscores the positive evaluative content of the law as Right (*Recht, droit, derecho, diritto*):[14] a state of affairs incompatible with the Right is wrong. It is that simple. Moore's effort to link wrongdoing to causing harm defies common sense.

Yet the question remains whether wrongdoing is aggravated by the occurrence of harm. Virtually everybody insists that this is true. Legislatures routinely punish drunk driving that causes death more severely than simple drunk driving.[15] The usual pattern of liability imposes a greater sanction on attempts that succeed as opposed to attempts that fail.[16] Yet there is a great temptation in the academic world to support a skeptical position about the relevance of harm to the degree of wrongdoing.[17]

The skeptical view goes something like this. Individual actors can be culpable only for matters within their control—their absolute control. The only thing we have absolute control over is the movement of our bodies. We have no control over what happens to a bullet after it is fired, over what happens to poison placed in someone's drink, over whether someone hired to kill actually carries out the plan, or over whether a woman consents or does not consent to a seduction with gentle force. Crimes should be defined, therefore, independently of these consequences. It follows that attempted homicide and attempted rape—crimes defined solely on the basis of what the actor intends at the time of acting—should be punished no less than the completed offenses.

It is clear, however, that this academic effort runs afoul of the public's sensibilities of wrongdoing and its degrees. The average person regards an actual killing as worse than a miss, an overcoming of the partner's will as worse than a case in which the woman happens to consent. Some theorists claim that this common view reflects a penchant for neurotic guilt, that if the average person were well informed, he or she would come around to the sophisticated view advocated by the academics.

There is no basis for thinking that this common view is neurotic, that it reflects some displacement of guilt. Yet the popularity of the common view has little impact on the theoretical conviction that control over one's bodily movements determines the outer limit of culpability and liability. This ongoing dispute presents, in the end, a conflict between two cultures in criminal law, one tied to common sense, the other reflecting what Bruce Ackerman once dubbed "scientific policy making."[18] I put little stock in the latter, but I am aware how difficult it is to address and convince those who do. If punishment is tied to shared cultural judgments of wrongdoing, then harming is clearly a greater wrong than trying or preparing to harm. It follows that the result, when it occurs, is part of the action for which an offender is punished.

The ordinary language of crime as well as religious sin supports the view that the result is part of the action. Prohibitions are always directed against killing, maiming, destroying, and other harmful actions. The Ten Commandments are directed to results such as dishonoring one's parents and desecrating the sabbath. The interesting exception is the Tenth Commandment: thou shalt not covet that which belongs to thy neighbor. Still the imperative is against actually coveting, not against trying or attempting to covet. No one would formulate a moral imperative simply against trying to commit these harms. In the culture of crime and punishment, as we know it, the harmful result inheres in the action prohibited.

Inchoate offenses are always derivative. They are designed to catch the offender in the preparatory stages where he may merely frighten the potential victim or take an excessive risk of harming someone (drunk driving). Because they are derivative and less intrusive in the rights of potential victims, they understandably receive a lower punishment. Admittedly, this sensible conclusion has yet to generate a compelling philosophical foundation. Moore believes that he has furnished one in this symposium, but Russell Christopher's Reply to Moore demonstrates that though Moore's intuitions are in the right place, his logic is wanting.[19] The search for a convincing account of our intuitions in this area remains unsatisfied.

3. The Relevance of Culpability

To speak of culpability is presumably to speak of culpability *for* something, for an act, a state of affairs, a violation of the law. In this respect, the structure of culpability parallels the concept of punishment. As the latter is not simply imposed without an object of punishment, culpability does not exist in the abstract. One is culpable *for* something untoward that has happened—for causing harm, for violating the law, for wrongful behavior. Similarly the excuses that negate culpability—mistakes of fact and law, duress and personal necessity, insanity—are excuses *for* having brought about the same untoward state of affairs.

Yet one often hears theorists of the criminal law say that offenders deserve punishment only if they are culpable—culpable in the abstract, without specifying what it is the actor is culpable for. This is notable among those who reduce culpability to an event of consciousness, such as intending or choosing to do something. This way of speaking suggests that the punishment is imposed for culpability itself. Those who take this line of thought characteristically have difficulty recognizing negligence as a genuine form of culpability. This is the position that Michael Moore finds himself in.[20] In a less sophisticated way, Jerome Hall took this line a generation ago.[21]

Some trends in criminal law support this way of thinking. The venerable requirements of *mens rea* and *actus reus* are treated as independent, parallel pillars of liability. This seems to imply that *mens rea* or "culpability" can be analyzed separately from the realization of an *actus reus* in the external world. This disposition is reflected in the current practice of penalizing impossible attempts. The actor thinks that sugar is cyanide and puts it in the intended victim's coffee. If there is a conviction in this case, what would the punishment be imposed for? The criminal act, it is said, is the taking of steps toward the execution of criminal intent. Yet it would not make sense to punish the act as it appears to others, namely as putting sugar in coffee. From the perspective of possible victims, the act itself is innocent and harmless. The only thing untoward in the situation is the intent to kill. The intent renders the act criminal, and then this act doubles as that for which the actor is deemed culpable. The circularity disquiets.

Maybe we would never have arrived at this state of criminal law if we took the rights of victims seriously in thinking about retributive punishment. Punishing harmless impossible attempts that frighten no one would hardly make sense if we take the victim's perspective. The particular act is not dangerous. If anything it is the actor who may be dangerous. But this shift from a dangerous act to a dangerous actor is morally monumental. Impossible attempts come into relief as the expression of a wicked intent. The would-be poisoner shows himself to be dangerous and therefore punitive intervention is supposedly justified. Yet this is a curious form of retributive thinking. It is in fact early intervention and preventive confinement masquerading as punishment.

The significant feature of culpability, as it bears on punishment, is that it comes in degrees. The person who kills under provocation or while suffering from diminished capacity acts with partial culpability. In sentencing, the presumptively reduced culpability of those who are contrite or who have made amends has the impact of reducing punishment. This, as I pointed out earlier, is the feature that renders criminal liability different from tort liability.

The intersection of two factors, then, determines the level of punishment that justly fits the crime. One is the scale of the wrongdoing; the other is the degree of culpability. They come together in this formula devised by Robert Nozick: $P = r.H$. The level of punishment equals the degree of responsibility (varying from 0 to 1) times the scale of wrongdoing. Causing rather than just risking harm increases the scale of the wrongdoing. Bringing about the harm negligently rather than intentionally reduces the "r" factor.

Punishment is imposed, therefore, for wrongdoing as reduced by the extent to which culpability is diminished. This way of understanding punishment is lost on those who think of culpability as an independent factor or even as the central factor in structuring criminal liability. Yet it may be lost on others as well. For as I argued at the outset, thinking of punishment as imposed *for* something attributes to punishment the capacity to rectify some untoward state of affairs. We live, however, in an era of skepticism about whether it is really possible to bring out harmony in the moral order or metaphysically to vindicate right over wrong. In these anti-mystical times we need to bring punishment back to the people who are directly affected by whether it is imposed or not.

4. The Duty to Punish as a Double Negative

It may be easier to justify punishment not as a positive remedy for wrongdoing but rather as the absence of an evil. The evil is abandoning victims in their suffering and isolation. Recently, I argued that blackmail should be understood as a paradigmatic crime, wrong because, like other crimes of violence, it establishes a relationship of dominance and subordination between the criminal and the victim.[22] I continue the argument here. The claim is that punishment is imposed in order to avoid the evil of not punishing.

Blackmail, theft, embezzlement, all leave a wake of dominance and subordination. Rape victims have good reason to fear that the rapist will return, particularly if the rape occurred at home or he otherwise knows her address. Burglars and robbers pose the same threat. Becoming a victim of violence beyond the law means that what we all fear becomes a personal reality; exposure and vulnerability take hold and they continue until the offender is apprehended. It would be difficult to maintain that all crimes are characterized by this feature of dominance. The most we can say is that this relationship of power lies at the core of the criminal law. It is characteristic of the system as a whole.[23]

The way to counteract the power of the criminal over the victim is for the state to intervene with power over the person of the criminal. It is not enough to make the offender pay damages or a fine, for all this means is that she purchases her ongoing status beyond the prohibitions that apply to others. The state must dominate the criminal's freedom, lest the criminal continue his domination of the victim. The deprivation of liberty and the stigmatization of the offense and the offender—these means counteract the criminal's dominance by reducing his capacity to exercise power and symbolically lowering his status.

Punishment expresses solidarity with the victim and seeks to restore the relationship of equality that antedated the crime. This may not be so obvious in a culture that has become accustomed to thinking of punishment as a utilitarian instrument of crime control. The way to appreciate the psychological significance of the state's standing by the victim is to think about the cases in which the state refuses to prosecute and thereby abandons the victim in solitary suffering. During the terror in Argentina that led to approximately 9000 *desparecidos* prior to 1983, many victims' families realized, to their horror, that they could not turn to the police. The police were often the ones engaged in the roundup of suspected terrorists. The failure of the state to come to the aid of victims, as expressed in a refusal to invoke the institutions of prosecution and punishment, generates moral complicity in the aftermath of the crime. The failure to punish implies continuity of the criminal's dominance over the victim. Not only the criminal can trigger a relationship of dominance and subservience. The state can effect the same relationship by failing to invoke the customary institutions of arrest, prosecution and punishment.

The problem is whether this argument is offered as a rationale for retributive punishment or as identification of the nexus between punishment and the criminal act. Does it make sense to focus on the relational aftermath of the crime as that for which punishment is imposed? Significantly, the plaintiff's injury, also an aftermath of the liability-creating incident, provides the requisite nexus for compensation. And we noted at the outset that we sought an account of punishment that would be as clear as the proposition that tort compensation is awarded for injuries sustained. Attempting to draw the parallel in the context of punishment, however, encounters grammatical problems. One cannot quite say that the punishment is imposed *for* the dominance the criminal acquires over his victim. The sanction may be imposed to counteract or neutralize this dominance, as compensation is awarded to rectify injuries sustained. But this might not be enough.

The factors of desert as well as remedy seem to control the grammar of "compensating for" and "punishing for." The victim deserves compensation for the full extent of her injuries, provided liability is established. The criminal may deserve punishment on the basis of what he has done, but not, it seems, for the advantage that he acquires in the crime. Also, focussing on the relational aftermath of the crime rather than on the crime itself might not generate the fine gradations we have noted in the formula $P = r.H$. The scale of wrongdoing and the degree of culpability are features of the act, not of the relationship of dominance the act establishes. We are drawn to the aftermath of crime in order to understand why we impose punishment, but to grasp what punishment is imposed for we must stick to the crime itself—in all its subtlety and fine grained distinctions. That we no longer grasp punishment as a remedy for the crime is a contradiction that we cannot so easily escape.

Reply: The Importance of Asking the Right Question: What Is Punishment Imposed For?

*Douglas Husak**

"What Is Punishment Imposed For?" surely is among the most provocative titles George Fletcher attached to any of his several remarkable contributions in criminal law theory. This exact question, he correctly notes, seldom is raised. This fact alone is significant. The question *seems* straightforward, important, and intelligible (despite ending with a preposition). It is noteworthy that legal philosophers are unlikely to confront this question until they read Fletcher's work.

Progress in philosophy often depends on asking the right questions. When the most brilliant minds throughout history fail to resolve a controversy, we have reason to suspect that something may be wrong with the question they ask . Perhaps our deepest concerns about free will, for example, are not really about *the will* at all. A simple reformulation of the issue may stimulate a major advance in philosophical thinking. Are we in a better position to grasp some important insight about the many perplexities that surround criminal law and punishment if we address the question Fletcher has posed? Maybe. We all know that the intuitive reactions of respondents can be altered by how a particular question is framed. Arguably, our judgments about punishment are influenced when we ask: What is punishment imposed for?

What exactly do we want to know when we ask Fletcher's question? The query conceals some important ambiguities. I will distinguish three possible interpretations. The first alternative is that the question asks for a *justification* of punishment. Of course, legions of legal philosophers have struggled to offer a normative defense

*Distinguished Professor of Law and Philosophy, Rutgers University.

of punitive sanctions. None, however, seems to have framed the question simply by asking what punishment is imposed *for*. Typically, they ask: "Why should we punish?" or "What justifies punishment?" Might we better answer the set of concerns that have vexed philosophers if we adopt Fletcher's formulation of the issue? I am tentatively optimistic that Fletcher's question may facilitate our understanding of the normative issues surrounding the justification of punishment.

On the one hand, attempts to answer Fletcher's question seem to tilt us strongly in favor of a nonconsequentialist (i.e., a retributive) solution. As H.L.A. Hart pointed out in his celebrated attempt to define what punishment *is*, punishment must be "for an offense against legal rules."[1] When one inmate (Jones) asks another inmate (Smith) what the latter is punished *for*, we would expect Smith to respond by identifying the particular crime(s) for which he has been convicted. It would be strange if Smith replied that he is punished to promote some future good, such as general deterrence. Jones would naturally suppose that Smith had misunderstood the nature of his query. Thus the question "What is punishment imposed *for*?" seemingly invites us to look backward at past acts of criminality. Suppose, however, that Jones had phrased his question differently, asking what justified the punishment of Smith, or asking why Smith's punishment was justified. Smith would be somewhat less inclined, I believe, to suppose that the answer to Jones's question must lie in the past. If I am correct, one plausible way to phrase the central issue about punishment leads naturally toward a retributive solution.[2]

Alas, matters are not quite so clear, for Fletcher's formulation of the question may not discourage us from embracing consequentialism after all. Frequently, when we inquire what someone did something *for*, we are asking *why* he acted. These *why* questions—why someone (Black) inflicts a punishment on another (White), for example—inquire about Black's reason for acting as he did, which often direct us to the end or objective he sought to achieve by his action. Once we identify this end or objective, we can try to decide whether it is capable of justifying Black's behavior. Suppose that Fletcher's question is understood similarly: For what end or objective is punishment imposed? This question, I think, directs us toward a consequentialist position.

In other words, I claim that the notorious "for" relation must be disambiguated in order to answer Fletcher's question and to understand how both past and future considerations contribute toward its resolution. If we want to know *for what* punishment is imposed, our answer necessarily looks backward at past behavior. As consequentialists and nearly all retributivists appreciate, however, it is perfectly coherent and eminently sensible to impose punishment *for the purpose of* attaining a future good. One *might* hold that the very purpose of imposing punishment is to implement a principle of retributive justice, but this claim seems improbable to me. At any rate, we are not precluded from imposing punishments to achieve special or general deterrence even though we answer the *for what* question by looking backward to crime.

Notice that our intuitions about the retributive or consequentialist perspective depend not only on *how* the question is framed but also on *who* the addressee of the question happens to be. When one inmate asks another inmate what he is punished for, the latter will naturally look toward the past. But when someone with the authority to dispense punishment is asked what he imposes punishment for, he is more likely than the inmate to look toward the future. If White is a defendant who asks Black, a judge, why he is being punished, White would not assume his question had been misunderstood if Black responded that he is imposing a penal sanction to prevent White (or others) from committing similar crimes in the future. I am unsure whether this observation parallels Hart's famous insight that it is coherent to provide different justifications of punishment if we ask different questions about it: a question about its general justifying aim (why do we have an institution of punishment?) as opposed to a question about its distribution (who should be punished and to what extent?). Still, we come close to replicating Hart's insight if I am correct that different justifications of punishment are likely to be given if we address Fletcher's question to persons who play different roles in our system of criminal justice.

Perhaps I have misunderstood Fletcher's original question by supposing it is designed to raise such familiar issues. His question need not be interpreted to demand a justification of punishment but instead may be construed to ask what it is *about* what is punished—that is, criminal behavior—that makes punishment a suitable response. In other words, the question "What is punishment imposed for?" might be interpreted as "What is it about crime that allows us to punish it?" One possible way to approach this difficult issue is as follows. Paradigm cases of core criminality involve wrongdoing, culpability, and harm. Is there some reason to privilege one of these three components? Is it sensible to believe that punishment is *for* one of these ingredients rather than for another? How should we decide?[3] A promising strategy is to reflect on cases in which punishment is inflicted when one or more of these three components is absent. If we still would regard punishment as an appropriate response to a (real or imaginary) crime that did not involve culpability or harm, for example, but would not regard punishment as an appropriate response to a (real or imaginary) crime that did not involve wrongdoing, we have some reason to conclude that punishment is imposed *for* wrongdoing. The other components of core criminality—culpability and harm—seemingly would play a less central role in our thinking about what it is about crime that allows us to punish it.

If we employ this strategy, I believe we come to conclude that wrongdoing is the most salient element in our thinking about why crimes merit punishment. I cannot demonstrate this claim to be true; it rests almost entirely on intuition. Many crimes impose strict liability, including at least one material element that requires no culpability on the part of the defendant. Although most such crimes are objectionable, others are not.[4] Even more obviously, many crimes do not require actual harm. Inchoate offenses prescribe only a risk of harm, rather than harm itself, and no sensible commentator contends that all such offenses should be repealed. In fact, Fletcher (and a host of other theorists) has expended considerable ingenuity trying to show what the occurrence of harm could possibly *add* to the case for punishment. In any event, it is hard to think of any acceptable crimes that dispense with wrongdoing. Possible counterexamples include the enormous number of *mala prohibita* offenses jurisdictions have enacted. I contend, however, that the only way to defend these offenses as involving a legitimate imposition of the penal sanction is to argue (appearances notwithstanding) that they involve wrongdoing after all.[5] If a given *malum prohibitum* crime were not really *malum* in any intelligible sense, no adequate theory of criminalization would allow it to be enacted. If all criminal offenses should require wrongdoing, the question Fletcher raises (as I have construed it) may help us to find a principled limit on the criminal sanction.[6]

Even if I am correct that wrongdoing has special salience in understanding what punishment is imposed for, we still need to know what it is *about* wrongdoing that merits punishment. This inquiry invites us to consider why some wrongful acts should *not* be punished. To resolve this problem, I think we need a theory of *public* wrongs. A wrong is public not because it is done *to* the community but because it is the *proper concern* of the community in which the punishment is imposed.[7] Unless we understand why some but not all wrongs properly concern the public, we will be unable to decide why some but not all wrongs merit punishment by the state. Suppose, then, we succeed in producing a theory of public wrongs. Why is punishment an appropriate response to persons who commit the offenses that conform to this theory? Is the state permitted to punish these wrongs simply to achieve retribution—to implement a principle of retributive justice? Could the value of achieving retribution possibly justify the massive expenditure of resources required to maintain our system of criminal justice? Or do consequences somehow enter into the case for punishing public wrongs? If so, exactly how and why are consequences relevant?[8] To provide a comprehensive answer to *these* questions, I believe we require nothing less than a theory of the state. Clearly, this is no small undertaking.

We have returned yet again to the issue that has divided punishment theorists for centuries. The debate between consequentialists and retributivists has resurfaced. Still, it has resurfaced at a somewhat different place, so the inquiry has been advanced. Fletcher's question, as I have construed it, helps to identify wrongdoing as salient in our effort to understand exactly what it is about criminal behavior that makes punishment appropriate, and sharpens our understanding of where the disagreement between consequentialists and retributivists may lie. An account of why some wrongs concern the state, and why this concern should take the form of punishing those who perpetrate these wrongs, may reveal whether and why consequences are relevant to the justification of penal sanctions. I conclude that

Fletcher's question "What is punishment imposed for?" may assist us in finding a solution to these problems. Or so I hope.

I will briefly suggest a third and final interpretation of Fletcher's question. We may want to understand the deep structure of criminal responsibility by asking "What is punishment imposed for?" Superficially, it is clear that criminal liability and punishment are imposed *for* conduct that is proscribed by a criminal law. But what is the significance of conduct? At the most fundamental level, theorists are (somewhat unevenly) divided between "choice" and "character" models of criminal responsibility. According to the first model, punishment is appropriate only when imposed for the *choices* persons make in their conduct.[9] According to the second model, punishment is warranted only when conduct reflects on the agent *qua* agent. Even though persons are held criminally liable for their actions, they are not responsible or subject to punishment unless these actions reflect on them as agents.[10]

Despite its importance, I will not dwell on this third interpretation of Fletcher's query. Even though it may invite an investigation into the deep structure of criminal responsibility, I do not see how his question helps us to better understand this structure. In any event, I do not believe that either a "choice" or a "character" model is wholly correct; no single, unified theory explains all of criminal responsibility, either descriptively or normatively.[11] Fletcher has persuaded me that the penal law contains at least three distinct models, structures, or (what he calls) *patterns* of criminal liability,[12] and that any attempt to eliminate or reduce one to another is doomed to failure.[13] Still, I have tried to show how addressing the novel question "What is punishment imposed for?" may help us to gain insights about some of the fundamental issues in criminal theory that have bedeviled philosophers for centuries. We should be receptive to proposals to move the debate forward by reframing our basic questions.

CHAPTER 6

Punishment and Compensation

░

George P. Fletcher

When novelists and philosophers turn to the work of lawyers, they tend to gravitate toward certain issues and ignore others. Two processes—punishment and compensation—lie at the heart of our legal system, but only the former has drawn the attention of literary and philosophical minds.

The issues of wrongdoing, guilt, and expiation are of endless fascination not only for Dostoevsky and Duerrenmatt, but for any writer who seeks to fathom the foundations of our moral life. For philosophers, the concept of punishment has become a proving ground of the even broader conflict between deontological and utilitarian moral theories. Deontologists hold that punishing crime is right and just in itself.[1] Utilitarians insist that the good of punishing criminals depends on the beneficial consequence of deterrence and incapacitation.[2] For lawyers as well, the concept of punishment comes center stage as the standard for distinguishing criminal prosecutions from civil actions. When a sanction constitutes punishment, the state must provide the procedural trappings of a criminal trial. Thus, the courts confront the question whether particular sanctions, such as deportation[3] and punitive fines,[4] constitute the kind of punishment characteristic of criminal trials.[5]

The equally important notion of compensation enjoys none of this glamour. Philosophers do not probe the meaning of compensation as they write unceasingly about the nature of punishment. As lawyers we speak daily about compensating the victims of accident and of governmental programs, but the question whether transferred funds constitute compensation or something else rarely concerns us.[6] That we ignore the nature of compensation should not puzzle us. Offsetting injuries by compulsory compensation lacks the dramatic appeal of crime and punishment. Yet the distinctions among institutions for transferring wealth are important, both morally and politically. The criteria for marking off compensation from welfare and redistributive taxation warrant our attention. These criteria bring into focus critical, undiscussed features of our legal institutions.

If punishment occupies the intersection between deontological and utilitarian moral theories, compensation can claim the same distinction. Do we require tortfeasors to compensate their victims because the victims deserve a monetary surrogate for their injuries or, alternatively, because we wish to stimulate changes in the behavior that generates accidents? Deontological theories insist that compensation for damages done is right and an end in itself. Utilitarian theories hold that compensating victims makes sense only as a means of furthering social objectives, such as reducing the costs of accidents and encouraging socially useful behavior.

A proper analysis of compensation does not require us to commit ourselves, as a moral matter, to either a utilitarian or deontological theory. In this article, I shall offer a conceptual account of compensation, which turns out to include the elements of a deontological theory. The method of inquiry resembles philosophical work on the concept of punishment. The result of the inquiry conforms, structurally, to those views that stress the intrinsic retributive component of sanctions properly called punishment.[7] The question that guides our inquiry, then, is not "What is the purpose of compensation?" but rather "What is the nature of compensation?" This question invites a conceptual analysis of compensation rather than an explicit moral choice between utilitarian and deontological moral theories.

Extrinsic and Intrinsic Perspectives

At the outset I wish to introduce a terminological distinction that will assist me in referring to various theories of compensation and punishment. The extrinsic aspect of punishment and of compulsory compensation refers to the impact of the sanction on future behavior, either of the defendant or of other people. The intrinsic aspect inheres in the relationship between the sanction and the wrongful or harmful act for which the sanction is imposed. This aspect of both punishment and compensation finds expression in inquiries about whether the sanction is fitting or appropriate. The intrinsic question about punishment is whether it responds justly to the actor's wrongdoing. The analogous concern about compensation is whether it serves to rectify the injury as suffered by the victim. Note that both of these intrinsic questions carry intimations of magic in the legal process. Punishment magically expunges the wrong; it enables the criminal to repay his debt to society. Compensation similarly expunges the damage done to the victim; the mere payment of money turns back the clock and puts the victim in the position she would have been in had the injury not occurred.

This intrinsic magic prompts some observers to doubt whether either punishment or compensation makes sense in any way except its extrinsic potential impact on future behavior. These sanctions presumably have an external impact, while the intrinsic, magical component remains open to doubt. The concreteness of the extrinsic perspective tends to support utilitarian theories, both of punishment and of compensation. These theories take the extrinsic perspective to be the only relevant consideration.

Focusing exclusively on the extrinsic aspect of punishment and compensation may avoid certain soft arguments about rectifying the wrongs of the past, but only at the expense of imprecise and unprovable claims of social impact. No one has yet figured out a way to determine the relative deterrent impact of a single incident of punishment or of requiring compensation. Even more critically, the extrinsic point of view blurs important distinctions among parallel sanctions that may have the same hypothetical social impact. From the extrinsic point of view, one has considerable difficulty distinguishing between punishment and civil commitment. In the field of compensation, the same extrinsic perspective obfuscates the contours of compensation both from the defendant's and from the plaintiff's point of view. If impact is all that matters, then the defendant's paying compensation and his paying a fine appear to be of equal moment. If receiving money is all that matters, then the plaintiff's receiving compensation hardly differs in nature from her receiving incentive payments, relief, or welfare. The underlying question is whether we must build these distinctions into any account or model we generate of our legal processes. I will argue that any theory of law that ignores this intrinsic side, either of punishment or of compensation, fails to capture our legal reality.

Though no one, so far as I know, has offered a theory of compensation parallel to the elegant theories of punishment, several influential writers have taken implicit stands on the nature and relevance of compensation. In fact, two of the more important schools of contemporary jurisprudence build on implicit stands about the nature and role of compensation. In the school of economic jurisprudence, as typified by the work of Calabresi[8] and Posner,[9] compensation as such turns out to be irrelevant.[10] In the opposing philosophical literature, typified by the work of Robert Nozick, the distinction between compensation and redistribution proves to be a critical premise of a libertarian political theory.[11] In order to gain some perspective on the concept of compensation, we should digress to consider these divergent views on the relevance of the intrinsic perspective and of the concept of compensation.

Is the Intrinsic Perspective Necessary?

As Calabresi and Posner approach tort law, the relevant inquiry consists in the external impact of monetary sanctions, never in examining the intrinsic aspect of compensation. Forcing a defendant to pay money might stimulate similarly situated risk-takers to invest more in safety or to be more careful in the future, but it is irrelevant that in the particular case the compensation flows from the defendant to the victim. The money could, as well, have been paid as a fine to the state.[12] If economic efficiency were the sole concern of the tort system, this conclusion would be plausible. The shift of assets from one party to the other has no economic significance. Of course, the reallocation of wealth poses distributional issues, but economists concede that in their professional goals, they know nothing about distributional justice, or for that matter, any other form of justice. Thus the economic approach to tort law suppresses the intrinsic question whether the damage award rectifies the loss suffered.

An analogous system of thought has arisen in analyzing whether the government should pay compensation to persons whose property is allegedly taken in the course of regulation and other governmental actions. The fifth amendment requires just compensation to those whose property is taken, either directly or indirectly, for the public good.[13] But as Michelman[14] and Ackerman[15] develop their versions of economic jurisprudence, the obligation to compensate should turn exclusively on whether buying off those who file claims is the socially least costly way of resolving the conflict.[16] The social cost of compensating or not compensating includes the administrative costs of processing the claims and the potential demoralization costs to those who are not compensated. But the social costs do not include the out-of-pocket expense of shifting assets from the government to the individual. Again, from the economic point of view, the mere redistribution of wealth does not represent a social cost. Again, we observe that economic jurisprudence systematically ignores the intrinsic aspect of compensation.

If economic jurisprudence ignores the compensatory aspect of required payments, the contrasting school takes the intrinsic aspect of compensation to be a central concept in determining the functions of a just state. To appreciate this point, we must turn to the theories of Rawls and Nozick.

In the wonderfully simplified world of economics as applied to the law, all legal questions fall into two categories: economic efficiency and the distribution of wealth. This bifurcation ignores the critical distinction between corrective and distributive justice. Corrective justice requires the transfer of assets in order to correct some injury for which the paying party is properly held accountable. Distributive justice, in contrast, dictates the distribution of assets in establishing the starting point for voluntary social cooperation. In Rawls' monumental work, the central concern is distributive rather than corrective justice. Rawls' basic premise is that all deviations from the equal distribution of wealth must be justified.[17] He ignores the question of corrective justice, for these issues arise not in establishing the framework for social cooperation, but only to correct concrete disturbances that occur in the course of social life.[18]

In Nozick's powerful retort to Rawls, however, the concept of corrective justice becomes the plumb line for staking out a plateau of just, voluntary relationships free of unjust coercion. For Nozick, taxing the rightfully held assets of the rich amounts to a violation of the natural right to hold property.[19] In contrast, requiring compensation for a harm caused stands as an acceptable form of coercion. Compensation merely corrects a harm for which the paying party is justly held responsible. Although it is coercive, required compensation does not violate anyone's natural rights. Indeed, the failure to require compensation, when justly due, would represent a violation of the victim's right to a redress of his injuries.[20]

In the structure of Nozick's argument, the distinction between corrective and distributive justice, between compensation and redistribution, figures most prominently in developing a model of voluntary, just processes that would lead to a minimal, Night Watchman state.[21] The challenge for libertarians is to develop a model of the state that entails neither the unjust loss of liberty nor the redistribution of wealth.

The stumbling block to a purely voluntary state would obviously be those citizens who preferred not to join the central state and instead to run their own courts and enforce their own judgments. Forcing these independents to give up their courts and their private police would, according to Nozick, intrude upon their natural rights.[22] And if they were coercively absorbed into the state, the state would have to accord to them its peacekeeping protection and its dispute settling services. Persons involuntarily subjected to the state's monopoly of force would presumably not pay for access to the state's courts. But if they did not pay, the implication would be that other voluntary citizens would have to pay a surcharge in order to support the services extended to the involuntary members. Nozick concludes that this surcharge would represent a redistribution of wealth. The voluntary members would in effect subsidize the involuntary members. A state based on the principle of subsidization would be tainted by the unjust redistribution of wealth.

To overcome these two impediments to a just, minimal state, Nozick borrows principles of compensation and prohibition from the common-law tradition. The argument for prohibiting independent courts and police is that these independent courts would expose the voluntary citizens of the emerging state to excessive risks of arbitrary judgments. As some dangerous activities are prohibited as nuisances, an emergent state could legitimately prohibit independent courts and police "not known to be, both reliable and fair."[23]

There remains the problem of characterizing the free services to involuntary members so as to avoid the taint of redistribution. Nozick's argument is that because individuals are deprived of their natural right to enforce their own claims, the free services of the state should be seen as a form of compensation. Nozick draws the analogy between epileptics prohibited from driving and independents prohibited from running their own courts.[24] Both prohibitions are based on the fear that the exercise of a basic right excessively endangers other people. Nozick argues that epileptics should be compensated for being deprived of the right to drive, and therefore, by extension of the same principle, independents are entitled to compensation for being deprived of their courts. The compensation consists in the free services offered by the state.[25]

Nozick's argument needs some shoring up at several turns.[26] My point in outlining this argument is not to endorse his conclusion that a state might evolve without the redistribution of wealth, but to demonstrate the importance of distinguishing between redistribution and compensation in developing a political theory.

It is fair to say that the writers I have mentioned shape the basic debate in our law schools today. Yet among these influential thinkers we find divergent postures on the relevance of compensation. The school of economic jurisprudence ignores the intrinsic aspect of compensation, for as their premises imply, a shift in wealth has no economic significance. In contrast, theorists who hold to the distinction between corrective and distributive justice tend to regard coerced compensation as immune to traditional libertarian concerns. It is imperative that we take a stand on this conflict. The issues are both substantial and methodological. At stake is the way we think about our legal institutions. And the way we think has long-range implications for what we regard as acceptable uses of legal power.

Philosophical Accounts of Punishment and Compensation

How do we go about determining whether the intrinsic perspective is necessary for an adequate account of compensation? I suggest we follow the lead of the philosophical literature on punishment and attempt to apply its teachings to the related concept of compensation. The two notions, after all, are closely related. From the extrinsic perspective, both function as sanctions imposed against persons, who, in general terms, cause harm or endanger others. From the intrinsic perspective, punishment seeks to rectify the public imbalance generated by the defendant's wrongdoing; compulsory compensation seeks to rectify the private imbalance generated by the defendant's causing harm. The problem in both contexts consists in refining this general account of the two remedies.

In the philosophical literature on punishment, two recurrent issues present themselves. The first focuses on the required relationship between the punishing person and the wrongdoer; the second, on the reasons for requiring the wrongdoer to suffer. Let us work through both these issues, first with regard to punishment, and then by extension to the process of requiring compensation.

Assume that someone has done something morally wrong. We want to do something about it. If we take action against a wrongdoer, the suffering we inflict does not always amount, conceptually, to punishment. For an example of self-help that does not amount to punishment, think of the proposed boycott against the Nestle Corporation's marketing its infant formula in underdeveloped countries.

Many people have argued that Nestle's expanding its market in this way constitutes a moral wrong. The effect is to induce poor women in underdeveloped countries to expend their resources for formula rather than to nourish their children
with their natural milk. The proposed remedy is to boycott Nestle products in the
United States. If the boycott succeeds, it would unquestionably inflict economic
harm on the Nestle Corporation. From the external point of view, this harm seems
very much like punishment. The effect of lost profits on the Nestle Corporation
would resemble the government's imposing a fine for wrongdoing. Yet, regardless
of their economic power, private individuals conducting a boycott cannot, in the
nature of things, punish the Nestle Corporation.

Similarly, the United States' boycott of the Olympic Games could not, conceptually, amount to punishment of the Soviet Union for invading Afghanistan.
The reason that these boycotts do not amount to punishment is that the person
seeking to punish stands as an equal with the alleged wrongdoer. Equals cannot
punish each other. Punishment presupposes a superior authority who judges the
conduct of the other as wrong. God can punish man; the state can punish its citizens; parents can punish their children. This point about authority is a conceptual
point.[27] It is a claim about the nature of punishment, not a normative thesis about
how we ought to construe the concept.

The concept of compensation lends itself to an analogous conceptual restriction. If someone has suffered injury in an accident or natural disaster, anyone might
offer assistance to help reduce the suffering of the victim, but not everyone who
offers money or other forms of wealth is in a position to compensate the injured
party. Suppose a fire strikes a Navajo village and we send money to help relieve the
suffering of the deprived villagers. We can help the victims with our funds, but as
a conceptual matter, we do not compensate them. Had an arsonist set the fire and
been required to pay for the damage, however, her payments would constitute
compensation. This subtle distinction invites others. Suppose the villagers have
fire insurance and they collect the proceeds on their policies. We would not ordinarily refer to the funds paid by the insurance company as compensation. Why
not? I submit that these variations of the problem fall into a pattern described
by a required relationship between the paying party and the injurious event. The
paying party must bear some responsibility for the harm caused. If we offer relief
to the villagers, we do so without any suggestion of responsibility for the fire. The
same is true of the fire insurance company, which merely acts to fulfill its contractual obligation. But the arsonist obviously stands in a relationship of responsibility and therefore her paying does constitute compensation.

The conceptual alternatives to compensation take a variety of forms. We might
call the funds we offer to the villagers "charity," or if the government came forth
with the funds, "relief" would be the right term. The proceeds paid by the insurance company would be neither compensation nor relief, neither welfare nor charity. The distinguishing feature of the insurance transaction is the insured parties'

right to receive the proceeds under their policies. Note that most cases of obligatory payment constitute compensation, but the fire insurance example stands as an exception. In that instance the policyholder's contractual right takes the payment out of the categories of welfare and relief, but the company's not having a responsible relationship to the fire inhibits us from describing the payment as compensation.

In the second perspective that we derive from the philosophical literature on punishment, we focus on the reason for judicial or administrative action. A range of sanctions meets all the external criteria for punishment. Impeachment, deportation, disbarment—all of these, in H.L.A. Hart's words, "involve pain or other consequences normally considered unpleasant."[28] All of them occur in the required relationship of authority and they all otherwise meet Hart's necessary and sufficient conditions for punishment. Yet we know intuitively that none of them constitutes punishment.

Consider impeachment and conviction of civil officers of the United States. This sanction is imposed for "high Crimes and Misdemeanors,"[29] and yet removal from office does not constitute punishment for these crimes. If it did, we would expect the double jeopardy clause to prevent subsequent criminal prosecution of the removed officer. Yet the double jeopardy clause does not apply. If impeachment represented a way of paying one's debt to society, we might expect the President's pardoning power to apply to the relevant crime and thus remove the debt that need be paid. By express exception in the Constitution, however, the pardoning power does not apply to impeachments.[30] How do we explain that a sanction can border on punishment and yet fall short? The explanation, I believe, resides in the reason for impeachment and removal from office. The point of this remedy is not to cancel out the wrong, but to protect the public by removing the offending civil officer. The significance of the high crime or misdemeanor is that it provides evidence of unreliability and untrustworthiness in office. It may be that the stigma of impeachment is greater than that for recall by popular election, but the weight of the sanction falls on the side of social protection rather than retribution for wrongdoing. As a measure of separation and protection, impeachment fails to qualify as punishment. The same analysis explains why legally and philosophically, deportation and disbarment fall beyond the range of punishment and thus may be imposed without all the procedural protections of a criminal trial.[31]

In referring to this cluster of issues as the reason for the sanction, I do not mean to say that individual judges necessarily have a particular reason in mind when they impose a sentence. Rather the reason should be inferred from the attributes of the sanction, both as they have been designed, and as they have crystallized in practice. The quality of impeachment and deportation becomes evident by comparison with a related sanction, expatriation, which the Supreme Court properly treats as punishment.[32] Expatriation for wrongdoing is subjected to the type of scrutiny ordinarily reserved for criminal sanctions. The difference between deportation and expatriation is important. The pain and deprivation implicit in deportation is incidental to the aim of separating an offending alien from the country; the compulsory separation accomplishes its end of protecting society. Expatriation, in contrast, does not accomplish anything except the disgrace of the dishonored citizen. The expatriated citizen remains at home; if he is dangerous, he remains dangerous even as a resident alien. If there is a social benefit that derives from expatriation, it is only as the result of the additional mechanism of example and deterrence. If others witness the dishonoring of a citizen, they might arguably abstain from the same crime.

The emergent thesis is that if a sanction automatically protects society by removing someone from a position in which he endangers us, then the sanction bears a nonpunitive component. If, in contrast, the sanction functions primarily to disgrace and stigmatize the offender, then we are inclined to see the sanction as punishment. Impeachment, deportation and disbarment fall into the category of sanctions that in their very imposition achieve a socially desirable goal of separating the offender from a role or a place where he might be dangerous. Expatriation more closely resembles flogging, capital punishment, and penitential confinement. These are sanctions designed to disgrace and stigmatize the offender, and through this act of labeling, perhaps to reform the offender and encourage others to abstain from similar behavior.

The difficulty of this analysis, I must note, is that it fails, at first blush, to explain why we regard imprisonment as a form of punishment. So far as confinement in prison serves merely to separate dangerous offenders from society, imprisonment functions very much like deportation for a specific term. Perhaps the stigmatizing effect of imprisonment is sufficient to explain why this form of separation differs from those cases that we regard as nonpunitive. Alternatively, confinement might be a special form of separation, far more intrusive upon liberty than merely removing someone from a position or from a particular society. Though I think my general account of punishment is correct, I concede that the central case of imprisonment may require a distinct analysis.

My aim here is to illustrate a method of analysis which I believe carries important lessons for understanding the structure of compensation in the law of torts and eminent domain. Recall Nozick's reliance on the distinction between compensation and redistribution. How do we decide whether a particular payment constitutes one or the other? It is not enough to point to a prior incident of causing harm as the stimulus for the required payment. We have to pose the additional question: what does the payment do? What is it designed to do? The analogy with mechanisms of separation breaks down at this point, for there is no easy way to inspect a monetary payment in order to determine what it accomplishes. We have to reflect on the criteria for assessing the amount of the payment. Do we look to the relative wealth of the parties in assessing damages? If we do, we can hardly avoid the suggestion that the payment effectuates a redistribution of wealth. On the other hand, if we limit our focus to the transaction causing harm, the payment functions more as a measure of compensation. Do we apply the principle that the defendant must take the victim as he finds him? If so, again it appears that the reason for the sanction is to correct the effects of the harm on the particular victim. Redistributive measures do not take the victim in his or her concrete particularity; rather they treat the victim as a member of the class of persons who warrant a greater share of society's wealth. Thus, if we consider the particular victim's age and earning capacity, we structure the obligatory payment to highlight the compensatory effect.

In our systems for requiring compensation to victims of torts and governmental takings, we do not permit evidence of the parties' relative wealth. Rather we require, particularly in the tort system, that the defendant take her victim as she finds him.[33] This suggests that the function of tort payments is to render compensation rather than to redistribute wealth. Of course, we could change the system so that it operated differently, but my aim here is to analyze the requirements of a model that would explain our practices. Revolutionary arguments are reserved for those who can convince us, as a matter of principle, that what we are now doing is wrong.

Conclusion

If I have offered an adequate account of compensation as that concept has crystallized in our legal practices, then one feature of that account takes us back to the conflict between the economic and philosophical analysis of compensation. The criteria for gauging the payment—critical in understanding whether it is compensation or redistribution—coincides with what we referred to earlier as the intrinsic aspect of compensation. The extrinsic perspective tells us merely that compensation is like many other actions that have the effect of transferring wealth from one person to another. The intrinsic perspective informs us whether the payment responds fittingly to a particular victim injured on a particular occasion.

Now recall the contrast at the beginning of this article between economic jurisprudence, which ignores the intrinsic perspective on compensation, and the philosophical school typified by Nozick's work, which relies on the intrinsic perspective in elaborating a political theory. If my account of compensation is correct, then it follows that economic jurisprudence cannot possibly offer a faithful account of the concepts that we actually employ in discussing legal problems. No system of thought that ignores the intrinsic perspective, on either punishment or compensation, can possibly capture the distinctions that we use every day in approaching legal problems.

This categorical rejection of economic descriptions of our legal system could well provoke a pointed objection. How is it possible, one might say, that by engaging in conceptual analysis, I can solve the normative questions that concern every reflective lawyer? What is the purpose of tort law? Is it merely to provide compensation or is it to minimize the costs of accidents? What is the purpose of the eminent domain clause? Is it to secure private property against redistribution or is it to minimize the social costs of governmental programs? These normative issues are at the forefront of every theoretical discussion. How can one simply brush them aside with an argument about the structure of compensation?

The objection is a powerful one, and indeed it goes to the heart of contemporary disputes about justice and efficiency as legal values. The pursuit of the "right" purpose of criminal law, of torts, of the first amendment, indeed of every institution in our legal system, dominates theoretical discourse. Yet in my opinion this pursuit is misconceived.

First, the pursuit of the "right" purpose directs our attention to the impact, or the extrinsic perspective, of our legal institutions. The "right" purpose consists always in the pursuit of some goal that the theorist posits. The preoccupation with these goals or policies obfuscates the boundaries among parallel institutions, all of which favor the same goal. From the point of view of social protection, we can hardly distinguish among punishment, impeachment and deportation. Yet the life of legal argument consists precisely in elaborating distinctions of this sort, probing essences of related concepts and staking out the boundaries between them. That is the simple fact that we confront every time we think about speech under the first amendment, about searches under the fourth amendment, about the concept of testimony in analyzing the privilege against self-incrimination, and about criminal punishment under the sixth amendment. The habit of drawing distinctions defines the lawyerly craft, and any mode of thought that blurs the boundaries of related concepts speaks not to lawyers, but to others who care more about functional similarities than about the structure of ideas. The preoccupation with purposes and goals, in short with the extrinsic perspective, blurs distinctions; for it directs us away from those intrinsic considerations that are necessary to distinguish among institutions that tend to have the same external impact.

My second response to those who favor focusing on purposes rather than on conceptual distinctions begins with a point of political theory. I start on the assumption of a heterogeneous society, in which we all pursue diverse purposes. The function of legal institutions is precisely to enable individuals with diverse goals to engage in peaceful and effective cooperation. It follows that our legal theory should not enthrone particular purposes as criteria of legitimation. In the doctrines of contracts, torts, and criminal law we find a systematic tendency to de-emphasize purposes and motives. The validity of a contract does not turn on the parties' purposes. It matters not why an individual borrows money, merely that she borrows it. Similarly, tort liability for battery does not turn on why A kicked B, but merely that A intentionally kicked B. As a general matter, motives are equally irrelevant in assessing criminal liability. Disregarding ultimate purposes enables us to establish a set of principles that function as the lowest common denominator among diverse purposes and motives. That is precisely what we need in a society in which we seek to cooperate despite our cherishing private purposes.

By like token, we should recognize that every theorist has a favored explanation of why we punish criminals, why we require compensation for takings, and why we protect free speech. Precisely as the validity of contracts does not turn on the parties' ultimate purposes, the analysis of our institutions should not incorporate the favored purposes of this or that group of theorists. Rather, we should view the criminal law, tort law, takings law, and other institutions as the common denominator of competing purposes. That is why I have urged a conceptual analysis of punishment and of compensation rather than a view of these sanctions hitched to some goal that we should all take for granted. The intrinsic perspective does not start from a goal, but from the reality of crystallized concepts in everyday legal discourse. It is in examining this discourse that we discover the implicit structure of our concepts and further a vision of law free of officially approved purposes. As we turn away from private purposes, we elaborate a legal method that conforms to the way lawyers actually think and argue. But most importantly, by recognizing that a proper analysis of punishment and of compensation need not incorporate a particular social goal, we encourage diversity of purpose behind a common institution. We maintain the unity of our legal system at the same time that we favor individuality and human freedom.

CHAPTER 7

Reply: "Punishment and Compensation": A Comment

❧

*John Gardner**

George Fletcher observes, in his 1981 article "Punishment and Compensation," that a great deal more philosophical attention has been paid to the punishment of offenders than to the compensation of victims (58). In the intervening years, there has been some rectification of this imbalance. In particular, there has been major new philosophical work on the payment of compensatory damages in the law of torts and the law of contract.[1] So we now have finessed versions of many of Fletcher's insights. Nevertheless, Fletcher's essay remains important as one of very few philosophical works that compare and contrast the compensatory and the punitive, giving evenhanded attention to both. In the following remarks I will attempt to augment and refine Fletcher's comparisons and contrasts.

A preliminary question is whether compensation is really the subject that interests Fletcher. His analysis seems to be of a narrower concept, which might more naturally be called "reparative compensation," or "reparation." Fletcher thinks that when an insurance company covers its policyholder's losses arising out of a fire, that is not compensation, since the insurance company did not "bear [causal] responsibility for the harm caused" (64). Presumably the various government schemes in modern welfare states that are said to compensate people for the adverse effects of industrial diseases, criminal injuries, and so on, are by the same token misnamed in Fletcher's view, for they too are paid without "any suggestion" that the diseases and injuries in question can be attributed causally to the government (64). My own conceptual intuitions differ from Fletcher's here. To my mind all these insurance-type payments are straightforwardly compensatory. What

* Professor of Jurisprudence and Fellow of University College, University of Oxford.

they are not is reparative. Reparation is a special kind of compensation with the added feature that it is paid by or on behalf of someone who bears causal responsibility for the injury or loss that is being compensated. This added feature is the one that particularly interests Fletcher. So in my view his article might more illuminatingly have been called "Punishment and Reparation."

Nevertheless, there is something helpful about beginning with the wider concept of compensation. For even before one begins to ask who should be paying compensation, there is a prior question of why anyone should be receiving it. This question forces us to spell out a unifying feature of all compensation schemes, reparative or otherwise. As Fletcher says, such schemes aim to restore their beneficiaries, so far as it can be done, to the position they would have been in had a certain misfortune not befallen them (59). I add "so far as it can be done" to accommodate both conceptual and practical limitations. Some misfortunes cannot be (wholly) undone even in an ideal world. Others could be (wholly) undone were there no budgetary caps or policy exclusions. Both types of limitations afflict most compensation schemes. In spite of such limitations, however, all compensation schemes by their nature have the aim just mentioned, the aim of "expung[ing] the damage done to the victim" (59). This is, in Fletcher's useful terms, their "intrinsic" aim as compensation schemes (59). They are more perfect as compensation schemes, the closer they get to eliminating the effects of the specified misfortunes on those whom they compensate.

Because he dives straight into discussing the special case of reparative compensation, Fletcher does not stop to point out how odd this intrinsic aim of compensation is. Why set about restoring the unfortunate to the position they *would* have been in rather than the position they *should* have been in? Of course in some cases it may come to the same thing. In some people's lives, apart from the misfortune that now stands to be compensated, things would have been as they should have been. But in other cases the two come apart. Since I should not have been so rich and you should not have been so poor, why (following some misfortune that afflicted us both) restore me to riches and you only to poverty? This is the perennial challenge issued by those who doubt the sanity, or even the intelligibility, of distinguishing corrective from distributive justice. Surely, the argument goes, it cannot be just to restore a distributive injustice. So corrective justice has no separate work to do. Compensation following a misfortune can be just only inasmuch as it puts us into the distributively just position that we should have been in anyway. There are many objections to this line of argument, some of which are outlined by Fletcher (61–63). The most important, however, is one that he does not mention. The proposed assimilation of corrective to distributive justice overlooks the independent negative value of disruption in human life. All else being equal, there is a stronger case for protecting people in the lives they already have than there is for giving those same lives to people who have not had them before. So the question of whether someone should receive fifty dollars by way of compensation for the loss of fifty dollars is not the same as the question of whether, had he never had the fifty dollars, fifty dollars should now be found for him.

Like it or not, this conservative principle is the main moral basis for the payment of compensation. But how can it be applied to cases of reparation? In reparation cases the loss is not automatically spread thinly across a large group of contributors, as it is with government compensation schemes or first-party insurance, but rather is shifted in its entirety (so far as this can be done) from the person who first suffered the loss to someone else who made some causal contribution to it. Why is this? Why eliminate disruption from one person's life, only to move it to another person's life? It is no answer to say that the person who is liable to pay reparative compensation (we can call her "the defendant") may in turn take out third-party insurance to spread her loss thinly and thereby reduce the disruption to her life. The question remains: Why shift this burden of loss-spreading to her in the first place? Why make it her problem?

The common response is to say that, as between someone who suffers a loss and someone else who makes a causal contribution to it, it is fairer (all else being equal) to shift the burden to the latter. The former is a patient and the latter is an agent, and this makes a moral difference to which of them should bear the disruption (or the burden of avoiding the disruption).[2] This seems right to me. Economists of law have tried to cast doubt on whether the distinction between agents and patients can be sustained. In my view their attempts have failed.[3] Nevertheless, the same writers have succeeded in raising a deeper challenge to the common response. Why should the pool of possible loss-bearers be restricted in advance to these particular people, to the person who suffers the loss and the person or people who made a causal contribution to it? Why not begin with a much larger pool of possible loss-bearers?

This is a genuine puzzle. It is the puzzle with which Fletcher grapples when he characterises the intrinsic aim of reparative compensation in the following way:

> [Reparative] compensation seeks to rectify the private imbalance generated by the defendant's causing harm. (63)

This is clearly along the right lines. But the formulation is too impressionistic to do the work that Fletcher needs it to do. Talk of "rectifying imbalances" suggests that it is just as important to eliminate the defendant's gain as it is to eliminate the plaintiff's loss. Sometimes, of course, the two go together. If I stole your car, then (all else being equal) taking the car from me and giving it back to you annuls my gain as well as annulling your loss.[4] But sometimes annulling your loss will not be enough to annul my gain. Suppose that I won a lucrative bet by stealing your car successfully. Should we care to annul this gain too? Some people believe that there are valid principles of corrective justice that require such surplus gains to be annulled by their "disgorgement" to the plaintiff. On this view gains, even without corresponding loss, are part of the "private imbalance" that needs to be "rectified" under the heading of corrective justice.[5] I doubt whether this view is right. But be that as it may, such annulment of gains is not compensation, and nor therefore is it reparation. Reparation aims to eliminate the plaintiff's losses, never mind the defendant's gains. In that respect talk of reparative compensation "rectifying a private imbalance" is apt to be misleading.

This matters for the contrast with punishment. Fletcher rightly argues that there are sanctions and remedies that meet the "external criteria" (65) for punishment, but which are not truly punitive. Such sanctions and remedies are not punitive because the "pain and deprivation implicit in [them] is incidental" to other aims (66). It is not itself part of their aim. Reparative compensation is such a non-punitive remedy. Whether it succeeds *qua* reparation does not depend on whether the defendant suffers or is deprived by being bound to pay it. Permitting him to rely on third-party insurance to meet his reparative obligations does not defeat the object of the reparative exercise, even if the insurance company declines to recoup the payment from the defendant through increased premiums. But the same indemnity would defeat the object of the punitive exercise. The object of the punitive exercise is (or includes) that the punished person should suffer or be deprived. Where does disgorgement of gains fit into this contrast? Is there any sound reason to extinguish a surplus gain from the defendant's holdings other than to subject him to suffering or deprivation? Maybe there is. But one wonders what it is, since *ex hypothesi* the transfer of surplus gains does not put the plaintiff back in the position she would have been in but for the defendant's actions, and so cannot be explained as an instance of compensation, reparative or otherwise. One cannot account for it by pointing to the need to mitigate disruption. So it is at least tempting to think that those who are against the retention of surplus gains are being punitive in their attitude.

I am not sure that Fletcher makes enough of this distinction between the incidental pains of reparation and the intentional pains of punishment. He prefers to emphasize, as his master-contrast, the private rectification of reparation as against the public rectification of punishment. On his view, punishment seeks to rectify the public imbalance generated by the defendant's causing harm (63).

But in what sense are the imbalances tackled by punishment "public"? This (I think) is Fletcher's explanation:

> Equals cannot punish each other. Punishment presupposes a superior authority who judges the conduct of the other as wrong. (64)

Once again I do not share the conceptual intuition. Many people respond to wrongs committed by their friends and relatives by sulking, withdrawing favors, and so forth. I see no reason to doubt that this is punishment, nor to regard it as a less central case of punishment than, say, criminal punishment. *Pace* Fletcher, a consumer boycott of the Nestlé Corporation by "private individuals" (64) is straightforwardly punitive, so long as the intention of those individuals is that Nestlé (or its directors, shareholders, etc.) should suffer for the corporation's wrongs.

More generally, I am skeptical about the idea that the rectification of imbalance is part of the very idea of punishment, as opposed to one possible reason (among many) for punishing. Why punish? People may say "to get even" or "to settle scores" or to have the wrongdoer "pay her debt to society," but they may equally say "to teach him a lesson" or "to give him a taste of his own medicine" or "to make an example of him." Are the latter nonrectificatory reasons for punishing in some way parasitic upon or secondary to the former rectificatory ones? Do they presuppose an undisclosed rectificatory objective on the part of those who cite them? I think not. Punishment's intrinsic aim is only that the wrongdoer should suffer or be deprived on the ground of her wrongdoing. Beyond that the possible aims of punishment are various.[6] In this respect punishment and reparation are more asymmetrical than Fletcher seems to allow. For rectification as between the defendant and the plaintiff is part of the very idea of reparation—part of reparation's intrinsic aim—and not merely one possible reason for exacting it.

I confess that I have not said anything so far to solve the puzzle of how rectification by reparation works. So I have not managed, so far, to improve on Fletcher's impressionistic formulation of reparation's intrinsic aim. Let me end by floating a suggestion about how one might make progress with this. When I fail to perform a duty that I owe to someone, there is something that I still owe that person afterward. Strictly speaking, I still owe him performance of the duty, which continues to bind me. But if it is too late to perform—the dirty deed is done—I now owe him the next best thing.[7] I owe it to him to put him back, so far as it can now be done, into the position he would have been in if I had done my duty in the first place. So how does the negative value of disruption fit in? The negative value of disruption is part of the rationale for the original duty, the one that I failed to perform. It was, at least in part, a duty of nondisruption. This means that the "next best thing" I now have a duty to do includes mitigating or alleviating, so far as possible, the disruption that I left behind. Often but not always the best way to mitigate or alleviate is to compensate. In short, the compensation is needed because of the disruption, and the duty to compensate is owed by me because I was the disrupter. That means it is the special kind of duty to compensate that, at the outset, I called a reparative duty.

Needless to say, this line of thought requires a great deal more work before it holds up.[8] But, properly developed, it explains a lot. In particular, it helps to bring out the most fundamental asymmetry of all between reparative compensation and punishment. For there is no way to represent punishment as the fallback performance by the wrongdoer of the duty that he originally failed to perform. Unlike reparation, punishment is not something that the wrongdoer owes. For it is not something that he can give. It is something that is inflicted upon him by others, and the norms regulating it belong, in the final analysis, to their normative position and not to his.

If this is right, then Fletcher's article makes reparative compensation and punishment seem more fundamentally alike than they are. Nevertheless, the article casts a great deal of light on both concepts and on the relationship between them. It was primarily this article by Fletcher that inspired me, as a graduate student, to think about the similarities as well as the differences between crimes and torts, and between criminal law and tort law, which in turn inspired me to invest philosophical energy (ever since!) in writing about both areas of law.

MENS REA AND MISTAKE

CHAPTER 8

The Fault of Not Knowing

George P. Fletcher

Introduction

Despite the outpouring of interest in tort and criminal theory over the last thirty years, we have not made much progress toward understanding the basic concepts for analyzing liability. We operate within the paradigm of the opposition of fault and strict liability and assume that this basic dichotomy lies at the foundation of the system. This dualistic assumption is to be found in the literature of both corrective justice and law & economics. All the treatises and casebooks follow this basic format, adding as well the distinction between intentional torts and negligent torts. The latter are two forms of fault, while strict liability, generally defined negatively as the absence of fault, covers everything else.

The difficulties of the tort theoretical system are evident in the use of the phrase "strict liability" as though it states a ground or rationale of liability.[1] Of course it does not. It merely says that there is no fault (whatever that term might mean), and surely the absence of something cannot state an argument for imposing liability. Economists argue that fault consists in acting in violation of the Learned Hand Formula of cost/benefit analysis. Faultful conduct is inefficient in the sense that its costs exceed its benefits. Liability for efficient conduct is called strict (the argument being that liability might be efficient because it would internalize the costs of the conduct). The only problem is that there are an infinite number of cases of efficient conduct, and they typically do not entail liability. The use of the term "strict liability" is obviously a conclusion that tells us nothing at all about the criteria for distinguishing between those cases of efficient conduct that result in liability (e.g., flying airplanes and crashing, with damage to structures and people on the ground) and those cases of efficient behavior that entail no liability (driving cars and crashing, with damage to structures and people next to the highway).

The same basic structure—intention and negligence versus strict liability—extends to criminal law, except that the criminal theorists play on a more restricted board of possibilities. They start from the assumption that strict liability is an improper basis for liability. Perhaps it might be necessary on utilitarian grounds in exceptional cases, but no one seriously argues—not even economists—that it provides a potential rationale for routine cases of criminal punishment. In contrast to tort theorists, American criminal lawyers make a radical assumption about the distinction between recklessness and negligence.[2] This constructed distinction, based on whether the actor is aware of the risk being run, turns out to be a structural feature of today's criminal law. Recklessness is an acceptable form of *mens rea*; inadvertent negligence is a dubious deviation from the principle that *mens rea* consists in choosing to do wrong. The assumption is that those who are aware of the risk they run are on the same side of some crucial barrier as those who choose; those who are unaware of the relevant risk are on the other side of the line.[3]

In the way that many criminal theorists picture the world of fault and mental states, there are three relevant categories: (1) real *mens rea*, including intentional, knowing, and reckless behavior; (2) inadvertent negligence; and (3) strict liability, or no fault at all. It is this picture that led Glanville Williams to describe negligence as "a half-way house" between real fault and strict liability.[4] The Model Penal Code (hereinafter MPC) implicitly takes the same line by restricting the application of inadvertent negligence to cases explicitly authorized by the provision defining the offense. If the statutory provision is silent about the required *mens rea*, then at least recklessness is required.[5] Some people still defend the view, once argued with great vigor by Jerome Hall, that inadvertent negligence is an improper basis for criminal liability.[6]

The sharp divide in American criminal theory, then, is between conscious and inadvertent risk-taking, but this architectonic distinction plays no role in torts, where the great divide runs between fault and no-fault, between negligence and intentional conduct taken together, on the one hand, and strict liability, on the other. These boundaries that carve up these respective disciplines have a whiff of the conventional about them. It would be entirely possible, for example, for the system of criminal law to be more casual about the distinction between conscious and inadvertent risk-taking, between recklessness and negligence. In German criminal law, for example, they are both treated as variations of negligence. Or it might be possible to structure the system of tort law with the same assiduous attention to mental states that the MPC shows in the field of criminal liability. For example, instead of relying on the concept of "gross negligence" to trump certain claims by the defendant, e.g., in guest statute cases, tort law could rely on the MPC's concept of reckless conduct instead.

Despite these differences in approach to the question of culpability in defining liability, common law theorists of torts and criminal law tend to accept the conventional distinction between objective and subjective standards and concur with the view that objective negligence is not really fault in the way that subjective negligence is. My own view, argued on many occasions, is that this distinction between objective and subjective standards is misunderstood and that, in fact, so-called objective negligence is a test of fault or culpability in the same way that subjective standards are.

Within the framework of all these debated points of doctrine, I want to defend inadvertent negligence as a proper basis for blaming someone for causing harm, and this is true whether we are speaking about torts or criminal law, whether the standard is regarded as objective or subjective. I will approach the problem first by engaging in an extended analysis, in the first part of the paper, of Oliver Wendell Holmes' writings on negligence. These merit attention for several reasons. First, Holmes set forth the basic categories of analysis that remain with us today, and further, his texts easily lend themselves to misreading. At least, my sense today is that I have misread him in the past, and this is an opportunity to set the record straight. In the second part of the paper, I will address the general question of how people can be considered at fault and be blamed for not knowing critical attributes of their conduct. These critical features might be either matters of fact or matters of moral evaluation. The first part, then, is historical; the second part philosophical.

Before beginning this exploration, I should note that the problem of inadvertent negligence pervades the criminal law. It arises not only in thinking about the basic mental state required for conviction, but surfaces also in considering the problem of mistakes with regard to claims of justification and excuse. Any time a defense of consent or self-defense is denied on grounds that the defendant's belief in the underlying facts was not reasonable, we encounter a problem of inadvertent negligence. The same is true with regard to claims of mistake of law. Whenever the defendant acts in good faith but is subject to blame on the ground of having deviated from the standard of the reasonable person, we collide with the same conundrum of imposing blame for not knowing that which one is supposed to know.

I. Holmes on Negligence

When carefully read, Holmes' argument in *The Common Law* turns out to be at odds with conventional views on tort theory that prevail today. Let us take the very distinction between fault and strict liability. His first cut at this distinction is that fault is the "personal fault"[7] characteristic of criminal liability and that this personal fault is located "in the state of the party's mind."[8] The alternative to fault is acting "at one's peril." The basis of this strict liability, apparently without fault, is that someone has chosen voluntarily to act and damage ensues. "If the act was voluntary, it is totally immaterial that the detriment which followed from it was neither intended nor due to the negligence of the actor."[9] Thus we find the basic distinction between fault and strict liability that governs the discussion today.

A careful reading reveals, however, that this dichotomy reflects the way "others" interpret the history of tort law, not the way Holmes thinks is correct. If you follow his argument carefully, you realize that Holmes' view is that the principle of acting at one's peril, or strict liability without fault, never really existed at common law. Going back to the yearbooks and *The Thorns' Case* in 1466,[10] Holmes argues that in every case of supposedly acting at one's peril, some element of "fault" or "blameworthiness" is implicit in the judgment of liability. In *The Thorns' Case*, the defendant trimmed his rose bush and the thorns fell onto his neighbor's land. Liability was affirmed on the basis of trespass, and it looks very much like liability based on no more than a voluntary act producing an invasion of another's land. Yet Holmes reasoned that the bush-trimmer could have prevented the thorns from falling. "The defendant ought to have acted otherwise, or in other words, he was to blame."[11]

This is a very revealing sentence. The notions of fault and negligence shift from the sense Holmes attributed to John Austin's analysis of criminal liability—namely, negligence as a state of mind—to a "personal" fault to the fault of not having acted otherwise. The basic ground for "blaming" someone for causing harm, as Holmes writes, is acting voluntarily to cause harm. Since the notion of voluntary conduct is built into the conditions of "acting at one's peril," the standards of fault and of strict liability collapse into one another. The only requirement is that "voluntary action" contain a sufficient element of foreseeable consequences to conclude that the actor ought to have done otherwise. This conclusion should come as no surprise, for the purpose of Holmes' argument was to show that strict liability never really existed at common law. The proper reading of tort history leads to the view, Holmes claims, that the defendant was always "to blame," even in the cases once thought to be examples of acting at one's peril.

The closest Holmes comes to recognizing strict liability in the conventional sense is in his description of damage done by grazing cattle. The owner is liable for intrusion on another's land, fault and foreseeability seemingly playing no part. Holmes concedes that this case from the common law is on the borderline between fault and strict liability.[12]

The discussion so far has generated two distinct senses of fault. One is that fault is personal and identified with a state of mind. The second is that fault is equivalent to breaching a duty to act otherwise and amounts to no more than acting in a way that is properly subject to blame. Each of these generates a conception of strict liability as its opposite. The first opposite is that liability is strict when it does not require a state of mind, a personal fault. The second opposite is strict when it applies regardless of whether there is any basis for blaming the defendant for causing the harm in question.

These different senses of fault and strict liability come into play in trying to understand what Holmes is getting at when he introduces the idea of "objective" negligence. The critical pages are 108 and 109, and these repay a careful examination of the logic and the context of the argument. The argument begins with the claim that the law consists of "standards of general application."[13] It follows, in Holmes' view, that the law cannot take into account "the infinite varieties of temperament, intellect, and education which make the internal character of a given act so different in different men."[14] It seems that in this remark, Holmes is rejecting the idea that negligence is a form of fault based on the "internal character" or "state of mind" of the individual. This is the first of a series of remarks that has generated the dominant picture of "objective" negligence as being a standard of liability that falls short of true fault. True fault is personal. It is linked to a "subjective" state of mind. As the criminal lawyers say, fault points to "a guilty mind," that is, to a form of consciousness that is self-consciously guilty.

Objective negligence is the fault that satisfies the fictitious standard of the reasonable person under the circumstances. According to the conventional view, subjective fault is a moral standard, but objective negligence is not. Holding people to general standards, exacting this "sacrifice" from them, is justified on the supposedly utilitarian standard of promoting the "general welfare."[15]

A whole series of remarks in these two pages support this claim that objective negligence—disregarding the "infinite variety" of personal characteristics—is something other than a moral conception of fault. Here are some of them:

1. "[The law] does not attempt to see men as God sees them."[16] Presumably the way God sees men exemplifies morality. The law is an institution necessary to serve the welfare of society.
2. "If a man is born hasty or awkward," he cannot claim this "congenital defect"[17] as an excuse. His being prone to accidents will be recognized in the "courts of Heaven,"[18] but not in the courts of this life. Why? Because his slips are just as troublesome to his neighbor "as if they sprang from guilty neglect."[19]
3. The reference to "guilty neglect" in this last passage reinforces the difference between objective and subjective negligence. The latter is based on guilty neglect.
4. An objective standard, one based on laws of general application, expresses the needs of potential victims to "require" the accident prone "to come up to their standard."[20]
5. If the "hasty or awkward" person fails to meet the standards of his neighbors, he should be held liable "at his proper peril."[21] The use of the word "peril" in this context reinforces the association between objective negligence and strict liability.
6. The alternative to requiring the "hasty or awkward" to meet the standards of his neighbors is for the courts "to take the personal equation in account," but

this the courts decline to do. The phrases that stand in opposition to objective accumulate. The image of what negligence in tort law is not now includes not only the "personal equation," but reference to the "courts of Heaven" and to acting with "guilty neglect."

7. The conclusion that derives from these premises is the "law considers…what would be blameworthy in…the man of ordinary intelligence and prudence, and determines liability by that."[22]

Given all of these mutually supportive comments, one cannot be surprised that the tradition has read Holmes to have introduced a standard of liability that in fact has more in common with strict liability than with true fault. The orthodox view that prevails in the profession today is that negligence is based on the projected behavior of the reasonable person. This standard is "objective" rather than "subjective."

Holmes did not use the terms "objective" and "subjective," but lawyers are drawn to them to capture the difference that Holmes sought to elaborate. The only difficulty with the opposition of objective and subjective is that these terms obscure two possible approaches to negligence that can be classified as "subjective." The opposite of objective negligence either can be the "state of mind" that Holmes associated with John Austin's view of negligence or it can be the standard that takes into account the "infinite variety" of individual differences among different actors. To distinguish between these strains of thinking in Holmes, I prefer to use the two sets of opposites: external versus internal and general versus individualized. Holmes apparently thought that negligence is external and general and neither internal nor individualized. As I will show later, Holmes believed that negligence can, at one and the same time, consist of standards of general application and be individualized in the assessment of personal responsibility.

Holmes has been systematically misread. And I confess that I have misread him in some of my earlier work.[23] Part of the misunderstanding is of his own doing. He held a restricted and rather primitive view about the contours of morality. In his lexicon, the general welfare is a safer, more sensible standard than ultimate issues of right and wrong, virtue or vice. Phrases like "guilty neglect" and the "courts of Heaven" supposedly refer to a moral standard, while the general welfare serves as a concept that people can understand without waxing ideological about natural law and ultimate truths. As I have argued elsewhere, Holmes' pragmatism is closely related to the moral fatigue that beset the United States in the wake of the Civil War.[24]

There is no doubt that Holmes' language accounts for, or at least provides support for, the massive shift toward the theory of negligence-as-inefficiency that has occurred in the law and economics movement. Vast numbers of scholars today actually think that negligence means no more than violating the rules of efficiency, of acting in a way that the costs of one's conduct exceed its benefits. In the efficiency-minded part of the profession, at least, the link to blameworthiness and the criteria of responsibility in a just society have been lost.

Despite the evidence to the contrary, I want to argue that Holmes did not mean to disengage negligence from just criteria of responsibility and this approach to negligence has nothing to do with the prevailing view that objective negligence is more like strict liability and "acting at one's peril" than it is like fault as a state of character or a state of mind of the individual actor.

This then is the thesis: *Negligence, even if it is objective rather than subjective, is a basis for attributing fault in the fullest sense of the word.* I intend to demonstrate this thesis by showing first that this was Holmes' view and then further that this view is correct. In order to make the second part of the argument, I shall have to defend the idea of fault in the absence of consciousness of fault. This is what I call the fault of not knowing.

With regard to the correct interpretation of Holmes, we have to keep in mind that in the first part of the chapter, Holmes seeks to interpret the history of tort law to show that the standard of blameworthiness has always applied, despite the suggestions to the contrary in the idiom used to discuss the writ of trespass. If that is the overall thrust of his reading of history, it would be odd—to say the least—for him to reintroduce the dichotomy between blameworthiness and strict liability and argue that negligence lies someplace between the two.

Three points direct toward a sounder interpretation of the law of negligence, both as Holmes wrote about it and as negligence in fact has evolved over time. First, we should leave aside the reference to promoting the general welfare. There is nothing wrong with a system of tort law or criminal law that has the overall effect of promoting the welfare of society, but this utilitarian appeal does not justify imposing liability in particular cases against those who are unjustly held accountable for the harm they do. Everything in Holmes' work—except his distancing himself from "moral" readings of the law—leads to the view that liability is imposed solely in cases where the defendant is blameworthy for not having done otherwise.

Second, we should understand the references to the "man of ordinary intelligence and prudence"—the forerunner of the reasonable person—as a heuristic device necessary to explain how one could be blameworthy without having acted in bad faith or with a wicked motive. One way to explain the fault of having fallen short of community expectations is to invent a hypothetical person and then to reason, as did Holmes, that negligence is "the failure to exercise the foresight of which [the reasonable person] is capable."

Third, Holmes never said that the standard of the hypothetical person is a fictitious standard or that all people are simply presumed to be capable of acting the way a reasonable person would act. His recurrent phrase is that "the law presumes or requires a man to possess ordinary capacity to avoid harming his neighbors." If "presumes" were the only verb in this phrase, I would have to concede that Holmes was willing to rely upon a fictitious standard of fault that would simply camouflage strict liability for failing to meet the standards of the reasonable person. But the word "requires" carries an entirely different connotation. To be required to do something is to be subject to a duty, and to fail to meet that duty can be a basis, as Holmes argued, for concluding that the actor ought to have done otherwise and was thus to blame for causing harm to his neighbors. The practice of "requiring" also carries a subtle connotation of "ought implies can." It makes sense to require something of someone only if the addressee is capable of doing the thing required. It is hardly coherent to require of the insane or the feebleminded that they act like reasonable people. One can "presume" or "pretend" that they are reasonable persons, but one cannot, plausibly, require them to be what they are incapable of being.

This explains the recognition of exceptions to the principle that negligence should be judged by standards of general application. Holmes argues that these exceptions illustrate the "moral starting-point of liability in general."[25] He gives three examples: (1) a blind person,[26] (2) infants,[27] and (3) insanity.[28] Blindness both excuses and aggravates. The blind person is not required to act as though he could see, but if he might anticipate the consequences of being unable to see in a dangerous situation, he is bound to take precautions in advance. If he encounters a hazard that he could not expect, e.g., a hole that a seeing person could easily avoid, he is not at fault if he is injured. But if he tries to drive a car, he cannot complain after a collision that a seeing person could easily have avoided. These are obvious points, and they follow readily from the principle of personal responsibility for risk-creating conduct.

The second exception is for infants, which, according to Holmes, cannot be held to the same standard as adults.[29] This clearly validates a principle of individualization in holding risk-creators responsible for causing harm. The third exception for the insane brings home the point. Whether an insane person should be excused depends, Holmes argues, on whether the individual is "capable of taking the precautions and being influenced by the motives, which the circumstances demand." If the "insanity is of a pronounced type, manifestly incapacitating the sufferer from complying with the rule which he has broken,"[30] then of course he should be excused.

This last sentence is particularly well-crafted, for here Holmes recognizes two critical points about denying liability in cases of insanity. First, in the cases in which the "sufferer" fails to comply with or violates the rule of law, the standard is one of general application. Second, the proper word to describe the law's disposition toward those who cannot comply with the legal standard is not "justification," but "excuse."

Had Holmes been clearer about the relevance of both "the man of ordinary intelligence and prudence" and "excuses" in defining negligence, he might have spared the tradition an enormous amount of confusion. With a little more care (perhaps more than "due care"), he might have hit upon the fundamental distinction between defining a permissible risk and holding someone accountable for creating it. Thus he might have ended up with the structure introduced much later in German law and found today as well in MPC § 2.02(d):

> A person acts negligently with respect to a material element of an offense if he should be aware of a substantial and unjustifiable risk that the material element exists or will result from his conduct. The risk must be of such a nature and degree that the actor's failure to perceive it, considering the nature and purpose of his conduct and the circumstances known to him, involves a gross deviation from the standard of care that a reasonable person would observe in the actor's situation.

The insistence on standards of general application is found in the phrase "substantial and unjustifiable risk," and the inquiry about responsibility and excusability is found in the concluding phrase "a gross deviation from the standard of care that a reasonable person would observe in the actor's situation." There is nothing in this definition of negligence that would make Holmes uneasy.

If this is true, we should be troubled by only one question: Why does Holmes confuse the issue with language like, "The law considers...what would be blameworthy in the average man...If we fall below the level in these gifts it is our misfortune"?[31] Holmes' difficulty lies in two propositions: (1) that falling below the common standard can be a basis for finding fault; and (2) some people—those of less intelligence and less prudence—may find it harder to comply with the community standard than do others.

It is not surprising that Holmes had difficulty with what is appropriately called the fault of not knowing. It is a rather common difficulty, even today among thinkers with a greater claim to philosophical sophistication. For example, Jules Coleman claims that negligence is not really liability for fault, because "failure to measure up to the standard of reasonable care, whether or not one is capable of doing so, suffices to render one's conduct negligent."[32] He also says that, "[A]scriptions of fault (negligence) are not normally defeasible by excuses."[33] Ernest Weinrib shares this view about the irrelevance of excuses because, for reasons that I have never been able to comprehend, he thinks that excuses are incompatible with the theory of corrective justice.[34] These are views that make one appreciate Holmes' account of the common law.

Explaining why "falling short" of the required standard is a form of fault or negligence—properly subjecting a person to blame—is not so easy. The very difficulty of this philosophical puzzle led Holmes to his reliance on blameworthiness in the average person as a surrogate explanation. There is ample evidence, however, that Holmes regarded this account as a heuristic device for two purposes: to explain to the reader how someone might be blameworthy for not knowing and to explain to the jury how they adjudge someone at fault for failing to meet the community standard. The proof of this claim lies in the general structure of the Third Lecture in *The Common Law*. Within a few pages of his discussion of blameworthiness and excuses, Holmes turns to the procedural problems of administering criteria of negligence before a jury.[35] The jury exemplifies the "neighbors" of the defendant, and it can decide whether someone is at fault by comparing his conduct with the standard that it takes to be the community level of care. Holmes did not define negligence in a way to make it appear divorced from personal blameworthiness, but he did use language in the borderland of substance and procedure that has been falsely understood as a substantive theory of objective and faultless negligence.

As far as the law goes, there is very little evidence that the law of negligence today is much different from the way Holmes described it as a general standard supplemented by criteria of excuses denying responsibility for running the risk. Perhaps the law of insane actors is less accommodating to the excuse than in Holmes' reading of the law,[36] but by and large, it is simply false to argue that the law of negligence applies regardless of individual capacity to conform with the community standard. Much is made of the case of *Vaughan v. Menlove*,[37] in which a defendant was held liable for a fire that resulted from his keeping a flammable hayrick on his land. The court had ruled against the defendant, and in the rule *nisi* for a new trial, the defendant's counsel alleged that his client did not possess "the highest order of intelligence." The defendant was at fault for falling short of the ordinary standard of care, and though he might have been less intelligent than his neighbors, there was no proof that it was impossible for him to meet the required standard. Chief Justice Tindal of the Court of Common Pleas made the oft-quoted remark "[L]iability for negligence should [not] be co-extensive with the judgment of each individual, which would be as variable as the length of the foot of each individual."[38] But this point merely anticipates Holmes' statement that the analysis of risk should consist of "standards of general application."

As do most lawyers today, Holmes tried to resolve the puzzles of negligence by relying on the projected behavior of a reasonable person—called in his idiom "the average man." This language is unfortunate because it introduces an element of fiction in the "objective" standard of negligence. Since the concrete defendant is not "the average man"—no one embodies the average man—this way of speaking suggests that one is no longer judging the actual defendant on trial. Of course, the jury always judges the defendant, even if they employ the heuristic of "what a reasonable person would do under the circumstances." The language of the reasonable person may be useful in practice, but it has misled theorists since Holmes in their efforts to understand what negligence is about.

We rely on the crutch of the reasonable person because we find it hard to understand the fault of not knowing—the fault of someone like the farmer in *Vaughan* who paid no attention to the risks latent in keeping his haystack in combustible condition. In my view, this fault is not fictional. It is as well grounded as any other form of fault or culpability recognized in torts or criminal law. In order to understand the fault of not knowing, we have to turn to the general problem of how and why people can be blamed for not knowing the truth about their potentially harmful conduct.

II. Guilt in an Innocent Mind: The General Problem

A good transitional case for illustrating the general problem came before Holmes when he was a Massachusetts Supreme Court judge.[39] A doctor named Pierce treated a patient by applying kerosene-soaked rags to her skin. The patient died from the treatment, and though there was no suggestion of ill will on the doctor's part, the state prosecuted him for murder. Holmes wrote the opinion confirming the conviction on the ground that as judged against an "external" standard, the doctor had been reckless (meaning: grossly negligent) in providing this treatment. The case is both similar to and distinguishable from *Vaughan*, where the defendant was a passive possessor of the dangerous haystack. Yet the culpability of both lies in not understanding the dangers latent in their conduct. Arguably, the doctor was more culpable because he presumably received stronger signals that there might be something harmful in using kerosene-soaked rags as a method of medical treatment. Yet the brunt of Holmes' opinion for conviction was that the doctor's good faith could not be a justification for his conduct, just as the defendant in *Vaughan* could not claim good faith as an excuse. This was the relevance of judging Pierce's conduct against an external standard.

It is not clear from the facts in *Pierce* whether the defendant had simply been oblivious to the danger of using kerosene-soaked rags or whether he had made the wrong cost/benefit judgment about whether the danger outweighed the potential benefit. In the pure case of not knowing of the danger, the fault lies in having failed to investigate the risks attendant upon his affirmative conduct of treating the patient.

Looking at the doctor's fault as an aspect of a larger activity says something important about how we have to think about negligence in torts and criminal law. If we look just at the doctrines of negligence, the structuring of issues very much resembles liability for omissions. That is, as every first-year law student knows, a finding of negligence requires a finding of duty and breach of duty.[40] The analysis of intentional torts and of intentional (affirmative) crimes does not require a finding of duty. The only field of law that is structured in the same way as the standard analysis of negligence in torts is liability for omissions—both in torts and criminal law. No one is liable for an omission unless there is a duty to intervene and prevent the harm from occurring.

The duty requirement reflects liberal anxieties about making people come forward and take initiative. We can easily blame aggressors who interfere with the rights of others (those who do not recognize that their liberty ends where the nose of their neighbor begins). But it is hard to blame people for failing to take initiative—for not recognizing an outstretched hand. The classic way of understanding negligence—not in Holmes but in the case law—was to stress the analogy between taking steps to learn of the risk and taking measures to avoid the occurrence of harm to others. This accounts for the emphasis on duty and breach as the doctrinal cornerstones of negligence and omissions. Duties arise only in special relationships. The guiding premise of the law was that a special relationship should be required to blame someone for not informing himself of the risks implicit in his action or for failing to rescue someone in distress.

As the law of negligence evolved, however, the failure to exercise due care—an omission—came to be seen as part of affirmative risks to others—the risks of driving, of medical care, of handling weapons, of manufacturing goods. In the context of these larger activities, the omission is but an epicycle on the arc of risk generated by the affirmative conduct. The omission becomes a minor part of the actor's assertive conduct. This is the way criminal lawyers think of negligence—as a way of killing or committing assault or destroying property. Thus, Dr. Pierce created a risk of death by the way he administered medical treatment. His gross negligence appeared to be less of a failure to realize a certain risk and more, as the MPC would describe it, of introducing in the world a "substantial and unjustified risk" for which there was no excuse.[41] The fault was not the passivity of an omission, but the affirmative wrong of creating an unreasonable risk.

It is not surprising, then, that criminal lawyers rarely speak of duty and breach when they discuss negligence. The survival of this terminology in torts reflects a throwback to a previous way of looking at risk-creation as a wrong that inheres in the fault of not knowing of a danger lurking in one's conduct.

The doctrine of unforeseeability reflects, I believe, the former way of looking at negligence as a fault of not knowing. Thus when the risk is too bizarre and the outcome so unexpected that no one can be faulted for running it, the appropriate way of talking about fault is to focus on the difficulty of knowing the unforeseeable. A good example is the nitroglycerine case decided by the Supreme Court.[42] At about the time TNT was invented, agents for the Wells-Fargo Company received a mysterious crate that was leaking a liquid that they could not identify. They tried to open the case with a hammer and chisel. After the crate exploded and caused injury to bystanders, the company found itself being sued. The Court affirmed a finding of non-liability on the ground that the explosion was unforeseeable.

In all three of these cases—*Vaughan*, *Pierce*, and *Wells-Fargo*—the defendants acted on a good-faith belief that there was nothing wrong, nothing risky, with their conduct. The case of inadvertent negligence provides a bridge, therefore, to the more general problem of good-faith beliefs in the justification of knowingly harmful conduct. An example that never ceases to engage my imagination is the German case known in the profession as the *Katzenkönig* or *The King-Cat Case*. The facts reveal a situation in which somebody was at fault for not knowing and not understanding the wrong that he had committed. Two women in a sadomasochistic cult manipulated a psychologically weak, gullible man, the defendant, into fearing a demon called King-Cat. For personal reasons, one of the cult leaders wanted to get rid of a woman named N. She induced the defendant into believing that if he did not kill N, "King-Cat" would claim a million victims. The defendant came to the conclusion that the lesser evil was to kill N, and he actually attacked her and stabbed her three times. All three parties were indicted and convicted of attempted murder.[43]

For our purposes, the intriguing question is whether the defendant could have mounted a good claim that his good faith belief should have insulated him from criminal liability. Had the threat been real, he might have had a good argument based on necessity as a justification[44] (although killing an innocent is always problematic under the theory of necessity, even when really necessary to save a million people). Could he have argued that he was not at fault because he did not realize that the threat was false? He was in a situation like that of Lot's daughters who thought that the destruction of Sodom and Gomorrah had brought the world to an end; they had no reasonable choice, as they understood the world, but to get their father drunk and sleep with him in order to continue the human species.[45] Faced with the possible death of a million innocent people, the defendant in *The King-Cat Case* had no reasonable choice, as he saw the world, but to sacrifice one innocent person.

Remarkably, the German Supreme Court conceded that the defendant's claim should be taken seriously as a mistake of law. He had been mistaken in good faith about the necessity of his actions. In the end, however, the Court rejected the claim of mistake of law, because the mistake was not unavoidable as required by the Code.[46] The teachings of *The King-Cat Case* were eventually used to aggravate the liability of accessories,[47] but buried in the opinion is the idea that good-faith mistakes by ideological offenders should be taken seriously as a ground of mitigation, if not as a complete excuse.

The great danger of this principle of mitigation is that it could easily apply on behalf of virtually all ideological offenders. Timothy McVeigh, Ted Kaczynski, Yigal Amir—they all tendered good-faith beliefs about why their homicidal conduct was necessary under the circumstances. They all thought they were acting for the greater good. And these are the offenders who live among us as one of us. Threatening us as well are outsiders, terrorists convinced of the rectitude of their actions and yet perceived by us as evil incarnate.

It is hard to know whether we live in an age in which ideological crimes have become more common than in the past, but understanding why we condemn and punish good-faith offenders has become an urgent matter on the agenda of criminal theory.

There are basically two ways to account for the attribution of wrongdoing and guilt to offenders who believe in their hearts that they are doing the right thing. One argument is based on an analogy with inadvertent negligence, the other on abstract principles of right and wrong. I call the first the "sociological" argument and the second the "moral realism" argument.

The sociological argument is based on the observation that a little effort in consulting people in the neighborhood can avert the risks that led to the burning of the haystack in *Vaughan* or the use of kerosene-soaked rags in medical treatment in *Pierce*. The idea that the harm was "foreseeable" means that the actor was put on notice that there might be something risky in his conduct or in the state of the things in his charge. There is warrant for talking to others, for being open to advice about the correct path of conduct. When, as in the nitroglycerine case, it is extremely unlikely that anyone would know of the danger, the case falls under the excuse of "unforeseeability." The sociological approach has some bearing on cases like King-Cat, McVeigh, and Kaczynski, where the slightest consultation with others outside one's immediate circle would lead to doubts about the suitability of the conduct in question. In such a situation, the fault of not knowing that the conduct is wrong is the fault of separating oneself from the potential self-correction one receives from being embedded in a community of opinion.

Of course, there are some cases of ideological conduct where everyone in the available environment supports the conduct as right, even honorable. This is the situation of Yigal Amir and Palestinian suicide-bombers. They know others outside their circles think the conduct to be wrong, but these diverse opinions have no bearing on their convictions that they are doing the right thing. In these cases, the sociological argument runs dry. The only basis for condemning these good-faith actors is the "moral realism" argument: That their killing of innocent people is wrong is simply beyond question. It is a moral universal, and as the tradition of moral argument holds, ignorance of a universal truth is no excuse.

The argument of moral realism may well be right, but it has the ring of dogmatism. One person's universal moral truth may well be another's conventional piety. Yet in the extreme case, some recourse to this argument is necessary to preserve our convictions that ideological actors are nonetheless guilty of wrongdoing. The analogy with inadvertent negligence helps, however, in the broad range of cases. Our moral lives are not so different from our learning about the risks latent in our conduct. If we are open to the opinions of others, we increase our capacity for self-correction. And having the opportunity to correct one's belief and failing to exercise that capacity lie at the foundation of the fault of not knowing.

CHAPTER 9

Reply: Fletcher on "The Fault of Not Knowing"

Larry Alexander*and Kimberly Kessler Ferzan**

George Fletcher is one of the preeminent theorists of criminal law, and he has been so for as long as we have been doing criminal law theory—which (for Larry at least) is a long time. There are many theoretical positions that Fletcher has taken with which we agree. And there are some with which we disagree—which, of course, is to be expected, given the breadth of topics Fletcher has addressed.

One theoretical issue on which we disagree is whether inadvertent negligence is culpable and deserving of blame and punishment. Fletcher believes that it is, or at least can be, whereas we do not. Fletcher's most recent defense of the culpability of negligence is in "The Fault of Not Knowing." In the article he spends a lot of time doing exegetical work on Oliver Wendell Holmes's views of negligence and strict liability and relatively little on making his case for negligence's culpability. Indeed, he reserves his case for the last five pages of the article, some of which he devotes to the failure to know moral standards rather than to the failure to know the risks one's conduct is imposing. And the case he does present is uncharacteristically conclusory and elusive.

Before dealing with what Fletcher does say on behalf of the culpability of negligence, let us set forth how we see the problem.

The orthodox account of the negligent act is that it is an act that imposes a risk of harm that is of such a magnitude that imposing it is unjustified given the actor's reasons for so acting—and, crucially, the actor is unaware that the risk he is imposing is of that magnitude. (If the actor were aware that the risk was that high, he would be acting *recklessly*, not negligently.) Notably, the negligent actor believes the risk of harm he is imposing is sufficiently low that were he correct,

*Warren Distinguished Professor of Law, University of San Diego School of Law.
**Professor of Law, Rutgers University School of Law, Camden.

imposing that risk would be deemed justifiable. What presumably makes the negligent actor culpable is that he underestimates the risk his act creates, whereas a "reasonable"—that is, nonculpable—person would not have underestimated the risk and, as a consequence, would not have acted as did the negligent actor.

Risk, however, is an epistemic notion, not an ontic one. Or, to make the same point a different way, from God's epistemically privileged point of view, all risks are either one or zero. When the negligent actor mistakenly drives in the lane for oncoming traffic, God knows whether he will or will not collide with an oncoming car. If he collides, the risk he was imposing from God's point of view was one. If he does not, it was zero.

So suppose he avoids a collision. He estimated the risk of his driving as ordinary—greater than zero, of course, but quite low—because he failed to realize he was in the wrong lane. God, on the other hand, being omniscient, knew the risk he created was zero. Yet, we are supposed to believe the driver is culpably negligent for underestimating the risk.[1] How can that be?

In order for the charge of underestimating the risk to make sense, given that the "real" risk was zero, we must posit as a standard the risk some other actor would have estimated—the so-called reasonable person in the actor's situation (RPAS). However, there is no principled and rationally defensible way to define the RPAS. There is no moral difference between punishing for inadvertent negligence and punishing on the basis of strict liability, and the lack of a moral difference evidences itself in the inability to draw a distinction between strict liability and negligence on any basis other than arbitrary stipulation.

There are two clear boundary lines for the RPAS. First, the RPAS could be a person apprised of all the facts about the world that bear on a correct moral decision. At the other possible conceptual boundary, the RPAS could be someone with all the beliefs that the actor actually held. Put somewhat differently, where action falls below the standard of recklessness—the *conscious* disregarding of an unjustifiable risk—the action will appear reasonable to the actor and thus to the RPAS if the RPAS has exactly the same beliefs as the actor.

The two possible boundaries that provide the frame for characterizing the RPAS present us with this dilemma. If the RPAS knows all the facts, the RPAS always chooses the action that averts the harm (in the absence of justification, of course). But if this is the standard of the RPAS, then every case of strict liability will be a case of negligence as defined by the RPAS standard. It will never be reasonable not to know. (Notice, as well, that because risk is epistemic, the omniscient actor deals only in certainties: for her, the "risk" of a particular harm entailed by any act is either one or zero. On this construct, then, not only is there liability for every avoidable and regrettable—unjustifiable—harm, but there is also no negligence where harm does not occur.)

On the other hand, if the RPAS knows only what the actor knows, there is never any negligence either, only recklessness. The RPAS will always act as the actor acted where the actor is not conscious of the level of risk, and will act differently only where the actor is conscious of the level of risk, that is, is reckless.

At either conceptual boundary, therefore, the RPAS collapses negligence into either strict liability or recklessness. The question, then, is where between those boundaries the RPAS is to be located.

The answer is that any location between these two boundaries will be morally arbitrary. Between the boundaries, any RPAS will be a construct that will include some beliefs of the actual actor together with beliefs that the constructor inserts. Which beliefs are inserted other than the ones the actor actually had will determine whether the RPAS would act as the actor acted. But there is no standard that tells us which of the beliefs of the actual actor should be left intact and which should be replaced by other (correct) beliefs. The RPAS standard, cut loose from the alternative moorings of the actor's actual beliefs or of the world as it really was at the time the actor acted, is completely adrift in a sea of alternative constructions, none of which is more compelling than others.

Some commentators at this point assert the possibility that the RPAS is like the actual actor in all material aspects, but that the RPAS "would have" adverted to and properly assessed the risks because the actual actor "could have" adverted to and properly assessed them.[2] But there is an equivocation here in the reference to what the actor "could have" adverted to and assessed in the actor's situation. If we take the actor at the time of the "negligent" choice, with what he is conscious of and adverting to, his background beliefs, and so forth, then it is simply false that the actor "could have" chosen differently in any sense that has normative bite. For although it may be true that the actor "could have" chosen differently in a sense relevant to the free will/determinism issue, it is false that in that situation, the actor had any internal reason to choose differently from the way he chose.

As Michael Zimmerman and Ishtiyaque Haji have written, one is culpable only for acts over which one has control.[3] If one is unaware that, say, someone has replaced the sugar on the table with poison, then one is not culpable for placing that poison in another's coffee and thereby killing her. For although one is in control of the conduct of placing the white substance in the coffee, the mistaken belief that it is sugar deprives one of the kind of control necessary for culpability. And what holds true for conduct taken in ignorance of its nature or likely consequences also holds true for the ignorance itself. One is not culpable for one's ignorance unless one is in control of it. And one can be in control of one's ignorance only indirectly, say, by deliberately refraining from learning something while being aware that one is running an unjustifiable risk of dangerous ignorance.

We are not morally culpable for taking risks of which we are unaware. At any point in time we are failing to notice a great many things, we have forgotten a great many things, and we are misinformed or uninformed about many things. An injunction to notice, remember, and be fully informed about anything that bears on risks to others is an injunction no human being can comply with, so violating this injunction reflects no moral defect. Even those most concerned with the well-being of others will violate this injunction constantly.[4]

Because the purpose of the criminal law is to prevent harm by giving us reasons to act and to refrain from acting, the criminal law does not reach the negligent actor. The negligent actor is not aware that her action unjustifiably risks causing harm, and thus cannot be guided to avoid creating that risk by the injunction to avoid creating unjustifiable risks.

Let us return now to Fletcher's defense of negligence as a form of culpability. He employs the Massachusetts case of *Commonwealth v. Pierce*, the opinion of which was written by Holmes, to make his case. In that case, Pierce, a doctor, used kerosene-soaked rags as a medical treatment, apparently sincerely believing that such a method, which killed his patient, was not too risky given his belief in the rags' curative powers. Holmes upheld Pierce's conviction of homicide despite assuming Pierce's sincerity. Fletcher concurs with Holmes, arguing that in a "pure case of not knowing of the danger, the fault lies in having failed to investigate the risks attendant upon [Pierce's] affirmative conduct of treating the patient" (89).

Notice, however, that even if Pierce believed the rags posed only a slight risk, he might also have believed that he might improve his estimate of that risk by further investigation, and that the direct costs of such an investigation—costs to Pierce in time and effort, and costs to Pierce's patient in terms of delay of treatment—were sufficiently low that it would have been unjustifiable for Pierce not to investigate further. If that were the case, then Pierce *was* culpable; he was *reckless* for not undertaking that investigation.

To convert Pierce's case to a case of negligence, we need to assume that Pierce was not aware of risks or opportunity costs that would make his choice a reckless one. Fletcher does not disclose how he would make out the case for culpability were Pierce deemed culpable for merely not knowing the risk rather than for not investigating it further. Given that the risk is an epistemic notion related to actor's beliefs, not an ontic one, we see no way for Fletcher to redeem his assertion that there is culpability in not knowing.

Finally, we turn to Fletcher's assimilation of the fault of not knowing the risks of one's conduct to the fault of not knowing that those risks are unjustified. For us, there is a chasm between the actor who sincerely says, "I didn't realize the gun was loaded," or "I didn't know the chlorine was combustible," and the actor who says, "I didn't know it was unjustifiable to risk others' lives and limbs to make it home in time to see my favorite soaps." It is true that at the margin, mistakes regarding justification can be nonculpable. However, most cases of mistakes about the justifiability of imposing risks on others *reveal* the culpability of insufficient concern for others rather than negate it. Doxastic failures are not intrinsically culpable; failures of proper concern for others' welfare are.

CHAPTER 10

Mistake in the Model Penal Code:
A False False Problem

George P. Fletcher

No solution seems more gratifying to the modern theorist than to claim that an apparently serious problem is not really a problem at all. By branding non-falsifiable propositions as nonsense, the Vienna circle of logical positivists discovered that the metaphysical concerns of others were really false problems. By ridding philosophy of false problems, Wittgenstein thought that he could let the fly escape from the bottle; he could release the philosophical spirit from its confounding constraints. Brainerd Currie brought this method to the law with his justly famous theory of false conflicts in the conflicts of laws.[1] There was no need to worry about false conflicts; they were not real problems. The Model Penal Code [hereinafter MPC or Code] takes the same tack toward the problem of mistake. To understand the MPC's claim that mistake is a false problem, we must first understand why judges and theorists have been confused and troubled about when mistakes about the issues bearing on liability should constitute a defense.

One of the major conundrums in the common-law approach toward mistake is why courts differ on the kinds of mistakes that should bar liability. Sometimes the courts hold that any mistake, reasonable or unreasonable, negates liability. In its recent, controversial decision in *Regina v. Morgan*,[2] for example, the House of Lords decided any mistake about whether the putative victim of rape consented to intercourse should be a complete defense.[3] In other situations, the courts insist that for a mistake to constitute a defense, it must be the kind of mistake that a reasonable person would make under the circumstances. In *Hernandez*,[4] the California Supreme Court decided that in a statutory rape case, a mistake about the age of the girl would be a defense only if that met this standard of fault-less conduct.[5] By like token, the New York Court of Appeals held last year, in the highly publicized *Goetz* case,[6] that a mistake about the factual presuppositions of self-defense should be a defense only if the mistake were one that a reason-able person would have made under the same conditions.[7] Why is it that some courts recognize every mistake as a defense and others limit the defense of mis-take to reasonable misperceptions of the surrounding circumstances? Do differ-ent courts have different rules? Would the New York and California courts decide *Morgan* differently? Or is there some important theoretical distinction among the issues at stake in the cases—a distinction that would explain why in some cases any mistake will do, while in others, the mistake must be reasonable.

It is also difficult to understand why some mistakes are treated as totally irrel-evant to liability. If a criminal actor is mistaken about the applicable statute of limitations, he could hardly expect much judicial sympathy. If he believes, falsely, that he is exempt from prosecution when he sniffs cocaine on his yacht because he is beyond the three mile limit of state territorial waters, his claim of mistake would hardly get far in court. Nor would he do well in escaping liability if in fact he was two miles out to sea and he thought the territorial limit of jurisdiction was only one mile. Why should these mistakes be treated as irrelevant?

Mistakes get their relevance from the actor's innocent frame of mind. By virtue of his mistake, in all of these cases, the actor thinks that his conduct is perfectly legal. So far as his own good faith effort to comply with the law controls the analy-sis, he should be acquitted in all of these cases. Yet he is not. Obviously, the actor's own subjective perspective on his conduct, his own good faith, cannot always be decisive. The problem is figuring out why mistakes must sometimes be reasonable in order to count, and why sometimes they are treated as irrelevant to liability, even if they are reasonable.

To the drafters of the MPC, all of these theoretical issues constitute a false problem. Under the Code, claims of mistake, like claims of accident, stand in a conceptual relationship with the culpability required for the particular offense. The basic principle that mistakes acquire their relevance from culpability is spelled out in section 2.04(1) of the Code:

> Ignorance or mistake as to a matter of fact or law is a defense if:
> (a) the ignorance or mistake negatives the purpose, knowledge, belief, recklessness or negligence required to establish a material element of the offense; or
> (b) the law provides that the state of mind established by such ignorance or mistake constitutes a defense.

The mechanics of this provision are best illustrated by the connection between mistake and intention. If murder presupposes "an intent to kill a human being," then a good faith belief that one is shooting at a tree rather than a human being precludes a finding of intentional killing. In general terms, the intention required for particular offenses consists of two factors: (1) the action verb that is the object of the phrase "intent to," and (2) the physical act that is the necessary object of this action. The simple insight, then, is that if the actor's mistake makes him ignorant of the necessary object of his intentions, it cannot be said that he intends to do the act required for the offense.

For example, the intention required for common-law larceny is "intent to deprive the owner permanently of his property."[8] If the defendant takes bomb casings from government land on the mistaken assumption that the government has abandoned its property interest in the casings, then he does not have the intent to deprive anyone of "property."[9] The logical relationship between mistakes and intention is immune to value judgments about the moral quality of the mistake; unreasonable mistakes negate the required intent as much as reasonable mistakes do. The analysis is that simple—provided you know what the required intent is.

For many offenses, however, the required intention is surprisingly elusive. How could the House of Lords in *Morgan* be so confident that the required intent in rape should be defined as "the intent to have intercourse with a nonconsenting woman"[10] rather than more broadly as "the intent to have intercourse with [any] woman?" It should be clear that on the former view, any mistake as to consent is a defense; on the latter view, the mistake would not negate the intent and our rule of thumb for analyzing the effect of mistake would be inapplicable. One could hardly say that every relevant factual issue in the case is included within the scope of the required intent. If it were, then the issue of self-defense would be analyzed in the same way as consent. The required intent for homicide would be "to kill a nonaggressing human being"; even an unreasonable belief about the victim's aggression would negate the required intent and constitute a complete defense. If every relevant factual issue were intrinsic to the required intent, any mistake would be a good defense. There would never be a ruling, as there was in the *Goetz* case, that the particular kind of mistake must be reasonable under the circumstances.[11]

The drafters of the MPC also thought they had a solution to this problem of analyzing mistakes about elements extrinsic to the required intent. The drafter of every specific defense must allocate one of the four culpability elements—purposely (the Code's word for "intentionally"), knowingly, recklessly or negligently—to each "material element of the offense."[12] Hence, it would be up to the legislature to specify whether as to each element such as the age of the girl or the nonconsent of the woman, the suspected offender must act purposely or with one of the lesser modes of culpability.[13] If one of the lesser modes is specified, the problem of mistake reduces whether the mistake negates that lesser culpability element. Thus if the legislature specifies that recklessness or negligence is required as to the age of the girl, the defendant will be liable only if he disregards the risk that the girl would be under age[14] or if he is unaware of the risk,[15] under circumstances in which a reasonable person would have been mindful of the risk. In other words, in those situations in which the legislature has ruled on the matter, a mistake will negate the required culpability only if the actor has conformed to the standard of a reasonable person under the circumstances. Thus, a careful reading of the statute solves the problem of mistake as to material elements that are not covered by the required intention. Further, this solution explains when and indeed why the mistake must be reasonable.

But how do we decide, on the basis of the Code's approach, whether a mistake is relevant at all? In line with the drafter's basic strategy, the legislature makes that decision in deciding which culpability requirement to assign to each element of the offense. If the legislature assigns knowledge as the required culpability, any mistake will be a defense; if it assigns recklessness or negligence to the particular issue, the mistake must be reasonable to escape classification as one of these levels of fault; if it expressly assigns no culpability requirement at all to the particular element, then no mistake as to that element will constitute a valid defense. Another way to express the irrelevance of mistakes on a particular issue is to say that liability is "strict" on that issue.

The strategy for rendering mistake a false problem, then, is to require that the legislature define the culpability required for the offense. Of course, deferring to the legislature does not solve the problem of mistake as a matter of principle. Should the intent required for statutory rape include the belief that the girl is under age? Or perhaps, at the opposite extreme, should liability be strict on the issue of age? Should the intent for homicide include the belief that the intended victim is not an aggressor? Or should mistakes on the factual basis for self-defense be treated as extrinsic to intent, thereby opening the way to a defense of reasonable mistake? Taking the statute as authoritative on these difficult questions merely shifts responsibility for the theoretical work to a legislative committee. The MPC renders the mistake a false problem, but only by pushing the entire theoretical conundrum under the legislative carpet.

From the treatment of this theoretical issue, one might think that the MPC avoids taking a stand on questions of principle. But this is not the case at all. The Code contains several provisions that the drafters took to be elementary in fashioning a just penal code. One of these is the principled opposition to strict liability. The official commentators to the Code proclaim their "hostility" to strict liability.[16] The general rule for interpreting statutes is that if the legislature is silent about the culpability required for a "material element of an offense," the culpability level to be inferred from the statute is recklessness.[17] If, contrary to this general rule, the legislature explicitly imposes strict liability as to one or more material elements of any offense, the offense should be treated as a "violation,"[18] thus implying that imprisonment should be impermissible.[19] These provisions, taken together, substantiate a general aversion to strict liability in the MPC.

Taking a stand against strict liability revives the problem that the drafters thought they had dissolved by deferring to the legislative definition of the offense. If strict liability is to be avoided, whenever room for judicial interpretation permits, then serious theoretical work is required to know how far to press the principled aversion to strict liability. Does it extend to mistakes about jurisdictions and the statute of limitations? Should we say that disregarding mistakes of law is an instance of the disfavored institution of strict liability? For the Code to maintain its principled stand against strict liability, it must supply answers to these questions.

The beginnings of an answer are found in the Code provisions on mistake and strict liability. The general provision on mistake, as noted above, applies only to mistakes that negate the culpability "required to establish a material element of the offense."[20] The same phrase "material element of the offense" circumscribes the Code's presumptive prohibition against strict liability[21] as well as the provision establishing the minimal culpability requirement of recklessness.[22]

A great deal turns, therefore, on the definition of "material elements." The MPC defines this key term by first defining the broader term "elements of the offense" to include every possible factual issue, such as the substantive and procedural circumstances that could bear on liability[23] and then approaches the definition of "material element" negatively to mean: "an element that does not relate exclusively to the statute of limitations, jurisdiction, venue or to any other matter similarly unconnected with (i) the harm or evil, incident to conduct, sought to be prevented by the law defining the offense, or (ii) the existence of a justification or excuse of such conduct."[24] This provision hardly explains why strict liability should be acceptable as to issues unconnected to the "harm of evil" or claims of "justification or excuse."[25] Intuitively, we might think that a mistake about a procedural condition for prosecution should have little bearing on the justification for liability and punishment. But this intuition demands explication and clarification.

In general terms, the distinction at work in the definition of materiality tracks the more conventional boundary between substance and procedure. The statute of limitations, for example, bears only the procedural value of prosecuting offenses after the events have become "stale" and the witnesses are likely to become relatively unreliable. Presumably, the drafters did not wish to rely on this conventional distinction. The distinction between substance and procedure has become so blurred in the conflict of laws and in post-*Erie* jurisprudence that the drafters preferred a convoluted definition that merely hinted at what they were after.

Yet, the distinction between substance and procedure is what they intended. Although the distinction has become fluid, we have no better terms to explain why some mistakes (namely, those about procedural facts) should be regarded as irrelevant. But how do we account for this distinction? Why should mistakes about substantive issues excuse the actor, but mistakes about procedural conditions for prosecution be deemed beside the point? A simple, straightforward answer might be that the procedural issues bear on the fair prosecution of a crime, not on the definition of that crime. And if procedural rules are extrinsic to the focus of the prosecution, an actor's mistake about the factual preconditions of these rules should have no bearing on the actor's substantive liability.

Underlying this distinction, however, is a conception of guilt or blameworthiness that justifies the imposition of criminal sanctions. Mistakes about procedural issues do not detract from the actor's guilt, but mistakes about substantive issues (in MPC terms: the harm or evil sought to be avoided, justification and excuse)[26] somehow undermine guilt to the point that punishment is no longer justified as a matter of principle. Implicit in the Code's reliance on the term "material element of an offense," then, is a deep, unexplicated theory of guilt as it relates to deserved punishment.

The drafters of the MPC would not readily concede that the Code incorporates theories of guilt and of deserved punishment. They sought to exhaust the analysis of guilt, blame, culpability and related concepts of mens rea by specifying four "kinds of culpability." Two of these definitions—purposely and knowingly—proceed as though culpability were simply a matter of fact, reducible to what people believe, think and take as the object of their actions.[27] The gap is not so easily bridged between a factual description of a state of mind and the kind of moral condemnation that can support a judgment of deserved punishment. Yet the working out of this inference obviously did not engage the attention of the drafters of the Code. It is not discussed anywhere in the Code or in the Commentaries.

Rather than explicate the premises underlying their thinking, the drafters simply ruled out mistakes extrinsic to substantive issues. Though they avoided the terms "substance" and "procedure," they relied on the conventional intuition that only mistakes about substance should bear on the actor's susceptibility to liability and punishment.

The most daring stroke in the definition of "material elements" was the flattening out of the criteria of liability, so that elements of defenses (justifications and excuses) receive the same treatment as "the harm or evil, incident to conduct, sought to be prevented by the law defining the offense."[28] It does not matter whether the mistake is about the inculpatory criteria defining the relevant harm (e.g., a mistake about whether the subject of an organ removal is already dead) or about the exculpatory criteria for legitimate self-defense (e.g., a mistake about whether the person one violently disables was then in the process of committing aggression). Of course, there is the simple logical difference that the prosecution must assert that the victim was alive at the time of the defendant's action, while in cases of self-defense, the defendant typically bears the burden of asserting the issue and going forward with the evidence.[29] As the argument goes, however, this purely formal difference should have no bearing on the analysis of liability. There is no reason why one could not consider claims of justification simply as negative elements of the offense. The common-law definition of murder is then rewritten to cover the "killing of another human being with malice aforethought *and absent self-defense.*"[30] For the time being, let us limit our discussion to the thesis that the exculpatory elements required for a justification, such as necessity or self-defense, could be treated as negative elements of the crime. Let us call it the "negative elements" thesis. We shall take the special problems connected to claims of excuse (e.g., duress, insanity) later. The first notable thing about the structure of the MPC is that there are two distinct paths for adopting the "negative elements" thesis. There is the special set of provisions for analyzing mistakes made about the conditions of justification. Before turning to these provisions, we should seriously note the Code's claim that its elements of justification and excuse are "material elements of the offense." If they are, then the general rule on mistake[31] should apply to the analysis of mistakes about the claims as well. The first step, then, is to check the definition of particular offenses to determine the "kinds of culpability" assigned to the negative elements of justification attached to that offense. Under this approach, however, one discovers a remarkable fact about the definition of particular offenses. One would expect that the definition of homicide would specify the absence of self-defense as one of the elements of the crime. But such is not the case. The only elements that matter in the definition of homicide, manslaughter and self-defense are causing human death and culpability—not a word about self-defense.[32]

The same omission is evident in other offenses. From the definitions of assault,[33] and false imprisonment,[34] one gets no clue of the possible defenses. Perhaps this should not be a surprise. That is the way the common law treats the definition of offenses. The offense is conceptually distinct from the possible defenses—claims of justification, excuse and mitigation. Yet this is the divide that the MPC seeks to span with its all encompassing bridge of "material elements." Supposedly, there is no important difference between the inculpatory elements of the offense and the exculpatory criteria of defense. One can only be puzzled, then, that specific offenses are defined without specifying the possible defenses.

Is there any way to apply the general mistake provision in § 2.04 to the defenses without building these criteria of justification and excuse into the definition of the offenses? Two special fail-safe rules in the Code might come to the rescue. According to § 2.02(4): "When the law defining an offense prescribes the kind of culpability that is sufficient for the commission of an offense, without distinguishing among the material elements thereof, such provision shall apply to all the material elements of the offense, unless a contrary purpose plainly appears."[35]

One would like to interpret this provision to mean that if the drafters fail to mention possible defenses in the definition of the material elements, then the culpability specified for the offense would apply as well to the absence, say, of self-defense. One commits murder by knowingly causing the death of a human being;[36] it would follow that the requirement of "knowingly" would then apply to the absence of justificatory conditions such as self-defense. In general terms, the elements of self-defense are first, that another person is about to commit unlawful aggression against the defender, and second, that force is necessary to repel the aggression.[37] In order to be guilty of murder, then, the actor must at least know that one of these two conditions is not present.[38]

It would follow from this reading that in the case of negligent homicide, the culpability required as to the conditions of self-defense would be merely negligence rather than knowledge. There would be no reason, in the view of the drafters, to treat the elements of self-defense differently from the core elements of homicide.

The alternative provision that might apply to this problem of the Code's failure to include the absence of defense in the definition of particular offenses would be § 2.02(3), which states that in the failure to specify a culpability requirement, the minimal requirement should be recklessness—not negligence.[39] If this provision is applied, the culpability required for the conditions of self-defense would not vary with the culpability required for the core offense. Whether the prosecution was for knowing, reckless or negligent homicide, the prosecution would have to prove that the defendant was at least reckless in his belief, for example, that another person was about to attack him.

The first provision, which coordinates the culpability in the area of justification with the culpability for the core elements, is more in keeping with the effort of the Code to overcome the distinction between core elements and criteria of justification and therefore we should apply it. I have serious doubts, however, whether this reading is warranted on the face of the provision. The phrase "without distinguishing among the material elements thereof"[40] implies that the drafters were concerned about the problem of distinguishing among the elements internal to the legislative definition of an offense. Take the definition of murder: knowingly causing the death of another human being.[41] The purpose of § 2.02(4) is to make it clear that the term "knowingly" applies with equal force to all of the core elements of the offense: (1) causing, (2) death, of (3) a distinct and separate being, that is (4) human. The Commentaries do not hint that the provision might apply to the conditions of justification and excuse.[42] Also, the Commentaries strongly endorse the related New York provision,[43] but the latter clearly distinguishes between the culpability required for the "offense" (meaning the core elements of the offense) and the culpability required for a "defense," "exemption" or "justification."[44] New York rejects the "negative elements" thesis and treats claims of justification as conceptually independent of the definition of the core offense.[45] Nonetheless, as I have suggested, the better reading of the Code's general theory, articulated most clearly in the definition of material elements[46] and the adoption of the "negative elements" thesis leads us to reject § 2.02(3) and instead extend § 2.02(4) to cover the criteria of justification and excuse.

Consider how this provision would work in the analysis of the mistake that might be attributed to Bernhard Goetz: he thinks that he is about to be assaulted and robbed by four youths on the subway. Let us also suppose, for the moment, that he succeeds in killing one of the youths. Under the MPC, he could be charged with either knowing, reckless or negligent homicide. The prosecution would have to prove, depending on the level of the offense, that Goetz knew that he was not about to be attacked, that he was reckless or negligent in believing that an attack was imminent.

One reason the Commentaries may fail to discuss the extension of the general provision on mistake[47] to claims of justification is that the Code contains a special set of rules on the analysis of these mistakes. All of the provisions on justification are couched in the language of "belief."[48] The minimal requirement for a claim of justification, therefore, is that the actor believe that the objective factual conditions support his claim. Contrary to the recent proposal of the U.K. Law Commission, objective circumstances alone are never sufficient to make out a case of self-defense.[49]

Many lawyers and judges read this reference to "belief" as not only necessary, but sufficient for a valid claim of self-defense. This misunderstanding ran through the arguments in the *Goetz* case in which the lawyers and several of the lower court judges, pondering the problem of liability for an unreasonable mistake, described the MPC as endorsing a subjective standard of self-defense.[50] What they meant by a subjective standard is that a good faith belief in the conditions of self-defense should be sufficient for acquittal. They arrived at this mistaken reading of the Code because they looked at the basic provision in § 3.04 without attending to the exception for unreasonable belief in § 3.09(2).[51] With regard to all of the claims of justification other than necessity,[52] the defense is inapplicable if "the actor is reckless or negligent in having [his] belief... in a prosecution for an offense for which recklessness or negligence suffices to establish liability."[53]

Let us work through this provision as to the three relevant grades of culpability in homicide—knowing, reckless and negligent.[54] The exception in § 3.09(2) applies only if the required culpability is recklessness or negligence,[55] and therefore in the case of knowing homicide, there would be no exception to the good faith belief in the conditions of self-defense. If the defendant believed in good faith that he was about to be attacked, he would have a good claim of self-defense.

But what about the rare hypothetical situation in which the defendant had no belief one way or the other about whether he was going to be attacked? He knows that his action will cause death, but he has no awareness of danger from aggression. He is simply indifferent to whether he is being attacked. Absent a good faith belief in the imminence of an attack, self-defense will not apply. If the Code is to yield a defense, we would have to resort to general principles on the analysis of ignorance or mistake as to a material element of the offense. The actor would be ignorant of a material element of homicide, namely the absence of justificatory circumstances. Arguably, the general provision on mistake would apply.[56] Unlike the special regulations in the provisions on justification, the general provision encompasses ignorance as well as mistake,[57] at least if the ignorance or mistake negates the knowledge required for the particular material element. Admittedly, it is odd to resort to a general provision to solve a problem supposedly regulated by the specially hewn rules on justification. The better argument might be that the rules on justification should control, and that ignorance about the presence or absence of an impending attack would be insufficient to generate a defense to liability.

The problem of liability in cases of indifference (no belief one way or the other) arises from the logical character of defenses. The defendant asserts self-defense as a justification and therefore it falls on him to claim an active state of mind accompanying the alleged justification. It is not adequate for him to argue simply that he does not believe the contrary, i.e., that he is not being attacked. Let us suppose then that § 2.04 will not apply to the indifferent defendant.

It does not follow that the indifferent defender would be guilty of knowing homicide, for if the absence of self-defense is a material element of the offense, he must know—i.e., he must be aware[58]—of this absence. If he is indifferent about whether he is justified, he is not aware that he is not justified. The missing link in this argument, however, is proof that knowledge is the required culpability for the absence of self-defense. The proof can derive, it seems, only from the interpretation of § 2.02(4), developed above, that would extend the knowledge stipulated for the core elements of the offense to all the negative elements covered by the criteria of justification. It follows that ignorance or indifference about the conditions of self-defense would preclude convicting the defendant of knowing homicide.

Suppose that the actor recklessly believes that he is about to be attacked. The implication of § 3.09(2) is that self-defense would not be available in a prosecution for reckless homicide. If the actor has recklessly caused death, would it follow that he would be guilty of reckless homicide? It would seem so, though the prosecution would also have to establish that the defendant was reckless relative to the material element of justification. The same reasoning applies to negligent mistakes about the conditions of self-defense.

A significant conclusion emerges from this detailed analysis of the general[59] as well as the special provisions on mistaken self-defense:[60] The *MPC does not need the special rules on mistaken justification.* All the results generated by the special rules follow from the general rule. It is preferable, therefore, simply to rewrite the justification provisions so that they do not turn on the actor's belief of objective circumstances; eliminate the exception provided in § 3.09(2) for negligent and reckless mistakes and simply proceed on the assumption that the prosecution must prove, depending on the definition of the core offense, purpose, knowledge, recklessness or negligence as to the elements of justification. Without the encumbrance of special rules on mistaken justification, the Code would be simpler, clearer and more elegant.

In addition, this simplification would cancel the infelicitous implication that someone who believes, mistakenly, that he is acting in self-defense actually is justified in what he is doing. I have done battle elsewhere with this philosophically dubious conception of justification[61] and I am reluctant to repeat myself here. It should be enough to point out that the MPC does not generally take mistake to be a justification. The whole point of § 2.04(1), located in the "General Principles of Liability,"[62] is that mistake stands in a conceptual relationship with the criteria of culpability. For example, mistaken beliefs about the legal validity of military orders are treated in the same category of general principles.[63] If mistakes generally are treated separately from the standard about which one is mistaken, it is surely wrong to treat putative justification (based on a mistaken belief) as an instance of justified conduct.

One might defend the MPC's resting claims of justification on the actor's beliefs as a necessary hedge against an objectified theory of justification—one that would be based exclusively on objective events, such as whether someone was in fact attacking the defender. But surely that fear is misplaced. If the criteria of justification are stated in objective terms, it need not follow that the defender can invoke a claim of justification without having had a justificatory intent. The 1975 German Criminal Code formulates its standard of self-defense and necessity without requiring that the actor know of the danger to which he is responding.[64] Yet there is no doubt in German law that the actor must at least knowingly respond to a threat or to aggression in order to claim a justificatory defense.[65]

The complex of criteria bearing on the justification of self-defense consists of objective and subjective elements: the objective factors of aggression and necessary response, and a subjective requirement of intent or knowledge. None of these factors has anything to do with mistake, which bears on the actor's culpability for acting in the absence of objective justifying criteria and not on the intent required to make out a good case of self-defense.[66] This exercise has demonstrated, I hope, that the MPC provisions on mistaken self-defense are superfluous. If they were stricken from the Code, there would be no substantive change. My argument depends on the assumption that the drafters of the MPC seriously intended in § 2.04(1) to enact a general provision on mistake that would cover all the material elements of every crime.

Yet, there are some serious implications of taking § 2.04(1) at its face value. Note, for example, that the provision covers "ignorance or mistake as to a matter of fact or law."[67] Think of the implication in a case in which the actor is mistaken about whether a particular justification exists. Suppose that he thinks, mistakenly, that he has a right to shoot every unleashed dog that wanders onto his property. Could he invoke this mistake as a defense in a prosecution for purposely destroying his neighbor's property?[68] If his purpose must include a belief that his conduct is unjustified, his mistake would negate the required culpability; he would not in fact regard his conduct as unjustified. This conclusion follows from taking § 2.04(1) seriously as a general provision covering all material elements, including, as the provision declares, questions both of fact and of law.

A contrary implication derives from § 2.02(9), which provides that no culpability is required as to "whether conduct constitutes an offense or as to the existence, meaning or application of the law determining the elements of [the] offense."[69] This provision expresses the classic rule that mistake of law is no excuse. Why, then, does § 2.04(1) hold that mistake of law is a defense if it negatives the culpability required for the particular material element of the offense? With regard to a mistaken view about the existence of a justification, either of these provisions could apply. The problem with the negative rule (§ 2.02(9)) is whether a mistaken perception of justification should receive classification as a mistake about whether "conduct constitutes an offense." There is no doubt in the mind of the man shooting the stray dog that the willful destruction of property is an offense, but he views his own conduct as a justified exception to the general prohibition. However, if we take seriously the MPC's commitment to treating claims of justification as negative elements of the offense, then the dog-shooter is mistaken about whether his conduct constitutes an offense and the negative rule of § 2.02(9) should rule out the defense.

But does the general rule, § 2.04(1), favoring the recognition of mistakes of law about material elements come into play? The problem is the meaning of the phrase "required to establish a material element of the offense."[70] Is justification in general a "material element" or does the Code apply only to particular, legally recognized justifications? That is difficult to fathom from the language of the Code. The definition of "material elements" hints at the latter view: it suggests, with confusing indirection, that all elements are material that are not unconnected with "the existence of a justification or excuse."[71] The use of the word "existence" in this context rather than, say, "application," supports the interpretation that justification in general is a material element of every offense. It would follow that the culpability required for the offense of destroying property should extend to the existence or non-existence of a justification. If this culpability level is purpose or knowledge, any mistake would qualify as a defense.

This is the better reading of the MPC. I have no doubt, however, that an American court would hold the mistake about the right to shoot the stray dog as irrelevant.[72] The problem is not with common-law intuitions about the relevance of mistake of law. In this situation the aversion to mistake of law is plausible, if not self-evidently sound. The problem is rather with a model code that designs its rules for the core elements of offense and assumes, uncritically, that the same rules apply, by extension, to criteria of justification and excuse.

So far the analysis has been limited to problems in the field of justification. Before we turn to the complexity of mistakes about excusing conditions, let us summarize the results so far. The schema (on the next page) illuminates the kinds of mistakes about material elements that require individualized analysis.

The basic problem in the theory of mistake—the real problem that the MPC took to be a false problem—is whether all six categories of mistakes are to be treated like mistakes of type 1. The MPC theorists supposed they could extend the model set by type 1 to type 2 and 3 without particular difficulty. The easy

Mistakes about Material Elements

	fact	law
core elements	1	2
justification	3	4
excuse	5	6

cases in category 2 would be a mistake, say, about whether bomb casings are or are not the "property" of another or whether one is still "married" at the time of entering into a second marriage. Though "property" and "married" are attributes raising legal issues, they still function as elements of their respective offenses to which the actor's knowledge and intention are obviously relevant. They are to be distinguished from mistakes about whether bigamy is a crime or whether bigamy requires that one engage in a second religious as opposed to a second civil marriage. These latter mistakes are the type the negative rule in § 2.02(9) seeks to banish from consideration in assessing criminal guilt.

If we assume that claims of justification are simply negative elements of the offense, extending the principles of type 1 to type 3 follows easily. Problems begin, however, when we seek to extend the same principles to type 4. Arguably, there are some easy cases in type 4, closer in structure to type 2 than the case of a hunter mistaken about the existence of a justification for shooting stray dogs. Let us suppose there really is a justification that permits every property owner to shoot dogs that wander onto his property. The hunter now shoots a dog on the sidewalk in front of his house on the assumption that this is legally part of his "property" (after all, he has to keep the sidewalk clear of snow during the winter). This looks like a mistake in category 2, except that it is transplanted into the realm of justification. The logic of the Code seems to say: treat it just like a mistake about whether allegedly abandoned bomb casings are the property of another. Again, I doubt whether any American court would recognize this mistake, however reasonable under the circumstances, as a good excuse. The analogy between type 1 and type 4 simply does not carry.

Now let us turn to the more difficult problems posed by categories 5 and 6, namely mistakes both about fact and law in the context of excuses as material elements of the offense. The first problem is figuring out the defense that the MPC classifies as an excuse. This is no place to rehearse the general discussion about the distinction between a claim that conduct is objectively right (justification) and an argument that though the conduct is wrong, it is not blameworthy (excuse).[73]

Although the MPC makes no effort to clarify this distinction, it obviously incorporates it in the organization of the general principles of liability. Article 3 explicitly specifies the domain of justification, and Article 2, covering "General Principles of Liability," includes most of the issues that both the general principles and the general practice of Western legal systems would treat as excuses.[74] We can be relatively sure that duress in § 2.09 and involuntary intoxication in § 2.08(4) qualify as excuses. The Code also seems to treat mistake about the unlawfulness of a military order as an excuse[75] and, I shall argue below, it recognizes a limited excuse of mistake of law.[76] Entrapment[77] is a borderline case. The issue bears on criminal responsibility; it relates to duress just as seduction relates to intimidation. However, the Code's decision to have the matter tried by a judge rather than by a jury would be constitutional only if the Code's conception of entrapment is extrinsic to the substantive criteria of liability—analogous, therefore, not to duress, but to the Fourth Amendment exclusionary rule.

Let us focus, then, on duress as undisputed in instances of an excuse under the MPC. A mistake of type 5 would be a mistake about whether one faces "a threat to use unlawful force against his person or the person of another."[78] Someone approaches the actor and threatens to kill him unless he strikes a third party in the face; he complies and is charged with battery. The threat, however, was merely a research project in the susceptibility of ordinary people to intimidation; the threatening party had no intention of carrying it through.

Though one would think that a provision on duress would address itself to the actor's subjective condition, the wording of § 2.09 requires us to assess whether the actor is in fact coerced by a threat. The result is unclear if the actor merely feels coerced by a mistaken perception of a threat. True, the provision adds a requirement that "a person of reasonable firmness in his situation would have been unable to resist"[79] the threat, but there is no suggestion that if the actor mistakenly thought he was under threat, the mistake must be one that a reasonable person would have made. There is no hint of a solution within Article 3 and therefore we have to seek the guidance of § 2.04(1). Before we do that, however, let us consider what a sensible solution would be to the problem of a mistaken perception of a threat.

Basically, the question is whether the criteria for duress should depend on the crime the actor seeks to excuse. The basic rationale for duress is that the external coercion undermines the actor's blameworthiness in committing the offense. If he could not fairly be expected to resist the threat, he cannot be fairly blamed and punished for the violation. If he is culpable in responding to the coercion, he cannot plausibly claim that the coercion negates his culpability. The strong connection between culpability and duress is borne out by the requirement that the threat be one that a person of "reasonable firmness" not be able to resist. This conclusion is buttressed by an additional provision rendering the defense unavailable if the actor "recklessly placed himself in a situation in which it was probable that he would be subjected to duress."[80] The analogous treatment of a mistaken perception of a threat would lead to the conclusion that the actor culpably made a mistake about whether he was threatened, and he should not be able to invoke the defense.

This is not the result, however, of applying the instructions of the MPC. The only provision leading to a result is the general provision on mistake.[81] Offenses under duress are typically committed purposely or at least knowingly because the actor chooses to commit an offense rather than suffer personal harm. In these situations, the implication of § 2.04(1), together with § 2.02(4), is that the actor must at least know of the absence of duress as a material element of the offense. If he thinks that he is under threat, however unreasonable his assumption might be, he cannot know or be aware of the absence of coercion. The implication is that the MPC would acquit in those cases in which the actor concludes that he must violate the interests of an innocent person in order to avoid an imagined threat.

This conclusion flies in the face of what we took to be the sensible solution to the problem of mistaken duress. More significantly, for the purposes of this essay, it highlights the internal contradictions in the Code. Excusing the unreasonably mistaken actor runs afoul of the general principle of not excusing unreasonable actors for other excesses such as unreasonably responding to the threat, or recklessly placing himself in the situation. Also, because the characteristic offense under duress is intentional, there is no way of holding the actor accountable for a lesser offense, as suggested by the compromise in § 2.09(2). There is no way of escaping the conclusion that extending § 2.04(1) to all material elements, including excuses like duress, represents a deep flaw in the structure of the Code.

This is not the only evidence of this flaw. Additional problems crop up in the analysis of type 6 mistakes. Suppose that someone is mistaken about the legal scope of duress. He thinks that the term "unlawful force to his person" includes the threat of damage to his car. A defendant in a criminal case threatens to blow up the actor's car unless he commits perjury. Confident that he will have a good defense of duress, the actor submits to the threat. It turns out that he is wrong about the scope of the statutory defense. Can he assert a good claim of mistake?

The problem is similar to the conundrum posed above in the analysis of type 4 mistakes,[82] but there are some new twists. First, it is not clear that § 2.02(9) should have any relevance. Is a mistake about the scope of duress about "whether conduct constitutes an offense"?[83] True, the mistake is about a material element of an offense, but it is hard to believe that drafters used the term "offense" to encompass all material elements, including excuses. The heading to § 2.02(9) is Culpability as to Illegality of Conduct. The better interpretation seems to be that duress would not be included within the issues bearing on illegality.[84] It follows that § 2.02(9) would not preclude recognition of the mistake about duress as a mistake of law.

The Code contains a general principle on mistake of law[85] which conceivably would apply in the case of mistake about the scope of the duress. Suppose that the actor came to his view about cars and persons by relying (or his lawyer's relying) on a judicial decision that treated banging on a car as a battery against the driver inside. It would be fair to call this "reasonable reliance upon an official statement of the law" that led him to the conclusion that duress included threats to his car. All § 2.04(3) requires is "a belief that conduct does not legally constitute an offense."[86] This phrase is more encompassing and therefore more tolerant to the inclusion of excuses, it would seem, than the reference to illegality in 2.02(9). The implication is that the mistake of law provision could well apply in a type 6 mistake. This strikes me as counter-intuitive. Individuals are not expected to govern their conduct by the legal criteria of excusing. These provisions are designed not as "conduct rules" to guide human behavior, but as "decision rules" for judges adjudicating liability for unlawful behavior.[87] Therefore, it seems wrong to treat the rules of excusing as rules about which individuals are entitled to reasonably rely in planning their conduct. Type 6 mistakes should be irrelevant to liability.

Of course, there is no clear indication in the Code that mistakes about the law of excuse would defeat liability. The basic concepts of "offense" and "illegality" are simply too vague to permit any clear conclusions.

This exercise could continue. I could pose the question: Does § 2.04(1) apply to mistakes about the scope of § 2.04(3)? Suppose the actor is mistaken about whether a lawyer's advice is included within the scope of legal sources on which an individual may reasonably rely. In fact, lawyers are not included in § 2.04(3).[88] But the latter provision sets out a general excuse of mistake of law, and if the actor is mistaken about its scope, it would seem that he would be mistaken about a material element of an offense. If this is a type 5 mistake, merely believing that lawyers are included in the provision would be sufficient for any offense that must be committed knowingly or purposely. If it is a type 6 mistake, the conclusion might be different—or at least it would seem that § 2.04(1) and § 2.04(3) would be in conflict. There is no point, however, in pressing the attack with questions of this theoretical refinement. It is obvious that the drafters of the Code have never thought about any of these problems.

Important consequences follow from the structure of issues that bear on liability. For some purposes, the Code recognizes these consequences: issues of justification are treated separately, excusing criteria are excluded from the definition of "unlawful force."[89] This is not the place, unfortunately, to develop an alternative theory of mistake. My task has been simply to critique the Model Penal Code's erring so profoundly. Six types of mistakes cannot be reduced to one. The legislature should not be expected to solve the problem of mistake in all six categories simply by stipulating criteria of culpability for the core elements. The Model Penal Code is wrong. Mistake is not a false problem.

CHAPTER 11

Reply: The Model Penal Code's Mistakes About Mistakes: An Analysis of George Fletcher's "Mistake in the Model Penal Code: A False False Problem"

Heidi M. Hurd

George Fletcher's 1988 article on the Model Penal Code's understanding of the role of mistakes in the assignment of criminal liability is a vintage example of what I think of as the first stage of Fletcher's impressive scholarly career—his long and influential period of theoretically informed doctrinalism. It well illustrates why Fletcher became and has remained a defining figure in criminal law jurisprudence, and it serves as a timeless model of what it means to bring relentless rigor to the examination of code provisions and to invoke background theoretical claims in order to resolve the tensions and conflicts revealed by a careful analysis of the law's black letter. Were one asked by an aspiring scholar for an example of scholarship that combines both critical doctrinalism and applied theory, one could find no better model than Fletcher's "Mistake in the Model Penal Code: A False False Problem."

Fletcher's essential claim is that the Model Penal Code (MPC) fails to do what it claims to do, which is to consistently treat mistakes as relevant to criminal liability if, but only if, they defeat the culpability required for conviction. Under the MPC, a mistake is thought to defeat culpability when its object concerns a material element of the crime charged. Thus, if a man mistakenly believed that a woman had

* David C. Baum Professor of Law and Philosophy, University of Illinois.

given consent to intercourse, he cannot be held liable for her rape if the statute under which he is charged predicates liability on a finding that he had knowledge of all the crime's material elements (for lack of consent is surely material). That his mistake was unreasonable is neither here nor there, so long as he is prosecuted for knowing, rather than negligent, rape. Similarly, if a Vermont woman mistakenly believes that her bedroom companion is her husband (because she went through a marriage ceremony with him in Nevada after he was there divorced from his former wife, and she does not realize that Vermont refuses to give full faith and credit to Nevada divorces), and if the adultery statute under which she is prosecuted makes the marital status of her companion material, then her mistake about her companion's marital status will preclude her conviction if knowledge is required of all material elements.

But while this much is straightforward under the MPC, Fletcher convincingly demonstrates that this strategy for dealing with mistakes breaks down when extended to justifications and excuses. If the absence of a justification or excuse is a material element of a crime (as he argues it both is and ought to be on the MPC's own "negative elements thesis"), then it would seem that a defendant could not be convicted of a crime unless she had the same mens rea as to the absence of justifications and excuses as she is required to have had as to the material elements of the substantive crime charged. Thus, if a defendant were charged with a knowing killing, he could not be convicted unless he also believed that his victim was not an aggressor and was not subjecting him to a hard choice that no person of reasonable firmness could resist. So, a defendant who was indifferent as to whether his victim was an aggressor (and who thus neither believed that force was necessary to prevent an attack nor believed that it was not necessary) would seemingly be *in*eligible for punishment—at least if the MPC's approach to mistakes about prima facie elements were carried over to justifying and excusing conditions. And a defendant who resorted to force in answer to an unreasonably imagined threat would be excused on grounds of duress, for he would not know that his actions were done in the absence of duress—at least, again, if the MPC were to resolve the conflict between sections 2.09 and 2.04 in favor of extending the general approach to mistakes articulated in section 2.04.

It is a virtue of Fletcher's analysis that it is impossible to summarize succinctly or to motivate quickly these reductio ad absurdum arguments and numerous others that he deploys in charging the MPC with redundancy, ambiguity, inconsistency, incompleteness, and moral absurdity, for they work at a level of specificity that defies broad-brush descriptions. Rather than dwell on petty complaints about a small handful of such arguments, let me instead raise questions that would have to be answered before one could construct an alternative theory of mistake of the sort that Fletcher explicitly postpones at the end of his article.

First, should there be *any subjective requirements* for justifications? If justifications had no mens rea requirements, Fletcher's questions about the nature of relevant mistakes would be made moot by the resulting irrelevance of mistakes.

While we are rightly averse to strict liability in the criminal law because we take it to be unfair to punish people who had no inculpatory beliefs about matters material to blame, there are no similar objections to justifications being "strict." For there is no symmetrical unfairness in exonerating defendants when they have, in fact, achieved the goods that justifications are thought to honor, whatever their beliefs or motivations. So why not consider the unwitting defender justified when he, in fact, killed someone who was culpably aggressing against him, even though he did not believe, at the time, that he was facing imminent peril? And why not accord the unwitting Robin Hood the defense of necessity, when in stealing from the rich to give to the poor he objectively did the lesser of two evils, because his beneficiaries were snatched from death's door by his deed? It would seem that to punish such persons proportionate to their culpability, we would impose upon them attempt liability, for under the facts as they believed them to be, they were committing unjustified deeds. Since their deeds were objectively justified, they cannot be said to have committed completed crimes; but attempt liability should be a satisfactory reply to the intuition that they acted culpably, even as they did no (objective) wrong.

Second, and inversely, should there be *any objective requirements* for excuses? If excuses had no objective (actus reus) requirements, Fletcher's questions about the nature of relevant mistakes would again be made moot by the irrelevance of mistakes. In a case of alleged duress, for example, we would not care whether the defendant was in fact subjected to a threat, or whether the threat was one that another (of reasonable firmness) would find hard to resist, or whether the defendant believed that his choice would be excused by the criminal law: we would only care whether the defendant subjectively felt himself to be between a rock and a hard place so as to make his choice nonculpable. Inasmuch as excuses are best explained as compassionate responses to those whose choices are made nonculpable by constraining or debilitating conditions they did not create, it is puzzling indeed (on any grounds other than evidential ones) that we attach objective conditions to their application. Why demand that a defendant have been provoked before according him a partial excuse for killing in the heat of passion? And why not accord people (partial) excuses for crimes other than homicide if they are committed in a heat of passion? If people are less culpable for the (bad) choices they make when reason has been displaced by passion, why not make this the only question? And if it were the only question, mistakes about objective circumstances would become irrelevant, because such circumstances would be irrelevant.

Third, how should the law treat mistakes about values that lead people into thinking that they have served, rather than dis-served, the law's implicit moral agenda (as made explicit in what courts take to be the lesser of competing evils, for example)? How should it handle the person who genuinely believes that it is the lesser evil to kill an abortionist, or to cultivate marijuana for medical purposes, or to distribute hypodermic needles to avoid the spread of AIDS, or to protest a war by disrupting a government office's functions? If mistakes of value are like mistakes of law, then the reasons that dictate that mistakes of law should not excuse (reasons that have little to do with considerations of culpability and much to do with considerations of deterrence) should similarly make us indifferent to mistakes of value. And it would seem that even if one agreed with the preceding arguments so as to strip justifications of their subjective requirements and excuses of their objective requirements, one could still, with consistency, refuse to allow mistakes of law, and analogous mistakes of value, to exculpate (except in exceptional circumstances of the sort the law now recognizes). But if mistakes about values are like mistakes about justificatory facts, then ridding justifications of subjective requirements and focusing solely on whether a defendant in fact responded to a credible threat to bodily integrity or chose what is objectively deemed to be the lesser of two evils would again make moot the current conundrums over how to treat defendants who have made good faith moral mistakes. We could purge justifications of references to so-called cultural defenses and syndromes that are currently advanced to support claims of necessity or the reasonableness of beliefs about imminent peril to self or others, for example, leaving them to support (subjectively defined) excuses when particularly compelling. And by so doing, we would eliminate a good deal of the mistakes that Fletcher assigns to the MPC's provisions about mistakes.

Fourth and finally, Fletcher describes the MPC as embracing a thin theory of culpability—a theory that does not patently reveal a theory of guilt or deserved punishment. As he puts it, its drafters "sought to exhaust the analysis of guilt, blame, culpability and related concepts of *mens rea* by specifying four 'kinds of culpability.' Two of these definitions—purposely and knowingly—proceed as though culpability were simply a matter of fact, reducible to what people believe, think and take as the object of their actions" (102). Certainly rich theories of moral responsibility and criminal punishment can be assigned to the MPC by way of vindicating its four-part analysis of culpability. But I have always agreed with Fletcher that the MPC worked a reductive strategy that significantly impoverished the criminal law in its ability to parse, analyze, and match punishments to distinctively different culpable mental states. It has left adjudicators without a means of reflecting concern for the motivations that drove actors to crime and the emotional states within which they committed their crimes. True, the MPC employs concepts that permit the preservation of the common law category of specific intent crimes (e.g., attempt crimes, burglary), and so it allows legislatures and courts to punish defendants not just for what they have in fact done (e.g., stalking, breaking and entering) but for the (further criminal) goals that inspired their actions (e.g., to kill, to steal). But while those kinds of motivations are surely worthy of legal concern and accorded such by the MPC, the MPC makes no room for the role of other motivations and attendant emotions that are unlike the goals punished by strict liability crimes—deeper features of character, rather than choice, that do far more to inform our sense of moral vice and virtue. And so jealousy, spite, sadism, narcissism, racism, sexism, and other character defects find no place in the MPC's taxonomy of the core concepts of culpability, nor do mercy, kindness, generosity, self-sacrifice, pity, bravery, or other such virtues that may motivate lawbreaking in extraordinary circumstances.

What role would mistakes play if the relevant mental states within the criminal law did not allow for easy cancellation by factual inaccuracies within our beliefs? Perhaps the fact that this question is hard to answer provides one (of probably many) good reasons why the MPC is wise to avoid entanglements with mental states that are far more complex than the four it specifies. But just as mistakes about defenses may be irrelevant, because justifications need no subjective elements and excuses need no objective ones, so mistakes about matters of prima facie liability might be of reduced relevance if defendants' goals and beliefs were ultimately deemed less significant in the assessment of their guilt than their deeper reasons for action.

The thrust of my four general questions is to suggest that while Fletcher successfully proves that mistakes are not a false problem for the MPC, they may, in the end, prove to be a false problem for the criminal law. This is not because mistakes should be thought relevant only if they negate the mens rea of crimes charged, as the MPC would have it. Rather, it is because mistakes may be largely irrelevant to the questions that ought to be asked—questions that would be asked if the MPC and the codes that it seeks to inform were clearheaded about the objective and subjective conditions of prima facie guilt, justification, and excuse.

JUSTIFICATION AND EXCUSE

The Individualization of Excusing Conditions

George P. Fletcher

I. The Concept of Excusing

The excusing conditions of the criminal law are variations of the theme "I couldn't help myself" or "I didn't mean to do it."[1] In this respect the defenses known as necessity, duress, insanity and mistake of law are but extensions of homely, routine apologies for causing harm and violating the rules of social and family life. While we use the plea "I couldn't help myself" to cover the full range of excusing circumstances, each of the formal excuses of the criminal law has a limited sphere. As a general matter, these spheres are dictated by the type of circumstances rendering the conduct excusable. If the excusing circumstances are natural phenomena, the appropriate excuse is necessity.[2] Standard cases are those of the starving man who steals a loaf of bread or the shipwrecked sailor who dislodges another man from the only life-sustaining plank at sea. If the excuse derives from intimidation exerted by another human being, the appropriate excuse is coercion or duress.[3] Thus, if the actor steals or rapes only because a gunman threatens to kill him if he does not, the defense of duress would come to play. In a third type of case, the distortion in the actor's conduct is attributable neither to natural circumstances nor to another human being, but to his own psychological make-up. It is here that we speak of legal insanity as a defense. Whether the formula of insanity is the restrictive *M'Naghten* rule[4] or the more liberal *Durham* test,[5] the inquiry is the same: Is there something about the defendant's psychological condition that makes it credible for him to say, "I couldn't help myself."

The excuse of mistake of law warrants special notice. An individual might engage in seemingly innocuous conduct, such as carrying a pocket knife, and find himself in violation of the criminal law. Nothing compels him to carry the knife. If he has an excuse, it would be that he "didn't mean" to violate the law. In this type of case, the distortion of the actor's conduct derives not from internal or external pressures, but from ignorance—ignorance that might be beyond his control.

These four excusing conditions bear several common traits. They all speak in the idiom of involuntariness. The claim is not that there was no act at all (as if the actor suffered an epileptic seizure), but that the actor, in Aristotle's words, "would [not] choose any such act in itself."[6] Were it not for the conditions of necessity, duress, insanity or ignorance of the law, the actor would not have violated the law. Therefore, his act seems to be attributable to circumstances rather than to his character. The act does not tell us what kind of person the actor is. The premise seems to be that if a violation of the law does not accurately reveal the actor's character, it is unjust to punish him for what he has done.[7]

According to this account, the practice of excusing men for their deeds is interwoven with a felt distinction between condemning the act and blaming the actor.[8] It is always actors who are excused, not acts.[9] The act may be harmful, wrong and even illegal, but it might not tell us what kind of person the actor is. And precisely in those cases in which there is no reliable inference from censuring the act to censuring the actor, we speak of excusing the actor for his misdeed.

II. Thesis: The Common Law's Aversion to Excusing Conditions

If this account of excusing conditions seems plausible, it is nonetheless a view that has hardly won favor among English and American jurists. German scholars and courts have cultivated a full range of excusing conditions, but common law courts have been loath to recognize necessity, duress, insanity and mistake of law as defenses relating to the character of the doer rather than to the quality of the deed. If they have recognized these defenses at all, it is only after converting the claims of excuse into other types of defenses. Necessity and duress sometimes emerge as justificatory defenses; that is, as claims that the act is right and commendable, rather than that the actor should be disassociated from wrongful conduct. Mistake of law occasionally slips by as a defense, but only as a denial for the special mental state required for conviction; common law courts rarely, if ever, ask whether the defendant's ignorance of the law was beyond his control and therefore excusable. Even insanity, which is universally recognized as a defense, is often taken not as an excuse, but as a jurisdictional challenge to the court—something akin to the defense of infancy.

Even where common law courts and legislators recognize defenses like duress as excuses, they nonetheless shy away from equating the issue of excuse with an assessment of the actor's character. Thus, even reform-minded forces like the Model Penal Code (hereinafter MPC) tie the defense of duress to the expected conduct of the "person of reasonable firmness" rather than to the individual character of the accused.[10] The "reasonable man" is so familiar a figure of common law rhetoric that he is hardly out of place in the MPC. Yet, as will become clear in the course of the analysis that follows, the common law reliance on "reasonable men" relates to the system's more general aversion to excusing conditions.

The ensuing sections focus in detail on the common law's abuse and transformation of four excusing conditions: necessity, duress, insanity and mistake of law. I shall devote special attention to the first; for the variations of necessity are complex and the comparative history of necessity in German and Anglo-American jurisdictions illuminates the difference between justifying and excusing criminal conduct. In conclusion we shall turn to an account of the common law's aversion to excusing conditions. To anticipate that account briefly, I shall attempt to show that this feature of the common law derives from misleading assumptions about the indispensability of rules in formulating legal judgments.

A. NECESSITY: THE PROTOTYPICAL AMBIGUITY

The byways of necessity are so intricate that we need a roadmap of the possible types of case. At least four landmarks stand out in the variations of necessity: (1) the harm threatened; (2) the harm done by the actor in eliminating the threat; (3) whether the actor acts in his own interest or in the interest of others; and (4) whether the danger emanates from the object damaged or from another source. Let us examine these four variables in greater detail.

The harm threatened. The interest threatened might be life, health, sexual integrity, property or personal liberty. For example, a man's life might be in danger if he is starving, a pregnant woman's life or health might be endangered by the fetus, or an individual's home might be in the path of a raging fire.

The harm done. The actor can eliminate the danger only by inflicting harm on another interest. To pursue the same examples, the starving man can save his life by stealing food, a doctor can save the mother's life or health by aborting the fetus, and the homeowner can save his home only by blasting a firebreak to contain the fire.

The status of the actor. Someone must decide whether the threatened interest should prevail over the interest that would need to be sacrificed. Sometimes, as in the case of the starving man, the decision-maker is the person whose interests are at stake. At other times, as in the case of the doctor aborting the fetus, the decision-maker is a non-involved third party.

The source of the risk. The harm inflicted by the necessitated act sometimes accrues to the source of the danger, as in the case of aborting a fetus, and sometimes to an interest independent of the danger, as in the case of stealing a loaf of bread to avoid starvation. It is obviously difficult to distinguish neatly between these two kinds of interests. If a house is blown up to check the spread of a fire, it might be viewed under either rubric. One might argue that either the fire or the continuing presence of the house is the true cause of the danger.

With these variations of necessity in mind, we can begin to probe the most troublesome aspect of necessity as a defense, namely, its capacity to function both as a justification and as an excuse. When necessity figures as a justificatory rationale, the issue is whether, on balance, the act is right or wrong. The rightness of the act typically turns on a comparison of the utility of acting (the value of the interest saved) with the disutility of acting (the value of the interest sacrificed). Rightness is thus a matter of maximizing utility, or furthering the greater good. This is the view of necessity—indeed the only view of necessity—that has crystallized in the MPC[11] and in the Soviet codes and literature.[12]

The following cases are readily justified as cases of necessity (of furthering the greater good):

1. A starving man steals a loaf of bread.[13]
2. A doctor aborts a fetus to save the life of the mother.[14]
3. A homeowner blows up a house to prevent a fire from spreading and destroying many other houses.[15]
4. A policeman kills a lunatic who is shooting wildly and uncontrollably into a crowd of people.[16]
5. Three desperate shipwrecked sailors select a fourth to be sacrificed and eaten so that the three may survive.[17]

In all of these cases, the decisive factor is determining that one interest (the starving man's life, the mother's life, etc.) should prevail over the other (the grocer's property interest, the life of the fetus, etc.), and that determination is made simply by asking which interest is worth more. The decision has nothing to do with the personality or character of the actor. In principle, the decision may be abstracted from the individual case to formulate a new rule of law: any time an actor is faced with this same conflict of values, he may legally and properly choose the value the court has preferred.

The theory of necessity becomes muddled when we note that most of these five cases also lend themselves to interpretation as cases of excused, rather than justified conduct. In cases (1), (3) and (5), one might think of the actor as surrendering to overbearing pressure rather than as furthering the greater good. Starvation causes a man to steal; the threat of destruction causes a homeowner to blow up the neighboring house; and the fear of imminent death causes sailors to cannibalize one of their number. As the inquiry moves from justification to excuse, the emphasis shifts from assessing the act in abstraction to assessing the actor's response to unusual circumstances. The relevant question is no longer whether other people should act the same way in the same situation, but whether this defendant can be justly blamed for having succumbed to overwhelming pressure.

Now one might properly note that the question whether an actor may be fairly blamed for yielding under the circumstances is very much like comparing the utility and disutility of counteracting impending harm. If a man inflicts great harm to avoid a slight injury to himself, he would be hard-pressed to show that his conduct was involuntary. Whether conduct appears to be involuntary depends, in part, on the competing interests at stake. Yet it would be a mistake to suppose that perceptions of involuntariness are tantamount to judgments that the act furthers the greater interest. For conduct to be excused as involuntary, it is neither necessary nor sufficient that the actor act to further the greater good. If the actor's life is at stake and he must kill an innocent man in order to survive (e.g., he must dislodge another shipwrecked sailor from the only plank at sea), he does not act to further the greater good, for the two competing lives are of the same value. Nonetheless, his instinctive effort to save his life would presumably be excused.[18]

Conversely, acting to further the greater good does not in itself generate an image of involuntary conduct.[19] Suppose a farmer shoots and kills moose attacking his crops.[20] The value of the crops may well exceed the value of the several moose, but it does not follow that the shooting was involuntary. The question of involuntariness turns on the competing interests at stake, but the question is always whether the impending harm is so great relative to the cost of acting that we cannot fairly expect the actor to abstain from acting and suffer the harm. The comparison of interests is but the vehicle for determining what we may rationally and fairly expect of the actor under the circumstances.[21]

There may be substantial overlap in the applicability of the theories of necessity, as in cases (1), (3) and (5) above, but it is important to note that there are three traditional areas where only one theory of the defense applies. These areas warrant our attention, for they establish the indispensability of both theories of necessity in a well-developed system of criminal theory.

The first area is typified by cases (2) and (4) above. Whenever the decision-maker is a third party, like the doctor who must decide whether to perform an abortion, the only relevant doctrine of necessity is that of justification. A finding of involuntary conduct is precluded because the actor's personal interests are not at stake.[22]

There are two important types of case in which the only available defense of necessity might be a claim of excuse. The first is the case in which the actor takes human life, perhaps even to save a greater number of human lives. One might divert a river to flood a town and kill innocent people in order to save a large city from destruction. Or in the classic situation posed in *Regina v. Dudley & Stephens*, a group of shipwrecked sailors, facing imminent death, might cannibalize one of their number so that the rest may survive.[23] If these cases did not involve the sacrifice of innocent lives, they would be readily justified as instances of furthering the greater good. But the taking of life has traditionally posed special problems. The Queen's Bench acknowledged this in *Dudley & Stephens*; if, as Lord Coleridge put it,

> the broad proposition [advanced is] that a man may save his life by killing, if necessary, an innocent and unoffending neighbor, it certainly is not law at the present day.[24]

The Kantian argument for this position is that sacrificing an innocent man for the sake of others is to treat him as a means to an end and thus to violate the imperative of respecting persons as ends in themselves.[25] The argument has had considerable impact in Western thought and helps to account for the common law's hostility to necessity and duress as defenses in homicide cases.[26]

The other type of case unamenable to analysis as justified conduct is that in which the harm done exceeds or is equal to the gain from acting. This is the case any time someone kills one or more persons to save his own life. The problem is well put in a hypothetical devised by Kadish and Paulsen:

> X is unwillingly driving a car along a narrow and precipitous mountain road, falling off sharply on both sides.... The headlights pick out two persons, apparently and actually drunk, lying across the road in such a position as to make passage impossible without running them over. X is prevented from stopping... by suddenly inoperative brakes. His alternatives are either to run down the drunks or to run off the road and down the mountainside.[27]

Suppose that the driver runs over and kills the two drunks in order to save his own life. Could a humane and just legal system do anything but acquit him? Yet his conduct is hardly justified as a maximization of utility: he sacrifices two lives to save one. The problem is the same any time a man is compelled to protect vital interests by inflicting greater harm than he stands to suffer. We can think of these situations as cases of necessity, but the necessity is not a form of justification. It is a form of excuse. It appeals to our sense of compassion for human weakness in the face of unexpected, overwhelming circumstances.

B. NECESSITY: CONFLICTING GERMAN AND ANGLO-AMERICAN APPROACHES

It is useful to contrast the German experience of devising a defense for all three types of case with the continuing common law confusion about necessity and its nature. The German Criminal Code of 1871 contained only one sentence on the issue of necessity; in section 54, the Code provided:

> A criminal act is not present whenever, apart from cases of self-defense, the act is done out of necessity to overcome an imminent risk to the life or bodily security of the actor or one of his dependents, provided that the actor is not responsible for the necessity and there is no other way of overcoming it.

Like other sections of the 1871 Code bearing on defensive issues, this provision does not specify whether the defense functions as a justification or an excuse. Yet there are several indications that the underlying rationale of section 54 is that of excusing involuntary conduct. First, the provision does not impose a limit on the harm that may be committed in the name of saving one's own life (or that of a dependent). Thus section 54 would apply to the case, posed above, of the driver who had to choose between running over two drunks and driving off the road to his own death. Secondly, the provision does not apply unless the actor's interests are at stake (or those of someone close to him); this requirement would not attach unless the underlying rationale were excusing those who succumb to self-interested action.

It was not until the early 1900s that German scholars perceived the two dimensions of necessity. In a landmark article published in 1913,[28] Professor Goldschmidt identified section 54 as a rule pertaining not to the rightness of the accused's conduct, but to the excusability of his engaging in wrongful conduct.[29] Provisions of the Civil Code, on the other hand, provided for a justification of necessity where the actor violated the property interests of another in order to further the greater good.[30] Goldschmidt's analysis brought a semblance of structure to the theory of necessity, and it also demonstrated a serious gap in the statutory scheme. The excuse of necessity was limited to cases in which the actor's or a dependent's serious interest was at stake, and the justification of necessity was limited to cases of inflicting property damage. Neither theory of the defense covered the case in which a third party furthers the greater good by violating an interest other than property rights. Thus there was no basis in the statutory scheme for acquitting a doctor who aborted a fetus to save the life of the mother. It was up to the *Reichsgericht* to round out the statutory scheme. In a dramatic 1927 decision, the German Supreme Court held that implicit in the criminal law was an extra-statutory justification based on necessity, and that this justification applied to render a life-saving abortion legal and proper.[31] Since 1927 the German courts have proceeded on the assumption that the Criminal Code regulates necessity as an excuse and that the Civil Code, supplemented by the extra-statutory defense of necessity, governs the justificatory dimension of the issue. The newly enacted Criminal

Code, effective January 1, 1975, provides separate and comprehensive sections on the two dimensions of necessity.[32]

Common law attitudes toward necessity have been much the opposite of those in the German tradition. Whenever the issue of necessity has arisen, the courts have assumed that the only applicable theory of necessity was that of justification. In the leading case of *Dudley & Stephens*, the Queen's Bench assumed that if necessity were to apply as a defense it would render the homicide lawful and justified.[33] The court had little difficulty concluding that killing an innocent man was morally wrong and therefore unjustifiable.[34] Thus the judges excluded necessity as a possible defense. What eluded the Queen's Bench in 1884 was that a killing might be unlawful, unjustified and murderous, but nonetheless be excused under the unique circumstances of the case.[35] This was a manner of legal thinking that perturbed the judges. It symbolized "a divorce of law from morality which would be of fatal consequence."[36]

The court assumed that if the defendants were to be acquitted, it would have to be under a rule clarifying the elements of murder—a rule that would be applicable in future cases as well.[37] The only such rule the court could imagine was the repugnant proposition "that a man may save his life by killing, if necessary, an innocent and unoffending neighbor."[38]

The Queen's Bench had no difficulty making another type of decision without relying on rules. It intimated that although it favored conviction, it would welcome the Queen's clemency.[39] Indeed the Crown subsequently did commute the death sentences to six months' imprisonment.[40] The decision to solicit executive clemency was much like a decision to excuse a case of unjustified killing.[41] It was based on an individualized assessment of the facts and of the character and propensities of the defendants. But it was not the kind of decision the Queen's Bench could call part of the "law"; therefore, the court regarded the decision to excuse the killing as beyond its province.

Common law jurists now regard *Dudley & Stephens* with uneasiness.[42] There is something inescapably odd about a court's simultaneously affirming a conviction and recommending clemency. The MPC sought to correct the mistake in the *Dudley & Stephens* syllogism, but it did so by tampering with the wrong premise. Necessity should be a justification, the draftsmen concluded in section 3.02, any time an actor favors the greater good; this principle, the draftsmen point out in commentary, would permit a court to conclude "on utilitarian grounds"[43] that killing one man to save three was justifiable. By extending the principle of necessity as a justification to homicidal conduct, the draftsmen thought they had corrected the error of *Dudley & Stephens* and had fashioned a comprehensive rule of necessity.

It will be remembered, however, that there are two areas in which necessity might have to function as an excuse in order to generate just and humane results. The first is the area of homicidal behavior, and the second is the area in which the actor saves his own life at a cost greater than or equal to one human life. The MPC disposes of the first by assimilating it, without qualm, to cases of conduct justified under a utilitarian calculus. The Code cannot so easily distend theories of justification to accommodate the second type of case: killing two men to avoid driving alone off the road is not supportable under any theory of justification.[44] The remarkable fact about the MPC is that it provides no solution at all to the second type of case. It is hard to believe, but the draftsmen ignored the problem. This was the tariff for maintaining that necessity was exclusively a justificatory rationale.

The common law theory of necessity has hardly matured since *Dudley & Stephens*. Witness a routine case decided by the Supreme Court of Missouri.[45] A convict named Green suffered a series of homosexual rapes and attacks by fellow convicts. He sought help from the prison guards; they ignored his pleas. On the day of his alleged offense, four other convicts told him they would rape him that evening. "Snitching" in the prison meant that he was likely to be killed. There was no available protective confinement other than the disciplinary "hole." As you or I would have done under the circumstances, Green went over the wall. Upon being caught, he was charged with escaping from a state institution, convicted, and sentenced to an additional three-year term. The Supreme Court ruled that the trial judge properly kept all the data on the prior and threatened homosexual rapes from the jury. Green's peers were not even allowed to consider whether compassion for his situation required an acquittal.

In the *Green* case, as in *Dudley & Stephens*, the court assumed that there was only one dimension to necessity: the dimension of balancing interests.[46] The Missouri Supreme Court could have held the evidence of prior and threatened homosexual rapes admissible on the ground that it might have been right, on balance, for Green to break out of prison. The defense of lesser evils could well have pointed toward acquittal, yet there are several reasons why a contemporary Anglo-American court would be reluctant to label Green's conduct as right and proper. For one, it would be fashioning a rule that would seem to give other similarly maltreated inmates the right to walk out the front door. Further, judges today are likely to interweave two distinct questions of balancing: first, whether on balance the defendant did the right thing, and second, whether it would be right, on balance, to acquit the defendant. Looking at Green's conduct as a matter of interest-balancing readily blends with the court's balancing the benefits and burdens of deciding to acquit. Once the court starts focusing on the interests weighing against acquittal, Green's chances plummet.[47] He would have been far better off if he could have anchored the debate to the limited inquiry whether his escape was excused by the impending rapes.[48] He might then have kept the court's focus on the question of whether he could fairly be blamed for yielding to the pressure of the situation. By so directing the inquiry, he might have been able to divert judicial attention away from the prospective benefits and burdens of their decision and toward the requirements implicit in treating the individual defendant fairly. Yet at least for the last century, judges in England and the United States have been unreceptive to that mode of decision. The unequivocal preference is for a future-oriented assessment of the virtues of deciding for and against the defendant; there is little commitment to the imperative of treating the defendant justly—as a value independent of the resulting social benefits. As a result, a lawyer in a case like *Green* is hard-pressed to induce the court to focus on the question whether the defendant can be fairly blamed for yielding to overwhelming pressure, for that question is not tied directly to any social goal that would outweigh the benefits arrayed in favor of conviction.

Like the draftsmen of the MPC, American judges are prone to insist that the only relevant dimension of necessity is the defense of lesser evils; thus the theoretical rationale for acquittal is whether, on balance, the defendant acted in the social interest. Yet that dimension rarely yields acquittals.[49] And whenever a strong interest—like maintaining discipline in the prisons—emerges on the opposing scale, the judges are likely to frustrate the defendant's appeal to the greater good.[50]

Thus one sees the extent to which the common law approach to necessity diverges radically from the German historical development. Anglo-American jurists are now inclined to hold that the defense of lesser evils ought, in principle, to justify violations of the law, yet the system remains averse both to applying this defense in practice and to recognizing a general excuse based on human frailty in situations of extraordinary pressure. The German pattern, in contrast, is rooted in the theory of necessity as an excuse; the defense of lesser evils emerges later as a way of covering those cases in which the actor's own interests are not at stake. This divergence manifests a deeper jurisprudential rift, which runs to the core of each system's conception of the law and appropriate judicial roles. The common law pattern reflects the influence of 19th century positivism blended with a commitment to decide each case instrumentally—a commitment to justify each decision as a means of optimizing the community's welfare. We shall return in conclusion to this account of the common law's posture toward necessity; but first we should broaden the analysis by turning to a comparative survey of duress, insanity and mistake of law.

C. DURESS: NECESSITY REVISITED

If common law judges have failed to acknowledge the excusing dimension of necessity, they have not fared so poorly in the field of duress. Jury instructions on duress frequently build on words like "coercion," "compulsion," and "involuntariness."[51] There is at least some recognition that the issue posed by a claim of duress is not whether the act was justified, but whether the actor's will was overborne by circumstances.[52] Stressing the issue of involuntariness makes it clear that the law's dominant concern is not the act in the abstract, but the extent to which the act reveals the kind of person the actor is.

Yet there are also contrary indications in the common law of duress. There are some signs that courts and legislators are inclined to recognize duress as a defense only when they feel that the act is right and justified. First, duress is frequently recognized as a defense only when the actor's life is in danger;[53] and secondly, it is rarely and only recently admitted as a defense in cases of homicide.[54] These two requirements, taken together, mean that the defense of duress is available only to those who protect an interest (namely life) that is greater than the harm caused (which must be less than the taking of life).

These restrictions on the common law defense of duress belie efforts to label the issue as an excusing condition. If the issue were exclusively the involuntariness of the deed—and not its rectitude—there would be no reason to reject claims of duress in homicide cases. German law recognizes the applicability of duress in homicide as well as other cases,[55] and so it must if it distinguishes rigorously between the issues of justifying a deed and excusing it. Yet the common law is obviously ambivalent about the distinction. It uses the idiom of excuses in characterizing duress, but it insists that the party relying on duress act to further the greater good.

The MPC has fashioned a defense of duress free of some of the inconsistencies of the common law tradition. It is classified as an "excuse," it requires merely a threat of unlawful force against the person, and it is available as a defense to every crime, including homicide.[56] Yet the MPC also betrays the common law's reluctance to inquire straightforwardly into the connection between an improper act and the actor's character. Section 2.09 of the Code provides:

> It is an affirmative defense that the actor engaged in the conduct charged to constitute an offense because he was coerced to do so by the use of, or threat to use, unlawful force against his person or the person of another, which a person of reasonable firmness in his situation would have been unable to resist.

"Reasonable men" and "persons of reasonable firmness" are ubiquitous in the language of the common law, and yet the same rhetorical figures are strangers to German legal idiom. This is not a fortuitous difference between the two systems. There is a close connection between each system's orientation toward excusing conditions and its reliance on fictitious standards like that of the reasonable man. The common law's aversion to excusing conditions is coupled with the felt indispensability of the reasonable man standard; the German law's cultivating excusing conditions is tied to indifference toward fictitious standards of exemplary men. This correlation is not at all mysterious, for the standard of the reasonable person provides a substitute for inquiries about the actor's character and culpability. This means that a system willing to assess character and culpability has no need of reasonable men; and a system afraid to look squarely at the character and culpability of the defendant must do so indirectly, by relying on standards like "the person of reasonable firmness." Let us see exactly why this is so.

What is the operative significance of the phrase "person of reasonable firmness" in section 2.09? The point of the requirement is that not every case of alleged duress is sufficient to excuse the defendant. Suppose someone kills another in order to avoid a slap in the face. Or suppose a government employee discloses official secrets to avoid having his car stolen. These are cases in which we would not be inclined to recognize the defense. It may well be true that these two actors felt "compelled" or "coerced" to act, but their sense of being compelled is hardly enough to warrant excusing their conduct.

There are two equivalent ways of explaining this result. The first approach would be to ask: Are these actors culpable for not resisting the threats? The first step in resolving that issue is to account for the actors' feeling compelled to act as they did. Unless we have additional facts about the psychological make-up of these defendants, we may suppose that the first actor was simply afraid of being slapped in the face. The second was presumably selfish; he was simply unwilling to make a personal sacrifice for the sake of governmental secrets. Do the traits of cowardice and selfishness excuse criminal behavior? Hardly. In the typical case, we can fairly expect of a man that he conquer his cowardice in the interest of saving human lives, or of a government official that he overcome his selfishness when governmental secrets are at stake. Of course, if the conduct of either was indeed beyond his control, it would be appropriate to excuse the conduct. But it would take some discernible pathology to cause us to believe that either of these men could not have done otherwise. Thus, according to this first approach, we relate the act to the actor's character traits and then assess whether the actor should be expected to control his propensities to act in the particular way.

The second path to the same result is the conventional common law formula: Would a reasonable person under the circumstances have acted in the same way? This test seems deceptively simple, yet its application requires the same logical steps and the same moral judgments as the first approach discussed above. Is the reasonable person cowardly? Is he selfish? If he were, our two allegedly coerced actors would have good defenses. Common law courts would obviously hold that the reasonable man is neither cowardly nor selfish. Why? Because these are traits that men can be fairly expected to surmount to save the life of another or to protect other vital interests. Thus, the definition of the reasonable person requires the same analysis and moral sensitivity as the frontal assessment of the actor's character and culpability.

To demonstrate this point more satisfactorily, let us suppose that our first hypothetical defendant kills to avoid being struck in the groin, and that it can be shown by reliable medical evidence that he has a pathological fear of castration and genital injury. The case for excusing him now seems more convincing; for we can now attribute his conduct to a personality disposition beyond his control.

Would it also seem more convincing under the standard of the "person of reasonable firmness"? It all depends, does it not, on the characteristics attributed to this fictitious character? If the applicable standard is the reasonable man with a pathological fear of castration, the jury might well acquit the defendant; if the applicable standard is the reasonable man without such fears, the jury would probably convict. How, then, does one decide how to instruct the jury?

There is only one sound way to determine the traits attributed to the reasonable man, and that is with an eye to the justice of blaming the accused for having displayed weakness of character. If we keep from the jury an important fact bearing on the homicide, namely the accused's pathological fears, we distort the jury's attempt to assess the causes of the killing. We skew the jury's inquiry toward finding that it was a culpable weakness of will, rather than uncontrollable pathological factors that induced the killing. For the defendant to be treated justly, the jury instructions should refer to a standard of a reasonable man with the specific pathological fears of the defendant. There is no doubt that the reasonable man standard can be adjusted and manipulated to encourage the right kind of jury deliberations. But the only way to make these adjustments in the standards is to decide by the first method discussed above whether the personality disposition accounting for the act is one that the accused should be able to control. If the accused should be able to overcome his dispositions, as in the case of cowardice and selfishness, these dispositions should not be attributed to the reasonable man; if the accused could not control the relevant disposition, as in the case of documentable, pathological fears, the disposition must be included in the standard used to assess the defendant's conduct.[57]

There is no suggestion in this analysis that the reasonable man test need yield results different from those obtained by assessing the actor's character and culpability. Indeed, the appeal of the reasonable man is precisely that he permits one, covertly, to make the same judgment that one would make in openly discussing the defendant's moral responsibility for his conduct. Yet if that is the case, one wonders why common law judges bother with the circumvention; why not simply ask whether the accused ought to have been able to resist the pressure exerted on him. This is a problem to which I shall return in conclusion. As we shall see, it is part of the broader puzzle posed by the common law's distinctive anxiety about decisions not based on rules.

D. INSANITY

Insanity is probably the clearest case of an excusing condition in the common law tradition. The courts have never confused insanity with the criteria of justification. It would be absurd to suggest that a man's psychological incapacity renders his conduct right and proper. Thus, at least in the case of insanity, common law jurists admit the possibility that an act might be wrongful and unjustified,[58] even though the actor is not to blame for committing it.

Among some common law writers and legislators, however, the defense of insanity has suffered another kind of distortion. There is a tendency in some quarters to think of the criminal law as applicable only to normal adults.[59] On this view of criminal responsibility, insanity and infancy become preliminary questions that one must resolve before deciding whether the criminal law is applicable. The California Penal Code provides, for example, that:

> All persons are capable of committing crimes except those belonging to the following classes:
>
> One—Children under the age of fourteen....
>
> Two—Idiots.
>
> Three—Lunatics and insane persons....[60]

As this provision is drafted, insanity is a status, not a condition explaining and excusing a particular act. This provision dates to 1872, but the view is even more fashionable today. Commentators now realize that a verdict of not guilty by reason of insanity leads, operationally, to one form of commitment rather than another. This fact of life has led to considerable skepticism whether insanity functions as an excuse. As Herbert Packer argues in his thoughtful book, *The Limits of the Criminal Sanction*:

> The insanity defense cannot be viewed as an excuse in the ordinary sense. It would be more useful to say that its successful invocation is a direction to punish but not to punish criminally....
> The insanity defense has no more to do with *mens rea* than does the defense of infancy....[61]

The defect in this argument seems rather elementary. It confuses an empirical concomitant of civil commitment with the grounds and justification for that commitment. Let us suppose that men acquitted by reason of insanity are regularly and routinely committed. It certainly does not follow that the verdict of not guilty is a "direction to punish" by civil commitment. The rationale for the commitment is a prediction of future dangerousness, not the finding that the actor was insane at the time of the act charged.[62] That courts rely on one index of dangerousness at one point in history hardly warrants the claim that the insanity defense does not perform an excusing function. Yet one is invariably struck by the widespread willingness of common law writers to reject the excusing function of the insanity defense. This willingness may well be further testimony to the deeply rooted hostility of the common law to the excusing conditions of the criminal law.

E. MISTAKE OF LAW

Mistakes about the legality of conduct impose the hardest strain on a legal system's sensitivity to individual justice. It is so easy for courts and commentators to slip into the mindless rhetoric about everyone's being presumed to know the law. Common law courts regularly intone that liturgy,[63] as German courts did about a hundred years ago.[64] In this century, German theorists have been engaged in intense debate about the appropriate doctrinal analysis of mistakes of law and about the kind of defense the courts should administer. After a landmark decision in 1952,[65] the German courts and theorists have converged on a fairly simple formula; translated into English legal idiom, the German rule is that reasonable mistakes of law excuse; unreasonable mistakes do not.[66] Whether a mistake is reasonable depends on whether the actor could be fairly and justly expected to perceive the wrongfulness of his conduct.

For good or ill, the common law is at about the stage of sophistication commanded by German theorists at the turn of the century.[67] We do not speak of mistake of law as a defense, though there are indeed isolated cases in which mistakes of law do bear on the state of mind required for conviction. In *People v. Weiss*,[68] for example, the defendant thought he had the authority to arrest one Wendel and take him out of the state. The defendant was prosecuted and convicted under a statute defining kidnapping as "wilfully seiz[ing]...another, with intent to cause him, without authority of law, to be...sent out of the state ...."[69] The New York Court of Appeals reversed the conviction. If the defendant assumed he had arresting authority, the court reasoned, he didn't have the "intent to cause [the victim], without authority of law, to be...sent out of the state"; therefore he was not guilty of the offense as defined by the statute.[70]

There are several remarkable features of this decision. First, there would have been no defense if the statute had read "wilfully seizing another, without authority of law, with the intent to cause him to be sent out of the state." Under this version, the defendant would have had the intent required for conviction; the only difference is that the phrase "without authority of law" is moved up six words in the formulation. It is inconceivable that the legislature would have located that phrase with an eye to whether mistakes about arresting authority should or should not constitute a defense. It is hardly exemplary of the judicial craft to place so much reliance on the fortuities of legislative drafting. Secondly, under the rationale of the decision, it is wholly immaterial whether the defendant's mistake is reasonable or unreasonable. Any mistake, even an irrational mistake, would negate the "intent to cause him, without authority of law...to be sent out of the state." It is scarcely sensible to resolve the case on the basis of a theory that leads to unacceptable results.[71] And in a system hostile to mistakes of law, it is an odd, unacceptable result to admit an irrational mistake of arresting authority as a full defense to the crime of kidnapping. These anomalies in the *Weiss* opinion should be enough to despair of this path for resolving the problem of mistake of law.

Yet there is no competitive approach in the Anglo-American literature. The MPC recognizes that relying on certain kinds of mistaken legal advice should constitute a defense, but the Code fails to integrate mistake of law into its theoretical structure, and indeed it discourages any association between mistake of law and other excusing conditions.[72]

It may well be that a legal system must develop some sophistication about the role of excusing conditions before it can engage the problem of mistake of law. It is only when courts appreciate the difference between excusing conduct and interpreting the law that they can avoid the snares surrounding mistakes of law. There is a common law tendency to say that recognizing mistake of law as a defense would be to allow the defendant to make his own law,[73] or to recognize a new exception to the pre-existing rule. But the law does not change when a jury finds that a man could not have been expected to know that his conduct was illegal. Thus there is an important and subtle difference between modifying a rule and finding that someone who violated the rule is excused and blameless for having done so. Yet this distinction has had little impact on common law thinking. And as a general matter, common law analysts have yet to see that mistake of law is an excusing condition parallel to necessity, duress and insanity.

III. Individualization and Rules

A recurrent theme in this discussion of the common law posture toward excusing conditions is that the common law, in the mind of its practitioners, consists of rules and nothing but rules. Judicial decisions must either follow rules or make new rules. Courts can handle the issue of justification, for recognizing a new justification is but to acknowledge an additional exception to the rule. Judges can think about what reasonable men would do, for abstracting the issue from the accused permits one to think of the case as a recurrent problem— the type of problem that is amenable to solution by rules. What common law judges find to be extra-legal are questions about the particular accused: What could we fairly expect him to do under the circumstances? Is he personally to blame for having succumbed to pressure? These questions are not about what the rule ought to be, but about whether a violation of the rule is fairly attributable to a particular individual. As questions about individuals in unique circumstances, they fall outside the dominant Anglo-American conception of law. The issue whether an individual is accountable for violating a rule fails to fit a model of analysis that limits the legal process to defining rules and determining whether they have been violated.

What the common law lacks is a concept comparable to the German notion of *Zumutbarkeit*—a term that is roughly translated as attributability or imputability. The German term captures the question whether an individual can be justly held accountable for violating a rule. It bears witness to the role of compassion as well as to the application of rules in the total process of judging an individual accused of crime. Anglo-American lawyers use words like "accountability" and "responsibility" but they come to life only when we speak of the insanity defense. And the special feature of insanity, as we have seen, is the tendency to think of the insane as a class apart—as people, like infants, who fall outside the ordinary jurisdiction of the criminal law.[74] There is simply no single term in the idiom of the common law that helps us focus on the question whether a normal person is responsible for having violated a legal obligation.

The common law tradition suffers a fundamental paradox. The tradition purports to be based on case-by-case evolution. In fact, the courts are systematically averse to considering the peculiarities of particular defendants. They are committed to deciding the ultimate issue of guilt or innocence according to rules that suppress the differences among persons and situations. In contrast, the contemporary German style of thought stresses the centrality of codification and legislative supremacy in defining prohibited conduct. Yet at the level of assessing individual culpability, the German courts cultivate a system of individualized excusing conditions. The indispensable inquiry in every case is whether the defendant, as a concrete individual, can be fairly blamed for having violated the law.

This radical difference between the contemporary common law and the German style of legal thought manifests a deeper cleavage between the two traditions. In an effort to approach these divergent perspectives, I shall try to state the arguments that a common law jurist might offer on behalf of the practices of his system. Each argument will invite a reply, and these replies will bring us close to the alternative view expressed in the German orientation toward the theory of excuses.

A. THE ARGUMENT THAT INDIVIDUALIZATION IS IMPOSSIBLE

It is a mistake, this argument would hold, to think that individualization is ever possible. Each decision is made with reference to a perceived set of facts about an individual, his conduct and the surrounding circumstances. This set of facts is always finite. If the decision is based on a finite set of perceived facts, that set of facts $\{F_1, F_2, F_3, \ldots, F_n\}$ generates a rule. The rule is that whenever $F_1, F_2, F_3, \ldots, F_n$ recurs, the defendant will be acquitted. Individualization, it follows, is an illusion. Legal acquittals invariably express rules that may be followed in future cases.

The first response that this argument invites is straightforward rejection. It is simply not true, one should maintain, that every factual situation is reducible to a finite set of variables. There is an irreducible uniqueness about every case of succumbing to pressure. There could never be another case just like *Green*. No other convict would be just like him. No other threat would affect an actor the way the threat of rape affected him.

Yet if one generates a description of the *Green* situation, one can imagine the same scenario occurring at another time and place. The time, place and defendant would be different, but presumably these facts would not matter in assessing the involuntariness of the escape. If the case can be definitively described, and the description transcends time and place, then one has no difficulty imagining the described set of facts obtaining in another context.

The individualization of excuses presupposes that each case of involuntary conduct is unique. Yet to maintain that claim, we are driven to claiming that the uniqueness consists in some feature of the case that goes beyond the factual description. The whole, one must argue, is greater than the sum of its parts: the situation of excused conduct is more than the sum of its component factors.

Yet this additional feature does not lend itself to articulation. And one of the first principles of legal decision-making is the commitment to articulating and explaining all that bears on the process of decision. One then confronts the antinomy of individualization, which resists verbal explanation, and the processes of the law, which are premised on the values of publicity and full articulation of the facts that inform decisions.

Given this conflict between legal values and the virtues of individualization, one would expect that courts would be consistently averse to deciding cases in their full peculiarity. We have already noted this aversion in the attitude of common law courts toward excusing conditions. But this attitude, surprisingly, does not pervade the thinking of American judges. One notable exception is the long line of Supreme Court cases on the admissibility of allegedly involuntary confessions. Since the late 1950s the Supreme Court has stressed that each decision should be rendered on a unique set of facts. The Court committed itself to deciding each case under the "totality of the circumstances."[75]

The way to understand the individualization of excusing conditions is to think of the process of individualization as akin to the assessment of allegedly coerced confessions in the "totality of the circumstances." In both instances, the ultimate issue is whether the conduct in question—violating the law or confessing—was undertaken voluntarily. What is so hard to fathom is that American courts can be so sensitive to individualization where the problem is the procedural fairness of relying on a confession, but so clearly averse to the same inquiry when the issue posed is the fairness of punishing a particular individual.

It is worth recalling that this line of analysis represents an effort to reply to the argument that individualization is conceptually impossible. The most that we have done is show courts can and do operate on the assumption that inquiries about voluntariness—of violating the law or of confessing—may be fitted to the "totality of the circumstances." We have not dispelled the claim that this commitment to individualization might be an illusion, and that decisions invariably reflect the perception of a finite set of factual variables. To counter that charge, we should have to argue that the whole is indeed greater than the sum of its parts, that each situation is indeed greater than the sum of its components. That would call for a much deeper critique of prevailing conceptions of rational thought. It is a critique that would require a work of much greater depth and sophistication than this limited paper on the theory of excuses.

We can, however, make a weaker claim that individualization, at least in one sense, is conceptually tenable. The argument would be that an acquittal on grounds of involuntary conduct is tied to the particular defendant. The acquittal is individualized in the sense that it fails to set a precedent that can be relied upon by other actors in the future. To appreciate this point, we should try to imagine the implications of an acquittal in a case like *Green*. Would other convicts, caught in comparable conditions of impending rape, be able to escape in the expectation that they would not be punished upon being caught? One would think not, for the fact that they expected to be immune from prosecution would partially undercut their claim that their conduct was a reactive response to impending danger. Their escape would come to appear to be attributable less to the present threat of rape and more to the promise of future immunity in the courts. On the other hand, after a conviction in a case like *Green*, subsequent escapes would appear to be even more the product of desperation and fear. If the convict fears punishment and he nonetheless escapes to avoid an impending rape, one senses even more that his conduct is the involuntary response to the terror of the situation.

Thus, so far as the problem in *Green* is treated as a matter of excusing conduct that is not fairly subject to blame, the outcome of the case bears an inverse relationship to the legal situation of actors who thereafter rely on the decision. If Green is acquitted on grounds of involuntariness, it becomes more difficult to acquit the next convict caught in a comparable situation. If Green is convicted, the mere fact of the conviction lends greater credence to the claims of those who subsequently claim that they are not to blame for yielding to the pressure of circumstances. In this weaker sense, excuses are individualized; for the mere fact of publicly excusing conduct under overwhelming pressure injects a new factor into the analysis of subsequent cases.

In this respect, excusing conditions differ fundamentally from justificatory claims. For the nature of a justification, say self-defense or necessity, is that it posits a right to cause harm under a defined set of circumstances. If a court should justify, say, the shooting of a stray dog to protect children in the neighborhood, it would in effect generate a new rule of law. Should the same circumstances recur, actors in the future could rely upon the decision, and guide their conduct accordingly. Excuses, in contrast, do not modify the applicable legal rule; they relate to the subsidiary question whether a particular individual can be held accountable for violating a rule that remains intact. Yet the fact of excusing changes the array of circumstances under which similar cases are to be judged in the future. The difference between justifying and excusing conduct, then, proves to be the difference between a legal process that is distinct from the world to be judged (the process of justifying conduct), and a legal process that is symbiotically tied to the world and irreversibly alters the factual background of succeeding cases (the process of excusing).

B. THE POSITIVISTIC ARGUMENT AGAINST INDIVIDUALIZATION

In this section of the discussion, I wish to assume the plausibility of individualization, both in the weaker and in the stronger sense. The point of making the assumption is to broaden the inquiry by reaching a range of other objections that might be made against the process of individualizing excusing conditions. The point of all these objections is to challenge the desirability of individualizing excuses, even if there is no conceptual barrier to doing so.

The first objection is that there is something characteristically "unlegal" about individualized decision-making. It might be appropriate to individualize administrative processes, like sentencing and even the exercise of prosecutorial discretion. But the rule of law presupposes decision-making under rules, and relying on rules runs against the rigors of individualization.

This is a powerful objection—one that is likely to appeal to many who would instinctively support the pattern of the contemporary common law. The argument reveals the extent to which the common law tradition identifies the phenomenon of law with the governance of rules. It bespeaks the essence of legal positivism and thus in the reply that follows, I shall refer to this strain of fidelity to rules as the positivist objection.

By way of constructing a reply to the positivist objection, we should note first that the process of individualization is not conducted without reference to a standard of decision. The standard in the cases of excuses, as in the case of allegedly coerced confessions, is whether the individual acted voluntarily under the circumstances. Voluntariness in the context of excuses means: Is the actor culpable for having succumbed to the pressure of the situation? Or to rephrase the question: Could one fairly and reasonably expect the actor to have resisted the pressure and to have abstained from violating the law? The standard is patently evaluative. There is no way to resolve the issue of voluntariness except by appealing to our sense of what we may fairly demand of each other under specified circumstances.

There is, no doubt, something odd about the claim that an individualized decision can be made under an abstract standard, even an irreducibly evaluative standard like that of voluntariness. One is invariably puzzled by the process of reasoning from abstract standards to results in concrete cases. The process is different from applying the rules of a game or the algorithms of a computer program.

It seems to be part of the legal process as we know it; yet it has yet to receive an adequate jurisprudential account.[76]

To meet the positivist objection at a deeper level, we should recall that the issue of excusing arises only after a determination that conduct violates the applicable legal norm. As it is formulated in German theory, the issue is whether illegal (*rechtswidrige*) conduct is fairly to be attributed to a particular individual. Thus one confronts an ambiguity about the legal status of excuses. In one sense, excuses are not decisions under the law (*Recht*), for they come to play only after one posits the illegality (*Rechtswidrigkeit*) of the conduct. The questions of excusing, therefore, cannot be resolved by appealing to criteria of the law; for those criteria have already applied in finding the conduct to be contrary to law.

Yet there is a broad sense of law and the legal process that seemingly encompasses the process of excusing. Excuses bear on guilt or innocence; the decision whether to excuse or not is a necessary stage in determining liability under the law. Thus one comes to see that the process of excusing and assessing blame occupies a hiatus between two concepts of law. Law in the narrow sense consists solely of the norms prohibiting conduct and laying down the conditions of justified, legal conduct. Law in the broad sense consists of the full range of criteria bearing on liability. It is in this hiatus that one seeks to individualize the judgment of liability by focusing on the individual and his personal culpability for violating a legal norm.

The thrust of the positivist objection is to banish this hiatus from the province of the law. For when it is banished, the sovereign of norms comes to rule over the entire kingdom. Once expelled, individualized determinations of culpability inhabit extra-legal domains. They are to be found in the discretionary processes of sentencing, pardoning, arresting and choosing to prosecute. The reply to the positivist objection turns on seeing that these borderland and admittedly individualized processes are part of the law itself. The task of the theory of excuses is to bring them within the law, and thus to provide a public and visible forum for the process of individualized assessment in the criminal law. There is no doubt that one can achieve individualization in the surrogate settings of prosecutorial charging, sentencing and pardoning. But every legal system, one would think, should be committed to maximizing that aspect of the criminal process that is public and subject to reasoned argumentation.

The positivist objection expresses a preference for a minimalist concept of law, a commitment to the dominance of rules, which leaves a maximum array of problems to be resolved in semi-secret, administrative processes. Though the prosecutorial bureaucracy may be the beneficiary of the positivist objection, it is hardly its author. There are many other biases of the age that militate against an expanded concept of law, a concept of the legal process that would encompass individualized excusing conditions as well as norms of conduct.

One of these biases is an empiricist preference for identifying the law with the collection of discrete official decisions of the system.[77] "The law is what the courts do in fact,"[78] as generations of Holmes' followers have learned to think. There is no law out there—hovering over us as a "brooding omnipresence in the sky."[79]

An even deeper bias that buttresses the positivist objection is the commitment to policy analysis, particularly as it is expressed in American legal circles. The relentless emphasis on policy objectives has created a condition of mind that sees the rationale of judicial decisions only in their consequences. A decision is right if and only if its prospective benefits outweigh its prospective burdens. What is lost in this unqualified embrace of the utilitarian calculus is a sense for the imperatives implicit in the situation of the parties before the court. The imperatives of a situation command our attention, not because our response will maximize utility, but because we have no choice but to respond to the perceived demands of justice. Why do we recognize the constitutional right to a hearing in a criminal case? It is not because we believe that providing hearings will redound to the long-range benefit of society.[80] We affirm a right to a hearing in a criminal case because, as human beings, we know what it means to suffer condemnation and punishment, and we can imagine the torture of being tried and convicted without the opportunity to answer the accusations against us. Once we identify with the criminal defendant and grasp that he is one of us, we cannot but affirm his right to a hearing. We respond to the imperative, not because it will inure to society's benefit, but because we know that not responding will betray what is human within us.

Excuses do not express policy goals. They respond to an imperative generated by the defendant's situation. Excuses are not levers for channeling behavior in the future, but an expression of compassion for one of our kind caught in a maelstrom of circumstance. If we sense that we would escape from prison to avoid a homosexual rape, do we have any choice but to acquit an escapee like Green? Should it matter whether the net impact of acquitting Green might be to undermine discipline in the prisons and produce a net social loss? Yet so long as we think of law as the pursuit of policies, we are inclined to think the probable consequences of our decision ought to mediate our sense of justice to the individual accused. The instrumentalist bias of the times thus converts the doing of justice into one among many policies, to be weighed and assessed along with the value of maintaining discipline in the prisons. This way of thinking about justice is so well entrenched in contemporary American legal thought that most students of the law find it hard to conceive of justice or compassion as an imperative, a demand to which we must respond without a view to the overall costs of our response.

There may be no compelling way to dispel the biases of empiricism and instrumentalist legal reasoning. There may be no definitive reply to the positivist preference for a legal system based on rules. The process of objection and reply must end with a sigh of resignation rather than the exhilaration of victory. The positivist can parry our every thrust. Yet his agile swordplay betrays a master we may not wish to accept. He serves a sovereign who rules from above and dominates his subjects with rules. If there is tolerance for individual weakness it is expressed in the processes of charging, sentencing, and pardoning. Yet the quest for a government of equals may lead us to reject a system of justice that depends so heavily on prosecutorial discretion and executive mercy. We may yet come to see the virtue of incorporating criteria of compassion into the criminal law. We shall then choose a public system of excuses instead of a semi-secret system of administrative grace. And then we shall understand that individualizing excuses complements rather than detracts from the rule of law.

CHAPTER 13

Reply: George Fletcher, Critical Feminist: Comment on Fletcher, "The Individualization of Excusing Conditions"

Susan R. Estrich[*]

I chose to write about George Fletcher's still famous law review article "The Individualization of Excusing Conditions" (henceforth "Individualization") not only for the obvious reasons—that it was published in my own school's law review, that it generated a debate that in turn produced some of the most important books and articles in the criminal law literature,[1] and that its sheer intellectual vigor has met the test of time—but also for some less obvious reasons that relate to my own passions for criminal law. The article was published in 1974, the year I entered law school, when the dominant theory that informed most law teaching had its roots in the work of Hart and Sacks on the legal process.[2] In this postrealist period, the idea was, to put it crudely and without disrespect, that even if the law was political, it was important that it not advertise itself as such; that even if its results were contextual, the context could be translated into a rule, or what looked like a rule; that the idea of the rule of law could be achieved through respect for precedent and reasoned elaboration; and that maintenance of that idea as something beyond the judgment of men was essential to the law's integrity.

Fletcher's seminal piece predated Duncan Kennedy's pathbreaking "Form and Substance in Private Law Adjudication";[3] it did not begin to imagine the work of Elizabeth Schneider, Holly Maguigan, and so many others, on battered women's

* Robert Kingsley Professor of Law and Political Science, University of Southern California Law School; B.A. Wellesley College, 1974; J.D. Harvard Law School, 1977. Professor of Law, Harvard Law School, 1981–90. My thanks to Anahit Petrosyan, USC Law Library, for her assistance in the research on this comment.

syndrome,[4] not to mention my own efforts, and those of others, to expose the inherent biases in the law of rape and the extent to which the law's standard of reasonableness was inevitably a gendered one.[5] I am not sure Professor Fletcher would take much pride in these associations, but in my view, his critique of the unwillingness of American common-law judges, as opposed to their German brethren, to see both the need and the inevitability of individualization in the definition of excusing conditions presaged these more tumultuous movements and underscores the importance of his contributions.

The cases that George Fletcher used as his prime examples in "Individualization" were about men. But the men he wrote about found themselves in situations where the question arose as to what kind of men they were, as to unique characteristics of their personality and experience that rendered their responses, even if unacceptable in some other, mythic reasonable man in reasonable circumstances, of a different moral character when committed by them.

Consider, for example, the case of Mr. Green, a man threatened with rape in a prison where snitching could bring even more awful consequences; having already been raped repeatedly, and having been told that he would be raped again that night, Mr. Green escaped from prison, which is of course a violation of the law prohibiting prisoners from escaping their confinement. Should the common law take account of the conditions of confinement the defendant was seeking to escape in deciding his guilt for the crime of prison escape? Could the act of escape be viewed as in some sense "involuntary" given the other choices, or at least less blameworthy than that of a prisoner who escapes because he is simply miserable in prison, or worse, because he hopes to wreak vengeance on those who put him there? Are the threats he faced even relevant, or admissible, in determining his guilt, and should the jury be instructed to weigh them or ignore them?

The Missouri trial court denied the defense the right to introduce any evidence of the past rapes or the threatened one; of Green's unsuccessful efforts to secure help from the guards; of the context that made this any different from a "typical" prison break. It denied the jury any instruction on whether compassion for his situation could be considered in determining whether an acquittal might be in order. A rule was a rule, and the rule was enforced. It is against the law to escape from prison. Recognizing the necessity of escape—and the court treated this as a case of alleged necessity—would undermine the larger interest in prison security. So reasoned the Missouri Supreme Court, which affirmed the district court's handling of the case and the resulting conviction of the defendant, a result that Fletcher rightly criticizes as unjust (129).[6]

Now, certainly one could argue that *Green* should be treated as a case of duress (an excuse) rather than necessity (a justification), and that seeing it that way might obviate at least some of the worry that the Court plainly had about ignoring or undermining the "rule" against escape. Under the Model Penal Code definition of duress, one might have argued that Green's actions were no different than those of any "man of reasonable firmness" facing the threat of repeated rapes, or the almost certain risk of death if he snitched. As to whether his choice represented the "lesser of the evils," measured objectively, an even more common formulation of the duress standard, one could argue that it should at least have been a question for the jury to decide. But that is not how the Missouri Supreme Court saw it, any more than the House of Lords in the famous chestnut of *Regina v. Dudley and Stephens* were willing to admit that starving men might blamelessly kill the weakest among them in order to survive. In *Dudley and Stephens*, as in *Green*, the larger issue for the Court was not the morality of the defendant's act but the rule that excusing it would appear to create: a rule that made discretionary the prohibition on escaping from prison, a rule that contextualized the prohibition on the intentional and willful taking of a human life, a rule that, in short, might be seen as undermining the capital R rule of law. The fact that the Lords in *Dudley and Stephens* recommended that the Crown pardon the condemned men only made explicit the price they were willing to pay to enforce the rule of law, with the emphasis on the rule.

Much of Fletcher's essay is devoted to the distinction between justification and excuse, and the difficult effort to classify various human responses and the potential defense of them into one category or the other. In this, he is not entirely successful, nor, as far as I can tell, are any of us, the Model Penal Code included, and much paper was spilled in the wake of this article and others that followed attacking the distinction on both a conceptual and a practical basis. As Professor R. A. Duff so aptly puts it:

> George Fletcher deserves much of the credit for persuading Anglo-American criminal law theorists to think seriously about justifications and excuses as two quite different ways in which a defendant can ward off a conviction for a criminal offense, and as two quite different kinds of elements in the structure of criminal liability. Or does he rather deserve much—or at least some—of the blame for luring theorists into a morass of unfruitful controversy about the precise contours of the distinction between justification and excuse? He surely deserves more credit than he does blame.... However, when one looks at the apparently interminable and irresoluble controversies that surrounded the topic, in particular those about so-called unknown justifications and putative justifications, one must begin to wonder just what of substance is at stake and how far the substantive issues may be concealed or distorted, rather than being illuminated, by such a determined focus on the question of what counts as a "justification" or "excuse."[7]

More significant, perhaps, at least for my purposes, was Professor Fletcher's recognition that, whether in the rhetoric of justification or excuse, "'[r]easonable men' and 'persons of reasonable firmness' are ubiquitous in the language of the common law, and yet the same rhetorical figures are strangers to the German legal idiom" (131). The difference, as Fletcher explained, is not "fortuitous" but rather based in the German comfort and the American discomfort in individualizing judgments of "character and culpability" (131). The reasonable man serves as the device for objectifying the inquiry, or at least appearing to, for avoiding looking at this defendant's decision as he saw it in preference for an external standard that more closely allies itself with the common law's concept of rule-based decision making.

Except it does not really work, as Fletcher recognized then, and a new generation of legal scholars were to vocally insist later. Fletcher's hypothetical is far different, almost amusingly so, from the ones that came later, but the point is strikingly similar. Suppose, Fletcher asks, that we are dealing with a defendant who kills to avoid being struck in the groin. Suppose further that it can be shown that the man has a pathological fear of castration and genital injury. The question that Fletcher posed was whether, in applying a standard of the person of reasonable firmness, it is appropriate to take into account the man's pathological fear. Is the reasonable man someone with a pathological fear of castration, or is he someone who has no such fears, or at least not the exaggerated version that Fletcher poses?

Fletcher's answer is that to deny the reasonable man the pathological fear that this defendant has of castration is to deny the defendant the opportunity to prove himself blameless. It would produce, in his view, an unjust result to treat this man as if he were, say, and this is my example now and not his, a woman, who might fear other sorts of injuries more than a kick in the groin.

So just how do we decide what characteristics of the defendant to attribute to the reasonable man, in order to produce what Fletcher considers a just result? When I took criminal law, in the year Fletcher's essay was written, we wrangled with the issue of whether the reasonable man was blind if the defendant was (yes), or impotent if the defendant was (no). Among the titters, the hard question of why blindness was the sort of characteristic that could be taken into account while impotence was not seemed unanswerable except by reference to the discomfort of the men in the class at the very idea of incorporating impotence into a normative standard of conduct. Fear of castration is easier to empathize with. Fletcher attempts a less machismo-based approach to this kind of line-drawing question, but he stops short of extending it to its logical conclusion. In "Individualization," he argues, the question is whether "the personality disposition accounting for the act is one that the accused should be able to control. If the accused should be able to overcome his dispositions, as in the case of cowardice and selfishness, these dispositions should not be attributed to the reasonable man; if the accused could not control the relevant disposition, as in the case of documentable, pathological fears, the disposition must be included in the standard used to assess the defendant's conduct" (133).

Now I might argue that a man whose fear of castration is so great that he would kill anyone who hits him in the groin should get help before he acts on it; that such a fear is the sort of character defect that, like undue excitability, imposes on the one who has it the responsibility to conform his conduct to the standards of the rest of us, not a right to be excused when he fails to do so. Or maybe the problem is that, being a woman, fear of castration is simply a foreign concept to me in the same way that life as a battered woman is foreign to most men and many women.

By the time I started teaching criminal law, and certainly for most of the time I have been writing about it, the explosive issues that have divided courts and scholars have gone beyond the question of the reasonable man's feelings about his genitals to questions of whether he is a man at all. What happens when the defendant is a woman? feminist scholars began to ask.[8] Is she expected to behave as if she were a man in the same situation? And what if she is not just any woman but a battered woman, or the mother of an abused child, or the victim of sexual abuse herself? The minute you argue, as Fletcher does so convincingly in "Individualization," that justice requires taking into account at least some of the unique characteristics of the individual man, and that the common law courts' refusal to do so in the name of preserving "rules" is not in fact essential to the rule of law, an increasingly diverse society is forced to confront claims of difference that go far beyond the preservations of potency, or lack thereof, of earlier days.[9]

The recognition of a defense for battered women is, in this sense, a logical next step from Fletcher's recognition of a defense for penis-obsessed men. But it is not simply a matter of gender; in the 1980s and 1990s, claims for individualized justice based on race, culture, poverty, and every form of abuse and disability became so common that many legal scholars, including my friend Alan Dershowitz, began decrying the plethora of "abuse excuses" that our own earlier work had in many ways provided the groundwork for.[10] The question became not whether the rules would be enforced but whether there were any to enforce anymore, whether we as a society could find a way to go beyond the deconstruction of an admittedly race-based, gender-based standard of judgment and find some middle ground between lawlessness and blatant unfairness, between anarchy and injustice. How do you frame the rules of law when you understand, finally, that rules are political constructs, both contextual and manipulable?

It is here that I find myself parting company with Professor Fletcher. On the one hand, his recognition of the injustice in judging someone according to a standard that she cannot meet has been a cornerstone of my own work. But individualization in a diverse society must be limited, lest the only guilty people be the hit men who kill for money (and even they may claim some pathologies of culture and identity). Defining the limits of individualization is a more complicated process than asking whether the defendant had the capacity to change his unique characteristics; certainly, years of therapy may change the psychology of the battered spouse, assimilation may modify the cultural constraints that would lead a jilted traditional Japanese spouse to walk her children into the sea, self-control might allow even the man most fearful of castration to avoid killing in the name of protecting his penis.

Reasonableness, properly understood, is not an answer but a way to frame the question, an inherently political question, of what we expect of each other, what deviance our society can tolerate, where the limits of sympathy must be drawn. It is, to borrow Duncan Kennedy's parlance, not a rule but a standard, a living standard, with all the strengths and weaknesses inherent in that recognition. There is no inevitable answer to the limits of individualization except to construct a process that is sufficiently inclusive and open-ended that its results will be seen as "fair" by the society that it governs. It is a question of trust, as much as justice.

CHAPTER 14

The Right and the Reasonable

George P. Fletcher

We lawyers should listen to the way we talk. If we paused to listen to our pattern of speech, we would be surprised by some of its distinguishing features. One of the most striking particularities of our discourse is its pervasive reliance on the term "reasonable." We routinely refer to reasonable time, reasonable delay, reasonable reliance, and reasonable care. In criminal law, we talk incessantly of reasonable provocation, reasonable mistake, reasonable force, and reasonable risk.[1] Within these idioms pulse the sensibilities of the reasonable person. For all the supposed concreteness of the common law, we can hardly function without this hypothetical figure at the center of legal debate. We cannot even begin to argue about most issues of responsibility and liability without first asking what a hypothetical reasonable person would do under the circumstances.

Our reliance on reasonableness is noteworthy because it distinguishes our legal discourse from legal discourse in other cultures. The fact is that French, German, and Soviet lawyers argue in a different idiom. Their languages deploy a concept of reason, and their terms for "reason"—*raison, Vernuft* and *razumnost'*—readily yield corresponding adjectives. Yet these parallels to our term "reasonable" do not figure prominently in legal speech on the continent.

In continental Europe, neither the adjective "reasonable" nor the figure of the "reasonable person" matters much in casting a legal argument. Whatever we sense as the common denominator underlying "reasonable reliance" and "reasonable mistake" is lost in continental legal debate. Whether we think differently from our European counterparts is not so easily assayed. That we speak differently, however, is quite clear.

In my view, it is no accident that we pervasively rely upon the concept of reasonableness while Europeans do not. This pattern of our speech serves a purpose, perhaps many purposes. I will consider some of these possible purposes and then bring the analysis to bear on the specific problem of reasonable mistakes in the criminal law.

I. Two Styles of Legal Reasoning

How should we go about developing an account of the common law's affection for reasonableness? I suggest that we listen carefully to the way in which French, German, and Soviet lawyers discuss legal issues. We should heed not only the language of legislation and of judicial opinions, but also the style of argument in textbooks, treatises, and the theoretical literature. Our aim in this empirical quest should be to isolate features of European discourse that are as prominent in their context as our pervasive reliance on reasonableness.

The argument in the offing is that the concept of Right (*Recht*)[2] shapes German legal thought as reasonableness directs common law reasoning. In order to develop this argument, I need first to introduce and clarify a distinction between two types of legal discourse, which, for want of better terms, I shall call "flat"[3] and "structured." Flat legal discourse proceeds in a single stage, marked by the application of a legal norm that invokes all of the criteria relevant to the resolution of a dispute. Structured legal discourse proceeds in two stages: first, an absolute norm is asserted; and second, qualifications enter to restrict the scope of the supposedly dispositive norm.

This distinction is readily grasped in context. Consider the problem of imposing limits on the right to use force in preventing encroachment on one's rights. German law approaches this problem in the style of structured legal discourse. According to the criminal code of 1975[4] (as well as the superseded code of 1871[5]), everyone who suffers an unjustified invasion of her rights has an absolute privilege to use whatever force is necessary to thwart the invasion. If the only way to stop a fleeing thief, even a child stealing fruit, is to shoot the thief, the courts[6] and the scholars[7] have supported the property owner's right to use deadly force. Countering this trend, some postwar commentators[8] and courts[9] have invoked the principle of "abuse of rights" to limit this right at a second stage of analysis.[10] At the first level, there remains an absolute right to use deadly force when necessary; at the second level, the exercise of that right comes under scrutiny. If the right is exercised at excessive cost, it is thought to be "abused" and therefore inoperative. Nothing in the criminal code supports this restriction. Nonetheless, the method of structured legal thought permits an additional level of argument, a level where extra-statutory considerations can limit the explicit provisions of the code.

In contrast, common law discourse typically avoids this bifurcation. We have no inclination to say, first, that the defending party has an absolute right to use all force necessary to vindicate his autonomy, and second, that invoking this right in particular circumstances would abuse it.[11] The advantage of the single term "reasonable" is that it packs into the initial norm criteria that are the same as or similar to those invoked in assessing "abuse of rights" at a secondary level of argument. The upshot of collapsing the two dimensions of argument is that the privilege of self-defense is no longer absolute. It is limited at the outset by the concept of reasonableness.

In view of this account of structured and flat legal thinking, we can see that our reliance on reasonableness facilitates flat legal thinking. With syntactically mobile modifiers like "reasonable" and "substantial," each rule of the common law can contain placeholders for everything that one needs to know to resolve a particular problem. Of course, the addition of open-ended modifiers sacrifices both the apparent precision and the apparent absoluteness of the stated rule. But a sophisticated American lawyer would presumably respond that these ostensible virtues of German law are illusory and that it is better to work with vague and qualified, but at least non-deceptive, legal norms. Structured and flat legal analysis each have their appeal. If they did not, they would hardly find expression in two of the world's leading legal cultures. Though my sympathies lie with the clarity gained from structured legal analysis, my primary purpose here is to probe the rhetorical and substantive differences expressed in these diverse modes of legal thinking.

A. JUSTIFICATION AND EXCUSE

Let us now look at the way in which our ubiquitous invocation of the reasonable person enables us to function without the fundamental distinction between justification and excuse. This distinction is basic in German criminal law. It was also indispensable to the common law of homicide as understood by Blackstone.[12] Today, however, only those common law theorists who read and respect the philosophical literature have high regard for the distinction.

The distinction between justification and excuse is not particularly difficult to understand. Claims of justification concern the rightness, or at least the legal permissibility,[13] of an act that nominally violates the law. If generally impermissible conduct is justified on grounds, say, of self-defense, lesser evil, consent, or the interests of law enforcement, the act is one that ought to prevail in a situation of conflict. No one is entitled to defend against a justified act, and third parties are permitted, indeed encouraged, to assist the justified actor.[14]

Excuses speak not to the rightness or desirability of the act but to the personal culpability of the actor. Excuses come into consideration only if it is first decided that some untoward (wrongful or unlawful) act requires excusing.[15] If an excuse, such as insanity, involuntary intoxication, duress, or mistake of law, applies in the case, the untowardness of the act remains unchallenged.[16] Yet the excuse implies that the actor is not personally to blame for the untoward act. Claims of justification direct our attention to the propriety of the act in the abstract; claims of excuse, to the blameworthiness of the actor in the concrete situation.

The distinction between justification and excuse is of fundamental theoretical and practical value. In framing a theory of liability or a rational criminal code,[17] one would presumably inquire whether a particular defense addresses itself to the propriety of the act or to the personal culpability of the actor. Yet the distinction has gone unmentioned in most of the English language textbooks of the last hundred years.[18] The indifference to the distinction emerges clearly in the recently published, four-volume *Encyclopedia of Crime and Justice*,[19] edited by Sanford Kadish. This work captures orthodox American sentiments toward criminal law as well as any document of the last two decades. But a surprising number of the entries pay no attention to how particular defenses might be construed differently if treated as justifications, excuses, or jurisdictional exemptions from liability. Though I might argue that these analyses are superficial, the question that arises is not whether they are right or wrong, sophisticated or unsophisticated, but a question of a different order: how do these writers analyze the criminal law without attending to a distinction that both German theorists and contemporary American analytic philosophers regard as fundamental?[20] My answer to this query will take us back to the point of departure: the pervasive reliance in American law on the concept of reasonableness and flat legal thinking.

B. STRUCTURED ARGUMENT

How, then, does the distinction between justification and excuse generate a structured form of legal argument? This is not so easily perceived, for in fact, the importance of the distinction lies in its mirror image: in the affirmative concepts negated by each claim. A justification negates an assertion of wrongful conduct. An excuse negates a charge that the particular defendant is personally to blame for the wrongful conduct. Although the defendant might have intentionally acted in violation of the law, he is not personally to blame for an unjustified violation if he acted under duress, while insane, or under certain types of mistake about the law. The structure that is implicit in this way of stating the analysis of liability ("excuses for *unjustified* violations") is that the concept of wrongful conduct logically precedes the concept of personal culpability. The analysis of justification must precede the analysis of excuse.

The question that properly engages us, therefore, is whether this ordering of the issues is logically compelled. In analyzing a problem of liability, might one not first consider an allegation of excuse, say of insanity or involuntary intoxication, and later a problem of self-defense or justified use of force in making an arrest? Why should not the issue of responsibility (as American lawyers often label the issue of personal blameworthiness) be the very first issue considered in analyzing liability?

For German lawyers, it seems natural to consider the issue of wrongfulness and then of responsibility (a W/R ordering). German textbooks do not even pause to justify the ordering. Yet even if we accept a clear distinction between the issues of wrongfulness (the absence of justification) and of responsibility (the absence of excuse), two other logical relationships between these issues are possible. It might be the case either that (1) that one must inquire into responsibility before wrongfulness (an R/W ordering), or (2) that no ordering of the two sets of issues is compelled. The latter possibility reflects the orientation of flat legal thinking. Consistently with my general thesis, I will attempt to show that an aversion to all ordering characterizes the orthodox American view toward analyzing criminal liability. First, however, I wish to consider the possibility of an R/W ordering and then account for the acceptance of the W/R ordering as a matter of course in German law.

1. *The R/W Ordering.*—There is some support in the common law tradition for the logical priority of the issue of responsibility over the issue of wrongdoing. The first issue for consideration should be whether the defendant is an addressee of the applicable legal norm. If an infant, the defendant is not a subject of the norm. If he is psychotic, or if, in the language of the common law, he behaves like a "wild beast," he should be treated like an infant—as someone who falls outside the scope of the criminal law. The analogy holds, more or less, for the criminally insane. But it is difficult to make the same claim for duress, involuntary intoxication, and mistake of law. Nonetheless this approach of the common law is still on the statute books. Section 26 of the California Penal Code lists six categories of persons who are not "capable of committing crimes."[21] The first two categories are infants and idiots. But the other categories involving mistake, accident, and duress speak not to the questions of the capacity of the actor, but to the way in which an act is performed. Those who invoke these excuses are unquestionably "capable of committing crimes," but they cannot fairly be held accountable for the particular act at issue.

There are some traces of an R/W ordering in the common law,[22] but as the California Code indicates, this ordering treats responsibility as equivalent to the general issue of personal capacity. If, in contrast, responsibility is negated by excuses, then a finding of wrongful conduct logically precedes the consideration of possible excuses. This is the conceptual relationship that I shall now try to explicate.

2. *The W/R Ordering.*—The analysis of justificatory claims logically precedes the consideration of excuses only if the corresponding affirmative concepts are ordered in the same way: W/R, with responsibility understood as referring not to the actor's general capacity, but to his culpability or blameworthiness for engaging in a particular act. Two arguments support the logical priority of wrongdoing over responsibility. The first is conceptual and draws on the implicit meaning of "excusing."

Excuses make sense only in the context of precluding blame and thus presuppose the possibility of blame. It makes no sense to "excuse" natural events such as a rainfall or an avalanche; these events raise no question of blame because there is no person to be held responsible. Nor do excuses perform their function when applied to beneficial acts, because again there is nothing to blame and therefore nothing to excuse. It would thus seem that the inquiry about blame and excuses is limited to harmful human acts. There must be something untoward for which the actor can coherently be blamed.

Among human actions, only those that warrant a prima facie negative evaluation require our attention. In the specific case of legal violations, a prima facie negative evaluation follows from the breach of a legal prohibition. This prima facie evaluation is subject to rebuttal in cases of justification. If the violation is justified, say on grounds of self-defense, lesser evils, or consent, the act is, on balance, right and good. It no longer has the negative evaluation necessary to render excuses relevant. There would be no more point in blaming or excusing a justified act than there would be in blaming or excusing a beneficial act. The justification sanctifies the act and renders excuses irrelevant.

All of this is plausible, one might concede, but it does not prove that the analysis of justificatory claims logically precedes the analysis of excuses. Why not consider the issues in this order: (1) violation of a statutory prohibition; (2) blame and excuse; and then (3) possible justification? This is a sensible challenge that poses the problem whether the violation of a statutory prohibition and the negative evaluation that it implies are sufficient, without a finding of wrongdoing, to make excusing a relevant issue. If so, it would be plausible to consider the excusability of a violation prior to its justifiability.

This argument has particular force so far as our criminal statutes conform closely to our moral norms. Because violations of these statutes carry strong negative implications, excuses can then come into play. Implicitly, this is to argue that the violation of a morally sound prohibition raises a strong presumption of wrongful conduct. Yet, this presumption is subject to refutation by a claim of justification. If the violation of the prohibition and the question of justification both bear on the wrongfulness of the act, it makes little sense to split the issues and consider them, respectively, at the first and third stages of the inquiry. As a matter of legal bookkeeping, one might consider claims of excuse prior to those of justification. But a method conforming to the logical structure of the matter would first consider all issues bearing on the negative assessment that renders both blaming and excusing relevant.

So far, the argument for the logical priority of wrongdoing has proceeded as a conceptual inquiry. The claim has been that the W/R ordering inheres in the nature of excusing. A second argument derives from retributive theories of punishment. These theories—as opposed to those that stress social protection—hold, simply, that punishment should be imposed for wrongdoing. Retribution requires that offenders be punished for their wrongs in order to rectify the imbalance represented by the unpunished wrong. Under retributivism, the primary issue is wrongdoing. The gravity of the wrong determines the maximum severity of the punishment. The punishment might be reduced in case of partial blameworthiness,[23] or eliminated in cases of blameless or excused conduct. The need to consider wrongfulness before responsibility follows from the structure of retributive thinking. The first inquiry is whether there is a wrong to be punished and, if so, how grievous it is. The second inquiry, whether the punishment should be mitigated, arises in considering whether the actor should be excused or should be punished to the full extent of her wrong.

The argument for mitigation might well be that the actor had incomplete control over the unfolding of the crime. The less control the actor has, the less his blame for the act. The diminution of control might result either from external pressures or from the actor's psychological condition. In cases of duress and personal necessity, such as breaking out of prison to avoid a homosexual rape, the actor's control over his actions is so far reduced that blaming him for wrongful conduct offends our sense of justice. Similarly, involuntary intoxication and insanity, at least in the conventional understanding of these states, reflect internal loss of control to an extent that makes blaming unjust. The analysis of mistake of law follows the same mode of reasoning: so far as someone does not know that his conduct might be wrongful, he can hardly be said to have control over a wrongful act he might commit. These remarks represent but the first cut at a difficult set of issues. Nonetheless, they point to a general account of excuses.

My analysis of excuses will remain at the superficial level of argument,[24] for the point of these remarks is simply to demonstrate the secondary nature of blame and excuse in analyzing liability. The theory of retributive punishment invites us to consider the relative desert of the offender, but only after establishing that he is an offender who has committed a wrongful act. The issues of blaming and excusing make sense only if we inquire: blameworthy or excusable for what? The "what" in this question requires us to specify the untoward act that makes the notions of blame and excuse meaningful.

3. *The Non-ordering: W or R.*—In a culture stressing flat legal reasoning, one would not expect to find either an R/W or a W/R ordering. And indeed we do not. The Model Penal Code (hereinafter MPC)—a vestige of the 1950s but still an orthodox document—makes no mention of either ordering. The provision defining a "material element of an offense" treats the absence of justification and excuse on a par with criteria defining the prima facie case of liability.[25] The MPC adopts the model of flat legal reasoning. All elements are of equal significance. If any element, be it affirmative or negative, is absent, the defendant is not guilty. It is of little importance whether we analyze the elements in any particular order, so long as we check them all before imposing liability.

C. FLAT LEGAL REASONING

Reasonableness—the ubiquitous modifier—provides the lever for this flattening of liability. The reasonable person enables us to blur the line between justification and excuse, between wrongfulness and blameworthiness, and thus renders impossible any ordering of the dimensions of liability. The standard "what would a reasonable person do under the circumstances?" sweeps within one inquiry questions that would otherwise be distinguished as bearing on wrongfulness or on blameworthiness. Criteria both of justification and of excuse are amenable to the same question. Concerning the justification of self-defense, we ask what amount of force a reasonable person would use. The inquiry is similar in analyzing the excuse of duress. We ask whether it is reasonable to rob a bank to avoid being killed,[26] or to escape from jail in order to avoid a homosexual rape.[27] Herbert Fingarette ingeniously argues that the key element in duress is that the defendant's act is "wrongfully made the reasonable thing to do."[28] The same formula works for self-defense. The aggressor wrongfully makes it reasonable for the victim of aggression to use force in self-defense. In this verbal matrix, we can slide back and forth between the criteria of justification and of excuse with the greatest of ease.[29]

I have argued, however, that Germans accept the W/R ordering not as a matter of policy, but because it is logically compelled both by the nature of excusing and the structure of retributive punishment. If this is true, we need to account for the failure of these considerations to entrench the W/R ordering in common law thinking. The two reasons for the German W/R ordering are not as distinct as they might seem. Excuses have a secondary status only if we assume the priority of wrongdoing in the analysis of punishment. But if punishment has some purpose other than censuring wrongdoing, then this relationship of logical priority might collapse.

Since the writings of Bentham[30] and the translation of Beccaria,[31] English legal theorists have been skeptical about censuring wrongdoing as an end in itself. The duty to punish the guilty does not comport with the Anglo-American quest for a productive purpose in every social practice. Inflicting injustice offends us. But doing justice for its own sake does not compel us. Although English and American lawyers might well believe that punishing the innocent is wrong, there are fewer votes for the Kantian principle that we have a categorical duty to punish the guilty.[32] According to the dominant view today, the requirement of blameworthiness functions at most as a limit on punishment carried out for the sake of deterrence and other social goals.[33] Yet, in a spirit of democratic tolerance, we loathe leaving out either the Kantians or the utilitarians.[34] We pick and choose among the purposes of punishment as we see fit.[35] In this tolerant muddle, we naturally fail to generate the logical two-stage structure of analysis that follows from a commitment to punishing the guilty as an imperative of justice.

It is not surprising, then, that orthodox common law theorists make so little of the distinctions between wrongdoing and responsibility, justification and excuse. These issues bear with equal force on the objective of social control. We should have little trouble picking up distinctions so easily stated, but we think and argue on a bedrock of instrumental concerns that renders these distinctions little more than philosophical curiosities.

II. The Concept of Right

We would hardly arrive at the concept of Right simply by seeking translations in particular contexts of the ubiquitous term "reasonable." Yet if we pay attention to those points of legal debate where flat legal thinking in the idiom of reasonableness corresponds to structured legal thinking in German law, we might be surprised at how often we encounter the notion of Right in German discourse. The concept of Right, then, becomes a candidate for the systemic equivalent of reasonableness. By "systemic equivalent," I mean to refer to a concept in German law that is as basic as reasonableness is in the common law and is pivotal in a system of structured legal thought that functions without the leveling effect generated by the reasonable person.

In the two issues from the criminal law that we have been discussing—the scope of self-defense and the distinction between justification and excuse—the concept of Right provides the wedge for breaking the German analysis into distinct, lexically-ordered levels of discourse. I wish to explain how this is so and to draw some inferences about structured legal argument in a system of Right.

We need at least a tentative account of what the Germans mean by *Recht*; the French, by *droit*; and the Russians, by *pravo*. These terms express a normative concept of just or sound law. Each legal system also has a term expressing a descriptive concept of enacted law: *Gesetz, loi,* and *zakon*. The normative principles of Right acquire their binding force from their intrinsic moral appeal. That no person should be a judge in his own case, that no one should profit from his own wrong, that no innocent person should be punished—these are all readily accepted principles of Right recognized in the common law as well as in other Western legal systems. By contrast, the rules of *Gesetz, loi,* and *zakon* are enacted. These are laws that get their binding force not from their content but from their form. The critical feature of their form is their pedigree: they must be enacted or declared by a law-giver recognized as authoritative within the legal system. The debate between positivists and their opponents turns on the exclusivity of enacted law within the system. As Thomas Hobbes, a seminal positivist, put it: "It is not Wisdom, but Authority that makes a Law."[36] The opponents of positivism hold out for part or all of the legal system as an expression of justice.[37]

The German legal tradition has positivist strains, but this strain has never been dominant in German thought, at least not to the same extent that the positivist message of Hobbes, Bentham, Austin, and Hart has commanded loyalty in the Anglo-American tradition. German legal thought, particularly in the postwar period, seeks to foster a living sense of Right, a conception of law that transcends the enacted legal materials.

Defining the Right by contrast to the positivist concept of law is unhappily negative. It tells us only that the Right is not reducible to the set of enacted laws. It is more difficult to say positively what the Right is. For Kant, whose influence is still felt in German legal thought, the Right is the set of conditions under which the choices of each person can be reconciled with the choices of others, under universal laws of freedom.[38] Kant's account distinguishes clearly between Right and morality. The former states the framework of freedom that enables people with diverse purposes to live together in civil society. Morality addresses itself, more demandingly, to our duty to respect the humanity in ourselves and in others.[39]

Kant conceived of the Right as guaranteeing the security and external freedom of everyone in civil society.[40] Provided that one respects these spheres of autonomy in others, one is legally free to be moral or not as one chooses. This narrow conception of the Right strongly resembles Rawls's first principle of justice.[41] It seeks to guarantee the basic structure of society without resolving the inevitable conflicts that occur in social and economic life.[42] A twentieth-century conception of the Right addresses itself to these conflicts and in the course of resolving them strikes a compromise between the moral duty to protect the interests of others and the autonomy secured by the basic structure. This modern conception of the Right thus compromises the values of security and external freedom, trading off these aspects of personal autonomy against other interests in an effort to resolve social conflict.

It is significant, however, that the traditional conception of the Right still informs the law of self-defense. Section 32 of the German criminal code provides:

(1) Whoever commits an act required by self-defense acts not-wrongfully.
(2) "Self-defense" refers to a defense necessary to ward off an imminent wrongful attack from oneself or another.[43]

The term "wrongful," appearing in both provisions, means "contrary to Right." Only attacks contrary to Right trigger the privilege or right of self-defense (including defense of self, of property, and of others);[44] the minimal force necessary to ward off a wrongful attack is not contrary to Right. In the same context, American legislation would use the term "unlawful,"[45] a term that risks confusion between law as the Right and law as reduced to enacted laws. In order to capture the point of the German term, my translation relies on "wrongful" as equivalent to "contrary to Right."

Limiting self-defense to warding off wrongful attacks means that if an attack is not wrongful, one has no privilege to respond. The attack itself might be justified on grounds of self-defense, in which case § 32(1) tells us that it is not wrongful. Similarly, § 34 provides that attacks justified on grounds of lesser evils are not wrongful.[46] It follows from the structure of these provisions that justified attacks, which are not wrongful, do not generate a right of self-defense. Recalling the distinction between wrongfulness and blameworthiness, however, we may infer that attacks excused on grounds of insanity, duress, and personal necessity do generate a full right of self-defense.[47] If the attack is merely excused, it is nonetheless "contrary to Right" and warrants the full measure of resistance. On this point there will be more to say later.

For present purposes, the important point is the failure of section 32, enacted in 1975, to incorporate the principle of proportionate force as a limitation on the right of self-defense. Even though important voices in the literature and the case law favored this limitation,[48] the code adopted the traditional German rule that all necessary force is privileged. If deadly force is necessary to prevent the escape of a petty thief, the code permits it. The common argument for this extreme position invokes a German maxim: Right need never yield to Wrong.[49] The very idea of being in the Right against an aggressor, of having a personal right encroached upon, means that one is entitled to resist. This is what it means to be an autonomous person in civil society. As Kant would put it, resisting an aggressor in the name of the Right reinforces the basic structure of civil society.[50] Forcibly repulsing the aggressor ensures that every individual may exercise his freedom consistently with the exercise of a like freedom by others.[51] It follows, then, that the legal system should not require that individuals surrender their rights to aggressors rather than use the force necessary to vindicate both their autonomy and the legal order.

Despite the wording of § 32, contemporary German theorists would require the surrender of rights in some cases—particularly if the aggressor is obviously drunk, an infant, or a member of the defender's family.[52] As noted earlier, the doctrinal rationale for this restriction is that although the defender has a right to use all necessary force, he "abuses" this right if he exercises it in certain cases.[53] What should lead to this restriction on the vindication of personal autonomy? At the outset we might say that some balancing is necessary between the interests of the defender and the interests of the aggressor. Deadly force would be all right to prevent a rape, but not to avoid a kiss; wounding the aggressor would be acceptable to prevent grand larceny, but not to frustrate an illegal attempt to tie up a parking spot.[54] The preliminary question, however, is why the defender, whose rights are under attack, should be concerned at all about the interests of the aggressor.

The answer, simply, is that the aggressor is a human being. Even though he is engaged in wrongful aggression, one cannot treat him simply as an intrusive force to be nullified at all costs. With its exclusive emphasis on vindicating personal autonomy, the German philosophy that Right need never yield to Wrong does indeed treat the Wrong as a force always rightfully negated. The humanitarian response is that sometimes the cost of defending the Right is simply too high; sometimes the Right must yield in order to preserve values found even in the person of a wrongful aggressor.

The humanitarian response leads directly to the modern conception of the Right, which incorporates the interests of the aggressor in asserting the limits of rightful self-defense. One finds this modern conception in Blackstone,[55] who argued that if we do not execute petty thieves for their crimes, neither should we permit the use of deadly force in resisting petty theft. The property owner should not be able to react more severely on the street than does the sentencing authority in the courtroom. Whatever the logical limits of this analogy, it does support an integrated standard for self-defense: on a single plane of argument, judgments about the merit of the defender's position interweave with concern for the aggressor's interests.

In the dominant German approach to the problem, these two levels are still kept distinct. The first level of the argument addresses itself to the criteria of security and personal freedom, the values embodied in the traditional conception of Right. The second level softens the harshness of this absolutist view by introducing criteria of human solidarity. In going from the first to the second level, we shift from rights to interests. According to the Kantian view, the aggressor has no *right* that a person exercising self-defense defer to his interests as a human being. So far as Right requires the vindication of autonomy, it is entirely on the side of the defender.

Those who would reject the recognition of humanitarian criteria at a second level might argue as follows. Of course, the aggressor has interests, but if Right is entirely on the side of the defender, then it is up to the defender to decide whether to defer to the interests of the aggressor. No victim is under a legal duty to exercise her privilege of necessary defense; she may choose to be compassionate, but the state has no rightful authority to force her to surrender her rights in the name of altruism. This is an important point, for it illuminates the extent to which the coerced surrender of personal autonomy in civil society does in fact reflect coerced altruism. The only disagreement would be whether it is the business of the state to ensure that people act altruistically and compassionately, even toward wrongful aggressors.

The same distinction between Right and compassion emerges in analyzing the criteria that bear on claims of justification and excuse. Looking at the converse side of these categories, we find that the analysis of wrongfulness raises questions of Right; the analysis of blameworthiness, questions of compassion. If the defendant's conduct is justified, it is not wrongful and the state's right to punish no longer obtains. There is nothing that warrants punishment. If, in contrast, the conduct is wrongful, the state does have a right to punish.

To summarize the argument thus far, I have attempted to show that the analysis of Right differs significantly from a secondary line of analysis that invokes considerations of compassion and altruistic concern for the interests of wrongdoers. In the field of necessary defense, the notion of Right generates an absolute right to use the force necessary to prevent wrongful aggression. In the analysis of criminal liability, the concept of Right provides the threshold for determining when conduct is wrongful and warrants punishment. In both fields of inquiry, humanitarian considerations come to bear at a secondary stage of analysis. In self-defense, these altruistic concerns restrict the scope of defensive force permissible against petty intrusions. In the analysis of liability, compassion comes center stage in the recognition of mitigating and excusing circumstances that reduce or eliminate the punishment deserved by the wrongdoer.

III. Putative Self-Defense: A Case Study of Flat and Structured Reasoning

The first two sections of this essay permit us to generalize tentatively about two styles of legal thought. One style is rooted in the notion of reasonableness; the other, in the conception of Right. The former generates flat legal rules that, with the inclusion of vague modifiers, refer explicitly or implicitly to all the relevant criteria that bear on a particular legal problem. The latter style of thought yields structured tiers of legal argument, with the argument of Right occupying one tier and humanitarian considerations, a secondary level.

There is probably no area of the criminal law that better illustrates the conflict between these two styles of thought than the problem of putative justification, particularly the problem of putative self-defense. The phrase "putative self-defense" refers to the problems that arise when someone reasonably believes that he is being attacked, but in fact is not, and uses force against a person who is not in fact an aggressor. The problem is whether in view of the actor's reasonable belief, the use of force will support a charge of battery or, if the victim dies, of homicide. The self-defense is called putative for it is not a case of real self-defense, but of force used against a putative aggressor.

Suppose that Dan reasonably, but mistakenly, believes that Allan is attacking him. The jurisdictions mentioned above concur that in this situation of "putative self-defense," Dan's use of force cannot be justified. Justification—harmony with the Right—is an objective phenomenon. Mere belief cannot generate a justification, however reasonable the belief might be. This is not to say that Dan has no defense. He may rely on his mistake to defeat liability for his use of force against the innocent Allan.[56] Now, suppose that Dan, still believing that Allan is attacking him, endangers Allan's life. Does the innocent Allan have a defense in response? Virtually everyone agrees that Allan has a right to defend himself against the person mistakenly trying to kill him. Dan's use of force is wrongful against Allan, and therefore, under section 32(2) of the German criminal code, Allan may use the minimal force necessary to ward off Dan's attack. In the final analysis, both Dan and Allan could be acquitted; Dan on the ground of faultless mistake and Allan, on the ground of self-defense.

The main propositions of this analysis are straightforward. First, mistakes cannot justify homicide. Second, the mistaken actor may rely only on his mistake; if the putative aggressor must defend himself, he, as the innocent party, may justify his act on grounds of self-defense. Yet these propositions do not present themselves as serious possibilities to American legislative reformers. Following the recommendation of the Model Penal Code,[57] American legislatures routinely equate reasonable belief in the existence of a justification with the actual existence of the justification.[58] They collapse the problem of putative self-defense into the analysis of actual self-defense. Therefore, in the case of Allan and Dan, the standard American response is that Dan has a full right of self-defense against Allan and Allan has a full right of self-defense against Dan. The reasonable is equated with the justifiable. There could be no better proof that American lawyers do not take seriously the distinction between justification and excuse.

It is worth considering whether a legal system founded on reasonableness is likely to generate the sharp distinction between objective justification and subjective belief required to distinguish between actual and putative self-defense. In order to approach these issues, I wish to reflect upon numerous discussions with American academic lawyers, both in print and in private exchanges, about two central propositions. Either of these propositions, if accepted, would lead to the distinction between actual and putative self-defense. The first proposition is that subjective belief cannot by itself render conduct justified. Believing that defensive force is rightful cannot, by itself, make it rightful.

One philosophical argument that subjective belief can justify conduct builds on a misreading of Kant's view that a good will is the highest conceivable good.[59] The good will is taken to be synonymous with good intentions, and because the putative defender acts with good intentions, his defensive conduct must be moral and is therefore presumably justified. An argument of this sort is found in the work of Charles Fried.[60]

This argument is flawed first in its reading of Kant's moral theory and second in its attempt to link the moral theory with the criteria of justification. According to Kant, the will is good only if one acts out of a sense of duty, which means that the act is rendered necessary by reverence for the moral law.[61] Let us suppose that the categorical imperative (the moral law) requires us to defend the Right against wrongful aggression.[62] This is our duty. It is conceivable that a putative defender might act out of this sense of duty and that his will would therefore be good. His conduct would be moral—in the Kantian sense. There is no warrant, however, for equating a good will in this special sense with good-faith intentions.[63] Nor is there any basis for the logical leap from good will to the concept of justification. The notions of Right and of justification arise in legal theory, which Kant properly keeps distinct from moral theory.[64] Morality is a characteristic of our inner attitude,[65] but the Right is an objective framework for regulating practical affairs in civil society. It seems to misrepresent Kant to appeal to his moral theory in arguing about the justification for killing an aggressor in the name of the Right.[66]

Furthermore, the argument that good intentions can justify our actions clearly proves too much. It would establish that the good-faith use of defensive force is always justified. Even an unreasonable, good-faith belief in the necessity of defensive force would establish that the will is good. It should take more than a misreading of Kant to convince us that good faith is equivalent to the Right. Yet the contrary view, that a principled distinction separates justified conduct from the mistaken perception of justifying circumstances, has yet to take hold even in sophisticated quarters of American legal thinking.

The second proposition that could lead us to the distinction between actual and putative self-defense derives from a claim about the nature of justified conduct. The claim is that in any situation of physical conflict, where only one party can prevail, logic prohibits us from recognizing that more than one of the parties could be justified in using force. I shall refer to this proposition as the "incompatibility thesis."

In the conflict posed above between Dan and Allan, the only plausible way under the Model Penal Code of protecting Allan against Dan's mistaken self-defense would be to recognize a privilege in Allan also to use defensive force.[67] The problem is whether this defensive response should be regarded as justifiable. Most commentators and colleagues seem to think that there is nothing implausible about recognizing that both sides to the conflict are privileged or justified.[68] These theorists do not even balk at saying that both sides could have a *right* to use defensive force. Indeed, when I argue this point, I rarely find colleagues who agree with me that only one side can be justified, only one side can be in accordance with the Right and have a personal right to use force. There is an obvious difficulty in any argument based upon conceptual analysis. My argument must rest on our common understanding of the concepts of justification and rights. It is embedded in our language, I would say, that incompatible actions cannot both be justified. In any situation of conflict, one or the other must be in the Right and have the right to act.

Several factors might explain the willingness of thoughtful American commentators to speak of both parties to a dispute as having rights or being justified.

Any of the following beliefs might be operative, and indeed operative in different degrees and in different combinations, among American theorists.

A. JUSTIFICATION AS SYNONYMOUS WITH "DEFENSE"

Quite possibly, American lawyers incline toward thinking of a justification as synonymous with any operative substantive defense recognized by law. They might think of a justification as a claim to be interposed ex post in appealing to a court not to convict. Of course, every justification and excuse could be conceptualized exclusively as a reason for not convicting the defendant. But the criteria of justification are supposed to function not only ex post as decision rules, but ex ante as conduct rules.[69] In an ideal state of affairs, everyone who contemplates harmful action could know whether her conduct is rightful. She need not guess how courts will subsequently evaluate the circumstances.

The prospect of knowing the law without judicial instructions reflects an ideal of a self-regulating criminal law. It is an ideal with anarchistic overtones. It suggests a body of norms rooted not in legislation, but in the tacit understandings of the community. From this perspective, claims of justification appear not as claims against courts, but primarily as claims of individuals against one another.

In order to think of justifying claims in this way, we must suppose that in a situation of conflict—say, Dan versus Allan—the struggling parties might argue about their claims instead of acting them out. They could make arguments and counter-arguments about who was in the wrong and who ought to desist from the struggle. This is conceptually untenable in the case of Allan's resisting Dan's mistaken self-defense, for by hypothesis Dan cannot tell Allan about the mistake. But if the ideal is the hegemony of the Right even prior to legislation, then all conflicts should, in principle, lend themselves to resolution. Every struggle comes to be seen as conflict between the Right and those who, by their acts, set themselves opposed to it.

The concept of justification is best understood as an expression of this ideal of self-regulation. Struggling parties should, in principle, be able to determine for themselves whose conduct conforms to the Right and whose does not. There is little evidence, however, that this ideal informs contemporary American legal theory. We are inclined to think of the entire criminal law as coercion imposed from above, as the product of intervention by police, prosecutors, and judges. If we think of the criminal law as dominated and defined by these official decisions, then of course we would be inclined to think of all defenses as appeals to officials. And there is no reason why officials, charged with finding reasonable solutions to practical problems, cannot find that two people in conflict—Dan and Allan—both have acted reasonably and therefore "justifiably."

B. JUSTIFICATION AS PERMISSIBLE CONDUCT

Another argument against the "incompatibility thesis" emerges from the sensible classification of actions into the rightful, the permissible, and the excusable. Self-defense and, particularly, lesser evils are better thought of not as rightful, but as permissible actions. There is indeed support for this view in German legislation, which labels these justificatory claims as not-wrongful rather than rightful.[70] German theory repeatedly stresses the distinction between conduct that falls outside the scope of the criminal law, such as killing a fly, and justifiable conduct that nominally violates the law, such as killing in self-defense.[71] The philosopher Judith Thomson highlights this distinction by treating justifiable conduct as the infringement of a protected interest but not a violation of that interest.[72] That cases of justifiable conduct are nonetheless infringements suggests that it is perhaps not correct to think of these acts as rightful.

The concept of the permissible enters to fill the apparent gap between the rightful and the wrongful. The common law notion of privilege also seems to capture this ambivalent middle ground. All reasonable options become privileged and permissible. Thus, the conduct of both Dan and Allan could be regarded as permissible, and, in this sense, justifiable. If that is all the claim of justification means, the incompatibility thesis must give way to a multiplicity of permissible actions.

The best argument against the view that justifiable conduct is merely permissible derives from the same thought experiment we used in assessing the view that claims of justification are merely appeals to courts. According to the ideal of the criminal law as a self-regulating set of conduct rules, the rules must generate a solution ex ante for every case. The "permissible" flows from a skepticism about the possibility of a single solution. It favors a limited range of reasonable outcomes. The notion of the permissible thus has no place in this idealized system of self-regulation. It follows that the incompatibility thesis can find no support in the reduction of justifiable conduct to the merely permissible.

C. RIGHTS AS PRIMA FACIE RIGHTS

German lawyers think of rights as absolute, although subject to defeasance on grounds of "abuse."[73] An absolute right occupies the available moral space. It is logically impossible for someone resisting the assertion of a right also to have a right. If a mother has a right to abort a fetus, the fetus cannot also have a right to be born. If a convict has a right to leave a burning jail, a guard cannot also have a right to keep him confined. If Dan has the right to use force against Allan, Allan cannot also have the right to use force against Dan. This strikes me as the natural way to speak about rights. The impossibility of inconsistent rights seems implicit in the grammar of rights discourse. So far as justifications generate rights, therefore, the impossibility of inconsistent justifications follows.[74]

It is not clear, however, that Americans think about rights in this way. There is a good deal of talk about rights "trumping" utilitarian incursions against the interests of right-bearers.[75] But the advocates of rights in contemporary jurisprudence typically concede that the rights themselves are "trumpable," or susceptible to being overridden in extreme cases. The innocent have a right not to be punished, but this right might be "trumped" by the necessity of saving the nation from a maniac who threatens to bomb us unless we punish a designated person.[76] We have a constitutional right to free speech, but this right might be "trumped" by a "clear and present danger" to the body politic. That rights can be "trumped" in this way is expressed by saying that the rights are merely "prima facie."[77]

There are at least two distinct interpretations of what it means to say that a right is prima facie, one interpretation for each of the modes of legal thought I have attempted to articulate. The advocates of a structured approach to rights insist that even if the right is trumped or overridden, we should retain a sense of loss in witnessing the overriding of the right.[78] The right remains intact, even though our common sense tells us that we must make sacrifices under exigent circumstances, such as sacrificing an innocent person in order to save the nation. The other interpretation appeals to the advocates of flat legal analysis. That a right is prima facie means that it occupies only a portion of the single plane of moral argument. When one right fails to govern the resolution of a particular dispute, another right on the same plane of moral space prevails. Once the right is trumped, it has no force at all. This, I take it, is the way many people think about overriding the right to free speech on the basis of clear and present danger to the common good.

If justifications generate prima facie rights in the first, structured sense, it would seem that the incompatibility thesis would still hold at the first level of analysis. But if "prima facie" is understood in the second sense of flat legal argument, there would seem to be no logical impediment to recognizing that both the mother and the fetus, both the escaping prisoner and guard, have prima facie rights. These rights would conflict but would still co-exist. In order to resolve the conflict, we would have to override one person's right and allow the other person's to prevail. Yet the basis for overriding the right is not that the other person's right is superior, for that would be to recognize that the latter party indeed had an absolute right. The trumping of a prima facie right is likely to turn on criteria of prudence and social interest—indeed whatever criteria rendered the right prima facie rather than absolute.

It is worth eliciting an additional ambiguity in talk about prima facie rights. The modifier "prima facie" could refer either to the degree of evidence about the existence of an absolute right, or to the nature of the right itself. When I say that a mother has a prima facie right to abort, I could mean: "I am not convinced that the mother has a right to abort on these facts, but there is a prima facie case made on her behalf." Or I could mean: "The right she has is qualified in its very nature." The former view, based as it is on the partial state of the evidence, would be compatible with the belief in absolute rights. The latter view is the one we need for the claim that after all the evidence is in, both the mother and the fetus have prima facie, but nonetheless conflicting, rights.

The divergence of common law thinking from continental thinking on putative self-defense derives from a matrix of interrelated assumptions. American lawyers tend to think of all available legal defenses as analogous, tend to assume that what is permissible is justified, and tend to view rights as trumpable claims. At the foundation of these assumptions lies the cement of reasonableness, a concept that enables Americans to blur distinctions between objective and subjective, self-defense and putative self-defense, wrongdoing and responsibility.

IV. Monism and Pluralism in Legal Theory

Although the Right and the reasonable lead us in different directions in criminal theory, the two concepts have much in common. They both represent efforts to transcend the sources of positive law and to reach for a higher, enduring, normative plane. Although both the Right and the reasonable permit the ongoing infusion of moral values into the law, these two architectonic concepts impose different structures on the legal order. The Right stands for a monistic legal order, for the existence of one right answer in every legal dispute. The Right requires us to believe that only one party can be justified in any situation of conflict. The reasonable, in contrast, urges us in the direction of a pluralistic legal order. Perhaps only one side can be in accordance with the Right, but both disputants might be reasonable. Both sides might indeed be justified.

CHAPTER 15

Reply: The Right and the Reasonable: Analyzing the Basic Idioms of American Criminal Law

Victoria Nourse

There is no more important concept in the criminal law than that of the "reasonable man": the law of murder and rape and robbery, not to mention duress and provocation and self-defense, depend upon it. Herein lies the great importance of George Fletcher's essay "The Right and the Reasonable," which remains one of the most erudite and penetrating analyses of "reasonableness" ever written. Here, as elsewhere, Professor Fletcher's project is to illuminate our most basic, unexamined, idiomatic conventions in the Anglo-American criminal law.

Fletcher begins by issuing a beautifully simple challenge: "We lawyers should listen to the way we talk" (150). In the Anglo-American common-law tradition, Fletcher writes, we cannot even "begin" to argue about most issues unless we invoke the concept of reasonableness. And, yet, this discursive habit is not mirrored abroad. Anglo-Americans' idiomatic reliance on the term "reasonable" stands in high contrast to the discourse of lawyers in Germany, France, and (then) Soviet Russia. In "continental Europe," urges Fletcher, "neither the adjective 'reasonable' nor the figure of the 'reasonable person' matters much in casting a legal argument" (150). It is not reasonableness, but Right (*Recht*), which plays the principal role, Fletcher argues, in the criminal law of Germany (151, 158–61). To clarify the distinction between Anglo-American and Continental discourses, Fletcher offers the notion of "flat" and "structured" legal reasoning, flat reasoning proceeding in a single stage, structured reasoning in two steps, first applying an absolute norm and then, in the second, qualifying that norm. For example, in the United States,

*Professor of Law, Georgetown University Law Center.

lawyers apply self-defense with a "flat" approach, asking whether the use of force is "reasonable," while in Germany, there is a two-stage inquiry: first, there is an absolute "right" to use deadly force when necessary, which is, at the second stage, qualified by various limitations, for example, if the right is abused (151).

Fletcher's "empirical quest" to discover the idioms of other cultures (151) highlights Americans' dependency on the concept of reasonableness and, at the same time, invites us to question our attachment to what Fletcher delightfully terms the "syntactically mobile" usage of "reasonableness" (152). If it is true that other countries manage quite successfully without the "reasonable person," then we must ask ourselves why Americans are so attached to this idea. As I have suggested elsewhere, one might even go so far as to ask whether one might eliminate the "reasonable person" from American criminal law altogether and consider what one might lose.[1] If Fletcher's comparison with European law is correct, then it seems more than plausible, and actually possible, to have a perfectly well-functioning criminal law without the "reasonable person" concept.

Fletcher's analysis aims at more than simply showing, empirically, the contingency of "reasonableness." It shows the intense need for greater theorization of a concept American lawyers find indispensable. As in other work, Fletcher focuses on the question of excuse and justification, arguing that the "flat style" of the "reasonableness" inquiry allows American lawyers to "function without the fundamental distinction between justification and excuse," a distinction far more central to continental lawyers (152). Fletcher chastises American lawyers for their indifference to the distinction, urging that the American position reflects "superficial[ity]" (153) and a "tolerant muddle" about the purposes of punishment (157). Structured forms of argument generate the proper distinction and priority of justification to excuse, according to Fletcher, because of the nature of retributive theories of punishment: "The theory of retributive punishment invites us to consider the relative desert of the offender, but only after establishing that he is an offender who has committed a wrongful act" (156).[2]

Even if one is skeptical of the value of the excuse/justification debate, Fletcher's analysis of the Anglo-American idiom deserves attention. First, Fletcher has asked a vitally important question and one theorists have traditionally evaded.[3] Standard scholarly debates have anthropomorphized the question, quite literally imagining the reasonable person to be a person and then asking what "characteristics" such a person would have. Particular attention has been devoted to whether the inquiry should be "objective" or "subjective."[4] This has, in turn, suggested questions taking the form of the "identity" of the reasonable person.[5] Although this is a much-debated question in the academy, it has an answer that is resolutely ambivalent. Almost all jurisdictions, on almost all questions, adopt a "hybrid," subjective and objective standard.[6] This is precisely what Fletcher's "flattening" argument predicts: that American criminal law evades direct analytic engagement with its most important concept.

Second, Fletcher's argument raises important questions of expressive condemnation—or, to put it differently, what the criminal law *means*. As Fletcher writes, the reasonableness standard sweeps together questions that should otherwise be quite distinct about whether an action was wrongful or merely excusable. Put in other words, questions of norms and exceptions, prescriptions and descriptions, aspirations and context find themselves all encompassed within the ubiquitously diffuse category "reasonableness." Meir Dan-Cohen once argued that there may be virtue to ambiguity in the criminal law,[7] and one is tempted to consider whether the flattened analysis of "reasonableness" can be justified on such grounds. Fletcher urges that the answer to this is no, that there are costs to flattening, costs measured in the value of simple due process: "In an ideal state of affairs, everyone who contemplates harmful action should know whether her conduct is rightful. She need not guess how courts will subsequently evaluate the circumstances" (165).

Third, and most important, Fletcher's analysis of the deep ambiguities of the reasonableness standard, its confusion of norm and exception, raises questions of moral evasion (and even moral perversion) in the criminal law. It is too easy for the Anglo-American mind to slip between what are analytically opposed meanings of reasonableness, from description (what do reasonable people do) to prescription (what should they do). Reasonableness in Fletcher's mind should be the equivalent of Right in the Continental tradition: it should reflect an aspiration to a "higher" law (168). And, yet, this is precisely the problem with the common-law tradition—arguments easily slip between "descriptive reasonableness" and "prescriptive reasonableness," between reasonableness that takes as its baseline the norms of the law-abiding and reasonableness that takes as its baseline the norms of the Holmesian bad actor.[8] In this slippage, in my view, lies moral hazard, specifically the hazard of importing within the criminal law the kind of biased norms it should be the law's aim to expose. Fletcher's purpose here may be different from mine (his is driven by the need for analytic clarity, mine by the need for normative clarity), but we agree that the "reasonableness" idiom of Anglo-American law deserves far deeper analysis. At the beginning of the twenty-first century, as at the end of the twentieth, no treatment of the concept, no treatment of the term, can begin without attention to Fletcher's "The Right and the Reasonable."

CHAPTER 16

The Nature of Justification

▦

George P. Fletcher

Since the unification of the two Germanies in October 1990, the West has begun to apply its principles of criminal justice to crimes allegedly committed by Eastern officials during forty-five years of Communist rule. That these proceedings are undertaken raises innumerable jurisprudential conundrums, among them the problem of justifying conduct under East German statutes that the West regards as unjust. This problem came to the fore in the prosecution of, among others, two border guards, Uwe Hapke and Udo Walther, for attempting the murder of fleeing citizens of the German Democratic Republic (GDR). A 1982 statute authorized border guards to shoot all persons trying feloniously to leave the country. The guards rather sensibly appealed to this statute—informally called the *Schiessbefehl* (order to shoot)—but the court would have none of it. The statute supposedly violated the generally recognized international right to leave one's country. And if the statute was unjust, the court reasoned, it could not provide a justification for shooting someone with the intent to kill. The court declared the guards guilty of attempted murder.

Many observers equate these proceedings to the Nuremberg trials, proceedings in which an international tribunal convicted German leaders for violating the newly coined crimes against humanity and conspiring to wage aggressive war. The Nuremberg process appears to have violated the principle *nulla poena sine lege*; the prosecution of genocide as a crime against humanity was not grounded in a pre-existing statutory definition. The same charge is made today against the German courts for disregarding a statutory justification valid in the GDR. The courts, in effect, created a new crime that was not punishable at the time of its commission. Though the prosecution is understandable as a passionate effort to punish injustice, the procedures and the rationale are the same as those of the Nuremberg trials. This negative assessment of the recent German conviction of the border guards seems to be the virtually unanimous opinion of Italian scholars, indicating the radically divergent styles of legal development in post-Fascist Italy and Germany.[1]

The jurisprudential problems raised by the case of the border guards are manifold. The first question is whether a statutory declaration should be conclusive on the issue of whether homicide or attempted homicide should be treated as justified. The second is whether the judicial disregard of a statutory declaration is tantamount to the judicial recognition of a new offence. Both of these questions raise a basic problem of whether there is a fundamental distinction between those issues that we would identify as the elements of the offence, and those that are raised by way of justification. If there is no basic difference, if a justification is merely a negative element of the offence (i.e. intentional homicide requires the *absence* of self-defence as well as an act intentionally causing death), then the critics of the German decision have a strong case. If the legislature has authority to define the "elements of the offence," then it should have the same authority over the negative elements we call claims of justification.

The claim that justificatory elements are like positive elements of the offence—except that the former require the absence rather than the presence of a factual element—has an enduring attraction. It comes in two basic forms—a conceptual and a positivist variation. My aim is to argue against both of these variations in favour of what I might call an ideal theory of justification. I will back into my argument for the ideal theory by trying to clarify its opponents.

The conceptual variation holds simply that whether courts or legislatures develop the criminal law, there is no important difference between affirmative and negative elements of offences; between, say, an act causing death and the absence of self-defence. This view is expressed in the doctrine that in homicide cases, for example, an unreasonable mistake about the factual presuppositions of self-defence should be treated just like an unreasonable mistake about whether an object being shot at is a human being or an animal. As the latter form of unreasonable mistake provides an adequate foundation for a charge of negligent homicide, so, the argument goes, should the former.[2]

The positivist variation of the theory holds that there is no conceptual structure in the criminal law at all, that all there is to the definition of crimes and defences derives from the authority of those charged with the matter. This view is positivist in the sense that it assumes that the entire criminal law is enacted law: there are no principles binding by virtue of their intrinsic merit. But if there is a structural distinction between elements of the offence and claims of justification, or between claims of justification and of excuse, these distinctions would acquire their appeal not from the will of the legislature, but from their intrinsic plausibility. Whether these distinctions obtain or not depends not on legislative authority, but on whether they provide a convincing account of the immanent structure of the criminal law. So far as positivism requires all legal rules and categories to derive from legislative authority, positivists cannot concede the existence of distinctions immanent in the law. Therefore, positivists are led to the conclusion that unless the legislature has spoken otherwise, there is no relevant distinction between elements of the offence and claims of justification. For the sake of brevity, I will refer to both the conceptual and positivist theses as the "unity" thesis.

The ideal theory of justification, by contrast, holds that despite the nominal realization of the elements of the offence, the conduct is not really wrong, not a violation of the *jus* or the Law in the ideal sense of *Recht, droit, diritto, derecho,* and the analogous forms in other languages.[3] A justified act conforms to the Right or the Law in a sense deeper than that captured in a legislative definition of an offence. A statutory definition should be understood as an approximation, by rule, of a principled understanding of wrongful conduct. It states the normal case of wrongdoing, but fails to account accurately for wrongdoing in the extraordinary cases that arise under conflict and under the pressure of circumstances. To deal with extraordinary situations, we must appeal to claims of justification, such as self-defence and necessity. Under ordinary circumstances, taking the property of another without consent should be treated as theft. Under circumstances of necessity, this conventional definition breaks down; it must yield to an understanding, based on principle, that in an emergency, taking property as the lesser evil is not wrongful behavior.

Similarly, killing is not wrong if committed in self-defence. Burning a dwelling-house is not wrong, if committed as an act of necessity to save more valuable property. Breaking and entering an abandoned cottage is not wrong if necessary to escape a life-threatening storm. To use Judith Thomson's distinction, the nominal *infringement* of the law in these situations does not amount to a *violation* of the law.[4] Satisfying the elements of the offence constitutes an infringement. An intervening justification prevents the infringement from being wrongful violation. It does not constitute full-blooded murder, arson, larceny, or burglary.

Of course they do not, the proponents of the unity thesis may respond. Killing in self-defence falls short of murder in precisely the same way that shooting and hitting a scarecrow with the intent to kill falls short of the crime. In this case, and in the other cases mentioned, one of the necessary elements of the offences—a negative element—remains unsatisfied. The ideal theory implies a structural difference between the two types of argument for non-liability. Denying an element of the offence is an assertion that there is not even an infringement that needs to be justified. Asserting a justification is, to use the term from common-law pleading, an argument in confession and avoidance. A claim of self-defence confesses the infringement of a significant human interest, and seeks to avoid the implication that the conduct is wrong.

To put the difference between the two theories simply: the unity thesis maintains that in the case of justified conduct, there is no harm relevant to the criminal law. An aggressor killed in self-defence, or a home destroyed as a matter of necessity, is not a relevant invasion of protected legal interest.[5] The ideal theory insists that in these cases there is some harm that should be registered in the criminal law, but that causing this harm is justified as a matter of principle.

It bears mentioning that we are not considering the theory of excuses. Claims of insanity, duress, mistake of law, and personal necessity take as their starting point the assumption that the conduct is wrongful. The thief who asserts starvation as an excuse does not deny that he has committed larceny. The insane killer does not deny that homicide is murder. These claims do not bear on the propriety of the act, but merely on the responsibility of the agent for authoring a wrongful act.

The two approaches to justification—the unity and the ideal theories— bear on a number of issues; their differing implications are worth rehearsing. *First*, as already mentioned, a mistaken claim about the factual preconditions of self-defence or necessity will be treated, on the unity theory, like a mistake about the elements of the offence. A mistake about whether someone is an aggressor is equivalent to a mistake about whether the person being shot at is alive. At one level, this can be understood as a point about the scope of the required intent. If the absence of self-defence is an element of homicide, then no one can be guilty of intentional homicide who mistakenly thinks that he or she is being attacked. If non-consent is an element of rape, then the required intent is the intent to have intercourse without consent. Further, if the mistake is unreasonable, then it will be treated as negligence as to an element of the offence. If the offence can be committed negligently, the negligent mistake renders the perpetrator liable. Thus, if Bernhard Goetz negligently thought he was about to be attacked, he could have been guilty of negligent homicide (had he killed one of the four putative aggressors). If the offence is not subject to negligent commission—as attempted murder is not—then the unreasonable mistake is insufficient to generate liability.

Second, the theory that claims of justification are merely negative elements of the offence leads to the view—the converse of the first implication stated above— that objective elements are sufficient to prevent commission of the offence. Think of the case in which the agent wants and intends to kill an innocent person, but in fact is subject at that very moment to a secret attack from his intended victim. The act of intended killing turns out to be an action in objective self-defence. If self-defence were just like an element of the offence, one would be inclined to think that the objective presence of aggression would be sufficient to prevent realization of the offence. If the objective fact that the intended victim is in fact a scarecrow precludes liability for homicide, then, by extension, the objective fact that the intended victim is an aggressor should have the same effect. Let us refer to this as the problem of objective justification, i.e. justification regardless of the perpetrator's ignorance of the justifying circumstances.

Though the matter continues to be debated in theory, virtually all legal systems—Italy excepted—adhere to the view that claims of justification represent good reasons for transgressing against the statute and the interest it protects. It

follows that only those who have acted with knowledge of the justifying circumstances—of self-defence, necessity, or for that matter consent—should be able to
claim a good reason for infringing a protected interest and rely upon a claim of
justification. Admittedly, there might be stronger arguments for a position that
seems so deeply entrenched in the world's legal culture. Generating a convincing rationale for requiring intent in cases of justification reminds one of other
practices of the criminal law that are widely shared and intuitively accepted—for
example, punishing completed crimes more severely than attempts, and retributive punishment generally—but for which theoreticians have yet to generate a
compelling justification.

Third, we may assume that the prohibitory norms of the criminal law protect
specific interests, and if the norms must be stated to include the absence of justifying circumstances, then it follows that the interest protected must be stated so as
to include the absence of justification. We normally say that the law of homicide
protects human life, but if objective self-defence precludes finding even a nominal infringement of the law, it follows that the purpose of the law of homicide is
to protect the lives of innocent, non-aggressing, human beings. Under this view,
killing an aggressor is no more an infringement of the law of homicide than fill-
ing a scarecrow full of lead. In neither case does the intent to kill an innocent
(non-aggressing) human being provide a sufficient basis for conviction.

Fourth, the doctrine of legislative supremacy, if applied to criteria of justification as well as to the elements of the offence, precludes the judicial recognition of
new justificatory defences. In fact, in most legal systems, the courts have taken
the lead in this century in developing the defence of lesser evils. Abortion cases
frequently emerged as a testing-ground. The German Reichsgericht's recognition
of lesser evils as an extra-statutory defence is perhaps the most dramatic example.[6] The German court's reasoning in this landmark 1927 case rests squarely on
the ideal theory of justification.[7] Criminal conduct, the judges argue, depends on
wrongdoing and wrongful behavior. Conduct is wrongful only if it violates *Recht*
in an ideal sense. The legislature is supreme in defining offences, but not in specifying the range of possible defences that can negate the inference of wrongdoing from the commission of an offence. Aborting a fetus to save the mother from
suicide, though not justified under the abortion statute, represents the lesser evil
under the situation, and therefore the act was justified in principle. As a justified act, it was not wrongful. There was no criminal liability. This kind of judicial
refinement of the law would not be possible under a coupling of the unity thesis
with legislative supremacy.

Fifth, legislation has a function in the field of justification (as well as in the
field of excuses) which is different from its role in rendering as precise as possible
the elements of the offence. Code provisions defining self-defence and necessity
have the function primarily of guiding judges in deciding cases. They function, it
seems, as decision rules rather than conduct rules.[8] Accordingly, these provisions

governing justifying criteria may admit of a degree of vagueness that would be intolerable under the due-process principle of "fair warning," requiring that criminal offences be defined with sufficient specificity to advise common people of their rights and obligations.[9]

The standard of necessity, for example, is defined generally to exact a comparison of the costs and benefits of following the nominal prohibition of the law. Imagine the vagueness of a crime defined to incorporate this cost/benefit judgment. It would read something like: Don't take things belonging to another unless, on balance, it is better for society to do so. When a California statute was interpreted as a prohibition against "unnecessary" abortions, the state supreme court declared the statute void as excessively vague under the due-process clause of the Fourteenth Amendment.[10] Cost/benefit standards and standards of necessity are suitable for claims of justification but, as a general matter, they infect the definition of elements of crimes with undue imprecision.

If the unity thesis were correct, then the absence of necessity would be an element of larceny, arson, burglary, and a host of other crimes that lend themselves to justification on grounds of necessity or lesser evils. It would indeed be correct to define the injunction of common-law larceny as:

Do not take an object from the possession of the owner, with the intent to deprive the owner permanently of his property, unless necessary to avoid an imminent risk that represents a greater cost than the damage represented by taking the object.

A crime so defined would fail the due-process requirement of fair warning: the principle *nulla poena sine lege* would be frustrated. The only way to save the common-law crimes from the vice of vagueness is to filter off the defence of necessity and to treat it as a different type of issue, to which relatively lax criteria of precision may be applied.

Sixth, if the legislature is not supreme in the field of justifying criteria, the courts are free to make statutory language conform to their ideal theory of justification. A good example in the German experience is the pruning back, in recent years, of the broad sweep of the German Code provision on self-defence. That provision, Article 32 of the 1975 Code, seems to recognize the traditional German doctrine that anyone may use any amount of force to uphold any right, however trivial. So understood, the provision implies that a property-owner may use deadly force, if no less drastic means is available, to prevent a thief from escaping with a minor bounty. No principle of proportionality restrains the use of necessary force. The guiding principle of the tradition is that the "Right need never yield to the Wrong."

In the last decades, German scholars and courts have begun to apply a principle of proportionality to restrain the scope of Article 32. The doctrinal label is *Rechtsmissbrauch* or *abus de droit*—a doctrine, peculiar to Continental legal thinking, which resembles, more or less, the common law principle of reason-ableness.[11] The difficulty posed by this development is precisely the charge that curtailing a justification implicitly recognizes a new area of criminal lia-bility, namely the set of cases that would be justified if the statute were strictly applied.

Seventh, there remains to be considered only the case of the German border guards posed at the outset of this article. This case differs from the problem con-sidered in the fourth point above, for here the court was willing to disregard a stat-utory justification to the detriment of the defendant rather than add a justification for the benefit of the defence. It differs from the sixth point, largely as a matter of degree, for in this instance the courts went further than adjusting a defence at the fringes. Disregarding an entire statutory defence poses the most difficult test for the ideal theory of justification.

Let us summarize the seven items and attempt to assay the balance of advan-tage between the unity thesis and the ideal theories of justification.

		Unity thesis
First	mistake about justifying fact	like mistake about element of offence
Second	objective justification	implied
Third	interest protected	includes absence of justifying factor
Fourth	recognizing new defences	not allowed
Fifth	problem of vagueness	not solved
Sixth	adjusting justification	not allowed
Seventh	disregarding statutory justification	not allowed

The ideal theory takes the opposing stand on all these counts. If justifications are asserted in a dimension of principle, while the elements are laid down by stat-ute, there would be no reason to treat mistakes about justifying facts as one treats mistakes about the elements. Also, if a claim of justification represents a good reason for violating the statute, it makes no sense to entertain the possibility of justification by objective facts alone. The interests protected under the criminal law are defined simply as life, property, etc., without considering the conditions that, if present, would justify a nominal infringement of these interests. The prob-lem of vagueness is solved, and further, courts have the authority to elaborate the ideal theory of justification by recognizing new claims of justification, curtailing other claims and disregarding legislative pronouncements at odds with the ideal theory.

It is hard to find a legal system that consistently adopts the implications of either the unity or the ideal theory. Because of the extraordinarily strong positivist bent of post-war Italian jurisprudence, the Italians seem to concur with the unity thesis on all seven points. The Model Penal Code takes the positivist line on most of these seven points, except that it explicitly rejects objective justification. German law follows the ideal theory on most points, except that the dominant view in German law concurs with the Model Penal Code in treating mistakes about justificatory facts as though they were mistakes about elements of the offence. Generally, the unity or ideal theories do no more than incline legal systems in one direction or another. Other arguments and theories intercede to yield different results on particular points.

As a matter of theory, the unity thesis appears to be harder to defend. Its major defects are the third and fifth points. It fails to provide an intuitively plausible account of the interests protected under the criminal law. As German theorists are fond of saying, it reduces killing in self-defence to the same format as killing a fly.[12] It also fails to solve the problem of vagueness introduced by claims such as necessity, which turn ultimately on broader questions of social costs and benefits. Of course, the advocate of the unity thesis could insist that these are mysteries of the criminal law. No one but the legislature knows what interests it seeks to protect. And if some of the defences are vague, so be it. These points hardly matter, the argument might go, as compared with the advantages gained by eliminating judicial power to curtail and disregard statutory defences.

It must be clear that, on balance, I favour the ideal theory of justification. More important than a decision for one theory or the other, however, is the way of thinking about criminal theory implicitly advocated in this essay. A case like that of the German border guards poses a problem in the foundations of criminal liability that goes beyond the immediate problem of whether a court may disregard a statutory defence. My suggestion is that the nature of justification should be assayed globally, as differing approaches to justification are manifested in the seven points, ranging from the analysis of mistakes to the problem of curtailing an overly broad statutory justification. When looked at in the light of its impact on these various points, the ideal theory cuts a more convincing figure.

The response might be: fine, we should apply the ideal where we have to, and rely upon the thesis of conceptual unity or the positivist variation whenever it serves the interests of the defendant to do so. Therefore, we will allow the courts to recognize new defences, but not to disregard a defence that protects the defendant. Although it seems to disregard the injustice of acquitting those who should be convicted, this position enjoys an undeniable appeal.

The best case for a defence-oriented version of the ideal theory would go something like this. When the legislature commits itself, in a statute, to a certain set of criteria defining criminal offences, the entire apparatus of the State, including the courts, is estopped from denying the defendant recourse to these criteria in his or her defence. Every citizen, every person subject to the jurisdiction of the State, has a right to rely on the statutory law as written. A statute is something like a promise to the citizen; the State cannot go back on its word. If the East German state promised a justification to its border guards in the form of the 1982 statute, the successor state of unified Germany cannot disregard the promise.

The problem with the theory of statute-as-promise is its overkill. It encompasses all statutes bearing on procedural matters that the State should be allowed to change retroactively, without falling foul of the principle *nulla poena sine lege*. Consider, for example, the statute of limitations. The German twenty-year statute of limitations on homicide was held to begin running first in 1945 at the end of the war, and then in 1949 when the Federal Republic took responsibility for crimes on German soil. When it was about to run out in 1965, it was extended for ten years, and before it ran out in 1975, it was abolished altogether. Is the statute of limitations a promise to the citizenry that estops the State from changing its laws retroactively? How should one decide whether it is?

The conventional starting point for considering when legislatures may apply new legislation to crimes already committed is to distinguish between procedural and substantive rules. The legislature is free to change the former but not the latter. Thus the question raised is whether the statute of limitations should be classified as procedural or substantive. But adding this problem of classification hardly advances the inquiry, for how should we decide whether it is one rather than the other? Some courts hold that the statute of limitations is procedural, some that it is substantive. For this distinction to be of assistance, we would need a theory of substance and of procedure, and an explanation of why the question of substance versus procedure should matter in resolving the problem of retroactivity.

A better approach is to shift the focus from legal categories to the question: what should the actor be entitled to rely upon at the time she commits the crime? We can agree that a criminal perpetrator should be able to rely on the definition of the crime at the time of acting. If a physician removes the organs of a moribund patient with a flat EEG reading—legally dead at the time of the operation—it would be unfair to change the definition of death retroactively and thus convert to homicide that which was not homicide at the time of commission. But should she be encouraged to think to herself: "If I commit this crime now, I am subject to prosecution, at most, for the next twenty years. This is a risk worth running?" I should think not. The purpose of the statute of limitations is not to shape the incentive structure of those considering crimes.

A case decided not long ago in California illustrates how the labels "substance" and "procedure" can be misleading.[13] The defendant Snipe allegedly beat his child, and the child died twenty-one months afterwards. At the time of the acts alleged, California Penal Code, § 194, expressed the common-law rule that the defendant could be guilty of homicide only if the victim died within a year and a day of the homicidal act. After the beatings but before the child died, the legislature amended the statute to permit prosecution if the victim died within three years and a day of the act causing death. The defendant argued that he should be held accountable solely under the statute that rendered his conduct criminal at the time of his beating his child. He argued, in effect, that he had a right to rely on the year-and-a-day rule.

The problem is more difficult than that posed by the statute of limitations, for the year-and-a-day rule appears to be substantive; it goes to the definition of the crime. If the courts may apply procedural but not substantive rules retroactively, the defendant in *Snipe* wins the argument. Yet the problem, in principle, is whether the defendant should have a right to rely on the year-and-a-day rule. It is as though he might have pondered whether to commit the crime by considering how long it would take her to die: "If I can beat the child so that she dies slowly, I will do so; but if she dies quickly, I will be liable for murder and therefore I won't do it." It is obviously absurd to think that the year-and-a-day rule should have entered the defendant's calculations about whether to commit the crime. Therefore he was not entitled to rely on that aspect of the law in force when he committed child abuse. The California court sensibly concluded that there was nothing wrong with retroactively applying the new three-years-and-a-day rule and holding Snipe liable for criminal homicide.

The same mode of analysis should shape our judgment about whether the rules of evidence or the statute of limitations properly influences a decision to commit a crime. Would we want a would-be murderer to reason to himself: "If I can commit this crime and lie low for twenty years, I'll be home free, and therefore I'll do it?" We employ a range of rules in the law—both procedural and substantive—that are not meant to be conduct rules. They are not meant to be relied on in steering a course to avoid criminal liability. We do want physicians to rely upon the statutory definition of death in deciding when it is safe to perform transplant operations, but we do not want to encourage the same mode of reliance on rules that are evidentiary in nature (as the year-and-a-day rule provides evidence of an adequate causal link) or otherwise irrelevant to the essential wrong of the statutory prohibition. Because these peripheral rules are not meant to be relied on— and there is no legitimate basis for relying on them—it is misleading to call them promises that preclude the State from changing its course of conduct.

The invocation of the notion of "essential wrong" is revealing, for it is not an expression that flows easily from the positivist's pen. But then again, positivists— for whom all enacted rules of the legal system appear to be of equal stature—could not distinguish between rules defining death and rules defining causation in the statutory elements of homicide. Using a term like "essential wrong" to explain when courts may apply statutory changes retroactively commits one to a certain view of the criminal law. It is a view that takes our pre-statutory understanding of wrongdoing to be essential in fashioning rules and principles that facilitate the resolution of foundational problems such as retroactivity.

Our pre-statutory understanding of wrongdoing may be of some assistance in grasping the roots of the ideal theory of justification. Claims of justification deny that conduct is wrong precisely in this sense of pre-statutory, principled understanding of right and wrong. The sensibility that permits a California court to disregard the statute in force when Snipe beats his child informs the intuitions that can convince a German court to recognize an extra-statutory claim of necessity or to disregard a statutory justification putatively permitting the killing of citizens fleeing their country. Both modes of thinking focus on the essential wrong of homicide and attempted homicide. Abortion is not essentially wrong if undertaken to save the mother from suicide, and attempted murder is wrong if committed against citizens whose crime is no greater than seeking, by the only means available, to cross their border. Rules that are peripheral to this core of wrongdoing do not fall under the ban of ex post facto decision-making. And statutory authorizations that do not, in fact, negate the wrong of trying to kill an innocent human being are not binding.

CHAPTER 17

Reply: Fletcher on Subjective Justification

*Peter Westen**

George Fletcher has done more than any other American scholar to clarify the norms of criminal law by examining what H.L.A. Hart calls our "conceptual apparatus,"[1] that is, the categories of thought by which we reason about norms, including norms of criminal responsibility.

Fletcher's most influential contribution has been introducing Anglo-Americans to the distinction between justification and excuse.[2] Most commentators now accept the importance of the distinction, though some disagree with Fletcher about the best normative understanding of justification.[3] "The Nature of Justification" is Fletcher's most extended effort to defend his normative view by grounding it in another substantive distinction he favors, that is, that between *elements of offenses* and *defenses*.[4]

Section I summarizes Fletcher's normative view of justification by contrasting it with Paul Robinson's. Section II discusses how Fletcher uses collateral normative claims regarding "elements" and "defenses" to defend his view. Section III states and criticizes Fletcher's collateral normative claims regarding elements and defenses.

I. Fletcher's Normative View of Justification

Fletcher's normative view of justification can be understood by juxtaposing it to Robinson's.

A. ROBINSON'S VIEW

Robinson argues that if wrongdoing consists of the harms and evils that the state seeks to prevent by means of the statute at hand, all things considered, anything that negates what otherwise constitutes wrongdoing is a "justification."[5]

*Professor Emeritus, University of Michigan School of Law.

Robinson's view has conceptual as well as normative benefits.[6] First, it reduces what are otherwise two conceptual elements of criminal liability, that is, wrong-doing and absence of justification, to one. For if justification negates wrongdoing, then the two foregoing elements of criminal liability consist essentially of wrong-doing alone, all things considered.[7]

Second, Robinson's view means that the relationship between the harms and evils framed as elements, and their absence framed as justifications, is entirely formal. That is, if justification is the negation of harms or evils the state seeks to prevent, legislatures can frame wrongdoing in alternative ways. They can define the elements of an offense more broadly than the harms and evils they wish to punish and, then, provide defenses of justification to reduce an actor's liability to precisely what they wish to punish, all things considered. Or they can define the elements of the offense to consist precisely of the harms and evils they wish to punish, all things considered.[8]

Third, Robinson's view produces what many commentators (albeit not Fletcher) regard as the normative benefit of giving equal treatment to actors who are equal in *not realizing* that they are actually causing the harm or evil that a statute seeks to prevent under the circumstances. An actor who kills a harm-less person in the mistaken belief that he is shooting at a scarecrow is norma-tively identical to an actor who kills in the mistaken belief that he must do so to defend himself, because each actor causes a harm that the state seeks to prevent under the circumstances, and, yet, neither does so intentionally. Accordingly, in jurisdictions that treat justifications as the negation of harms and evils, equals are treated equally. Neither actor is punished for intentional homicide, though both may be liable for negligent homicide. In contrast, Fletcher believes that a policeman who negligently kills a suspect in the false belief that doing so is nec-essary to defend himself ought to be equated with a policeman who purposefully kills a suspect whom he knows to be harmless by punishing both for intentional homicide.[9]

Finally, Robinson's view produces what many commentators[10] (albeit not Fletcher) regard as the normative benefit of giving equal treatment to actors who are equal in *trying but failing* to bring about a harm or evil that a statute seeks to prevent under the circumstances. An actor who shoots at an enemy not realizing that his gun is unloaded is normatively identical to an actor who lethally shoots an enemy not realizing that the latter is about to kill him, because each actor tries but fails to produce a harm that the state seeks to prevent under the circumstances. Accordingly, within jurisdictions that treat justifications as the negation of the harms and evils, equals are treated equally. The two actors are both punished; but rather than being punished for murder, they are punished for the crime of trying but failing to kill a person whom the state seeks to protect under the circumstanc-es—namely, the crime of "attempted" murder.[11] In contrast, Fletcher believes that the actor who lethally shoots a rival gang member (not realizing that the latter is about to kill him) ought to be punished for the harm-based offense of murder, despite the fact that the shooting is not a harm the state wishes to prevent under the circumstances.[12]

B. FLETCHER'S VIEW

Fletcher repeatedly states that justification "negates" wrongdoing.[13] Significantly, however, Fletcher does not mean that justification is merely the converse of harms and evils the state seeks to prevent by means of the statute at hand, all things considered. For if he did, his view would be interchangeable with Robinson's. Instead, Fletcher takes the two-part normative position (hereinafter his "two-part normative view") that (1) in order for an actor to be justified, he not only must act under circumstances that negate such harms and evils but also must act *for those reasons,*[14] and (2) in order to excuse an actor of an intentional crime who mistakenly thinks his conduct is necessary to prevent such a harm or evil, the actor must not only think so, his belief must also be *reasonable.*[15]

How, then, does Fletcher reconcile his statements about "negating" with his two-part normative view? A full answer would address the several ways in which Fletcher defines "wrongdoing" and "justification" differently than Robinson.[16] However, it is unnecessary to discuss those differences here because, even apart from differences in definition, Fletcher believes that wrongdoing consists in part of two components—one that is negated by justification, the other that is not.

Wrongdoing for Fletcher consists, in part, of (1) conduct by *A* that harms *B* by infringing interests of *B*'s that the statute at hand recognizes and *generally* seeks to protect by means of punishment, albeit not under certain exceptional circumstances, and (2) the absence of such exceptional circumstances, the absence of which leaves *B* not only harmed under component 1 but *unlawfully* harmed, all things considered.[17]

Fletcher further believes that component 1 forms part of the *elements of an offense,* while circumstances that negate component 2 form part of *defenses of justification.* The boundary between them is "fundamental" (173), "structural" (173), and "substantive,"[18] Fletcher says, because, although justification—which consists in part of exceptional circumstances that render *A*'s harm to *B* lawful and, hence, not "wrongful"—does negate component 2, it does not negate component 1. That is, justification does not negate the fact that *A* has harmed *B* by infringing an interest of *B*'s that the law recognizes. Instead, justification "defeats"[19] such harm by rendering *A*'s conduct lawful *in spite of the harm* that it inflicts upon *B* (174), provided that (1) *A* acts for those reasons, and (2) *A* reasonably believes the extraordinary circumstances obtain.[20]

II. Fletcher's Invocation of "Elements" and "Defenses"

With one exception, Fletcher does not try in "The Nature of Justification" to defend his two-part normative view directly.[21] He does not explain why the relationship between elements of offenses and defenses should have the two-part normative effect on justification that he expounds. Instead, he defends his view *indirectly* by criticizing what he believes are the collateral normative consequences of Robinson's view that the relationship between elements of offenses and defenses of justification is entirely formal.

Robinson, it will be recalled, argues that justification should be understood to consist of anything that negates a harm or evil that the state seeks to prevent under the circumstances—from which it follows that, burdens of proof aside, anything that is framed as a defense of justification can be framed in the negative as part of unified elements of the offense. Fletcher criticizes this "unity theory" of elements and defenses by enumerating certain collateral disadvantages he believes it produces.

III. Fletcher's Collateral Claims Regarding Elements and Defenses

Fletcher enumerates seven collateral consequences that he believes Robinson's unity theory produces. The first two, however, are precisely the normative features that are at issue, that is, the features that distinguish Fletcher's view of justification from Robinson's.[22] The remaining consequences can be reduced to four.

1. UNITY THEORY EQUATES HOMICIDE WITH "KILLING A FLY"

Unity theory equates an actor who intentionally kills a rival without realizing the latter is about to kill him with an actor who intentionally shoots a scarecrow thinking the latter is alive by convicting them both of "attempted" murder. Based on this, Fletcher argues that unity theory equates the harm of homicide with actions that are as trivial as "killing a fly" (179, see also 174).

With due respect, this argument is a straw man. Unity theory asserts that everything the state seeks to prevent by means of a statute can be conceptualized in the form of a single prohibition, for example, statutes prohibiting "the *unlawful* killing of a human being." But that is not to assert that conduct that complies with such a prohibition, for example, the *lawful* killing of a human being, is costless. To the contrary, everyone, including Robinson,[23] acknowledges that homicide is an irreparable loss that survivors will mourn and is presumptively to be prevented— while shooting scarecrows is not.

To understand why unity theory punishes both actors for attempt when one of them admittedly produces an irreparable loss, we must address what Fletcher ignores—namely, why the state punishes murder more severely than attempted murder. The state punishes murder at the highest level to give vent to the righteous and untrammeled indignation its residents feel when malefactors not only act with homicidal intent but actually kill the very persons whom the law seeks to protect.[24] The controlling question, therefore, is whether a defendant killed a person whom the law wishes he had not killed under the circumstances. By that standard, a malefactor who shoots a scarecrow and a malefactor who lethally shoots a rival are identical because, despite the fact that one causes an irreparable loss that survivors will mourn, neither produces the kind of untrammeled indignation that society reserves for those who actually succeed in killing persons whom the state wishes they had refrained from killing, all things considered.

2. UNITY THEORY PROHIBITS COURTS FROM FASHIONING EXCULPATIONS

Fletcher argues that elements must be framed by legislatures, and that since unity theory regards everything as an element, unity theory prohibits courts from the current practice of creating judge-made exculpations, such as necessity and self-defense.

This argument misstates what unity theory is. Unity theory is an analytical assertion about the formal relationship between elements and justification that obtains when justification is understood as the negation of the harms or evils the state seeks to prevent. Unity theory claims that anything that is presently stated as a justification of the foregoing kind *can* be framed in the negative as an element. It does not claim that justifications "must" (176) be—or even *should* be—restated as elements. On the contrary, economies in drafting and burdens of proof may well militate in favor of stating justifications separately.[25]

Nor does unity theory claim that *legislatures* rather than courts must act in the event that justifications are reframed in the negative as elements. Quite the contrary, as long as courts are allowed to frame justifications, they may surely frame them in the negative as elements.[26]

3. UNITY THEORY REQUIRES "FAIR WARNING" TO WHICH ACTORS ARE NOT ENTITLED

Fletcher argues that justifications are "decision rules" to which actors have no right to fair warning, and that since unity theory regards everything as an element—and, hence, as "conduct rules" that do require fair warning—unity theory requires fair warning to which actors have no right.

Again, this misstates what unity theory is. The unity that the theory asserts is a formal relationship between elements and justifications, not a substantive change in normative entitlements such as rights to notice. Unity theory is entirely consistent with whatever rights to notice defendants otherwise have.

Contrary to Fletcher, I believe, along with others, that justifications are conduct rules that do indeed vest actors with rights to notice.[27] Indeed, that is precisely why it was unjust for Germany to punish GDR border guards for complying with order-to-shoot rules. Once the GDR guards were officially told that they were obliged to shoot unlawful border-crossers, it was unjust to punish them for conducting themselves accordingly, because in contrast to the Nazi extermination policies punished at Nuremberg, the order-to-shoot rules were normatively plausible under the demographic and political pressures the GDR faced at the time.

Nevertheless, if Fletcher is correct that justifications are decision rules that involve no fundamental rights to notice, justifications do not become conduct rules—and, hence, implicate fundamental rights to notice—simply because, as a conceptual matter, they can be reframed in the negative as elements.[28]

4. UNITY THEORY PROHIBITS UNAVOIDABLE "VAGUENESS"

Fletcher argues that "vagueness" is a fatal flaw in elements rather than in defenses of justification, and that since vagueness is unavoidable if states wish to take account of whether an actor's conduct is a "lesser" or "greater" evil under the circumstances, unity theory, by regarding everything as an element, bars states from taking account of whether an actor's conduct is a lesser or greater evil.

The fallacies here are twofold. First, justice does not bar states from employing vague terms such as "unreasonable"[29] and "greater evil" to define prohibited conduct, provided that the terms are confined to conduct that it can confidently be said that conscientious members of the community regard as punishable. When such terms are applied more broadly than that, the flaw is not in denying actors notice but in punishing actors for conduct that it cannot be said with sufficient confidence the community regards as punishable.[30]

Second, if vagueness is, indeed, a flaw in elements, it cannot plausibly cease to be a flaw simply because the harm or evil the element defines is framed in the negative as a justification.

In sum, the formal relationship between elements and justifications that unity theory espouses involves no collateral normative consequences at all, much less collateral consequences that could undermine Robinson's two-part normative view and leave space for Fletcher's contrary view.

CHAPTER 18

The Psychotic Aggressor— A Generation Later

George P. Fletcher

Some twenty years ago my imaginary character the "psychotic aggressor" made his debut in the pages of the *Israel Law Review*.[1] Of all the hypothetical cases I have devised over the years, the story of the psychotic aggressor in the elevator, attacking someone who must defend herself, has become one of the most vigorous and long-lasting. This unlikely case has proven to be a useful medium for understanding the difference between claims of justification and claims of excuse in structuring criminal liability. Everyone assumes that the person attacked should be able to defend herself; the problem is whether the defense is right and proper (justified) or whether it is simply the human response and therefore free from blame (excused). This classification has implications, in turn, for whether third parties may come to the aid of the person attacked and whether the psychotic aggressor, in turn, has a right to defend himself against efforts to kill him. These issues have given rise to considerable debate over the last two decades, and much of it can be traced to the conundrum whether resisting a psychotic but purposeful aggressor should be treated as right in itself or, alternatively, wrong but free from blame.[2]

If there is anything I have learned about legal studies over the last generation, it is that for thinking people, legal cultures set no limits. The problems that we face as theoretical lawyers are universal. They arise in every legal system, and there is no culture-driven necessity in the way we think about them. From one legal system to another, there may be differences of argumentative style and attitudes toward sources of law. But in thinking about a theoretical legal problem, these matters of style recede into the background. What counts are the arguments that are mustered, not the language or culture in which the arguments are made.

So it is with the theory of justification and excuse. No legal system begins with a theoretical distinction between these two kinds of defense. The historical evolution springs from the recognition of particular defenses—insanity, mistake, self-defense, necessity. The architecture of the law comes after the building is more or less built. The grand distinctions by which we organize our legal thought today—between contract and tort, between person and object, between intent and negligence—are not laid out in some plan before the legal structure begins to take shape. As the beams and boards are added to the barn, we notice that a certain structure lies implicit in what we have been doing. The task of the theorist is to explicate the plans that make the building possible.

Thus thinking about the defenses generally recognized in the criminal law, we recognize that insanity differs fundamentally from, let us say, killing a thief breaking into a residence at night. At an earlier stage of legal thought, there was a tendency to think that insanity was different from self-defense because insane persons were not subject to the criminal law at all. They were like infants— outside the jurisdiction of the criminal courts. This is the view that you find in Blackstone. Some people today continue to think of the insane as a class apart. In Communist legal theory, which is still being used in the post-Communist societies of Eastern Europe, insanity was officially classified as bearing on the "subject" of the crime rather than on any of the other three categories recognized in that over-simplified structure.[3]

The hypothesis that the insane are not bound by the criminal law is precisely what makes the attack by the psychotic aggressor so puzzling. Is this not an act of human aggression? Does it not trigger a right of self-defense on the part of the potential victim? Some people have argued that insane aggressors should be treated like rabies-stricken animals, mad dogs that have to be done away with to protect more valuable interests. Twenty years ago I sensed that this way of thinking about the insane reflected a depreciation of their lives, and I wrote:

> Those who solve the problem of the psychotic aggressor by depreciating the life of the insane depart from the basic premise of equality before the law.[4]

The point is that the way we solve these conundrums carries moral implications. It strikes me as a moral advance to bring the insane within the law, to treat the psychotic aggressor as an addressee of the norm against aggression and then to search for the proper basis for not holding him criminally liable. That basis, I take it, is that although he has violated the norm against aggression, we cannot fairly blame him for his violation. Perhaps he has no control over himself; perhaps he cannot appreciate the wrongfulness of attacking another. Yet under these criteria of self-control and knowledge, he might be accountable for some acts and not others. Each act must be examined on its own terms, and in each situation the question must be whether he is fairly to blame for the violation. But if we cannot blame him for a violation, what sense does it make to say that he has actually violated the norm? With this question we land in a thicket of philosophical puzzles.

What do we have to establish in order to say that someone has violated a norm of the criminal law? I should like to think that what we need to know is (1) that some objective event has occurred that is incompatible with the norm, and (2) that this objective state of affairs is traceable to human action. Thus an act causing death violates the norm against homicide; an act causing unwanted physical contact violates the prohibition against battery. If the result accrues without an act, as if someone is pushed off a cliff and falls on me, there is no act and therefore no violation. Rabies-stricken dogs may threaten interests protected by legal norms, but their animal actions do not transgress these norms. The law does not speak to dogs, but it does speak to all human beings, including the insane.

Admittedly, the proposition that the law speaks to all human beings has an ideological cast to it. This is not a factual proposition, easily verified by looking at the world. It is the way, I maintain, that one should think about the law: the legal system itself expresses a principle of human equality by addressing all those it regards as potentially responsible adults. The norms of the criminal law do not embrace minors as subjects of obligations and, of course, do not treat objects, such as animals, as subjects bound by law.

A second moral or ideological premise is implicit in what I have just written; the insane are assumed to be potentially responsible. They are a not a breed apart, not lunatics (as once believed) under the permanent control of the moon, but mentally ill humans who can, in principle, return to a normal state of responsibility. Insanity is not a condition that removes the person from the scope for all cases and under all situations, but only a ground for denying responsibility for a particular act under a particular set of influences.

The necessity of a theory of excuses derives from this moral aspiration of the law: if the norms of the law address the insane, then there must be some available account of why the psychotic aggressor is not responsible for his aggression. The theory of excuses comes on the scene to fill this gap: to account for how individuals can violate norms and yet not be held accountable.

Excuses are a relatively recent development on the stage of legal thought. In the eighteenth century, even the most advanced thinkers, such as Immanuel Kant, sought to solve the problem of responsibility not by applying excusing conditions but by limiting the scope of the relevant norms. Or at least this is one way to read Kant's treatment of the problem.

In an oft-cited passage in Kant's *Philosophy of Law*, he poses the case of the shipwrecked sailor who, lost at sea, saves his life by pushing another person off the only available plank. Our intuitions tell us that we should not punish this person who acted in order to save his own life. The question is why. Kant writes:

> In other words, there can be no penal law that would assign the death penalty to someone in a shipwreck who, in order to save his own life, shoves another, whose life is equally in danger, off a plank on which he has saved himself. For the punishment threatened by the law could not be greater than the loss of his own life. A penal law of this sort could not have the effect intended, since a threat of an evil that is still *uncertain* (death by judicial verdict) cannot outweigh the fear of an evil that is *certain* (drowning). Hence the deed of saving one's life by violence is not to be judged *inculpabile* (*inculpable*) but only *unpunishable* (*impunible*), and by a strange confusion jurists take this *subjective immunity* to be *objective immunity* (conformity with law).[5]

This passage lends itself to alternative interpretations: either that the statutory norm prohibiting homicide does not address the shipwrecked sailor if it cannot influence his behavior, or that the rationale for not punishing the sailor's life-saving act is the exculpatory effect of necessity. Kant's views mediate between these two positions. Even if the statutory norm does not apply to the shipwrecked sailor, his act is still a wrong in violation of general principles of law. This is the point of the last sentence, which stresses that the act is contrary to *Recht* or law as principle. It is a wrong because it violates the general norm against interfering with the rights of others, and the first occupier of the plank presumably has a right to stay there.

Though the life-saving act of the shipwrecked sailor is wrong, the actor enjoys a subjective or personal immunity from punishment. Thus the life-threatening situation comes into relief as a basis for excusing conduct in the same way that the inner compulsion of the psychotic aggressor renders his conduct wrongful but excused. Both acts occur under overwhelming pressure. In one case it is the imperative of staying alive that causes the sailor to aggress against the first occupier of the plank; in the other case, it is the distorting effect of mental illness that commands the act of aggression. We see, then, that there are two types of excuse, one based on external and the other, on internal circumstances. In neither case can one say that the aggressor would choose to do the act if the situation were "normal." The aggressor's true personality or character remains concealed behind the overlay of circumstances that compels the action.

Linking the theory of excuses to the actor's character raises numerous problems, and it is not clear that I need to concede the linkage.[6] It should be enough, it seems to me, to stress the involuntary nature of excused aggression. We cannot blame either the psychotic aggressor or the shipwrecked sailor because they are acting in extremis. They are not choosing freely to commit aggression. Yet the very language I am using—the vocabulary of voluntariness and free choice—troubles some theorists skeptical about whether action is ever truly free, whether there is such a thing as free will. The skeptics, it seems, are inclined to ground the theory of excuses in their negating inferences from wrongful action to the actor's character. They think that by relying on the notion of character, they can justify criminal punishment without making what they take to be dubious assumptions about free will.[7]

The conventional position on these matters is termed "incompatibilist." It holds that fairly blaming human conduct would be impossible if the determinist hypothesis were true: if no one could have acted otherwise, then no criminal could be justly blamed for his or her actions. In the subset of cases where conduct is determined by circumstances, namely where the actor is excused, the basis for blame disappears. Determinism, then, is the extrapolation of the theory of excuses to the entire spectrum of human action. According to the incompatibilist, determinism is tantamount to the claim: all action is compelled and therefore excused.

The competing "compatibilist" position holds that the truth of the determinist hypothesis has no bearing on the justice of punishing criminal offenders. The condition for just punishment is the attribution, the bringing home, of the criminal act to the character or personality of the offender. If the action is attributable to the physical circumstances that shape and define the action, it is not an expression of who the actor really is. Punishment is justified, on this view, only if it is pitched to an action that expresses a person's true nature or character.

My sympathies lie with the incompatibilist position. There are, to be sure, problems making sense of what it means to be a choosing agent, a self-actualizing being, an autonomous agent—in short, a being with "free will." Actions that do not express the actor's personality would be random and arbitrary. In order to be coherent, our decisions must be grounded in who we are. This much can be conceded about the relationship between action and character. It does not follow, however, that tracing an action to the actor's character provides a sufficient rationale for punishment. If aggressive and harmful "action in character" were sufficient for just punishment, as compatibilists argue, there would be no apparent reason not to punish a wild horse for throwing its rider or a vicious dog for biting in conformity with its character. This, I take it is a reductio ad absurdum of the compatibilist position. No one wants to punish animals, but if there is no sound distinction available about the difference between the determined behavior of animals and the determined behavior of human actors, the practice of punishing one would justify punishing the other.

The tentative conclusion at this stage of the argument is that insanity and personal necessity represent parallel excusing conditions that negate the voluntariness and thus the responsibility of a wrongful act. Before we take this conclusion as the premise for further argument, however, we need to dispose of a recurrent objection. There is a tendency to think that the shipwrecked sailor has a stronger claim than a mere excuse akin to insanity. After all, he is acting to save his life; he has good reasons for displacing the first occupier from the plank. The claim is that perhaps his action is not wrong at all. He is doing what he has a right to do. While the psychotic aggressor is clearly wrong in his attacking an innocent person, the shipwrecked sailor may well be able to justify his conduct, at least partially.

At this point in the argument, the analysis of the shipwrecked sailor's defense interweaves with our intuitive assessment of the kind of defense that the first occupier of the plank should have to resist and defend his position. Kant argued that the first occupier should have a right not merely of personal necessity but of self-defense against wrongful aggression.[8] The difference, as he perceived it, was that while the shipwrecked sailor acts out of personal necessity, his aggression against the first occupier is nonetheless wrongful, a violation of his rights, and thus the first occupier is entitled to defend himself.

Admittedly, the distinction between these two Kantian characters fighting for their lives is not as sharp as it could be. A more compelling illustration of the relevant point presents itself in a variation of the famous cannibalism case, *Regina v. Dudley and Stephens*.[9] Two marooned and starving sailors, without food for eight days, decide to nourish themselves on the ailing cabin boy Parker. Suppose that as they are about to stab poor Parker, he comes to his senses and seeks to defend himself. Obviously, he should not be guilty of assault if he does so. How are we to explain the conflicting claims of the parties?

It would make sense to recognize an excuse of personal necessity on behalf of the two starving sailors; they are acting out of inner necessity. That the Queen's Bench convicts them and recommends mercy testifies only to the judges' lack of doctrinal imagination; it would have been better had they expressed their compassion in the form of an excuse. The more troubling question is whether one could, in theory, recognize a justification for killing one ailing cabin boy in order that two men survive. Three arguments weigh in on the other side. A straightforward utilitarian calculus suggests that the killing might be all right; after all it is better that two survive than that all three die of starvation. The case against justification relies in part on the moral imperative against killing innocent persons. Whatever the benefit that might result, there is no justification for taking the life of the non-offending cabin boy. Using the boy as food represents as clear a case as one can imagine of betraying the humanity of another, of using another exclusively as a means to one's own ends.

Even if one had utilitarian leanings, a second, pragmatic argument enters the case against justifying the killing of Parker as the lesser evil. The killing might indeed have produced a net gain in human life. Parker was likely to have died in any event, and his death substantially increased the probability that two men would survive.[10] Yet there is a great *danger* in allowing individuals to justify their action on cost/benefit grounds where they receive the benefits and others bear the costs. Their self-interest obviously lies in exaggerating the former and minimizing the latter. Oddly, neither the statutory formulations of necessity as a justification nor the literature on the point recognizes this potential for distorting the cost/benefit analysis. Yet the cases on tort law do acknowledge the point: acting in the interest of others is called public necessity and the person so justified in inflicting harm remains exempt from liability for the resulting damages. But private necessity, or causing harm to others in one's own self-interest, fails to generate the same exemption from liability.

A third, more controversial argument against recognizing a justification on behalf of Dudley and Stephens derives from the impermissibility of logically inconsistent claims of justification. If Dudley and Stephens are justified on grounds of lesser evils to kill Parker, then, according to a widely shared understanding of the concept of Right, Parker cannot also be justified in invoking self-defense on his own behalf. This thesis—call it the "one Right" thesis—is among the propositions about the criminal law that seem self-evident but are notoriously difficult to establish to everyone's satisfaction. The thesis holds that only one side to a zero-sum conflict (where one *gains* as much as the other loses) can act justifiably and thus be in the Right. Kant gives expression to this thesis in considering whether the shipwrecked sailor could have a right to endanger another in order to save his own life: "It is evident that were there such a right the doctrine of Right would have to be in contradiction with itself."[11] Those who reject the "one Right" thesis simply say that they see no reason to reject the possibility that two inconsistent claims might be both instances of justification.

Two strategies support this move. One strategy is to demote the significance of justification so that it comes closer to meaning something like "defense." The "one Right" thesis treats claims of justification as equivalent to the assertion of a right. If it cannot be the case that Dudley has a right to kill Parker and Parker has a right to defend himself, then nor could it be true that both are justified in their use of force. Treating justifications as rights derives from the term the implicit meaning of rendering an act compatible with *jus* or Right. The implication is clear as well in the German term *Rechtfertigung*, which, like justification, means bringing an act into harmony with higher principles of Law or Right. By depreciating the meaning of justification, however, one can create logical space for simultaneous and inconsistent claims of justification. This is Greenawalt's strategy in arguing that claims of self-defense, lesser evils, and law enforcement simply betoken "warranted action."[12] In Greenawalt's view, the shipwrecked sailor could be "warranted" in trying to gain control of the plank, and the first occupier could also be warranted in trying to protect his position of safety. Using the term "warranted" in this way brings the notion of justification close to the purely procedural idea of a "defense."[13]

An alternative strategy for rejecting the "one Right" thesis expresses a tragic vision of the legal and moral order. The thesis itself trades on our yearning to believe that all competing moral and legal claims can be ordered so that we can know in *any* particular situation of conflict who is right and who is wrong. In the conflict between Creon and Antigone in Sophocles' play, we want to assume that there is a right answer. Either Creon is right in declaring a ban on burying a fallen enemy solider; or Antigone is right in appealing to the higher law of Hades in insisting that she was right in violating the ban and burying her dead brother. Martha Nussbaum has argued compellingly that this yearning misconstrues the nature of tragedy.[14] It could well be the case that both Creon and Antigone are right in some significant way, or at least that we cannot fathom the full depth of the moral conflict and identify which side is right.

This view of the tragic nature of moral conflict has become increasingly fashionable. Abortion disputes are now a prominent example. The pitched battle about when fetuses are entitled to be treated like born children offers, it seems, little hope of resolution. Both sides stake out their positions, and adhere to them with little opening for a dialogue of reason. In conceding the tragic nature of the dispute, one need not slip into moral relativism and proclaim that all values are subjective and beyond rational criticism. The problem in the abortion controversy today is not that neither side has "right" on its side but rather that both do.[15] The arguments for protecting the fetus are compelling, but so too are the arguments for liberating women from unwanted pregnancies.

The sense of tragedy in moral disputes is catching. If there is tragedy in abortion disputes, there could also be tragedy in Kant's case of the shipwrecked sailor and in *Dudley & Stephens*. There might even be tragedy in the necessity of killing the psychotic aggressor. Yet the idea of moral tragedy is at odds with one of the most basic aspirations of legal and moral thought: If we ponder the matter long enough, if we engage in sustained reasoned discourse with our opponents, we should be able to arrive, eventually, at an acceptable moral consensus. The faith in a consistent moral and legal order dies hard, and that is the way things should be. No one has the wisdom to declare the quest pointless. Insisting on the truth of the meta-proposition, namely there is no right answer, seems to be as arrogant and dogmatic as the absolute faith that one has found the right answer.

Close moral conflicts, such as that between Creon and Antigone, make for good drama. The drama may even be enhanced by the belief that the conflict is irreconcilable. But what is true for the stage is hardly true for the world we live in. In my view there is no need ever to assume that moral conflict is insoluble, even though admittedly in some situations, such as abortion, the temptation is great to do so.

We have located two, perhaps three defenses that we can unhesitatingly treat as excuses for wrongful conduct. The internal compulsion of the psychotic aggressor excuses his conduct, and the external life-endangering circumstances of *Dudley & Stephens* should have excused their homicidal attack. There seems to be no difference, in principle, between the non-human compulsion of circumstances and the human compulsion represented by a gunman pointing his gun at a bank teller; the intimidating effect of the situation is the same, whether the source is the deprivation of food and water or a gun pointed at one's head. Thus the range of excuses should include not only personal necessity but the defense ordinarily called duress. Some writers would prefer to regard duress as a justification, but the three arguments against treating *Dudley & Stephens* as a justification apply as well in the case of conduct induced by human threats. The list of excuses includes, therefore, insanity, personal necessity and duress. All three of these defenses negate the actor's personal responsibility or blameworthiness for unjustifiably violating the law.

This analysis and grounding of excuses provides a foundation for considering the difficult question whether mistakes of fact and law generate excuses or whether they provide some alternative rationale for exempting a nominally criminal actor from responsibility and punishment. The problem is illustrated by the complexity of analyzing the mistaken perception of the conditions required for a justification of self-defense, consent or lesser evils. A good example is the mistaken judgment that one is about to be attacked and that deadly force is necessary to avert the attack. These might well have been the mistakes that Bernhard Goetz made when he shot four youths in the subway.[16] He thought they were about to attack him and that shooting was necessary to protect himself. Yet no one knows what the four youths would have done had Goetz not shot and there is no way of proving that more was necessary to contain the danger than merely drawing and pointing the gun.

There are at least three distinct ways of analyzing this dissonance between the truth of the matter and Goetz's perception of this truth. One approach is to assimilate the claims of putative justification to the claims of actual justification, as exemplified by the language of Model Penal Code §3.04 and the state codes enacted in its train. The reasonable perception of an attack is treated as equivalent to an actual attack for purposes of self-defense as a justification. Yet it is not entirely clear why the mistake need be reasonable; voices are often heard for the so-called subjective view of justification, which would treat as sufficient good faith belief in the conditions of justification, regardless of whether this faith is reasonable or not.

Alternatively one might argue that a mistake about the conditions of a defense negates the intent required for commission of the offense. Thus the House of Lords concluded in a controversial decision that any mistake, reasonable or not, about a woman's consent would negate the intent required for rape. If you assume that the intent required for rape is "the intent to have intercourse with a nonconsenting female," then indeed a man cannot formulate this intent if he believes, however irrationally, that the object of his sexual aims has consented to intercourse. There are many who would advocate an analogous intent for homicide, thus rendering any mistake about the conditions of self-defense a complete defense. Note that the position provides an alternative grounding for the subjective theory of justification.

A third way of approaching a putative justification concedes that many mistakes fall outside the intent required for the offense and yet balks at assimilating these mistakes to cases where objective facts generate good reasons for nominally criminal conduct. The residual possibility of analysis is that a mistake about the conditions of justification constitutes an excuse parallel to the excuses of insanity, personal necessity and duress. The argument would be that the mistake negates the voluntariness of the act in the same way that overwhelming pressure undercuts the voluntariness of choice. This was Aristotle's argument about mistake:

> Therefore that which is done in ignorance, or though not done in ignorance is not in the agent's power, or is done under compulsion, is involuntary...those done in ignorance are *mistakes* when the person acted on, the act, the instrument, or the end that will be attained is other than the agent supposed...Of involuntary acts some are excusable, others not. For the mistakes which men make not only in ignorance but also from ignorance are excusable, while those which men do not from ignorance but...owing to a passion which is neither natural nor such as man is liable to, are excusable.[17]

If the defense of mistake is in the nature of an excuse, it follows that it should be governed by the general requirements governing excuses. The most significant of these requirements is the principle that no excuse may be asserted by those at fault. This demand follows from treating voluntary conduct as a component of the actor's responsibility or blameworthiness. That which negates voluntariness, therefore, also negates responsibility and desert. And as the argument goes, no one should be punished who does not deserve it; desert and blame are implausible if the actor does not act voluntarily, that is, if he or she could not have been expected to do otherwise.

It follows that the conditions for excusing wrongful conduct must themselves be free of grounds for blaming the actor. Yet if his or her mistake reflects an unreasonable and irrational judgment of the facts, the conditions of the excuses are hardly fault-free. The lack of restraint, the indulgence, the failure to discipline one's reactions—these are the grounds for blaming the person who claims that his wrongdoing is excused. And if this is true, it must be the case that only reasonable mistakes can generate excuses in the cases of putative self-defense, consent and lesser evils. This seems to be the right result in cases of mistaken perceptions of consent in rape cases. Excusing all mistaken perceptions of consent rewards the brutal and the callous. There is no less need to sanction thoughtless, negligent overreaction in cases of self-defense and lesser evils. This seems like a plausible argument for treating mistakes about the conditions of justification as excuses. It follows that as there is a psychotic aggressor who may be resisted as a matter of self-defense, there is also a mistaken aggressor whose conduct is merely excused and not justified. If the stranger in the elevator reasonably thinks that I am about to attack him when I pull my handkerchief from my pocket, his falling upon me in an effort to disable me is a reasonable response and therefore excused.

There are some who think these cases of putative self-defense are justified. They would not claim that the psychotic aggressor is justified: insanity hardly gives one good reasons for acting. Yet the mistaken aggressor, they claim, does have good reasons. Kent Greenawalt has offered us the most sustained and sophisticated defense of this position and therefore I turn to a detailed analysis of his argument.[18]

Greenawalt imagines a case in which Roger intentionally destroys property in order to prevent the spread of a forest fire.[19] The decision to blast a fire break in one place rather than another depends on the actor's predicting the direction of the fire's spread, and that in turn depends upon his assessment of wind movements. "Employing the most advanced techniques" for making this judgment, Roger thinks that the wind is going to blow one way and in turn it blows the other way. His destroying the property is for nought. And yet Greenawalt thinks that though this conduct turned out to be wasteful, it was reasonable and therefore justified at the time of decision. How is this case different, one might ask, from a reasonable judgment that my companion in the elevator is about to attack me or a reasonable judgment that my date really wants sex even though she protests to the contrary?

Greenawalt has no qualms about saying "the risk Roger took was justified" and infers that his action was therefore warranted and justified.[20] A clever set of moves is afoot in pitching the idea of justification to the notions of risk and warranted behavior. The latter notion, as pointed out above, reduces the moral content of justification and therefore makes it easier to sustain the claim that a particular defense is a justification. More subtle, however, is the shift from harmful "action" to "reasonable risk" as the foundation of the defense. In deciding to destroy property in one place rather than another, Roger acts against a backdrop of reality defined by "the most advanced techniques for predicting wind patterns." The appearance of risk determines the parameters of his action. The implicit assumption of Greenawalt's analysis is that Roger is not mistaken at all. He competently and reasonably understands the risk and though there is later an "unfortunate outcome," he acts according to the circumstances. Given this way of thinking about risk and reality, Greenawalt's conclusion that the conduct is justified follows ineluctably.

Would he make the same argument about the man who reasonably thinks that his date has consented to sex (suppose he is told that she gets turned on by dissembling resistance)? Is this not also the case of acting on the basis of apparent reality, of a risk that she has consented in fact? My hunch is that Greenawalt would balk at this extension of his argument, and well he should. For in this case, there is a clear fact of the matter. She has not consented. This is a fact knowable at the time of the action. By contrast, there is no way of knowing, definitively at the time of the action, which way the wind will carry the forest fire. All that can be known is the risk, as perceived by the "the most advanced techniques for predicting wind patterns." In the case of rape, the fact of the matter is the woman's nonconsent; in the case of the forest fire, ultimate reality is the probability that the wind will shift this way or that.

Greenawalt picks an easy case to lay the groundwork for the argument that a reasonable choice based on a reasonable perception of reality justifies the resulting action and consequences. The next step is to extend the argument to a situation in which there is a fact of the matter knowable at the time of the action. This he does in contemplating the fact pattern in the *Young* case in New York.[21] The defendant came upon a street fight in which a youth was struggling with two middle-aged men. Reasonably concluding that the young man was the victim, he intervened on his behalf. It turned out, however, that the two middle-aged men whom he assaulted were police officers engaged in properly affecting an arrest. The New York trial court convicted Young of assaulting the officers. This seems clearly unjust because, as Greenawalt concludes, "Young is to be praised, not blamed, for what he did, and members of society would wish that others faced with similar situations would act as Young did."[22] It is clear that in view of his reasonable mistake, Young should not be blamed; he should not have been convicted. The linchpin of Greenawalt's argument, however, is the move from not-blaming to praising. Given the world as it appeared to Young, what he did was right. Even if the result was unfortunate, the action on the basis of appearance was correct. It was the kind of decision we would want others to emulate.

Two factors intersect in Greenawalt's defense of treating reasonable mistakes about justifying conditions as themselves claims of justification. The first is the shift from reality to appearances, from the fact of the matter to the contingent world of risk. The second is the judgment that the decision on the basis of appearances is worthy of emulation. When these two factors converge, the case is strongest that the defense should be classified as justification based on the world as we rationally perceive it. It follows that if it appears reasonable to me that I am about to be attacked, I am justified in responding with defensive force, even deadly force.

Yet there is an important difference between the case of fighting the forest fire and the mistaken use of defensive force. In the latter case, the innocent person reaching for his handkerchief suddenly finds herself the object of mistaken aggression. What should she do? It is clear that she has to be able to defend herself, and for all the reasons set forth in the analysis of the psychotic aggressor. The most plausible account of her defense is self-defense against the wrongful, but mistaken aggressor. If the mistaken aggressor is treated as justified, one can affirm self-defense on the part of the innocent victim only by denying the "one Right" thesis. It is not surprising, then, that theorists skeptical about the distinction between justification and excuse tend also to reject the thesis that only one person in a zero-sum game can act justifiably. The soft-edged world of the skeptic readily admits of inconsistent claims of justification.

The most compelling case for the skeptic is one with which Greenawalt begins his argument: the case of the forest fire where it is difficult to treat a judgment based on appearance as a mistake. I admit that when there is no apparent truth of the matter, as in the case of the forest fire, it is difficult to treat a judgment that turns out to be false as a mistake. As Greenawalt thinks about these judgments, they represent the "morally best possible act in the circumstances"[23] and if so, they could hardly be wrongful, and if not wrongful there is nothing that need be excused.

As soon as one falls the slightest bit away from the best possible act under the circumstances, however, the matter gets much more complicated. Greenawalt imagines a variation of the forest fire case in which the actor does make a mistake that "results from conscious indifference to relevant information or from inadequate care or effort in acquiring information."[24] Roger could have made a better prediction of the way the wind would blow but he failed to do so. His prediction is mistaken not relative to the fact of the matter (for that is apparently unknowable) but relative to the best possible meteorological prediction.

Greenawalt appears to agree with this basic proposition, for he concedes these cases of mistake should be treated as excused rather than justified.[25] Yet the distinction between these two categories becomes even more subtle when he claims that if Roger is less experienced than the average forest ranger and makes the wrong choice but "the best that could be expected of him,"[26] Greenawalt just does not know if this is a case of justification or excuse. He is equally perplexed about the case in which the prediction is reasonable for the average ranger, but the actor has greater expertise than average and could have made an even more refined judgment.[27] At this point in the argument Greenawalt brings his acute philosophical skills to a halt, for he claims that the distinction between justification and excuse does not matter in practice: "In either case, no criminal liability will be imposed."[28] He remains perplexed about the borders between justification and excuse, but he maintains faith that the distinction is sound.

Greenawalt fails to consider whether we could improve our practices by distinguishing systematically between defenses based exclusively on the rectitude of conduct (justifications) and defenses based upon the absence of personal responsibility (excuses). Had he thought more about the practical implications of the distinction, he might have maintained his efforts to work out the boundaries between the two types of defense. Upon further reflection, he might have taken the position that even in the case of the forest fire, there is a fact of the matter presupposed in the effort to make the best possible prediction under the circumstances and that a prediction that turned out to be wrong should be treated as an excusable mistake rather than a justified assessment of the risk.

The motive for further work on the distinction between justification and excuse is indeed practical. Distinguishing between the two kinds of verdict could make a noticeable difference in the way the public understands a verdict of acquittal.

Consider the findings of not guilty in the *Goetz* case or in the state trial of the four police officers who beat up Rodney King. None of these defendants argued that their conduct was objectively justified. Their arguments consisted, in effect, of excuses based upon reasonable perceptions of danger. As the situation appeared to them, the argument went, they had reasonable grounds to fear an assault. Yet the findings of not guilty treated them as though their conduct were really justified. It would have been far better—far more comprehensible in the public mind—for the jury to have found first that their conduct was unjustified, that they had violated the rights of the victim, but that they were personally excused. As we have a split verdict in all cases of alleged insanity, we should also have a split verdict in all cases of alleged excuses—whether it be of insanity, personal necessity, duress or reasonable mistake about the conditions of justification. The jury should first find and declare to the public that a defendant like Bernhard Goetz or Officer Laurence Powell in Los Angeles acted unjustifiably and wrongfully in using force against someone who was not actually engaged in attacking them as required by the law of self-defense. Then, as a second stage of the proceedings, the jury should be able to declare the defendants excused on grounds of reasonable misperception of the danger. Of course, a judge sitting without a jury could make the same findings and thereby contribute to an understanding in the public mind that an acquittal is not synonymous with justifying and approving the defendant's behavior. Clarifying the bases for these decisions might mitigate the rage that some people experience when they think of an acquittal as an invitation to others to shoot in the subway or pull their police batons at the slightest provocation.

As we look back on the "psychotic aggressor" a generation later, we can begin to see that the theoretical refinements begun in that article can have an enormous payoff in practice. When that payoff is realized depends on how many of us come to see that the distinction between justification and excuse refines our criminal justice system and makes it more comprehensible to the public at large.

CHAPTER 19

Reply: A View of the Psychotic Aggressor: Two Generations Later

■

*Alon Harel**

There is too much with which I agree with George Fletcher to justify writing this comment. Most fundamentally, I agree with his observation that "for thinking people, legal cultures set no limits" (189). In the words of George Fletcher, "What counts are the arguments that are mustered, not the language or culture in which the arguments are made" (189). This is an important observation; it should guide our investigation of criminal law, and, if I may add, there is no criminal law theorist who contributed more to establish the veracity of this statement than George Fletcher himself. Let me therefore endorse this insight and examine in light of it some of Fletcher's arguments.

Fletcher's essay "The Psychotic Aggressor—A Generation Later" raises some important conjectures but it is not aimed at fully answering all the questions it raises. It makes suggestions, raises questions, and provides insightful guidelines, but it also leaves a lot of questions unanswered. I wish to raise critical concerns with respect to two issues: the "one right" thesis and the reason provided by Fletcher at the end of his article as to why the distinction between justification and excuse is so central to criminal law and ought to be addressed by legal theorists.

Fletcher adheres to what he labels the "one right" thesis—the thesis maintaining that there are no "logically inconsistent claims of justification" (195). Fletcher takes this view to imply that in the famous *Regina v. Dudley and Stephens* case— the case of two starving sailors who saved their lives by nourishing on the ailing cabin boy Parker—either Parker was justified in resisting the two sailors or the sailors were justified in killing Parker. Under the "one right" thesis it cannot be

---

*Philip P. Mizock and Estelle Mizock Chair in administrative and criminal law, Hebrew University Law Faculty, Jerusalem, Israel.

the case that the sailors are justified in killing Parker *and* Parker is justified in resisting their attack.

I think Fletcher is wrong in describing the "one right" thesis as cases of "logically inconsistent claims of justification." The claims that both the sailors and Parker are legally justified are not two logically inconsistent claims. Fletcher also believes that to the extent that such a conflict between claims of justification arises, it is a tragic moral conflict. Fletcher rejects this conclusion and defends the "one right" thesis on the grounds that although such tragic moral conflicts make for a good drama, there is no need ever to assume that a moral conflict is insoluble.

While I do not have a compelling argument for why such conflicts exist, I see no a priori arguments precluding the possibility of such moral conflicts. To the extent that no such a priori arguments are provided, it seems to me that one ought to examine each case of alleged moral conflict on its own terms without presupposing either the existence or the absence of tragic moral conflicts.

At the end of his essay, Fletcher argues against a pragmatic approach to criminal law that fails to acknowledge the significance of the distinction between excuses and justifications. As an example of the importance of this distinction, Fletcher discusses the Rodney King case in which policemen used excessive force against King on the basis of a false conviction that King would use violence to prevent his arrest. The policemen were acquitted. Fletcher does not challenge the acquittal but argues that the acquittal "treated them as though their conduct were really justified" (202). In Fletcher's view: "It would have been far better—far more comprehensible in the public mind—for the jury to have found first that their conduct was unjustified... but that they were personally excused" (202).

Why is it so important in Fletcher's view to insist on the distinction between excuse-based and justification-based acquittal? Fletcher's answer is unconvincing. In his view, "[c]larifying the bases for these decisions might mitigate the rage that some people experience when they think of an acquittal as an invitation to others to shoot in the subway or to pull their police batons at the slightest provocation" (202).

While I believe the distinction is important, it is important for a different reason. Its importance cannot be based on the need to mitigate the public rage or to make the decision comprehensible to the public. Criminal law is not a means to appease the public or gain its sympathy or understanding. The distinction between justifications and excuses is an important legal distinction simply because a person who has an excuse has a different legal status than a person who has a justification. It is the task of courts to draw legal distinctions and use these distinctions in their reasoning. Mitigating rage or enhancing public comprehension provides no reason for courts to draw distinctions that have no basis in legal reality. At most the mitigation of rage or broad public comprehension is a desirable by-product of drawing the legally relevant distinctions.

CHAPTER 20

Domination in the Theory of Justification and Excuse

George P. Fletcher

I. Introduction

The major currents driving legal theory have largely bypassed the field of criminal law. Neither the economists nor the advocates of critical legal studies ("crits") have had much to say about the theory of criminal responsibility or the proper mode of trying suspects. The economists have fallen flat in applying their rationalist models to the problems of punishing wrongdoers.[1] The "crits" have had little to add beyond Mark Kelman's one original and provocative article.[2]

Of all the schools on the march in the law schools today, the feminists have had the most to say about the failings of the criminal law. The critique of rape law burst on the intellectual scene with Susan Brownmiller's best-selling book, *Against Our Will: Men, Women and Rape.*[3] Susan Estrich made her career by opening up the field of rape both to teaching and serious scholarship.[4] More recently, the field of self-defense has come under scrutiny as a body of law that, like rape, traditionally discriminated against the rights of women. In this context, we have heard much about the battered woman syndrome and how it supposedly should apply to improve the position of desperate women who kill their partners under borderline circumstances, such as the case of the partner being asleep. These are situations that have always fallen beyond the conventional bounds of self-defense. With sympathy for battered women, however, commentators have taken a closer look at the traditional contours of self-defense in an effort to make the doctrine bend in their preferred direction.[5]

This article addresses the debate about the proper structure of claims of self-defense and, in particular, whether special rules should apply on behalf of women who kill those who have persistently battered them in the past. In this context, the feminist arguments accrue to the benefit of (female?) criminal defendants. It is worth underscoring, however, that the feminist critique of criminal law does not always come out in favor of the accused. Witness the rape law reformers, who broke away from the Warren Court's pattern of consistently favoring the rights of the defendant. The interests of women in rape cases lie in enabling the state to convict more easily. Thus Susan Estrich and others have argued against the corroboration requirement to support the testimony of witnesses complaining of rape.[6] Estrich also argued against the ruling in the William Kennedy Smith case that three other women who complained of sexual abuse by the defendant would not be able to testify against him.[7]

The pro-prosecution slant of feminist influence has led to some questionable legal decisions, such as the ruling in the Mike Tyson prosecution that three witnesses would not be permitted to testify that they saw Desiree Washington necking with Mike Tyson a half hour before the alleged rape.[8] My aim here is not to assess whether feminist influence has gone too far in strengthening the position of the prosecution, but rather to assess the other side of the argument: the effort to expand the rules of self-defense to make it easier to acquit women who kill their husbands under circumstances that would not ordinarily qualify as self-defense. I shall assess these arguments with a view particularly to whether a history of domination between husband and wife (more broadly, batterer and the person battered) should bear on the interpretation of self-defense. In conclusion, I shall explore the application of the same in other contexts of alleged domination, particularly in the notorious first trial of the Menendez brothers.

To keep a real case of wife battering in mind, think of the prosecution of Judy Norman in North Carolina.[9] John Norman had engaged in systematic dehumanizing actions toward his wife Judy. Beginning about five years after the wedding, he started drinking and, while drunk, assaulting her, throwing glasses and bottles at her, putting out cigarettes on her, breaking glass against her face and crushing food on her face. In addition, he forced her to engage in prostitution to generate income for their household and mocked her streetwalking in front of "family and friends." If not satisfied with her earnings, he beat her and called her "dog" and "whore." On a few occasions, he made her eat pet food out of the pet's bowl and forced her to sleep on the floor. Apparently, according to her testimony, he kept up these degrading practices for about 20 years until the day in mid-June 1985 when she shot him in the back of the head.

There is ample corroboration of her story in the words of others. For example, her daughter Phyllis testified that her father had beat her mother "all day long" immediately prior to the shooting. Also, Judy Norman had appealed with complaints to the police and to a domestic abuse center at the local county hospital.

The police would not intervene unless Judy took out a warrant for John's arrest, and that she feared to do; she had experienced beatings in retaliation for prior efforts to leave the scene of her suffering. The situation went from bad to worse. John was enraged and out of control, as a boarder testified, for having been arrested on a drunk driving charge. At that point he forbad Judy from eating for three days prior to the shooting. The family tried to get food to her, the mother sent over groceries, but Judy Norman feared retaliation and a beating if she disobeyed her tyrannical husband. The words that we have availed to describe these anti-human conditions are too easily subject to abuse. This was a gulag she called home.

If there was ever a clear relationship of dominance, this was it. This is a case of obvious evil. And the legal system turned a blind eye. The temptation is to think that the oppressed and battered woman should take the law into her own hands. The victim of the shooting, John Norman, had it coming to him. But however tragically Judy Norman's appeals to the authorities went unheeded, she cannot put herself in the position of judge and executioner. If the authorities had responded and prosecuted John Norman, they could not for all his wickedness impose the death penalty. There may be justice in his dying, but it is not a form of justice that the legal system can readily accommodate.

One is reminded here of Joel Feinberg's useful distinction between an action that is just and one that is justified.[10] John Norman's fate may be just in some ultimate sense, but the legal system focuses solely on whether Judy's killing him was justified as a matter of self-defense. To be justified as self-defense, an action must fall under the rules governing the defense in the particular jurisdiction. In general terms, these rules address five distinct issues:

1. THE ATTACK MUST BE IMMEDIATE

Self-defense is about repelling attacks—or more broadly, about fending off possible violations of rights. The first question, then, is when the impending violation is sufficiently proximate to trigger a legitimate response. The most common formula is that the attack must be imminent; it must be about to happen.

The requirement of imminence means that the time for defense is now. The defender cannot wait any longer. This requirement distinguishes self-defense from the illegal use of force in two temporally related ways. A preemptive strike against a feared aggressor is illegal force used too soon, and retaliation against a successful aggressor is illegal force used too late. Legitimate self-defense must be neither too soon nor too late.

In the case of a preemptive strike, the defender calculates that the enemy is planning an attack or surely is likely to attack in the future, and therefore it is wiser to strike first than to wait until the actual aggression. Preemptive strikes are illegal in international law as they are illegal internally in every legal system of the world.[11] They are illegal because they are not based on a visible manifestation of aggression; they are grounded in a prediction of how the feared enemy is likely to behave in the future.

The line between lawful self-defense and an unlawful preemptive strike is not so easily staked out, but there are some clear instances of both categories. Because the general principles of international law are the same as those of domestic legal systems, we can ponder some dramatic examples among current international events.

Think about the various military moves that Israel has made against Arab forces in the last twenty years. The strike against the Iraqi nuclear reactor in 1981 was clearly preemptive, for the supposition that the Iraqis would use the reactor for military purposes was based on an inference from private Israeli military intelligence. Even if it is true that the Iraqis intended to manufacture a nuclear bomb, that activity hardly constitutes an attack against Israel. Israel has its own nuclear weapons, and its government would hotly contest the inference that this fact alone establishes its intention to bomb Arab territory. Preemptive strikes are always based on assumptions, more or less rational, that the enemy is likely to engage in hostile behavior. Israel could well argue that it did not wish to take the chance that Iraq would use nuclear weapons against the Jewish state as well as against Iran and other opponents of the Baghdad regime. Be that as it may, there is no doubt that the air attacks on the reactor constituted a preemptive strike. The possible attack by Iraq was not sufficiently imminent to justify a response in self-defense.

More controversial is Israel's attack against Egypt in June 1967, initiating the spectacular Israeli victory in the six-day war. Egypt closed the Straits of Tiran to Israeli shipping, amassed its troops on Israel's border and secured command control over the armies of Jordan and Iraq. In the two weeks preceding the Israeli response on June 5, Nasser had repeatedly made bellicose threats, including the total destruction of Israel. The question is whether Egypt's threat was sufficiently imminent to justify Israel's response under international law. Perhaps Egypt was merely bluffing; perhaps its leaders did not know whether they intended to attack or not. There is no doubt, however, that Egypt was attempting to intimidate Israel by behaving as though it were about to attack (unlike Iraq in the reactor incident). Israel took the Egyptians at face value; it responded to what appeared to be an attack in the offing. Could Israel have waited longer? Of course it could have. But the requirement of imminence does not require that guns actually fire, that bombs be in the air. And if anything short of letting the missiles fly constitutes an imminent attack, then that requirement was fulfilled in the June 1967 conflict between Egypt and Israel.

In cases of interpersonal as well as international violence, the outbreak might be neither defensive nor preemptive. It could be simply a passionate retaliation for past wrongs suffered by the person resorting to violence. Retaliatory acts seek to even the score to inflict harm because harm has been suffered in the past.

Retaliation is the standard case of "taking the law into one's own hands." There is no way, under the law, to justify killing a wife batterer or a rapist as retaliation or revenge, however much sympathy there may be for the wife wreaking retaliation. Private citizens cannot function as judge and jury toward each other. They have no authority to pass judgment and to punish each other for past wrongs.

Those who defend the use of violence rarely admit that their purpose is retaliation for a past wrong. The argument typically is that the actor feared a recurrence of the past violence, thus the focus shifts from past to future violence, from retaliation to an argument of defending against an imminent attack. This is the standard maneuver in battered-wife cases. In view of her prior abuse, the wife arguably has reason to fear renewed violence. Killing the husband while he is asleep then comes into focus as an arguably legitimate defensive response rather than an illegitimate act of vengeance for past wrongs.

We shall return to this requirement, as it applies in the *Norman* case, after surveying the other standard elements of self-defense.

2. THE ATTACK MUST BE UNLAWFUL OR UNJUSTIFIABLE

The general proposition is that self-defense is unavailable against the lawful use of force. If the police are properly executing an arrest warrant, defensive force is impermissible. The same is true of force that is itself justified as self-defense. The principle is that if force is exercised as a matter of right, it would be self-contradictory to recognize a right to resist the exercise of the right.[12]

The important corollary of this proposition is that if the attacker is merely excused and not justified, then the attack is nonetheless contrary-to-right and in this sense unlawful. A defensive response is justified. It makes a difference, therefore, whether we classify insanity, duress, or mistake as claims of excuse or justification. Later, I will show specifically why it is so important that self-defense based on a mistaken perception of the facts be treated as excused rather than justified.

3. THE LEVEL OF FORCE MUST BE NECESSARY

If we assume, in the *Norman* case, that the requirement of an imminent attack is satisfied, the question remains whether the other elements of justifiable self-defense are present in the shooting. Judy's shooting her husband in the back of the head must have been necessary under the circumstances. Was there a less drastic effective response? This inquiry calls for a counterfactual conditional response. One has to imagine what would have happened had Judy just wounded her husband in the leg. In view of his threats against her in the past, this might have been a dangerous option. But in every case, using lesser force incurs risks. The question is always whether it is fair to impose these risks on the person attacked. Our sympathy for the plight of the particular victim of attack undoubtedly influences our sentiments about the imprecise question whether using lesser force was mandated under the circumstances.

4. THE RESPONSE MUST BE PROPORTIONAL TO THE HARM THREATENED

The requirement of proportionality adds a problem beyond the necessity of the defensive response. To understand the distinction between proportionality and necessity, think about the ratio between the means of resistance and the gravity of the attack. Necessity speaks to the question whether some less costly means of defense, such as merely showing the gun or firing a warning shot into the air, might be sufficient to ward off an attack. The requirement of proportionality addresses the ratio of harms emanating from both the attack and the defense. The harm done in disabling the aggressor must not be excessive or disproportionate relative to the harm threatened and likely to result from the attack.

Some examples will illuminate the distinction. Suppose that a liquor store owner has no means of preventing a thief from escaping with a few bottles of scotch except to shoot him. Most people would recoil from the notion that protecting property justifies shooting and risking the death of escaping thieves. It is better from a social point of view to suffer the theft of a few bottles of liquor than to inflict serious physical harm on a fellow human being.

It is not simply that property rights must sometimes give way to our concern for the lives and well-being, even of aggressors. Suppose that the only way for a woman to avoid being touched by a man harassing her is to respond with deadly force by, say, cutting him with a razor blade. May she engage in this act necessary for her defense rather than suffer the personal indignity of being touched? Most people would probably say that a little unwanted touching is not nearly as bad as being cut or stabbed in response. Of course, if she were threatened with rape, she could use every necessary means at her disposal to protect herself. No legal system in the Western world would expect a woman to endure a rape if her only means of defense required that she risk the death of her aggressor.

Proportionality in self-defense requires a balancing of competing interests, the interests of the defender and those of the aggressor. As the innocent party in the fray, a woman defending against rape has interests that weigh more than those of the aggressor. She may kill to ward off a threat to her sexual autonomy, but she has no license to take life in order to avoid every petty interference with her autonomy. If the only way she can avoid being touched is to kill, that response seems clearly to be excessive relative to the interests at stake. In the *Norman* case, however, the threat to the wife was sufficiently great to warrant a deadly response.

If Judy Norman's response was necessary, it was presumably also proportional to the harm she faced.

Even if we have two thumbs on the scale in favor of the defender, however, there comes a point at which the aggressor's basic human interests will outweigh those of an innocent victim, thumbs and all. There is obviously no way to determine the breaking point, even theoretically. At a certain point our sensibilities are triggered, our compassion for the human being behind the mask of the evil aggressor is engaged, and we have to say "Stop! That's enough."

5. THE INTENT OF THE DEFENDER MUST BE TO DEFLECT THE ATTACK

Three of the preceding characteristics of self-defense—imminence, necessity and proportionality—speak to the objective characteristics of the attack and the defense in response. In order to establish that these requirements are satisfied, we need not ask any questions about what the defender herself actually knows about the circumstances of the attack and the defense. The relevant questions are purely objective.

The consensus of Western legal systems is that in order to invoke a sound claim of self-defense, the defender must know about the attack and act with the intention of repelling it. Surprisingly, some leading scholars think that in a case of criminal homicide, the accused should be able to invoke self-defense even if he does not know about the attack.[13] Their argument is that if you cannot be guilty of homicide by killing someone who is already dead (no matter what your intent) you should not be guilty of homicide by killing an aggressor (no matter what your intent). No harm, no crime. And there is arguably no harm in killing an aggressor.

Yet there is an important moral difference between pumping lead into a dead body and killing an aggressor in self-defense. We can comfortably say that there is no harm in the former case (except perhaps interference with a dead body), but injuring or killing a human being remains a harm, even if the harm is inflicted in self-defense. Justifying the infliction of harm against a human being acknowledges the harm but asserts that it was inflicted for good reason. The good reason is one that the defendant must personally entertain. It must be his or her reason for inflicting the harm.[14]

Note that the intention required is not to make the aggressor suffer but merely to thwart the attack, to ward it off, to prevent it from happening. Working out this distinction between making the aggressor suffer and fending off an attack was a critical advance in the Western understanding of self-defense. So far as I know, Thomas Aquinas was the first to note the distinction and to limit self-defense to an intention designed to repel the attack.[15] Without this distinction, it is tempting to think of self-defense as a form of private punishment, designed to make the aggressor suffer for the attack.

Yet the distinction between punishment and self-defense is fundamental. Without a clear understanding of the conceptual distinction between the two, we would find it hard to explain why it is possible to use deadly force even in those cases where capital punishment would be out of the question. For example, deadly force is permissible to defend against rape, but capital punishment for rape would be unconstitutional. When a nation abolishes capital punishment, as have most European countries, it does not thereby modify its law of self-defense. Also, self-defense is permissible against unjustified, but excused, aggression. This would not be conceptually tenable if defensive force were considered an act of punishment. The excused aggressor is never punished for his deed, but he may suffer serious physical consequences when his aggression is justifiably thwarted.

These five elements of self-defense—imminence, unlawfulness, necessity, proportionality, and intention—interweave in the standard legislative definitions of legitimate defensive force. Consider the Model Penal Code: "[Subject to certain limitations] the use of force upon or toward another person is justifiable when the actor believes that such force is immediately necessary for the purpose of protecting himself against the use of unlawful force by such other person on the present occasion."[16]

The requirement of imminence is reflected in the language "immediately necessary... on the present occasion." The element of "unlawfulness" is made explicit; the principle that excused attacks are unlawful is recognized in § 3.11, which explicitly limits the scope of § 3.04. The phrase "immediately necessary" also captures the necessity of the response. The element of proportionality is made explicit in § 3.04(2)(b), which limits the use of deadly force to cases of threatened homicide, serious bodily harm, kidnapping, or rape. The required intention to defend oneself comes through in the pivotal position occupied by the word "believes" in the drafting of the section.

The word "believes" is so centrally located in § 3.04(1) that it appears that what is at stake is not an actual unlawful attack, but merely the belief of the actor that an attack is under way. This mode of drafting captures what is in fact a deep misunderstanding about self-defense in American jurisprudence. The requirement of intention—number five in the list above—has become the necessary and sufficient condition for justifiable self-defense.

According to a strict reading of § 3.04, if the actor "believes that such force is immediately necessary... on the present occasion," then it is justifiable not only in his mind, but in fact. In other words, all that is required is the right intention. The correct mental state justifies the infliction of harm on an innocent bystander.

This is the approach to self-defense reflected in a jury instruction litigated in the 1977 Washington case, *State v. Wanrow*, now a leading precedent supporting expanded self-defense on behalf of battered women:

To justify killing in self-defense, there need be no actual or real danger to the life or person of the party killing, but there must be, or reasonably appear to be, at or immediately before the killing, some overt act, or some circumstances which would reasonably indicate to the party killing that the person slain, is, at the time, endeavoring to kill him or inflict upon him great bodily harm.[17]

This, it is fair to say, is the standard "subjectivist" view of self-defense in the United States. The defense comes into being on the basis of the reasonable belief of the defender. The requirement of reasonable belief is also implicit in the structure of the Model Penal Code: a later provision, § 3.09, makes it clear that § 3.04 is limited to beliefs that are nonnegligent and reasonable.

Note the subtle transformation that has occurred in the theory of self-defense. The intent requirement becomes a standard of belief, which in turn becomes the mirror for all the objective requirements of imminent and unlawful attack and the necessity and proportionality of the response. In the end, all that counts is the belief, albeit reasonable belief, that these objective facts obtain in the real world.

II. Two Propositions About Justification

Having surveyed this background material about self-defense as it is understood in American law, I wish to assert two propositions that I will defend as the relatively original contribution of this paper.

The first claim is that beliefs alone cannot justify the infliction of violence on another human being. Reasonable beliefs can excuse wrongful aggression against another person but they cannot justify that aggression. Some interaction in the real world is required for a claim of justified harm. The factor of reasonable belief bears properly not on justification but on the excuse of reasonable mistake in using defensive force.

The second claim is that past relationships of dominance cannot and should not affect the analysis of justification. The proper bearing of past relationships of power and dominance bear, at most, on the reasonableness of the mistaken belief in the necessity of defensive force.

At first blush it is difficult to understand how anyone would argue that beliefs alone could possibly justify harming an innocent person. But there are two arguments that seem to come forward from time to time to uphold the position of American law. One is a misinterpretation of Kantian moral theory that goes something like this. Kant writes in the first sentence of his leading work on ethical theory, *Foundations of the Metaphysics of Morals*: "Nothing in the world can possibly be conceived...which can be called good without qualification except a good will."[18] The common mistake is to read the reference to the "good will" as synonymous with a good intention and therefore to believe that Kant upholds a view of the following sort: If one's intentions are proper, one's action is proper. This view is a little more than a tendentious and clever misreading of Kant, whose conception of the will has nothing to do with intentions. Yet once this misreading is negotiated, the rest follows easily: The move from intentions to beliefs is not a great leap, and therefore it follows that believing in the necessity of self-defense seems, erroneously, to be a proper basis for concluding that defensive force is morally proper. And if it is morally proper, it presumably is also justified. There are at least a half dozen errors in this common line of argument. But somehow the argument hangs together well enough to convince a lot of writers.

The big factor missing from the above line of argument is why the belief must be reasonable. If any proper belief can find its warrant for justification in the first sentence of Kant's *Foundations*, then there is no reason to insist that the belief be not only in good faith but reasonable as well.

If, in contrast, the issue of belief bears solely on an asserted excuse of mistake, then the requirement of reasonableness does make sense. Excuses negate culpability or blameworthiness, and therefore a good excuse is one that is free from blame. Only reasonable mistakes have this quality of being free from blame and therefore adequate to negate the defender's culpability for unjustifiably injuring the putative aggressor.

The second argument squarely addresses the requirement of reasonable perception of the conditions for a justification and finds in the matrix of reasonableness the conditions for justifying the action. The best exposition of this argument comes in an article by Kent Greenawalt, in which he poses a case of necessity as a justification: forest ranger Roger intentionally destroys property in order to prevent the spread of a forest fire.[19] The decision to blast a fire break in one place rather than another depends on the actor's predicting the way the fire is going to spread, and that in turn depends on his assessment of wind movements. "Employing the most advanced techniques"[20] for making this judgment, Roger thinks that the wind is going to blow one way and in turn it blows the other way. His destroying the property is for nought. And yet Greenawalt thinks that, though this conduct turned out to be wasteful, it was reasonable and therefore justified at the time of decision.

Greenawalt has no qualms about saying "the risk Roger took was justified" and infers that his action was therefore warranted and justified.[21] Now the focus of the justification is no longer the action, but the risk Roger decides to run. In deciding to destroy property in one place rather than another, Roger acts against a backdrop of a world perceived according to "the most advanced techniques for predicting wind patterns."[22] The world of risk, as he understands it, is the world in which he acts. The implicit assumption of Greenawalt's analysis is that Roger is not mistaken at all. He competently and reasonably understands the risk and though there is later an "unfortunate outcome," he acts correctly under the circumstances. Given this way of thinking about risk and reality, Greenawalt's conclusion follows that the conduct is justified.

Greenawalt picks an easy case to lay the groundwork for the argument that a reasonable choice based on a reasonable perception of reality justifies the resulting action and consequences. The next step is to extend the argument to a situation in which there is a fact of the matter knowable at the time of the action. This he does in contemplating the fact pattern in the *Young* case in New York.[23] The defendant came upon a street fight in which a youth was struggling with two middle-aged men. Reasonably concluding that the young man was the victim, he intervened on his behalf. It turned out, however, that the two middle-aged men whom he assaulted were police officers engaged in properly effectuating an arrest. The New York court convicted Young of assaulting the officers.[24] This seems clearly unjust because, as Greenawalt concludes, "Young is to be praised, not blamed, for what he did, and members of society would wish that others faced with similar situations requiring instant judgment would act as Young did."[25] It is good for people to intervene in fights to protect the person they reasonably perceive to be the victim.

It is clear that in view of his reasonable mistake, Young should not have been convicted. The linchpin of Greenawalt's argument, however, is the move from not-blaming to praising. Given the world as it appeared to Young, what he did was right. Even if the result was unfortunate, the action on the basis of appearance was correct. It was the kind of decision we would want others to emulate.[26]

Two factors intersect in Greenawalt's defense of treating reasonable mistakes about justifying conditions as themselves claims of justification. The first is the shift from reality to appearances, from the fact of the matter to the contingent world of risk. The second is the judgment that the decision on the basis of appearances is worthy of emulation. When these two factors converge, the case is strongest that the defense should be classified as a justification based on the world as we rationally perceive it. It follows that if it appears reasonable to me that I am about to be attacked, I am justified in responding with defensive force, even deadly force.

Greenawalt's strategy converts mistakes about harmful actions into justifiable judgments about perceived reality. Yet the distinction between a reasonable and therefore justifiable judgment and a harmful but justified action is worth maintaining. Reasonable mistakes in self-defense cases are about actions that are harmful to innocent people—unjustifiable, unlawful actions that can, at the most, be excused on grounds of mistake.

III. Domination and Imminence

The central debate in the theory of self-defense for the last decade has been whether we should maintain a strict requirement of imminence in assessing which attacks trigger a legitimate defensive response. The traditional rule confronts a critique favoring relaxation of the rule primarily to make it easier for battered women to assert a claim of self-defense in cases of doubtful imminence. The typical case in dispute is like the *Norman* case—one in which the battered woman kills her batterer when he is asleep or otherwise quiescent. In her trial for the 1985 killing, Judy Norman was held to the strict imminence requirement and, as might be expected, her claim of self-defense failed. She was convicted of manslaughter, sentenced to six years in prison but released three months into her term after the governor commuted her sentence.[27]

To many critics it seems that Judy Norman had no practicable, reasonable choice. Her shooting her husband in the head was a necessary response under the circumstances. Thus, the argument goes, there must be something wrong with the imminence requirement. The critique of the imminence requirement is buttressed by additional considerations:

1. The shift in language in the Model Penal Code from imminence to "immediately necessary."
2. Hypothetical cases involving long range latent dangers that make killing necessary even though the attack does not seem to be imminent.[28]
3. The subjectivist interpretation of self-defense that seems to make the interpretation of imminence dependent on the perceptions of the defender.[29]

A number of these objections would be satisfied by recognizing an excuse of self-defense based on necessary action where there is no practicable alternative. Under this standard, Judy Norman would have been excused and acquitted.

The more difficult questions arise in the context of justification. Does the imminence requirement belong in a properly constructed standard of justifiable self-defense? And if it does, is it proper to condition the interpretation of imminence on the power relationship between the parties? Does it follow that the battered wife, subject to the domination of her husband, should be allowed a broader interpretation of imminence?

In response to these questions, I confess that the existing literature of criminal law has done a woefully inadequate job in constructing a case for the imminence requirement. The traditional rule, arguably based on patriarchy, hardly persuades feminist critics. Needed is an argument of principle about why only imminent attacks—those about to happen—should trigger a right of self-defense.

Explaining the imminence requirement confronts the initial difficulty of overcoming the subjectivist bias in current thinking about self-defense.[30] Generating a defense for a strict imminence requirement differs from an account of why the defender must believe, in the words of the Model Penal Code, that the use of force is "immediately necessary" to defend himself or another "on the present occasion."[31] So far, accounts of both the objective and subjective view remain wanting.

To gain some perspective on the problem, think of the analogous requirement in cases of necessity. In this context, the tendency of the courts is to insist on an actual situation of necessity—an actual emergency—to justify a departure from a criminal norm. There must be an actual danger to the public or private individuals before demonstrators can even hope to justify trespassing, violating a police order, or damaging property. The rationale for the defense is that the individual violates a nominal prohibition for the sake of a greater social good.[32]

The Model Penal Code, which has had an enormous influence in generating acceptance of the necessity defense, fails to mention an imminence requirement under § 3.02. Unless a contrary legislative intent appears, every criminal prohibition is subject to being overridden by the private judgments of individuals. Yet in the defense as adopted by several states, the requirement of imminent danger has sensibly reasserted itself.[33]

In the context of necessity, the standard of imminence provides a solution to the problem of limiting the competence of individuals to override legislative judgment about the social welfare. Limiting the privilege of necessity to cases of imminent risk means that the individual cannot pick the time, the place, or the victim of his judgment about what the law requires him to do. If an accident victim lies bleeding on the sidewalk and it is necessary to take someone's car to get him to the hospital, the range of car owners who might suffer the intrusion is limited. The situation of imminent risk prescribes the parameters under which an individual can assert his view of rightful conduct.

The limited range of competence to invoke the necessity defense stands in contrast to the free-ranging legislative power to prescribe general rules of socially desirable conduct. Every socially justified prohibition benefits some people and harms others, yet it is the legislature's prerogative to make these judgments that impose uncompensated costs on some people. The legislature is empowered, in short, to pick the victims of the common good. Yet these are not the costs that we wish private individuals to impose on each other, even if the private judgment of social welfare is correct. Thus the requirement of imminent risk insures that the stage be set before the individual play his part in furthering the common good.

The significance of the imminence requirement in cases of self-defense bears some resemblance to the account I have given of imminence in necessity cases. In the latter context, the imminence requirement expresses the limits of governmental competence: when the danger to a protected interest is imminent and unavoidable, the legislature can no longer make reliable judgments about which of the conflicting interests should prevail. Similarly, when an attack against private individuals is imminent, the police are no longer in a position to intervene and exercise the state's function of securing public safety. The individual right to self-defense kicks in precisely because immediate action is necessary. Individuals do not cede a total monopoly of force to the state. They reserve the right when danger is imminent and otherwise unavoidable to secure their own safety against aggression.

Several implications follow from this account of the imminence requirement. First, the requirement properly falls into the domain of political rather than moral theory. The issue is the proper allocation of authority between the state and the citizen. When the requirement is not met, when individuals engage in preemptive attacks against suspected future aggressors, we fault them on political grounds. They exceed their authority as citizens; they take "the law into their own hands." Precisely because the issue is political rather than moral, the requirement must be both objective and public. There must be a signal to the community that this is an incident in which the law ceases to protect, that the individual must secure his or her own safety.

Now so far as the issue is objective, the interpretation of attacks as imminent depends exclusively on the qualities of the attack—on its proximity to success and on the danger latent in the threatened use of force. The background relationships of the parties, whether one is dominant and the other subordinate, should not matter. This seems to be obvious in relations between states. Whether Egypt is engaged in an imminent attack against Israel depends exclusively on what they are doing. The general power relationship between the parties might have some bearing on the interpretation of the danger expressed by amassing troops at the border. But whether one state does the bidding of the other should not give the subordinate party either an advantage or disadvantage. If this proposition applies as between Israel and Egypt, it should also govern the relations between Judy Norman and her battering husband.

In cases like *Norman*, however, an additional element seems to influence those who seek to relax the law in favor of the battered wife who strikes back. The political issue at stake in interpreting the requirement of imminence is whether the state's authority to keep the peace should yield to the individual's authority to use force in self-protection. The argument is often made that in these cases the state fails to exercise its protective function. Judy Norman in fact sought protection from social agencies and she failed to receive it.[34] In other cases, the police fail to intervene to protect those who are victimized at home. In these situations, where there is a gap between the theory of state protection and the reality of police indifference, it becomes difficult to assess whether the courts of the state should be required to recognize a broader than usual right of self-defense. The problem, it seems, is to formulate a precise test of how badly the police have failed and to determine a proportionate adjustment in the law of self-defense.

This is about as good a case as I can make for the view that the underlying relationship of dominance and subordination should not bear on the analysis of self-defense as a justification. The deeper point that I have established, I hope, is that because the requirement of imminence is political rather than moral, the element of self-defense known as an "imminent attack" must actually occur in the real world. The attack signals to the community that the defensive response is not a form of aggression but a legitimate response in the name of self-protection. Self-defense becomes compatible with the state's supposed monopoly over the use of force precisely because the community can understand the exceptional nature of self-defense in response to imminent attacks.

IV. Lessons from the *Menendez* Case

The political analysis of imminence as a public event helps us to understand where the trial court went wrong in the notorious first trial of the Menendez brothers. At first it did not seem as though there would be much controversy about the guilt of Lyle and Erik Menendez, who in the summer of 1989, at the ages of 21 and 18, entered their own home with shotguns just purchased in San Diego and emptied fifteen rounds into their father and mother, Jose and Kitty Menendez. Yet as the trial unfolded, the televised parade of surprising and shocking witnesses became the emblem of the current fascination with relationships of abuse.

The plan to beat murder charges was this. The boys would testify that each was subject to years of sexual abuse by both father and mother, that immediately prior to the killings Kitty pulled Lyle's toupee off his head and this event supposedly generated sympathy in Erik, the younger brother, for Lyle's embarrassment. Erik then confessed to Lyle that his father had sodomized him for the last twelve years; this prompted Lyle to go to his father and insist that the abuse cease or he would make it public. Jose supposedly responded with a threat to kill the two boys. A defense of self-defense began to come into relief.

The problem that Erik and Lyle faced was the same as the typical problem in the battered wife cases. On the day they were killed, the parents did nothing to indicate a threat to their sons. They were sitting at home, watching television. They were no more overtly aggressive than the sleeping husbands in cases like Judy Norman's. How could the brothers overcome this obvious impediment? The basic rule in California was the same as in North Carolina. Erik and Lyle could claim self-defense only if they were in "reasonable fear of imminent death or great bodily harm."[35] And surely this was not the case.

Yet California recognizes a doctrine called "imperfect self-defense" that permits a defendant to rely on self-defense even if his fear is unreasonable. This defense derives its force from the assumption that if a killer fears an attack, however unreasonably, he does not act with the malice aforethought necessary for murder. The doctrine makes some sense: if a person kills in self-defense, then he acts, more or less, in good faith, and good faith is incompatible with hatred or malice toward the victim.[36] North Carolina recognizes this principle too, but it could not help Judy Norman on appeal. Even if the jury finds that this fear-based good faith prompted the killing, they should convict of manslaughter, and Judy had been convicted only for manslaughter.

Going into the *Menendez* trial, public outrage strongly backed the Los Angeles District Attorney who was committed to seeking the maximum conviction and punishment, including the gas chamber for the cold-blooded murder of the two people to whom, if morality means anything, the Menendez boys owed a duty of respect. Yet when Lyle and Erik began testifying about their sexual abuses at the hands of their father and the participation by their mother, the public began to sway to their side. Lyle gave such a good performance that as he stepped down from the stand several jurors were in tears. The appetite for the details only increased as Erik testified and defense lawyer Leslie Abramson tried to create the impression that some hard evidence corroborated their testimony. In fact virtually no evidence, except an ambiguous photograph of the defendants as nude children, supported their tales of abuse. And there was compelling silent evidence on the other side. They both complained of forced sodomy; yet there were no signs of bruising or tissue damage to their anuses. When they confessed their crime to their psychiatrist Jerome Oziel, they failed to mention their fear of a preemptive attack. No members of the family had witnessed any parental behavior that could qualify as physical or psychological abuse. In the end, the defense's case turned almost entirely on the persuasive but self-interested performance that Lyle and Erik gave on the stand.

Yet there were portions of the public and of the jury who were eager to believe. An abusive parent is an enemy—much more of an enemy, apparently, than a child who puts a shotgun to his mother's face and blasts away. The case for the defense degenerated rather quickly into an attempt to convict the parents. This was the real strategy from the outset. As Leslie Abramson said as the defendant's testimony began to make its impact: "If people would just think for a minute, there are some fundamental precepts of family life. Precept No. 1 is that children love their parents. Good parents do not get shotgunned by their kids. Period."[37] The nub of the defense, therefore, was that the parents must have done something to deserve their fate. This is the classic strategy of blaming the victim.

The most disturbing aspect of the transformation of the case into a trial of the parents for abuse is that journalists took this testimony of abuse seriously and accepted the wildcat defense theory that prior abuse somehow made the killing all right. As the distinguished New York Times reporter Seth Mydans formulated the "core question" of the trial, it was: "to what degree a history of child molestation can justify parricide."[38] This is a truly remarkable perversion of the trial and its doctrines. First, the formulation of the question presupposes that there was "a history of child molestation." At a certain point in their coverage, the mainstream press simply lost its critical judgment and assumed that where there was testimony, there must be facts. Even if we assume that there was a "history of child molestation," the suggestion that this history could justify the killings would come as a great surprise to Judge Stanley Weisberg. The most that could be said under the judge's instructions to the jury was that a fear of "imminent death or great bodily harm" would negate the malice required for murder. There was no reference in the judge's rulings to the possibility of justifying the double parricide.

On the legal questions as they were actually formulated by the judge, two juries—one for Lyle and one for Erik—could not make up their minds. After an average of three weeks of stormy deliberations (nineteen days for Erik, twenty-five for Lyle), the representatives of the people remained divided, roughly half voting for murder and the other half for manslaughter. Erik's jury split right on the gender line. Six women accepted the story of abuse and voted from the outset for the less severe verdict. The men remained skeptical until the end. Five held out for first-degree murder, and one was willing to compromise on second-degree murder.

It is not clear why the women were so easily persuaded. One would expect that they would have identified with the defenseless Kitty. The most likely supposition is that the cry of abuse resonates so strongly with women that two female defense lawyers, Abramson and Jill Lansing, could persuade them that this was another instance of the phenomenon that has plagued women as victims of rape and domestic battering. Yet associating the alleged abuse of Lyle and Erik with the condition of women who demonstrably suffered, as did Judy Norman, illustrates the tendency of good ideas to find their cheapest common denominator. Judy Norman could not escape without fearing being caught and beaten, as she had been beaten in the past. Nothing stopped the monied Menendez boys from getting in their Alfa Romeo, a recent present from their allegedly abusive father, and driving their way to freedom. If they motored their way to San Diego to buy a shotgun, they could find their way out of their silver-lined unhappiness.

Judge Stanley Weisberg made a tragic mistake in admitting the evidence of abuse in the first place. The legal point that governed his decision was exactly the same as in the Norman case. To claim a relevant fear of "imminent death or great bodily harm," the threatened attack must indeed be imminent. It must be about to happen in an objective sense visible to any observer. If Judge Weisberg had understood imminence to be an objective precondition for the argument of "imperfect self-defense," he could have ruled uncontroversially that the feared attack was simply not imminent. There was no evidence of a planned attack against the boys that evening or even that week. And if the attack was not objectively imminent, the defendants' supposed fear was irrelevant to the charge of first-degree murder. And if their fear was irrelevant, so was the evidence of supposed abuse. The judge should have ruled all of it inadmissible.[39]

Yet the subjectivist tendencies of American legal thought exercise an enormous attraction. The dissent in *Norman* succumbed to the same argument: "In the context of the doctrine of self-defense, the definition of 'imminent' must be informed by the defendant's perceptions."[40] In other words, if the defendants believed that the attack was imminent, they could escape liability for first-degree murder. It is not clear whether the jury even cared about whether Lyle and Erik believed the attack was imminent or not. So long as the defendants could devise an argument for treating the evidence of abuse as relevant (it supposedly explained their fear of attack) they could testify about their "history of child molestation," put their victim-parents on trial, and thus secure a balancing of their wrong against their parents' wrong. We should never forget the *Menendez* trial, for it illustrates the great myth that juries and the public care about legal questions as they are formulated in jury instructions. No matter how precisely the judge defined the issue of imperfect self-defense, the press and their readers would view the dispute as a question whether "a history of child molestation can justify parricide."

The Menendez debacle leaves two messages for us to ponder. First, there is no way to limit arguments of domination and abuse to the justification of force in situations of ongoing domestic violence between men and women (or between adult gay couples). Some feminists may have thought that advancing the battered woman's claims of self-defense would help women as a special class that deserved special protection after centuries of discrimination. The battered woman syndrome would represent something like affirmative action in the courts; it would compensate for all the prejudice that had accumulated against women, particularly in rape cases. But if there is any principle guiding legal thought, it is the egalitarian impulse toward generalization by analogy. The courts cannot recognize a defense for the blue-eyed and refuse it to the brown-eyed. There is no way of limiting a new defense to a privileged class. If the "syndrome" relaxes the criteria of self-defense for women, it must have the same impact for battered men and battered children. This was obvious to Leslie Abramson, Erik's lawyer, who made it clear from the outset that the defense would develop a defense for battered children that would draw on the innovations developed for battered women.

The second message of the Menendez trial is that if relationships of dominance are introduced in the context of self-defense and other claims of justification, the tendency of well-meaning observers will be to repeat Mydans' mistake: Treating the issue as an exploration of whether a history of abuse and domination justifies retaliatory action by the subordinated party. In self-defense cases, as they are now tried, this temptation is ever present.[41] There is no reason to confuse the law even further by inviting arguments about whether a history of domination could justify striking back by the victimized person.

V. Domination as It Bears on Excuses

The question remains: How should the law bring relief to people like Judy Norman? There must be a way to accomplish this end without triggering the kind of distortions represented by the Menendez trial. My view, which I have expressed many times, is that the law should make greater use of excusing conditions. The prior relationship between the parties should bear on aspects of self-defense that sound in the theory of excuses, namely the recognition that the action is wrongful but nonetheless not a fit basis for blaming and punishing the person who resorts to violence.

Two features of self-defense properly appeal to criteria that negate the blameworthiness of the defender. One is the theory of necessity. Where there is no reasonable choice but to attack someone who is sleeping or otherwise in a quiescent mode, the proper argument is not that the attack is right and lawful, but that the actor is not properly subject to blame for acting on the instinct of self-preservation. A prior relationship of dominance bears upon the analysis of necessity, for it assists us in understanding whether reasonable alternatives permitted an escape from the situation without resorting to the use of deadly force.

Relations of dominance also enter into the analysis of mistaken belief in the imminence of an attack. A good example is *State v. Wanrow*,[42] in which the defendant suspected a man named Wesler of having molested her son and violated her daughter. When confronted with these charges, Wesler went to the home of Yvonne Wanrow's friend. Wesler, "a large man who was visibly intoxicated, entered the home and when told to leave declined to do so."[43] A quarrel ensued. Wanrow, who was 5'4" and then on crutches, had a pistol in her purse. Suddenly Wesler appeared behind her. "She testified to being gravely startled by this situation and to having then shot and killed Wesler in what amounted to a reflex action."[44] Yvonne Wanrow was convicted of second-degree murder.[45]

The conviction was reversed partly because the trial court had admitted into evidence the tape recording of a telephone call in which Wanrow's friend made statements that apparently incriminated the defendant by making the shooting appear vengeful rather than defensive.[46] For our purposes, the more interesting grounds for reversal are the defects asserted in the instruction quoted above.[47] The instruction directs the jury to consider only those circumstances occurring "at or immediately before the killing." The Supreme Court of Washington responds: "This is not now, and never has been, the law of self-defense in Washington. On the contrary, the justification of self-defense is to be evaluated in light of all the facts and circumstances known to the defendant, including those known substantially before the killing."[48]

In particular, the court noted, the decedent's reputation for aggressive behavior, so far as it was known to the defendant, should enter into an assessment of the "degree of force which...a reasonable person in the same situation...seeing what [s]he sees and knowing what [s]he knows, then would believe to be necessary."[49] Note that the prior relationship of the parties, including factors leading to the aggressor's dominating behavior, bear properly only on the reasonable perception of danger. This is the aspect of self-defense that, as I have argued, should be considered grounds for excuse rather than justification. If Yvonne Wanrow was mistaken about the danger that the decedent represented, she could try to invoke the relationship of the parties in assessing whether her mistake was reasonable and therefore compatible with an excuse.

In an additional, arguably redundant paragraph, the court notes the concentration of the disputed instruction on the male gender as though the standard "to be applied is that applicable to an altercation between two men."[50] This arguably deprived the defendant of the equal protection of the laws. A correct instruction would enable "the jury to consider her actions in the light of her own perceptions of the situation, including those perceptions which were the product of our nation's long and unfortunate history of sex discrimination."[51]

These last lines have spawned a great deal of misunderstanding. There is no doubt, as I have argued since the early 1970s,[52] that excusing conditions should focus on the individual circumstances of the person asserting the excuse. If a female defender is substantially weaker than her assailant, this factor obviously should enter into the analysis of whether her perception of danger is reasonable under the circumstances. The problem, in my view, is not the "history of sex discrimination" (however malign that history may have been) but rather the unfortunate history of a system of criminal law that has paid too little attention to rendering justice in individual cases of excusable criminal actions.

CHAPTER 21

Reply: Battered Women, Sleeping Abusers, and Political and Moral Theory

*Joshua Dressler**

Even when I disagree with George Fletcher, I admire his scholarship. First, his writings frequently shape scholarly and legal debate. For example, his first major article as an academic provided an original (and now generally accepted) perspective on the criminal law implications of turning off life-support machinery on individuals in a chronic vegetative state.[1] Even more impressively, Fletcher almost single-handedly inspired attention to the distinction between justificatory and excusatory defenses.[2] Indeed, he inspired a scholarly renaissance in the field. At a time when constitutional criminal procedure received most of the attention of American criminal justice academics, Fletcher inspired many of the greatest legal minds to reflect on and write about substantive criminal law. A second reason for my admiration is that Fletcher does not shy away from taking unpopular positions. He is provocative. We need more scholars who force us out of our intellectual complacency, even if we ultimately disagree with them.

Fletcher's article on battered women demonstrates these admirable qualities of his scholarship. Focusing again on the justification/excuse distinction, he invites us to swim against the intellectual and political currents of his time. He calls into question the dominant view then (and perhaps now): that self-defense law should be changed—the traditional imminency requirement liberalized or abolished—to permit battered women to use lethal force against their abusive partners in nonconfrontational circumstances (i.e., when the batterer is not attacking the woman and may even be asleep).

*Frank R. Strong Chair in Law, Michael E. Moritz College of Law, The Ohio State University.

Fletcher provokes us: he calls into question preemptive strikes, and retaliative force disguised as self-protection, by having us question the justifiability of a homicide that at first glance seem so obviously appropriate, for example, Judy Norman taking the life of her violent and degrading husband, John, while he sleeps. And, Fletcher seeks to convince us of his position by having us consider matters as provocative as Israeli attacks upon Egypt and Iraq. If he were writing his essay today, I can imagine Fletcher using the highly controversial American invasion of Iraq, and President George Bush's defense of it as preemptive self-defense, to explain his position.

Fletcher begins by asserting the proposition—one he has made many times— that the conception of "justification" should be limited to real, objectively existing, conditions that render the actor's conduct morally right (or, at least, morally permissible).[3] Fletcher's rejection of "putative justifications"—a claim of justification based on a mistaken, albeit reasonable, belief that justifying conditions exist—has in turn been rejected by most scholars (including me)[4] and by virtually all courts and penal codes. Starting from a premise that few legal observers accept is not a great way to begin to make one's case about self-defense. But one can reject Fletcher on this point and still accept his conclusion that the law need not, and should not, approve of a battered woman killing her sleeping batterer.

As Fletcher sees it, the traditional imminency requirement belongs "in a properly constructed standard of justifiable homicide" (216). He sees this issue as a matter of political, rather than moral, theory. We ordinarily leave it to the legislature, he reasons, to "pick the victims of the common good" (217); however, when a deadly threat exists, that threat is imminent, and when deadly force is necessary to respond to that imminent threat, the government (through its police force) cannot protect the threatened party, so it is appropriate to allow her to respond in self-protection. The requirement of imminence, Fletcher nicely points out, "insures that the stage [is] set before the individual play[s] his part in furthering the common good" (217). The aggressor's "attack signals to the community that the defensive response is not a form of [retaliatory] aggression [by the battered woman] but a legitimate response in the name of self-protection" (219). In the absence of such imminence, Fletcher reasons, we fault the actor on political grounds for exceeding her authority as a citizen, for deciding for herself what is best for the community; or we may blame her for retaliating for a prior harm—for inflicting private punishment (indeed, executing her abuser) rather than allowing the public to handle the matter through the criminal justice system.

As Fletcher points out, we cannot justify an imminency (or, if you will, non-imminency) rule that is limited to battered woman. Why them and nobody else? What about other victims of domination—battered men, child abuse victims, women in general? We know that we cannot realistically create a rule that is so particularized: expanding the rule for battered women means that we are devising a rule that will expand the justification defense of self-defense for *all* persons.

I, too, would retain an imminency-type rule.[5] I, too, do not justify nonconfrontational homicides. But I follow a somewhat different route. First, unlike Fletcher, I recognize putative justifications. But rather than fight that battle here, it is enough to say that even if battered woman syndrome (BWS) evidence is admitted to prove that the battered woman subjectively believed that her sleeping abuser represented an imminent threat (and, thus, that her actions were intended to be self-protective and not retaliatory), it would be wrong to permit BWS evidence to try to show that her subjective beliefs were reasonable. To claim that a reasonable person might think that a sleeping man represents an *imminent* threat is virtually to defend the oxymoron of a "reasonable irrational person"; to suggest that a person *that* far out of touch with reality possesses a reasonable belief about the situation is to obliterate the distinction between "justification" and "excuse." So, even if Fletcher is wrong about putative justifications generally, the prevailing "reasonable belief" rule cannot "save" Judy Norman. So, let's look further.

Fletcher fears (I would have emphasized this point more than he does) that once the imminency requirement is watered down or abolished, it is easy to shift imperceptibly to a different question: Does this person, for example, Judy Norman's despicable husband, deserve to die? Is his death—when he attacks, when he is asleep, or *at any time*—justifiable because of his prior conduct and/or his despicable character or (if you will) evil soul?

Let's not fool ourselves. Many persons who advocate self-defense "reform" simply believe that abusers like John Norman deserve to die because of their past abusive conduct, without regard to the future (their potential threat to take a life). When my criminal law students read about Judy Norman, and I ask them to put aside discussion of BWS and simply tell me whether she was justified in killing her husband while he slept, often a majority of them say that she was. Why, I ask? Their answer comes down to this: because John Norman was a moral monster, he deserved to be crushed like a noxious insect. Explained in slightly more attractive clothing, these students are saying that John forfeited his right to life by his earlier, ongoing abusive conduct.

Yes, as Fletcher suggests, we can offer a political theory objection to this reasoning. We can say that none of us is qualified to determine when another person's character or soul justifies a private execution. But there is also a moral argument: we should not treat people like noxious insects whose lives are, permanently, socially worthless. We should never kill a person like we swat a fly—without a second thought.

Are we *really* prepared to assert the moral claim that a person forfeits his right to life, now and forever, because of his prior depraved conduct? If so, then Judy Norman had a right to kill John even if he had suffered a stroke a week earlier and no longer represented a threat to her life. And, if the moral forfeiture theory is accepted, Judy should be allowed to call on her brother, or a neighbor, or even a contract killer, to kill the noxious insect we know as J. T. Norman. Do we *really* believe this? I doubt it. Or, at least, I hope not.

One of the reasons for a temporal (e.g., imminency) requirement is the belief—the moral proposition—that even a bad guy should not be killed unless we are very certain that his death is necessary. An imminency requirement is the best way to enforce that moral proposition. Predicting the future is always a risk; but when an attack is under way or imminent, the risk of factual error is reduced to virtually nil. Any factual error at this point is a justifiable one—not because the decedent forfeited his right to life but because our natural right to life justifies defensive action based on reasonable appearances.[6]

Judy Norman's plight properly shocks us. We cannot believe that the law would punish her for killing her abuser, so many onlookers look to the most obvious target—the traditional imminency requirement—and argue for its abolition. But, as Fletcher reminds us, we can conclude that Judy was unjustified in killing her husband and yet potentially *excuse* her for her unjustifiable action.

Fletcher spends too little time on the excuse solution. I have argued elsewhere[7] that sometimes we should excuse a battered woman who kills in nonconfrontational circumstances—and we can do so without arguing that she is "crazy," as some lawyers used to argue in defense of their client. The basis for excuse would be a duress-type claim that suggests that some battered women lack a fair opportunity to conform their conduct to the law. It is wrong to expect a person to demonstrate saintly behavior; if jurors, representing the community, believe that there but for the grace of God go them, then moral condemnation and punishment of the battered woman is unjustifiable; she deserves to be excused for her unjustifiable conduct. *That* is the right moral message to send, one I think George Fletcher might find plausible.

DOMINATION AND PROTECTION OF VICTIMS

CHAPTER 22

Blackmail: The Paradigmatic Crime

George P. Fletcher

The ongoing debate about the rationale for punishing blackmail assumes that there is something odd about the crime. Why, the question goes, should demanding money to conceal embarrassing information be criminalized when there is nothing wrong with the separate acts of keeping silent or requesting payment for services rendered? Why should an innocent end (silence) coupled with a generally respectable means (monetary payment) constitute a crime? This supposed paradox, however, is not peculiar to blackmail. Many good acts are corrupted by doing them for a price. There is nothing wrong with government officials showing kindness or doing favors for their constituents, but doing them for a negotiated price becomes bribery. Sex is often desirable and permissible by itself, but if done in exchange for money, the act becomes prostitution. Confessing to a crime may be praiseworthy in some circumstances, but if the police pay the suspect to confess, the confession will undoubtedly be labelled involuntary and inadmissible. If there is a paradox in the crime of blackmail, these other practices of criminal justice should also strike us as self-contradictory.

Contrary to the popular view in the literature, I wish to argue that blackmail is not an anomalous crime but rather a paradigm for understanding both criminal wrongdoing and punishment. That is an ambitious claim, one that requires at least a clear plan of exposition. My project is to seek "reflective equilibrium"[1] across ten cases that are pivotal in the debates about the rationale for criminalizing blackmail. Reflective equilibrium requires a convincing fit between the agreed-upon outcomes in the ten cases and general principles that can account for these outcomes. After stating the cases and their legal resolutions, I will consider possible explanatory principles. The desiderata that I set for a sound analysis are not only that we explain the results but that we explain why blackmail is *criminal*—not only in the United States but in all civilized legal systems.

The latter requirement bears underscoring. It will not be sufficient, for example, to explain blackmail's status as a crime simply on the ground that it is immoral or that it leads to the inefficient use of resources. Countless immoral and inefficient activities are not punished.[2] Affixing these labels to blackmail could, at most, be a first step in explaining why it is a crime. The inquiry would then focus on why the immorality or inefficiency warrants punishment. As we shall see, explaining the simple phenomenon of punishing blackmail requires an excursus into the tangled web of theories justifying the entire institution of criminal punishment. In order to account for blackmail as a crime, I offer a novel retributive theory of punishment—a theory that, so far as I know, has never before been articulated in the literature on punishment. The task is complex but simple. Blackmail turns out not to be a paradox but rather a paradigm for thinking anew about the nature of crime and punishment.

I. Ten Cases

We begin, then, with standard cases that fall on both sides of the line, some constituting blackmail, others, falling illuminatingly in the category of lawful behavior.

1. *Crime case:* D threatens, if not paid, to report V's suspected crime to the local prosecutor.[3]

Blackmail

2. *Tort case:* V rams his car into D's. D threatens to sue if V does not compensate D for the resulting damage.[4]

No Crime

3. *Hush money:* D threatens to reveal a damaging truth, say a sexual peccadillo, about the celebrity V unless the latter pays "hush money." The threat is supported by incriminating pictures.[5]

Blackmail

4. *Late employee:* D, V's employer, threatens to fire V if he does not get to work on time.

No Crime

5. *Lascivious employer:* D, V's employer, threatens to fire V unless he sleeps with her.[6]

Blackmail

6. *Baseball case:* D offers to sell V a baseball autographed by Babe Ruth with knowledge that V's child, who is dying, would receive solace from having the ball. D demands $6000 for the ball.

No Crime

7. *Dinner kiss*: *D* says to *V*: "If you do not go to dinner with me, I will not kiss you." Alternatively, *D* says to *V*: "If you do go to dinner with me, I will kiss you."

No Crime

8. *Tattoo case*: *D* tells his friends that unless they pay him money, he will have his entire body tattooed.

No Crime

9. *Political embarrassment*: *V* is a black political candidate. *D* is a black activist with antiwhite views, whose connections to *V* are an embarrassment to *V*. *D* goes to *V* and tells him that unless he is paid off, he will speak out and repeatedly declare his support for *V*, thereby sabotaging *V*'s electoral chances.

Blackmail

10. *Paid silence*: Same story as in 9, but *V* goes to *D* and offers him $20,000 to "lay low" until after the election.[7]

No Crime

Of these ten cases, four represent clear instances of criminal blackmail; six are related cases where the consensus appears to be that the behavior is not subject to conviction either for blackmail or for any another offense. Yet the cases are very closely related. They all involve inducements by *D*, an offer of a benefit or the threat of a harm, designed to bring about a certain form of behavior in *V*. How should we go about distinguishing them? What categories should we use for classifying them?

Taking these cases as our guide, we can quickly dispose of several false leads. We will not take seriously, for example, the conventional distinction between threatening to disclose information (no. 3, *hush money*) and threatening other forms of harm, such as dismissing an employee (no. 5, *lascivious employer*). A principled distinction among the cases based on the mode of trying to get the behavior one wants is hard to imagine. Nor should we put much emphasis on whether the desired behavior consists in the surrender of property (no. 3, *hush money*; no. 9, *political embarrassment*) or sexual favors (no. 5, *lascivious employer*). Recognizing this distinction, as German law does,[8] suggests that blackmail is a crime against property—something like theft or acquiring property by false pretenses. But that seems to place excessive emphasis on the blackmailer's acquisitive end, with insufficient attention to the means of realizing that end.

The striking feature of blackmail is the way the defendant seeks to induce the behavior of another, not the peculiar interest that the victim sacrifices. Even if we did distinguish between inducing property transfers, on the one hand, and inducing other sorts of behavior, on the other, all we would gain would be two versions of blackmail running parallel to each other. Of course, the interest sacrificed must be significant, however vague that threshold may be: it is not enough that one is induced to go to dinner for fear of not being kissed (no. 7, *dinner kiss*). We may concede that blackmail in the narrow sense is limited to the acquisition of property; but blackmail in the broad sense encompasses all actions aimed at inducing the victim to give up something significant, something like money, property, sexual favors, or political liberties. We shall be concerned with blackmail in this broad sense.

II. Threats and Offers

It is tempting to stake out a path through the ten case results by distinguishing between threats and offers. The argument is that in the *baseball* case (no. 6) the refusal to sell at a lower price is not blackmail because it represents the withholding of an offer, not the making of a threat.[9] Threats are coercive, but withholding offers is not. Coercion is immoral because it deprives the victim of an option that she would have had, and this deprivation interferes with her autonomy, i.e., her freedom of action.

Yet not all threats, not all acts of coercion, are immoral or criminal; for example, the threat to sue in the *tort* case (no. 2), is considered permissible. So too the threat in the *tattoo* case (no. 8). An all too facile resolution of these cases is that they contain threats that D has the right to make. Joel Feinberg distinguishes these cases from the criminality of threatening to lodge a criminal complaint on the ground that one has a duty as well as a right to file the complaint.[10] There is no duty to sue in tort and no duty to tattoo or abstain from tattooing oneself. It is unclear why it should matter whether D is under a duty. True, Anglo-American contract law addresses whether demanding payment for the performance of a pre-existing duty constitutes valid consideration. But contract doctrines have little to teach us about the nature of criminal wrongdoing.

That the defendant's action constitutes a threat is clearly not a sufficient condition for blackmail, though it might be a necessary one. Accordingly, the distinction between threats and offers, if sound, could help us understand some of the cases. One could say, for example, that the precise difference between the *political embarrassment* case (no. 9) and the *paid silence* case (no. 10) is that in the former D makes a threat, while in the latter V makes an offer. Yet the distinction between offers and threats is not so easily drawn. The two versions of the *dinner kiss* (no. 7) are functionally equivalent. If you do not come, I do not kiss; if you do come, I do kiss. It appears to be the same deal. Is the kiss an offer or the withholding of the kiss a threat? The classification does not depend on whether it is good or bad to be kissed. If it is bad to be kissed, then withholding becomes the offer, and puckering up, the threat.

To make the distinction between offers and threats, one must first discern the normal state of affairs. If A kissing B is normal, then withholding the kiss is a threat rather than an offer; if two parties normally keep their distance, then the threat consists in making contact. If we know the baseline of normalcy, we may regard proposed changes for the worse as threats, and proposed changes for the better as promises to confer benefits. The baseline of normalcy is fairly obvious in the *baseball* case (no. 6), in which the seller proposes to give the parent the benefit of the autographed baseball, however outrageous the price. The baseline here is the seller's ownership of the ball; the proposed benefit, the definitive transfer of title and control. Because we are clear about the baseline, we readily perceive the transfer of title as an act conferring a benefit on the purchaser.[11]

This, I take it, is the point of Nozick's distinction between productive and nonproductive exchanges.[12] Selling the baseball is clearly productive in the sense that both sides gain something by the trade. In cases of blackmail, however, the exchange is not productive for "if nonproductive exchanges were impossible or forceably prohibited so that everyone knew they couldn't be done, one of the parties to the potential exchange would be no worse off."[13] In other words, in the paradigmatic *hush money* case (no. 3), the normal situation presumably is that the pictures and the information remain suppressed. Relative to that baseline, *V* would be no worse off if revealing the pictures were strictly enjoined. Of course, if the normal situation is that the information leaks out, then *V* is surely worse off if she is prohibited from paying hush money. Whether the exchange is taken to be productive or nonproductive depends on what we take to be the normal state of affairs apart from the blackmailer's offer.

I am skeptical about whether a coherent account is available for these parallel distinctions between threats and offers and between nonproductive and productive exchanges. The basic idea is that some things that we do to and for others increase their freedom (their "opportunity set") and other actions decrease their freedom. Whether *A*'s acts increase or decrease *B*'s freedom depends, however, on what would happen if *A* were not present in *B*'s life. Yet the latter condition, "if *A* were not present," is insuperably ambiguous. Does it mean that *A* does not have the information that *A* could release to the press or does it mean that *A* does not ask for payment to conceal the information? When the mugger *A* says to *B*, "Your money or your life," the same ambiguity is inescapable. If *A* never confronts *B* with a gun, *B* is of course better off, but if *A* does point a gun at *B*, *B* is also better off if she has the option of paying in order to avoid getting shot. In one sense the exchange is unproductive (as compared with *A*'s never pointing the gun at *B*), but in another sense, it is productive (as compared with *A*'s shooting *B*). The familiar problem of time-frame ambiguity—narrow or broad?—makes it virtually impossible to decide whether these transactions decrease or increase freedom.

III. Third-Party Chips

If the distinction between threats and offers is not likely to get us very far, maybe James Lindgren's effort to unravel the "paradox of blackmail"[14] hits closer to the mark. His comprehensive study reviews the literature, pans all competing theories, and then offers a test for distinguishing between blackmail and permissible commerce. The wrong, says Lindgren, is that the blackmailer seeks to bargain with something that does not belong to him or her: "In effect, the blackmailer attempts to gain an advantage in return for suppressing someone else's actual or potential interest. The blackmailer is negotiating for his own gain with someone else's leverage or bargaining chips."[15]

With this criterion in hand, Lindgren rolls through the cases. The *crime* case (no. 1) is blackmail because D is "bargaining with the state's chip."[16] The *hush money* case (no. 3) falls into the same category because D tries to sell the public's right to know the content of the pictures. Because V pays "to avoid being harmed by *persons other than the blackmailer*,"[17] D supposedly engages in an act that is criminally wrong. The *lascivious employer* case (no. 5) is not so easy to explain on Lindgren's theory, but I suppose he might argue that by misusing her authority (threatening to dismiss an employee for reasons unrelated to job performance), the employer is bargaining with chips that belong to her partners, clients, or stockholders. With similar imagination, one can dispose of the *political embarrassment* case (no. 9): D seeks gain by invoking the interests of the electorate or at least those of the competing political party.

There is no theoretical harm in this imaginative play about whose chips are really at stake in an alleged blackmail transaction. It hints at the difference, for example, between threatening to sue after an accident (okay) and threatening to file a criminal complaint (not okay), or between threatening to dismiss V if he does not get to work on time (okay) and threatening to fire him if he refuses sexual favors (not okay). Yet the argument does not go far enough. It fails to account for the difference between the *political embarrassment* and *paid silence* cases (nos. 9 & 10). In the intuitive response of most people, it makes a difference whether the candidate V is subject to the threat of political embarrassment, or whether he takes the initiative to keep the source of embarrassment out of harm's way. He is not the victim of blackmail if he initiates the transaction. In either case, however, D plays with a chip that seems to belong to someone else. Lindgren's analysis focuses entirely on the content of the transaction, and fails to consider who initiates the interaction or whether the transaction lends itself to repetition. As we shall see, the latter factor turns out to be critical in developing a proper understanding of blackmail.

Lindgren's criterion—emphasizing the unfair trafficking in other people's chips—calls into question our assumed distinction between selling the baseball at an outrageous price and the other stipulated cases of blackmail. In the *baseball* case (no. 6), the seller takes advantage of the sick child's vulnerable condition and her special love for Babe Ruth. The baseball might be worth no more than $600 on the collectors' market, but under these circumstances, the seller reaps an unexpected profit. She drives a hard, exploitative bargain, but one that is neither criminal blackmail nor any other form of crime. The windfall profits derive from her taking advantage of something that does not belong to her, namely, the child's and parent's consumer surplus in possessing the ball. She is bargaining with a chip that does not belong to her, and for Lindgren, that should be enough to render her demand criminal. Since by common agreement it is not criminal, there must be something awry in Lindgren's argument.

One might object that I am playing fast and loose with the notion of chips and the people to whom they belong. Perhaps, but so does Lindgren. After all, how does one know whose chips are at stake in the *lascivious employer* and *political embarrassment* cases (nos. 5 & 9), when one party makes an unfair threat against another? Lindgren's implicit theory of bargaining chips seems to turn on a notion of extra-legal moral rights. Some people other than the potential blackmailer have a morally defensible interest in the item being sold—whether the item is pictures in the *hush money* case (no. 3), a job in the *lascivious employer* case (no. 5), or an improved chance of winning the election in the *political embarrassment* case (no. 9). Even if we could solve these problems, it is not clear what should follow. Lindgren's claim about playing with other people's chips trades on a general principle of fairness: play only with your own chips and do not cheat. This may be a sound moral principle, but cheating and sharp dealing are, at most, tangential concerns in the criminal law. We do not penalize cheating on exams, committing adultery with other people's wives or husbands, or even stealing numerous forms of intellectual property protected under tort law. By like token, there is no reason to punish the particular form of cheating that Lindgren espies in cases of blackmail.

We are left with the problem posed at the outset: How do we generate a principle to cover these ten cases that, at the same time, connects with general criteria of crime and punishment? None of the tests and criteria proposed in the literature are capable of satisfying these desiderata. We must make a clean break with the conventional approaches to the problem. The break consists in broadening our focus from the intrinsic nature of the transaction to the kind of relationship that the transaction engenders between the parties. We must look at the aftermath of the suspected blackmail to determine whether the act is criminal or not. First, I will illustrate how this approach accounts for the ten cases; then broaden the thesis to suggest a general approach to crime and punishment; finally, I consider several objections to the thesis.

IV. Dominance and Subordination

The proper test, I submit, is whether the transaction with the suspected blackmailer generates a relationship of dominance and subordination. If *V*'s paying money or rendering a service to D creates a situation in which D can or does dominate V, then the action crosses the line from permissible commerce to criminal wrongdoing. The essence of D's dominance over V is the prospect of repeated demands. Consider the difference between the *crime* and *tort* cases (nos. 1 & 2). In one case D threatens criminal prosecution; in the other, a private law suit. The critical point here is that if V pays D an amount necessary to settle the tort dispute between them, D must release his claim. He cannot thereafter come back to V and demand more. But if V pays D money to suppress a criminal investigation, D retains the option of coming back for more. It turns out, therefore, that these first two cases neatly illustrate the thesis. Blackmail occurs when, by virtue of the demand and the action satisfying the demands, the blackmailer knows that she can repeat the demand in the future. Living with that knowledge puts the victim of blackmail in a permanently subordinate position.

Let us see whether the same test provides a guide to the other eight cases. The recurrent *hush money* case (no. 3) is readily resolved. If V pays D to keep the information to himself, the latter has every incentive to demand more money in the future. V places his life and fortune at the disposal of the blackmailer. Even if D says that she is surrendering the pictures and the negatives, there is no assurance that copies have not been made. Nor is there any way to expunge D's personal knowledge of the pictures and what they reveal. Scott Altman makes the same point after he fails to find an adequate explanation of why selling an embarrassing video at the market price to the victim should be punishable.[18] The case puzzles him because demanding only that the victim pay the price that a television station would have paid for the video insulates the transaction from the stigma of exploitation. Yet, he concedes, "there cannot be any guarantee that a first payment will not be followed by more demands."[19] And the maker of the video, even should she surrender all copies, "might later demand further payment not to tell people what she saw."[20] This is the essence of the blackmail—not the transaction itself, but the relationship of dominance implicit in taking the first step of inducing the victim to pay money for her own protection.

The *late employee* case (no. 4) illustrates the converse thesis that unless further threats are imminent in the transaction, there is no criminal blackmail. So long as V shows up on time, D can make no additional threat of dismissal. This case thus falls into the pattern of the *tort* case (no. 2). But, if in the following case (no. 5), V sleeps with D, he places himself in her power. The initial submission establishes a relationship of dominance and subordination that encourages further sexual demands. The thesis is clearly borne out by these two cases.

And what about the troublesome *baseball* case (no. 6)? The theory proves its mettle in neatly accounting for why a tough one-shot transaction cannot be considered criminal blackmail. Once the parent purchases the baseball, the seller D can demand nothing further. In no sense does the parent place herself in ongoing subordination to the seller, and there is thus no criminal wrong in demanding an exorbitant price for the baseball. This strikes me as a far more persuasive account of this case than one that focuses on the supposed distinction between offers and threats. Significantly, no analysis of "baselines" or "normalcy" is necessary to dismiss this case as exploitative commerce rather than criminal blackmail.

Neither variation of the *dinner kiss* case (no. 7) poses a problem of dominance and subordination. The threat and the demand are minimal. *V* can easily tell *D* to "take a walk" and be free of the minimal threat. Dominance requires something more than withholding a kiss or making unwanted bodily contact. Exactly what is required, however, is not clear. The message of the *tattoo* case (no. 8) is that no one can dominate someone else by asking for money to do or not to do that which is in one's recognized domain of freedom. The case resembles the problem of the landowner who threatens to build a wall on his own property that will deprive his neighbor of light. The neighbor has no easement to interpose against the landowner, and if the latter thus demands payment to forgo building the wall, the demand is within the landowner's rights; there is no blackmail in demanding payments to do or not to do that which one has a right to do. For the neighbor to complain of subordination to the whims of the wall-builder, he would have to have some legitimate interest that is put in jeopardy by the repeated demands for payment.

The great virtue of the dominance-and-subordination test is that it neatly accounts for the distinction between the *political embarrassment* and *paid silence* cases (nos. 9 & 10). Indeed, the test grows out of my effort to make sense of this distinction. Think of these two cases as posing variations on the interaction between the candidate and the activist who has the power to embarrass him. If the candidate submits to the activist's demand (no. 9) and pays him to keep quiet, the candidate comes under the sway of the activist who, like other blackmailers, would continue to make demands. On the other hand, if the candidate takes the initiative, seeks out the activist, and offers him "walk-around money" to stay out of sight until after the election (no. 10), the candidate is the master of the transaction. He certainly is not being blackmailed, and neither is the activist, who is simply being paid a salary for remaining quiet for a certain period of time. If our fictional candidate is smart, he will structure the payment in the *paid silence* case in staggered installments so that the activist has an incentive to keep his side of the bargain. Of course, the latter might realize that more money is to be had by selling his silence. If he starts threatening the candidate that he will speak if he does not receive more, however, the situation reverts to the pattern of the *political embarrassment* case (no. 9).

We have now generated a coherent and convincing fit between the principle of dominance and these specific cases. Unless some counterexample might challenge the principle, we should move to the next stage of the two-part test for what constitutes a convincing account of blackmail. Does the principle of dominance explain not only why blackmail is undesirable but also why it is conventionally regarded as a crime subject to punishment? The question invites us to consider whether punishment fulfills an important function in counteracting relationships of dominance. This inquiry, in turn, necessitates a slight detour to survey the theoretical positions typically considered in the literature on punishment.

V. Punishment as the Negation of Dominance

Punishment is one of those topics on which consensus eludes us. Since the eighteenth century, utilitarians and Kantians have been arguing about whether punishment is justified by the good it brings about or simply as an imperative of justice, regardless of its social costs and benefits. In the works of Beccaria[21] and Bentham,[22] we encounter the systematic utilitarian argument that the deterrent value of the penalty must outweigh the suffering of the prisoner. The welfare represented by a safer society justifies the pain inflicted on the offender.

Referring to this approach as the "principle of happiness" or "eudaemonism,"[23] Immanuel Kant found a loophole in the utilitarian argument. Justifying punishment by appealing to its beneficial consequences could readily justify differential punishment for the same crime—depending on the social needs of the moment. Kant dismissed this potential result of utilitarianism with outrage: "The principle of punishment is a categorical imperative, and woe to him who crawls through the windings of eudaemonism in order to discover something that releases the criminal from punishment...."[24] Kant insisted that punishment is an imperative of both morality and justice. And "if justice goes, there is no longer any value in men living on the earth."[25]

The opposition between Bentham and Kant provides the framework for most contemporary debates about punishment. For Benthamite utilitarians, the primary justification for punishment is deterrence; for Kantians, it is the retributive justice implicit in making the punishment fit the crime. Retribution seeks retrospective justice: it looks only to the crime, and not to the beneficial consequences of punishment. On this axis of time, utilitarianism is prospective: it looks to the beneficial consequences of punishment rather than to any imperatives urged by the facts. There are, we should note, many variations on the axis of retrospective and prospective or consequential theories. Let us distinguish among some of them:

1. *Purely retrospective*: The only permissible punishments are those based on events in the past, and particularly on the details of the crime.
2. *Factually consequential*: Punishment is justified by deterrence, both special (the criminal himself) and general (the rest of society). This argument represents a factual prediction; if neither the criminal nor the rest of society is

deterred, then the prediction is false. Whether punishment is justified on these grounds, therefore, requires careful observation of what happens in the aftermath of punishing. In testing a penalty's efficacy, the problem is distinguishing between those things that would have happened anyway from consequences solely attributable to the act of punishment.

3. *Conceptually consequential*: Some of the consequences by which punishment is justified are conceptually linked to the act of punishing; the desirable consequences follow logically from the punishment. For example, Hegel's argument for punishment is that it vindicates the Right over the Wrong represented by the crime.[26] This act of vindication is conceptually connected to the punishment in the sense that if one is convinced the vindication occurs, no facts can undermine this conviction.

4. *Mixed theories*: To avoid the conflict among these variations, many theorists today argue that punishment must satisfy both of these desiderata. It must have a deterrent effect and it cannot exceed the punishment that the defendant deserves for the deed, considered purely retrospectively.

As we shall see, the argument that punishment counteracts criminal dominance—the rationale that I have proposed for punishing blackmail—lies somewhere between the poles of factual and conceptual consequentialism. The claim is that punishing criminals restores the dignity of the victim. Whether this is a factual or conceptual consequence remains to be seen.

The debate about the rationale for punishment has appeared to be endless because none of the proffered positions escapes telling criticism. Utilitarians suffer the charge of not taking human autonomy and responsibility seriously; i.e., they treat criminals as organisms to be manipulated rather than as human ends in themselves. Yet retributivists do not agree on why it is right to punish somebody, whether a new social benefit follows or not. The best way to appreciate the defects in the standard retributive argument is to consider the many unconvincing arguments Kant offers for his position. After surveying these diverse approaches, I will seek to defend my own thesis—that criminal punishment negates the blackmailer's dominance—by invoking the least popular passage in Kant's defense of punishment. This passage calls for the execution of the last murderer languishing in prison before society voluntarily disbands.[27]

Most of Kant's arguments in favor of retributive punishment turn on the themes of equality and universality. First, in the context of the "woe to him ..." passage quoted above,[28] Kant develops a general critique of the inequalities engendered by a case-specific calculation of the social advantages and disadvantages of punishing a particular person. Kant believed, above all, that punishment required the equal application of the law. There should be no exceptions, not even for those whose punishment benefits society.[29] The term "categorical imperative" that Kant casually invokes is not, in this passage, used in its ordinary sense.[30] It means no more here, it seems, than a commitment to general and universal laws, equally applied.

In his second argument in favor of nonutilitarian punishment, Kant stresses the equality or equivalence between the crime and the punishment. Drawing on the teachings of the *ius talionis*, he insists that the scales of justice as well as the concept of law itself require this equivalence.[31] No other standard would, he claims, be sufficiently precise to meet the good identified as "strict justice" under law.[32]

The third argument elicits Kant's understanding of "retribution" as captured in the German term *Vergeltung*. The categorical imperative in its ordinary sense requires people to act on their maxims (subjective plans) only if these maxims can be universalized and made to apply (*gelten*) as a universal law.[33] If one applies a negative version of the categorical imperative that Kant, trading on the association with *gelten*, calls *vergelten*, the same should be true of criminals. The justification for punishment, as it emerges in this argument, requires that the criminal's maxim be universalized and applied to him.[34] If he kills, his killing should be universalized and applied to him. If he steals, his stealing should be regarded as a universal law, which would imply that all property would be subject to theft. If property is undermined, then the criminal should be treated as not having any resources of his own. If he has no resources, Kant concludes (playfully, it would seem) that he should be imprisoned, and forced to work for his sustenance.[35]

Though this argument blurs the distinction between the poorhouse and the prison, one should recall that, at the time of Kant's writing in 1795, imprisonment had yet to become the common mode of punishment. Kant struggles to find a rationale for putting people behind bars rather than executing, exiling, or castrating them. The latter forms of punishment he regards as fitting, respectively, for murder and treason,[36] sex with animals,[37] and rape.[38] The general theme in Kant's writing on punishment is that the crime should be turned back on the criminal. Sometimes this can be done by universalizing the criminal's maxim and making him suffer the consequences, or by making the punishment "fit" the crime, just as castration fits rape. The notion of a fitting punishment bears some resemblance to Michel Foucault's thesis that punishment was originally thought to expiate the crime by reenacting the horror of the crime on the body of the defendant.[39]

The most intriguing of Kant's arguments for retributive punishment is the most often derided. He imagines that a society is about to disband, but it has a problem: murderers, condemned to die, still languish in prison. What should be done about them? Kant insists that the murderers should be executed "so that each has done to him what his deeds deserve and blood guilt does not cling to the people."[40] Executing them seems to be pointless because no societal benefit could possibly follow. But this is precisely Kant's point.

The notion of a society's disbanding should be treated as a thought-experiment, very much like the idea of a society's coming together in a social contract. Neither of these events ever occurred in history, but they are useful constructs for testing our intuitions about the conditions of a just social order. Further, the biblical reference to blood guilt is highly suggestive. In biblical culture, a murderer acquired control over the victim's blood; the killer had to be executed in order to release the victim's blood, permitting it to return to God as in the case of a natural death.[41] The failure to execute the murderer meant that the rest of society, charged with this function, became responsible for preventing the release of the victim's blood.

Whatever the metaphysics of gaining and releasing control of blood, the biblical idea should be understood today as a metaphor for society's complicity in a crime for failing to punish the criminal. Once the institution of punishment becomes the conventional response to an obvious crime, the decision either to prosecute or not to prosecute carries social meaning. The state's intervention communicates condemnation of the crime and solidarity with the victim. By prosecuting, the state's officials say to the victim and his or her family: "You are not alone. We stand with you, against the criminal."

Conversely, refusing to prosecute and convict for an obvious crime also carries meaning. When the state court jury acquitted the four officers charged with beating Rodney King,[42] they communicated implicit approval of the police behavior, thus engendering rage among African-Americans in Los Angeles.[43] The existence of the institution of punishment creates an opportunity to counteract the criminal's attainment of an unjust position of power over others. The failure of police, prosecutors, and juries to invoke their established power, their inaction when there is an opportunity to act, provides the foundation for the perception of shared responsibility. If they willfully refuse to invoke the traditional response to crime, they effectively disassociate themselves from the victim. Abandoned, both the victim and the victim's community feel betrayed by the system.

Punishment expresses solidarity with the victim and seeks to restore the relationship of equality that antedated the crime. This may not be so obvious in a culture that has become accustomed to thinking of punishment as a utilitarian instrument of crime control. To appreciate the psychological significance of the state's standing by the victim, consider the cases in which the state refuses to prosecute and thereby abandons the victim to solitary suffering. For example, during the terror in Argentina that led to approximately 9000 *desaparecidos* in the early 1980s, many victims' families realized, to their horror, that they could not turn to the police. The police were often the ones engaged in the round-up of suspected terrorists.

The failure of the state to come to the aid of victims, as expressed in a refusal to invoke the customary institutions of arrest, prosecution, and punishment, generates moral complicity in the aftermath of the crime. The state's failure to punish also reaffirms the relationship of dominance over the victim that the criminal has already established.

This argument for punishment admittedly relies on a double-negative. It is less an argument *for* punishment, in fact, than an argument about why *not punishing* is sometimes tantamount to complicity in evil. And it is not an argument for punishment *ab initio*. Some other argument is necessary to explain why it is better for the state to punish than to impose civil penalties or simply to have its officials declare that they sympathize with the victim.

Generating a positive argument for punishment requires that we return to the theme of domination as I advanced it in the context of blackmail.[44] Extending the thesis to all crimes of violence and even to theft and embezzlement is not a difficult task. The argument is that all of these crimes carry in their train a relationship of dominance and subordination. Rape victims have good reason to fear that the rapist will return, particularly if the rape occurred at home or the rapist otherwise knows the victim's address. Burglars and robbers pose the same threat. Becoming a victim of violence beyond the law means that what we all fear becomes a personal reality; exposure and vulnerability take hold and they continue until the offender is apprehended. It would be difficult to maintain that all crimes are characterized by this feature of dominance. We can say, however, that this relationship of power lies at the core of the criminal law. It is characteristic of the system as a whole.

In order to counteract the power of the criminal over the victim, the state must intervene by exercising power over the criminal. It is not enough to make the offender pay damages or a fine, for all this means is that she purchases her ongoing status exempt from the prohibitions that apply to others. The state must dominate the criminal's freedom, lest the criminal continue her domination of the victim. The deprivation of liberty and the stigmatization of the offense and the offender—these means counteract the criminal's dominance by reducing his capacity to exercise power over others and symbolically lowering his status.

VI. One, Two, Many Objections

Any novel way of thinking about crime and punishment is likely to engender skepticism, and this is undoubtedly the case both with this account of blackmail as a paradigmatic crime and with my theory of punishment. Let me try here to anticipate and respond to probable objections.

Some may argue that not all crime generates a relationship of dominance. This is obviously true, and I could not possibly insist that every case conforms to the thesis. The most that I need to show, however, is that the core of the criminal law is expressed in an act of achieving dominance over others. If the thesis is persuasive, it provokes questions about nonconforming cases, such as homicide.[45]

Others may posit a much more serious objection, arguing that it is unclear how punishment counteracts the criminal's dominance over the victim. This objection challenges the notion that the consequence of punishment is conceptually connected to the act of punishment, that punishment negates the criminal's wrong and vindicates the right.[46] There should be some data, some factual consequence, that determines whether this objection is correct or incorrect. It might even be correct under some circumstances but not others. The data that would validate the claim would be the experience of victims, their testimony that apprehending, prosecuting, and punishing those who prey on them enables them to reintegrate into society and overcome their humiliation.

The testimony that one can come by is largely anecdotal. And it is easier to find stories that support the negative proposition that *not punishing* those who have committed crimes demoralizes victims and requires them to live under inhumane psychological stress. I was led to this thesis, in part, by a story that I have never been able to verify in the press. Upon President Raúl Alfonsín's replacing the military junta in Argentina, the father of an abducted child—a *desaparecido*— expected the newly elected government to take rapid action against criminal elements in the military. Nothing happened for several months. As a result, the father despaired and eventually committed suicide. In this particular case, of course, there may have been psychological factors that pushed the father over the edge. But I still understand and empathize with his distress, and that of a man I interviewed shortly after the verdict in the *Goetz* case. He called into a talk show and reported:

> I'm a New Yorker, black. Over the past seven years, three members, boys, in my family has [*sic*] been killed, the last one shot, with the killer that we see weekly—today—walking around. My wife has been mentally disturbed ever since this happened because no one is serving time for any of this.... The question is: where is the justice?[47]

The caller sympathized with Goetz. If the system does not respond to the plight of victims, they invariably fantasize that a vigilante will vindicate their dignity.

A third objection, raised by Stephen Latham at the Blackmail Symposium, is whether one can give a persuasive account of blackmail merely by focusing on the relationship of dominance induced by the interaction between the parties. The dominance might be justified. Determining whether it is requires consideration of the intrinsic merits of the act itself, not just its aftermath. The legal system is arguably a system of justified dominance. It must be the case, therefore, that the blackmailer's actions are somehow intrinsically wrong and unjustified.

Many words and expressions at hand express what is wrong with blackmail. In fact, too many things are wrong with it. Blackmail represents coercion of the victim,[48] exploitation of the victim's weakness,[49] and trading unfairly in assets or chips that belong to others.[50] It represents an undesirable and abusive form of private law enforcement.[51] It leads to the waste of resources so far as blackmailers are induced to collect information that they are willing to suppress for a fee.[52] None of these arguments, however, offers a convincing account of the difference between cases of punishable and nonpunishable conduct. All of them capture a portion of blackmail's evil, but none accounts systematically for the cases.

Of all the arguments about the wrong immanent in blackmail, only one accounts persuasively for the distinctions implicit in the ten cases considered above, and that is the impact of the alleged blackmail on the ensuing relationship between D and V. When D's demand is a one-shot affair, as when D threatens to sue in tort if V does not agree to the payment demanded, there is no crime. There is no way to explain this or the other cases of nonpunishable threats except to note that V's payment effects a settlement and thus negates the possibility of repeated demands. Conversely, all the cases of punishable blackmail generate a situation that invites repeated threats and exploitation.

Finally, some may argue that if the aftermath of the alleged blackmail is the determinative factor, why not define the crime as the second act of blackmail? Douglas Ginsburg and Larry Alexander raised this objection at the Blackmail Symposium, and though I was initially puzzled by it, I see now that it poses no serious challenge to my thesis. Ginsburg and Alexander obviously understood dominance as a state of affairs that crystallizes only as a result of repeated demands. Therefore, one must wait for the second demand to ascertain whether the blackmailer intends to exercise his power. But, in fact, the relationship of dominance and subordination comes into being as a result of the victim's making the first payment or engaging in the first coerced act of submission. The dominance consists in the knowledge that the victim is now fair game for repeated demands. Dominance and subordination are states of anticipation. When both parties know that the victim has submitted once and has no defense against submitting again, he is at the mercy of the blackmailer. His only hope lies in the intervention of the police or other agents of the criminal law.

The existence of criminal sanctions gives him the possibility of asserting a counter-threat of going to the police. Some might object to the permissibility of reciprocal blackmail, for threatening prosecution, considered by itself, violates the same criminal prohibition. Yet as a defensive move, as a way of protecting oneself from blackmail, the counter-threat of invoking the criminal law seems fully justified.

CHAPTER 23

Reply: The Crime of Trying to Dominate

Judge John T. Noonan Jr.*

The Case of the Interfering Niece

In 1971, a fifty-five-year-old San Francisco businessman, A, responded to an ad run by B in a Los Angeles newspaper. A flew to Los Angeles and had sex with B, a young man, for money. The transaction was repeated the next two or three times they met. They became friends. They had sex but not as a commercial transaction. The older man enjoyed the young man's personality. He came to consider him a very good friend. He employed B for several months in his business. That did not work out; instead B became dependent on A for financial assistance, and A, as he later stated, was "glad to help him out."

In 1987, A, now seventy-one, stopped traveling to meet B. Physical contact ceased. Psychological contact continued by telephone and by A's handouts to B. Transfers of money were made by Western Union. On April 5, 1991, for example, a total of $510 was sent by A to B in nine separate installments, ranging in amounts from $35 to $145. The money was sent in response to requests by B. The dribble was A's chosen method of response. In the course of 1991, A sent B $24,000.

A's business had chiefly consisted in the unlikely enterprise of selling ashtrays to hotels. With the change in public attitude toward smoking, his business dried up. A obtained a part-time job with a fraternal organization and borrowed $20,000 from relatives. He had a phone with an answering machine. In 1991, he received no business calls on it. The phone, in fact, was used only to receive messages from B.

One of A's relatives, a niece, N, had been aware that for several years A had been giving B money. She advised her uncle to stop. He did not, but when he found

---

* Judge, U.S. Court of Appeals, Ninth Circuit; Professor Emeritus, University of California, Berkeley School of Law.

himself out of money, he cut his wrists in a failed attempt at suicide. While he was in the hospital, N persuaded the FBI to bug his phone and answering machine.

While the bug was in place, three calls from B were imperfectly recorded. On September 4, 1991, B asked, "Please have $100 down here in 15 minutes. Or I'll be…on my way to San Francisco." A few minutes later, B called again stating, "I'll be calling the Fairmont and the St. Francis….You put me in this miserable motherfucking spot, Mister. So I'm going…put you in the same spot back." A third message, sent three hours later, began: "A, I'm sorry for being an asshole this morning. Could you please do that for me, A?"

On October 7, 1991, B left eight more messages on A's machine. The first, at 1:00 a.m., asked for $100 and told A that he was "the most caring and kindest person that I've ever met in my life." In later calls the same day B stated that he needed to pay the rent, and that if A did not help him, "I'm going to kill you," a few minutes later calling to say, "You don't deserve to live….I'm coming to San Francisco. When I get up there you're gonna die."

On October 9, B left three recorded messages, stating that he was desperate for money and adding, "I'm gonna call the Fairmont Hotel…and every person you do business with. I will call every account that you have." In other calls that day B called A a pig and his mother a liar, again threatened A with death, and in his last message stated that he, B, was being threatened with a knife and needed A's help.

On the basis of these three days of messages, B was indicted by a federal grand jury for extortion and attempted extortion. The trial jury acquitted B of the charges based on the messages of October 7 and 9 but convicted him on the basis of the calls of September 4. B appealed. The appeals court observed that an element of extortion was the fear aroused in the mind of the victim and that at trial the government had produced no testimony that the September calls had caused A to fear. But, the court noted, the crime of attempted extortion was different. Attempted extortion did not require instilling fear in the mind of the victim, it only required an effort to do so by a threat of economic loss. The court focused on B's threat to put A in the same miserable spot that B was in. Coupled with the threat to contact A's customers, this intention constituted sufficient evidence of an attempt to extort.

One of the three judges on the appeals court dissented. The jury had not believed that the death threats of October 7 and 9 were real. Why was September 4 different? The dissenter observed that what the evidence showed was a consensual game, in which B tried to dominate A by threats, and A tried to dominate B by doling out cash in small amounts that required B to beg for more. There was no evidence that A had any customers. B, who knew A well, was aware of his situation—on one message he even stated that he'd called the fraternal organization where A now worked. This call was not a threat but a taunt. How would A's gay lifestyle have endangered his economic well-being anyway? He lived in San Francisco where openly gay persons were routinely returned to public office. At most what B conceivably could have intended to provoke in A was the fear of embarrassment if his longtime liaison with B was brought to light. Threat to embarrass is not an

attempt to extort. A kept his answering service not to do business but to be sure
that he could continue this expensive game with B.

The Essence of Blackmail

I have set out details of *United States v. Marsh*, 26 F.3d 1496 (9th Cir. 1994),
because I believe that when a judge is seriously engaged in judging a criminal
appeal, he has an experience, however vicarious, that enlarges the judge's perception of the evil the law has forbidden. I was the dissenter in *Marsh*. When
I read George Fletcher's "Blackmail: The Paradigmatic Crime," I had a strong
sense of the congruence of his article with my dissent. I could have greatly
strengthened the dissent if I had had the framework of the article's analysis
as underpinning. He saw extortion as evil because it involved an inappropri-
ate attempt to dominate the victim of the blackmail. A and B were engaged in
alternate attempts to dominate each other. Their play, however irresponsible in
the eyes of the guardian niece, did not constitute a crime.

Essences

I have been stimulated by Fletcher's argument to think about whether blackmail is the paradigmatic crime. I am not persuaded that it is. Fletcher's article
has fulfilled the Socratic function of forcing me to say why I would answer his
question differently.

In the first place, again judging from my own experience, a common federal
crime is tax evasion. It is a stretch too far to say that the evasive taxpayer is trying
to dominate the federal government. He is trying to get away with something, not
set up a relationship where he can continue to avoid his obligations.

In the second place, dominance or effort to achieve it is not always wrong. Hospitals
and doctors dominate their patients, schools and teachers their pupils, courts and
judges the litigants before them. The dominators, whether public or private, have
legitimate reason by virtue of their social function to determine the behavior of those
before them. There is no such thing as a ban on dominance per se.

Thirdly, it is extraordinarily difficult to discover a paradigm that will work for
the variety of crimes that our law condemns—for example, attempts (all without
victims), conspiracy, drug dealing, gambling, insider trading, jury-fixing, obstruc-
tion of justice, perjury, price-fixing, and tax evasion. In the most famous analysis
of crime in literature, Dante made an effort to segregate crimes by their spiritual
essence, treating the fraudulent as deserving more punishment than the merely violent, because the fraudulent misused their God-given human intellects. But where
would he have put the purveyors of marijuana? Where would he have put the prostitute's patron? Where would he have put the player of a silly psychosexual game?

CHAPTER 24

Reply: George Fletcher on Blackmail

*Alan Wertheimer**

The "paradox of blackmail" has occasioned a philosophical literature out of proportion to its practical importance. This is not surprising. One does not need to do much theoretical work to explain why homicide, rape, or battery or robbery should be criminalized. It is more difficult and more interesting to explain why it should be criminal to propose to do that which one has a right to do. A striking feature of George Fletcher's fascinating essay is that he proposes to treat what might seem to be a marginal case as "[t]he paradigmatic crime" (231). Fletcher proposes a "dominance and subordination" test as a means to render coherent the legal status of the ten cases he describes (238). He then argues that dominance and subordination are the core criminal wrongs and that the negation of dominance and subordination is a core justification of punishment.

There are four questions that we can ask about Fletcher's analysis: (1) Is he right about the cases? (2) Does his theory render coherent the law's view of such cases? (3) Does that theory explain why the illegal acts should be regarded as crimes? (4) Does his theory help to explain the justification of punishment?

As a nonlawyer, I will assume that Fletcher is right as to which of his ten cases are crimes. I do have some worries. It is arguable that even if D commits blackmail in *crime* case, it is not a crime against V. I also wonder whether *lascivious employer* would be prosecuted under a blackmail statute as opposed to sexual harassment or sexual assault. But not much turns on words. Although "blackmail" typically involves a particular type of threat (information) that involves third parties (the public as in *hush money* and *political embarrassment* or the authorities as in *crime* case,), we do use blackmail as a synonym for coercion, and so D's friends might say, "You're trying to blackmail us" in *tattoo* case even if their claim is unsuccessful as a matter of law.

---

*Senior Research Scholar, Department of Bioethics, National Institutes of Health.

If Fletcher is right about the cases, I am less convinced that his "dominance and subordination" test offers the best explanation of the distinction between those that are crimes and those that are not. Fletcher offers what might be called an *internal* theory of crime as contrasted with an *external* theory of crime. An "internal" theory argues that behavior X is a crime because of features internal to the relation between the perpetrator and the victim. An external theory argues that X is a crime because of the effects of X on others or, perhaps, because it is thought that *permitting X* will have a harmful effect on others.

Although Fletcher favors an internal theory, his own examples point to the advantages of an external theory. Fletcher argues that "[m]any good acts are corrupted by doing them for a price," but the acts he mentions are best explained by an external theory (231). If we are justified in criminalizing consensual prostitution, it is because of the effects of prostitution on society and not because the prostitute or the customer is a victim of anything. And, *pace* Fletcher, I do not think we should object to paying people to confess because it would render a confession *involuntary* any more than paying people to work renders their work involuntary. After all, prosecutors may give defendants numerous nonmonetary incentives to confess or plead guilty, and we do *not* think that such incentives render their acts involuntary. If it should be a crime to pay people to confess, it is not because defendants would be victimized but because such a practice would corrupt the system of justice.

Second, if we adopt an internal approach to explaining the distinctions among the cases, I believe that, properly understood, the distinction between coercive threats and noncoercive offers explains most of these cases equally well. On my preferred view, A's proposal is a coercive threat rather than a noncoercive offer only if A proposes to violate B's rights if B does not do what A wants B to do.[1] The baseline by which to distinguish between threats and offers is set not by a "normalcy" baseline but by a moral baseline that refers to V's rights or, perhaps, to D's obligations. Although it is perfectly natural to say that "D threatens to sue" in *tort* case, D's proposal is—for moral and legal purposes—an *offer not to sue* if V settles because D is not proposing to violate V's rights if V does not settle, just as a plea-bargaining prosecutor is making a noncoercive *offer* not to take V to trial if V pleads guilty rather than threatening to take V to trial if V refuses, for the prosecutor would not be violating V's rights if he takes V to trial. Similarly, I believe that Fletcher's analysis of *late employee* is off the mark. It is not (just) that V can immunize herself against D's demand by showing up for work on time. Rather, D is not proposing to violate V's rights if she refuses to do so. Relative to a rights-defined baseline, D's "threat" to fire B can be recast as an offer to continue to employ V on condition that V come to work on time.

I do not think that Fletcher does quite enough to test his dominance principle against counterexamples. I do not think that dominance is either necessary or sufficient to establish blackmail or criminality. To see that dominance is not necessary, suppose that D's evidence in *crime* case and *hush money* consists of a Polaroid picture which V has seen D take, and that, absent that picture, V would be able to successfully deny the behavior. I take it that D commits blackmail in both cases even though D is not in a position to dominate and subordinate. Or consider a nondominating twist on *lascivious employer*:

> *Lascivious hiring officer.* D is a hiring officer. Although V is not the most qualified applicant, D tells V that he will hire V if V has sex with him.

Although this case seems to constitute blackmail, if D has no control over V's employment once V is hired, then D is not in a position to dominate and subordinate. Interestingly, it is not clear that "quid pro quo" sexual harassment is best understood as coercion, since V has no right to be hired, and thus D is not proposing to violate V's rights if she refuses. It might be argued that whereas V does not have a right to a job, V does have a right to be considered on her *merits*. But this, too, may not work to explain what is wrong with *lascivious hiring officer*, since V might prefer *not* to be evaluated on her merits and to exchange sex for the position. Indeed, we can tell a story in which V makes the proposal to D. It may be sensible to criminalize such practices, but this may be better explained on an "external" theory that appeals to the long-term consequences of a hiring process in which employers could exchange jobs for sex rather than the internal dynamics of the case.

If the dominance test is not necessary to establish criminality, it is also not sufficient. Contrast Fletcher's *lascivious employer* with my case of the *kinky cohabiter*:

> *Kinky cohabiter.* D is wealthy. V is a poor single mother. D invites V to move in with her child. After a few months, D tells V that he will allow V and her child to stay only if she agrees to have anal sex (which she abhors) once a week.

It appears that both cases meet Fletcher's view of blackmail, since D is in a position to repeat his demands in both cases. Yet whereas *lascivious employer* may constitute a crime, even if not the crime of blackmail, *kinky cohabiter* does not. Why? I suspect that this is not because of features internal to the relationship but because there are good external reasons to prohibit the demand for sex in exchange for employment but not to prohibit the exchange of sex for continued cohabitation. The general point is that one can "subordinate" another through repeated offers of benefits in exchange for favors, and, in general, such subordination does not constitute a crime.

Let us assume that Fletcher's domination and subordination test provides a plausible account as to why some behaviors should be illegal. We must still ask whether that theory explains why blackmail is a *criminal* wrong as contrasted with a *private* wrong. The core feature of a criminal wrong is that it is a *public* wrong. The case is brought by "The People." The guilty are punished by the state rather than being required to compensate the victim. We say that a criminal "pays his debt to society," not to the victim. These may all be convenient fictions. Perhaps the state is simply acting on behalf of individual victims rather than protecting society's interest in these matters, but I am inclined to take seriously the notion of a *public* wrong. After all, we treat some acts as criminal even if both parties consent and would have no private cause of action. We punish attempted crimes where no one is palpably harmed and where the target would be unable to bring a successful civil suit. Interestingly, it could be argued that Fletcher is exactly right to maintain that the "paradox of blackmail" illustrates why blackmail is a paradigmatic *crime*, but not for the reasons he advances. It may be that the combined acts of blackmail generate harmful public consequences that are not caused by either of its components.[2]

Along these lines, Lawrence Becker argues that we can justify punishing attempted crimes as harshly as successful crimes on the grounds that they impose just as much harm on *society* as successful crimes, even though they do not impose as much or any private harms on *victims*. Although the "private" harm of an attempted rape may be relatively low, the harm to the sense of security in the community may be just as great, and it is *those* sorts of *public* effects that explain why attempted rape is a serious *crime*. Similarly, one might say that *crime* case and *hush money* are crimes not because the victims have a complaint (*hush money* could involve a serious noncriminal offense such as plagiarism) but because we do not want to live in a society that gives people incentives to acquire the information that can then be used in blackmail. Or consider a society in which kidnapping is prevalent. The society might well criminalize paying ransom (as well as kidnapping) because paying ransom increases the incentive to kidnap and puts *others* in jeopardy and not because there is anything intrinsically wrong in paying money to get one's loved ones returned.

Finally, let us consider whether Fletcher's theory helps to explain the justification of punishment. Fletcher's attempt to explain how punishment might "negate" the victim's experience of dominance is imaginative and plausible (241). Unfortunately, it seems entirely unnecessary as a justification of punishment *even if we accept the dominance principle*. It is surprising that among the theories of punishment that Fletcher surveys, he does not even mention the sort of two-tiered theory offered by H. L. A. Hart and John Rawls.[3] On that view, what Hart calls "the general justifying aim" of punishment is justified by its consequences and, in particular, its tendency to reduce the prevalence of the undesired activity, whereas the application or distribution of punishment is guided by retributive considerations such as guilt and intent.

Applied to the issues at hand, we might say not that "criminal punishment negates the blackmailer's dominance" (241), when applied, but that the threat of punishment for blackmail reduces the cases in which prospective blackmailers come to dominate their victims. I do not claim that this account is correct, but it is certainly plausible, it is consistent with Fletcher's theory of the justification for the criminalization of blackmail, and it does not require the sorts of psychological evidence to which Fletcher appeals.

CHAPTER 25

Justice and Fairness in the Protection of Crime Victims

George P. Fletcher

I. Introduction

Sydney Morgenbesser, late professor of philosophy at Columbia, was well-known for his impious humor. He buttonholed us as we walked across campus and, like Socrates in the Agora, he posed questions that would both make his colleagues laugh and keep us pondering for the rest of the day. His wit also held great wisdom, as exemplified in the following encounter with a lawyer in court that occurred in the aftermath of the 1968 protests on the Columbia campus and the police intervention.

During a trial about alleged police brutality, a lawyer asked Sydney under oath whether the police had beat him up unfairly and unjustly. He replied that the police had assaulted him unjustly, but not unfairly. The lawyer was puzzled. "How is that possible?" he queried. "Well," Sydney reportedly said, "They beat me up unjustly, but since they did the same thing to everyone else, it was not unfair."

This anecdote reveals an important distinction between the concepts of justice and fairness. Justice is about what we deserve—individually. Fairness is about the way we are treated in comparison to others. In criminal procedure, we encounter this problem every time we acquit or reverse the conviction of someone who is in fact guilty of a crime. Criminals might, in principle, deserve punishment for their deeds, but they are subject to conviction and punishment only if the state has given them a fair trial and proven their guilt beyond a reasonable doubt.

By and large, in criminal cases, justice is associated with the interests of victims; fairness, with the interests of defendants. If we hear the slogan, "No justice, no peace," we know immediately that it pertains to the interests of victims.[1] Indeed, one pro-victim website now takes this slogan as its title.[2] Fairness speaks to the interests of defendants, without assuming guilt or innocence. A fair trial is one that satisfies two desiderata of equal treatment. First, as Sydney's anecdote reveals, the defendant must be treated the same way as are other defendants, and that means that we must accord the same treatment to those we strongly suspect are guilty as to those who are probably innocent. Also, there must be some effort to maintain "equality of arms" between the prosecution and the defense, though the proper balance between the two has never been clearly worked out.[3] The defense is permitted many privileges not available to the prosecution. For example, in the common law system, the prosecution must prove guilt beyond a reasonable doubt, and verdicts of acquittal are not subject to appeal—though verdicts of guilty are. By contrast, the common law prosecutor has many advantages in the field of substantive law; for example, the possibility of overcharging in order to induce a plea bargain.[4] However the balance of advantage between prosecution and defense is struck, the now widely accepted requirement of a fair trial speaks not to what the particular defendant deserves, but to how criminal defendants as a class should be treated in assessing individual liability.

II. The Undiscussed Boundaries of Victimhood

When we are discussing the rights of victims, we take it for granted that, regardless of whether the particular defendant is guilty, we know who the victim is. We rarely refer to an "alleged victim" in the way we routinely speak about alleged offenders. One reason for this disparity is that the person identified as the victim has actually suffered, and there appears to be at least a plausible connection between the suffering and the wrongful actions of some criminal suspect. Nonetheless, our confidence in who the real victims are should give us pause.

In fact, the easy assumption of victimhood camouflages a number of very difficult conceptual issues. First, it has always been difficult to figure out who the victim is in homicide cases. Of course, in one sense the decedent is the victim—but in another sense, he or she is not. We no longer believe that the blood of the victim cries out from the ground.[5] The decedent is gone. Given our modern sensibilities about rights, it is difficult to claim that the dead have rights or even interests.

It is more plausible to treat the family members as the victims, but this too is puzzling. Certainly they feel the loss and grieve for the decedent. But the number of people included in this category—as well as their ranking—remains elusive. Are cousins included? Are spouses more important than parents or children? Do friends count? What about mistresses and lovers? We encounter similar problems in defining the category of people who have standing to complain of wrongful death under the legislative variations of *Lord Campbell's Act*.[6] But there is no reason to assume that being harmed for purposes of tort law is the same as being victimized under the criminal law.

Further, not all persons who suffer count as "victims." Consider aggressors who are injured by legitimate actions of self-defense. Are they victims? What about those who are executed in conformity with a lawful judgment? The aggressor and the condemned criminal may suffer, but they are not victims in the ordinary sense.[7] Yet there might be other cases—say, of excused rather than justified conduct—where the object of the violent excused behavior would nonetheless be called a victim. When the offender is excused by reason of insanity, for example, the person he or she has killed is still called a victim. Even though the distinction between justification and excuse has not always been recognized in the literature of the common law, our usage of the term "victim" implicitly incorporates the distinction.[8] This is, of course, true in other languages as well.[9]

Other conundrums arise in the borderlands of the concept. Attempted offenses typically endanger specific persons. A person aims a gun and pulls the trigger, but the gun jams. Is the person being aimed at a victim? Probably not. Would the answer come easily if the person being aimed at were asleep? Yet, the defendant is guilty of attempted murder regardless of whether anyone else is conscious of the danger manifested in his actions. Perhaps it is the case that victims must actually be hurt and not merely threatened.

For most purposes, the analysis of victimhood remains outside the law applied in the courts. There is one instance, however, in which very strong assumptions are made about who is a victim and who is not—namely, in the law bearing on victims' impact statements in capital sentencing in the United States. The question is, who is entitled to make a statement to the court on behalf of the victims? I am afraid that this problem has not received the principled analysis it deserves. One could well argue that the relevant victim for purposes of sentencing should not be the particular decedent but the abstract person whom we protect by asserting that all human beings enjoy a right to life.[10] Whether the right to life is violated does not depend on whether the victim has a family, or whether that family will miss him or her. The right bears the same value whether it is instantiated in a young mother with three children or a gutter bum despised by all around him. Yet the way capital sentencing works in practice, it makes a tremendous difference whether the decedent had a family and whether they were closely attached.[11] In a case like the *Menendez* case in California, where two sons were prosecuted for killing their immigrant parents, no one appeared at trial or during the sentencing phase to bear witness to the victims' importance as human beings.[12] Does it make sense as a principle of justice that those who kill the unloved among us should receive a lighter sentence?[13] On the contrary, justice for victims requires that we abstract from the particular victim and focus on elements of humanity shared by all.

III. Two Types of Basic Laws

With one exception, the basic instruments of human rights ignore the status and rights of victims. None of the constitutions of the world, so far as I know, even mention the victims of crime. The American, German, and Canadian constitutions elaborate the rights of criminal defendants but ignore the other side of the equation. They are devoted to the problem of a fair trial for the accused, not the issue of justice for those who have suffered from crime. The one big exception to this pattern, which I take up below in detail, is the *Rome Statute* establishing the International Criminal Court (ICC).[14] The *Rome Statute* begins in its *Preamble* by referring to the twentieth century problem that "millions of children, women and men have been victims of unimaginable atrocities that deeply shock the conscience of humanity."[15] The purpose of the *Rome Statute* is to vindicate the interests of these victims.

The proper question we should ask ourselves is how and why this enormous gap in orientation has arisen. Why do the basic legal documents of human rights and civil liberties fall into these opposing categories—the many that focus exclusively on fairness for the accused, and the one that stresses the problem of justice for victims?

The European Convention of Human Rights (ECHR) represents an important middle ground between these two extremes. The jurisprudence of the European Court of Human Rights in Strasbourg is worth reviewing in some detail because it reveals the difficulties of generating principled recognition of the rights of victims. The absence of constitutional protection for victims is hardly an accident. Extending the concept of individual rights to encompass victims requires considerable legal imagination.

The text of the ECHR, adopted in 1949,[16] is silent on the rights of victims, but in 1985, the Strasbourg Court began to explore the doctrinal possibilities of recognizing a violation of the Convention when states fail to adequately prosecute criminal offenses. The first case was *X & Y v. The Netherlands*,[17] where a mentally handicapped young woman was induced by a young man to have intercourse while she was a resident in a mental hospital. The Dutch penal code provided for liability, but only if the victim herself filed a complaint. The prosecutor decided that the victim was not mentally competent to file the complaint, and they would not accept her father's complaint as a substitute. The father brought a complaint to the Strasbourg Court on the grounds that the Dutch authorities had violated his and his daughter's right to a "private life" under Article 8 of the ECHR. The Court decided that the failure to prosecute was indeed a violation of his right to privacy. The remedy, however, was merely to provide a minimal compensation (3000 guilders—about $1700) to the victim.[18] There was no order directing the state to prosecute and surely no way that the Council of Europe itself could have undertaken prosecution. Indirectly, however, the message was that the Netherlands must correct the flaw that led to the failure to prosecute the case—and in fact, they did so.

The legal theory of the case, however, based on the right to privacy, is a bit farfetched. It might have made sense to say that the young man who had sex with Ms. Y violated her personal privacy. But it is not clear why the failure to prosecute the crime in itself constitutes a violation by the state of the same article. In effect, the Court was applying the German constitutional theory of *Drittwirkung* (third party effect), by which private parties secure protection under the constitution against other private parties, but there was no explicit invocation of the German doctrine. Instead, the Court refers vaguely to the possibility of "positive obligations inherent in an effective respect for private or family life."[19]

In an even more intriguing development, the Strasbourg Court devised a way to regulate private relationships under a broad interpretation of Article 3 of the ECHR, which holds: "No one shall be subjected to torture or to inhuman or degrading treatment or punishment."[20] At first blush it seems that the terms "torture" and "punishment" should apply only to actions of the state, but the Court has read the provision to protect children against corporal punishment by their parents. In *A. v. United Kingdom*, decided in 1998,[21] a stepfather had beaten his nine-year-old stepson and was prosecuted for assault, but acquitted on the grounds that he was entitled to use a reasonable amount of force as chastisement. The Court found that the stepfather's beating the boy had constituted "degrading...punishment" and therefore the U.K. was in violation of the Convention for not having protected the victim.[22]

The reasoning of the Court takes a middle position between the imposition of duties under the ECHR on private parties and the stressing of the "positive obligations" of the state. Here is the general language:

> The court considers that the obligation on the high contracting parties under art 1 of the convention to secure to everyone within their jurisdiction the rights and freedoms defined in the convention, taken together with art 3, requires states to take measures designed to ensure that individuals within their jurisdiction are not subjected to torture or inhuman or degrading treatment or punishment, including such ill-treatment administered by private individuals.[23]

In its latest move to protect victims, the Strasbourg Court imposed a broad general duty, in *M.C. v. Bulgaria*, to enact an effective criminal law protecting women against rape.[24] The Court submitted a highly learned opinion that canvassed the recent legal developments of several European states, the United States, and the ad hoc international tribunals on the relevance of using or threatening force to the definition of rape. The conclusion was that Bulgaria breached its duty under Articles 3 and 8 (the two provisions invoked in the prior cases discussed) by failing to adopt a definition of rape that would provide women with protection against unwanted sex in the absence of the traditional emphasis on force or threat of force.[25]

This holding is a far cry from the two earlier cases. The case of *X. & Y. v. The Netherlands* was based on what appeared to be an arbitrary exception for mentally handicapped victims of rape. The case of *A. v. United Kingdom* reflected private conduct that could be properly called "inhuman or degrading punishment" as explicitly prohibited by Article 3 of the ECHR. In the most recent case against Bulgaria, the notion of degrading punishment has merged with the broader idea of ill-treatment. Though the Court did say, as quoted above, that the member states of the Union must take measures "designed to ensure that individuals within their jurisdiction are not subjected to ill-treatment, including ill-treatment administered by private individuals," the range of the former now seems to have no bounds. The Strasbourg Court has assumed the remarkable burden of supervising and rewriting the criminal codes of all the member states.

It is important to keep in mind, however, that in these cases the power of the Strasbourg Court is severely limited. They do not order states to change their laws, nor do they reverse judgments entered in the national court. The only remedy offered is monetary damages to the victim. Thus, a new species of international tort law seems to be emerging, based on the failure of states to protect their citizens against harm. Of course, there might have been a tort remedy available in Bulgaria against the defendants, but the Court holds, without much reasoning, that the member states must provide criminal sanctions for this type of harm.[26] In a separate concurring opinion, Judge Tulkens of Belgium properly expressed reservations about the propriety of insisting on a criminal remedy at the national level. She emphasizes that "criminal proceedings should remain both in theory and in practice, a last resort or subsidiary remedy."[27] One would think so, particularly because in these cases the Strasbourg Court itself recognizes only tort liability for breach of the Convention.

Though there are obvious anomalies in the jurisprudence of the Strasbourg Court, these cases represent a salutary development in the protection of victims' rights. The United States lags far behind in this area. Even if state officials are negligent in failing to provide protection for abused children, the courts refuse to find state action liable and treat the abuse as a constitutional violation.[28] American courts have not even considered invoking the concept of privacy to reach the result of the Strasbourg Court in 1985—namely, that an unjust and arbitrary decision not to prosecute is a violation of the victim's right to privacy.

IV. The Innovation of the Rome Statute

Against this background, we should consider the dramatic shift represented by the *Rome Statute* adopted by the International Convention of States Parties in Rome in the summer of 1998, and now ratified by more than 90 states. The United States signed the treaty under President Clinton and then, reversing this decision under President Bush, adopted a position of apparent hostility towards the ICC. In April 2005, however, the United States dramatically signaled a new policy of support for the ICC by abstaining from (rather than vetoing) Security Council Resolution 1593 referring the situation in Darfur to the Court for investigation and prosecution of offenses against the *Rome Statute*.[29]

The *Rome Statute* is the first major international document to place the interests of victims as fundamental to the pursuit of justice. The *Preamble* to the Statute stresses the atrocities committed in the wars of the twentieth century, a source of injustice compounded by the impunity of the offenders.[30] The rights of the accused are mentioned, but only later in the statute, beginning in Article 63, which gives the accused the right to be present at the trial.[31] The more significant rights constituting a "fair hearing" are detailed in Article 67.[32]

The ICC constitutes nothing less than a major victory for the victims' rights movement, a reversal of priorities between justice and fairness that is unprecedented in the history of criminal law. For this reason, it is important to examine precisely what justice requires for victims. What do the advocates of victims mean when they proclaim, "No justice, no peace"? They cannot mean that they have a right to see the accused convicted and punished, any more than the accused can translate the right to a fair trial into a right to acquittal. Yet the rights of victims consist in more than an echoing of the defendant's right to a fair trial. The key to understanding the special position of victims is the word "impunity" as used in the *Rome Statute Preamble*: "Affirming that the most serious crimes of concern to the international community as a whole must not go unpunished and... [d]etermined to put an end to impunity for the perpetrators of these crimes."[33] Of course, the question that any legal philosopher would ask is, "Why?" The *Preamble* lamely suggests that the issue is the "prevention of such crimes," but this is clearly a makeweight argument.[34] Even a complete skeptic about the possibility of deterring future crimes would insist that the Eichmanns and Milosevics of the world be punished for their crimes against humanity.

What is so terrible about impunity? This is the central question, I believe, in formulating a theory of justice to victims. An answer often given, and one that I advocated some ten years ago,[35] is that when the state tolerates criminality that it has the capacity to punish, it becomes complicit in the crime. The state, which derives its legitimacy in part from its mission to protect its citizens against crime, becomes an agent of criminality by failing to prosecute.

The concept of impunity relates closely to the complementarity underlying the jurisdiction of the ICC. According to the *Rome Statute* in Article 17(1)(a), the ICC may prosecute only if the state that would otherwise have jurisdiction "is unwilling or unable genuinely to carry out the investigation or prosecution."[36] Therefore, the ICC functions in a way that is complementary to the administration of criminal justice by nation states. Cases of impunity in the twentieth century were instances of states—mostly fascist or communist—that were unwilling to prosecute. Today, there are more likely to be instances in which states such as the Congo and the Sudan are "unable genuinely to carry out the investigation or prosecution." In either case the victim is left alone, effectively abandoned by the one power that should have prevented the crime and should insure that the offender is properly punished for his or her actions.

The paradox of the *Rome Statute* in the modern world is that it endorses a form of retributive punishment. The supporters of the *Rome Statute* would probably not want to identify themselves as adherents of "an eye for an eye" justice, but if deterrence is in fact dubious, then why must the state punish the offender? The only plausible reason is the retributivist claim that, as a matter of justice, crime must always be punished. Recall the words of the *Rome Statute Preamble*: "Affirming that [these crimes]...must not go unpunished..."[37] This is a simple claim of justice as an end in itself.[38] The guilty must be punished—that is simply what justice requires.[39]

V. The ICC as the Triumph of Victims' Rights

The proper question to ask ourselves is, "How did this transformation occur?" How did the leading nations of the world come to the conclusion that the impunity of those who commit crimes "of concern to the international community as a whole" must not go unpunished? How did the question of justice for victims gain a place equal, if not superior, to the commitment to a fair trial for the accused?

The roots of this transformation lie, I believe, in the legal events of the mid-1980s. We have already seen the way in which the European Court of Human Rights began to vindicate the rights of victims in the case of *X. & Y.* in 1985. At the same time, the concept of *impunidad* (Spanish for "impunity") became an influential value in post-junta Argentine legal politics under President Raul Alfonsin, elected in 1983. The prosecution of the generals responsible for the "disappearances" recorded in *Nunca Más*[40] became a major precedent for the ICC.[41] More than he realizes, Jaime Malamud-Goti, who has also contributed to this Symposium, is one of the heroes of this historic series of trials. As the Presidential Advisor responsible for the trials, Malamud-Goti fervently believed in the evil of *impunidad*. The point of trials, he explained to me at the time, was to demonstrate that no one was above the law. That is another way of saying that democratic Argentina could not tolerate the impunity of dictators who committed grave offenses against humanity. Of course, as a philosopher and academic, he is skeptical about the lasting significance of the Argentine trials.[42] When the history of this period is properly understood, however, the Argentine experience will stand in bold relief as a key legal event that led, fifteen years later, to the adoption of the *Rome Statute*.

Is it possible that the United States was not part of this major reorientation of legal thought? I believe we were indeed part of it, but that racial and gender politics have obscured the shift in our thinking. In a whole series of cases involving gays, blacks, Jews, and women as victims, we began to take more seriously those who belonged to these legally disadvantaged groups. These are cases known largely by the name of the victim, as in the Rodney King affair. No one remembers the names of the police officers who were prosecuted and eventually convicted for beating up Rodney King, but no one will forget King's name. To a lesser extent, the same is true of Harvey Milk, the gay city councilman assassinated in San Francisco; of Yankel Rosenbaum, the Hasidic Jew killed on the streets of Brooklyn; and of Desirée Washington, the woman who was allegedly raped by Mike Tyson. These were the headline-grabbing cases in America in the 1980s and early 1990s. They are our counterpart to the jurisprudential shift toward victims' rights in Strasbourg and the prosecution of the generals in Argentina. In the public responses to the cases of Harvey Milk, Rodney King, Yankel Rosenbaum, and of rape victims who took to the streets to "take back the night," we too participated in the jurisprudential transformation that has converted impunity for offenders into an evil we can no longer tolerate.

Yet, for Americans, the issue of justice for minorities seems to have overshadowed the question of justice for victims. The prosecution of the African-American celebrity O.J. Simpson was seen as a continuation of the injustice done to Rodney King. Indeed, the backlash from the King affair probably generated undue sympathy for Simpson. Since South Central Los Angeles rioted after the Simi Valley acquittal of the police officers who beat up King, the media speculated about racial unrest if the jury convicted O.J. As I have argued, the failure to do justice for victims generates a sense of second-class citizenship in the group as a whole. This loss of self-esteem, generated by the sense that offenders enjoy impunity, is typically absent when a member of the same group is subject to prosecution.

The same phenomenon of minority-group-identification accounts, in part, for the shift in American policy toward the ICC. The alleged crimes in Darfur are perceived to be atrocities committed by Arabs against blacks. African-Americans—indeed all Americans—bring a keen sense of injustice to these events, particularly after the shameful failure of the United States to intervene in the Rwandan genocide. American leaders have been even quicker than the Security Council to allege that the atrocities in Darfur constitute genocide.

VI. Conclusion

As in domestic criminal justice, ethnic identification with the victims of crime often enables people to give voice to their sense of justice. Their active engagement may begin with a sense that people of their own group have suffered and therefore, they personally feel attacked. To become effective in courts of law, however, they must transcend partisan identification and seek a form of discourse that protects all persons against similar forms of injustice.

CHAPTER 26

Reply: Justice for Victims and Justice for Society

*Stephen J. Schulhofer**

The United States, unlike many nations of continental Europe, grants the victim no formal right to become a party in a criminal prosecution of the alleged perpetrator. Indeed, from an American perspective, rights are almost always conceived in entirely negative terms. The government *must not do* certain things, such as abridge the freedom of speech or punish a suspected offender without first giving him a fair trial. A right, in this conception, is by its very nature a legal entitlement *to stop* the government from doing something, and a bill of rights is, again almost by definition, a catalogue of actions that the government *must not take* against individuals. Affirmative rights, the right to insist that the government must *do* certain things, are largely absent from the American constitutional framework, even when the needs involved are the most basic imaginable—for example, the need for adequate health care, the need for a decent education, and even a small, defenseless child's need to be protected from violent injury inflicted by his own father.[1]

The victims' rights movement that first emerged in the United States in the 1970s drew to a considerable extent on the ideology and momentum generated by the then-recent successes of the women's liberation movement and the movement to protect the civil rights of racial minorities. But the victims' rights movement nonetheless represented a profound political and conceptual revolution, insofar as its main thrust was the claim that government has an affirmative *obligation to act* and that citizens—in this case those victimized by crime—have a personal right to insist that certain affirmative things be done.

*Robert B. McKay Professor of Law, New York University

The victims' rights movement in the United States quickly gained political traction, and its goals were realized across a broad front. Victims obtained the right to be kept informed of the progress of the prosecution, to express an opinion about the propriety of a proposed plea agreement, to be heard at sentencing, and to receive restitution from convicted perpetrators.[2] Yet from an international perspective these achievements seem quite modest. Indeed, victims' advocates in America seldom even attempted to win the affirmative rights that have long been taken for granted in parts of Europe—the right to insist that a prosecution actually be brought and the right to become a formal party in the criminal litigation.[3]

Because American jurisdictions are unanimous in denying the victim "standing" to present a formal challenge to prosecutorial decisions,[4] victims in the United States cannot overturn decisions to forgo prosecution, even when such decisions are based on manifestly improper grounds. Thus, in the Supreme Court's notorious decision in *Linda R. S. v. Richard D.*,[5] the mother of an illegitimate child sought to challenge a Texas prosecutor who refused to bring charges against the child's father for refusing to pay child support, where it was conceded that the sole ground for the failure to prosecute was the fact that the child was illegitimate. Although the state was clearly engaged in invidious and unconstitutional discrimination, by denying the equal protection of its laws to children born out of wedlock, the Supreme Court, in a decision written by Justice Thurgood Marshall, dismissed the mother's challenge on the ground that neither she nor her child had standing to raise the claim or to compel the prosecutor to take into account only legally acceptable considerations.

Professor Fletcher's thoughtful essay "Justice and Fairness in the Protection of Crime Victims" draws attention to this sharp split between the United States and the rest of the world in terms of what passes for success on behalf of victims. And as Professor Fletcher perceptively notes, the split has grown wider. Existing American law and the prevalent agenda of groups seeking pro-victim reform all remain largely content to grant and perhaps reinforce the victims' "voice" in a criminal process that remains firmly under official control. Meanwhile, European nations and a variety of emerging international tribunals have taken large steps toward recognizing the victim's affirmative right to insist that a prosecution be brought and that justice be done.

These international developments, welcome though they are, mask some ambiguity and ambivalence about the jurisprudential basis for this improved position of the victim. The victim's enhanced leverage may be grounded in what we could describe as either a *modest* or an *ambitious* conception of what the victim's right is.

In the modest conception, the decision whether to prosecute is assigned to public officials who are expected to make prudent choices; they are entrusted with discretion to determine whether, all things considered, it serves public purposes, comprehensively understood, for a criminal offender to be prosecuted, convicted, and punished. The victim's right, in this conception, is merely the modest right to insist that such discretion be exercised on acceptable grounds. A decision to forgo a child-neglect prosecution, on the ground that the child in question was illegitimate, would be overturned. But the court would not necessarily have the power to insist that a prosecution be brought; the prosecutor would merely be forced to reconsider and, if she still refused to go forward, to provide a permissible reason for that decision.

The ambitious conception, in contrast, is based, as Professor Fletcher notes, on a very different jurisprudential theory, namely on "the retributivist claim that, as a matter of justice, *crime must always be punished*" (emphasis added)(261). In this conception, the victim has a right not merely to insist that charging decisions be made on legitimate grounds but, going further, to insist that the defendant, if in fact guilty, must be charged, prosecuted, and subjected to a punishment commensurate with the degree of his moral fault.

Professor Fletcher's provocative essay spotlights the evolution of international thinking on this subject and the subtle way in which the jurisprudence and the international documents have slowly moved from what I called the modest to the more ambitious conception. In its decision in *X & Y v. The Netherlands*,[6] the European Court of Human Rights (ECHR) held only that a prosecutor could not base a refusal to charge on the unconscionable ground that the victim of the crime was mentally handicapped. But lurking in the court's decision is also the possibility that a state's affirmative obligation to protect its residents from private violence may encompass a stronger right, the right to insist that criminal remedies be effective.

The ECHR's decision in *M.C. v. Bulgaria*[7] takes a further step in this direction. On the surface it is, again, not a ruling that the state was necessarily required to press criminal charges. Instead, it is simply a ruling that the reasons for not prosecuting were unacceptable. Prosecutors had declined to charge rape because the fourteen-year-old complainant did not allege that her attackers had subdued her by physical force. This, the court held, was an improper standard because women have a basic human right to state protection from unwanted sexual imposition, and this right, the court said, requires the availability of criminal sanctions for those who impose sex *without consent*, even in the absence of physical force.

Here, of course, we are a long way from the kind of ruling that finds an abuse of discretion in a prosecutor's decision not to charge on the sole ground that the victim is an illegitimate child or a mentally disabled adult. The reason that prosecutors relied on in the *M.C.* case is one that is the subject of much good-faith debate and disagreement.[8] To that extent, even the "modest" conception of victim's rights confers on victims and ultimately upon the courts a potentially sweeping power, the power to step into controversial policy debates and exert significant influence over the reach of the substantive criminal law. Still, the *M.C.* decision, at least on the surface, accepts the principle that a prosecutor's discretion *whether* to charge is legitimate, so long as it is exercised on permissible grounds.

Once again, however, there is also in the opinion an implicit suggestion that the fundamental human right to state protection may encompass an affirmative entitlement to vindication, to the imposition of criminal punishment when that right is violated. Professor Fletcher's analysis of the Rome Statute shows how that document appears to carry this evolution further still, implying that "[t]he guilty *must be* punished—that is simply what justice requires (261)."

Professor Fletcher properly asks *how* this transformation occurred. But the transformation he identifies is still a work in progress, and it is therefore pertinent to ask as well whether that transformation is desirable, and whether it should be encouraged, restrained, or even reversed. Adherents to the form of Kantian retributivism that insists that "the guilty must be punished" will not be swayed, of course, by the prospect that such a retributivism, scrupulously respected, could grievously damage social welfare and the prospects for effective law enforcement. They have heard that complaint before, and for them, what justice requires, no merely practical concern should forestall. (As Kant not so gently put it, "woe to him who creeps through the serpent-windings of utilitarianism to discover some advantage that may discharge him from the justice of punishment, or even from the due measure of it.")[9] But everyone who does not subscribe to this version of retributivism must acknowledge the obligation to explore with care the pragmatic implications of an affirmative state duty to punish all the guilty to a degree proportionate to their desert and, further, the pragmatic implications of endowing the victims of crime with the capacity to force officials to carry out that duty to its full extent.

In the case of relatively ordinary crime, including even such serious felonies as robbery, rape, and homicide, the urgent claims of sympathy and justice for crime victims can conceivably be met in adequate fashion by the relatively simple right to insist that discretion be exercised on legitimate grounds. The ECHR's decision in the *M.C.* case dramatically illustrates the far-reaching potential of this ostensibly "modest" conception of victim's rights, and it may be plausible to think that justice (in a world of limited resources) does not necessarily require that every single perpetrator be punished to the full extent of his or her desert.

In contrast, in the case of truly atrocious crime, mass murder and genocide, it becomes hard indeed to dismiss the contention that "the guilty must be punished" and that impunity is intolerable. Yet even here, pragmatic concerns have some claim on our attention. Do the goals of ending a cycle of violence and achieving social repair, reconciliation, and a peaceful future ever justify amnesty or forgiveness for the low-level foot soldiers who may, nonetheless, have perpetrated unspeakable crimes? And what of the very worst of the perpetrators, the leaders who initiate and orchestrate murder and rape on an unimaginable scale? They must be brought to justice, to be sure. But are there ever cases in which it should be permissible to moderate the demands of justice, to accept a negotiated end to civil war as an alternative to a just but uncompromising stance that may prolong the fighting and make it impossible for the leadership of one or both sides to surrender? The choices are all bad; no answer can be pretty under such circumstances. But there is much to consider before we can say with confidence where the path lies in the proper pursuit of justice and fairness for the victims of crime.

GEORGE FLETCHER REPLIES TO HIS CRITICS

CHAPTER 27

Remembrance of Articles Past

George P. Fletcher

Reading these essays of mine has left me in a reflective, trancelike suspension of time. They take me into a confrontation with a past that is even deeper and more arresting than the normal suggestions of memory. I cannot deny that I have written these essays, but the exact form of the arguments made thirty-five years ago surprises me in the way one might be amazed to encounter an old friend from college who reminds one of long-forgotten antics of rebellion. I relish this past and now have the distance to assess what I was doing and what kind of passions guided me.

A good deal of my early writing was in fact a form of rebellion—against American law, against the Model Penal Code, against the leading scholars of the prior generation, mostly on the East Coast (Herb Wechsler, Jerome Hall, Hart and Sacks). There was something slightly absurd in starting to write about the virtues of German criminal theory less than a generation after World War II. And adding Soviet law to my portfolio was bizarre so far as I attempted to include their views in normative articles about what the law should be. As early as *Rethinking Criminal Law* (1978) (hereinafter *Rethinking*), I even began a practice commenting on biblical sources as authority from which we could derive wisdom about the current state of criminal law. Fortunately, no one has followed me in these practices of relying on exotic sources. My critics have kindly deferred to my tastes and treated my eclectic interests with seeming respect.

When I began writing about the criminal law, I had the sense that the field was barren. The cases that one must teach—with one or two exceptions—are atrocious, certainly as compared with the elegant, influential precedents in constitutional law, torts, contracts, and most fields in the curriculum. Ask a criminal lawyer whether there is any case decided by an American court in the field of substantive criminal law that makes him proud to be an American lawyer, and you will encounter a long period of silence.[1]

In the last forty years, however, the field of criminal theory has become a major movement in American academia. As this and other volumes and projects attest,[2] the writing on criminal theory in English is now as good as if not better than any system abroad. I might complain that our scholars are not sufficiently interested in comparative law, but the truth is that virtually no one—here or abroad—takes the time and invests the energy to think about criminal law on a comparative global scale. Criminal law—as written in German, Spanish, or Japanese—tends to be equally parochial, oriented to local codes and court decisions. Textbooks on the Continent are written with almost no citations to foreign law.[3] There is still a tendency to think of one's own legal system as the entire world of law that is relevant.

This visit to my early essays—and most of this volume has focused on ideas present in essays written before 1985—gives me a certain amount of distance from my passions as a scholar. In this suspended, almost trancelike, state, my thoughts turn to the differences between taking a scholarly stand and arguing for positions as an advocate. I have never written about my experiences as an advocate. Therefore, in this essay I want to reflect about the differences between arguing for a scholarly position and arguing for a client.

1. Giving the Scholars Their Due

The first thing that impresses me about scholarly work is the high probability of consistency over a scholarly career of forty years and more. Very few scholars undergo the kind of transformation that occurred to Wittgenstein between his writing the *Tractatus Logico-Philosophicus*[4] and *Investigations*.[5] I have not changed my mind often, whether this is to my credit or discredit. Nonetheless, these essays—taken as a whole—highlight some points of dissonance. For example, I still believe in the claim in *Rethinking*[6] that the criminal law is best described in three patterns of liability. In a comment that is almost an aside, Douglas Husak reminds me of my commitment to the three-patterns thesis. Yet in my essay on blackmail, I claim that there is one paradigm of liability that runs through the entire criminal law, namely, the paradigm of domination. John Noonan correctly takes me to task on this part of my argument, but he seems to be sympathetic to my internal account of why blackmail is punishable. Alan Wertheimer takes the opposite approach. He delves into the details of the cases I pose and doubts whether the principle of domination can account for the proper results, yet, at the same, he thinks that blackmail, under a proper account, might be the paradigm for all criminal liability. On these issues I think that Noonan is right, and I adhere to my earlier view that the proper analysis of the criminal law requires us to distinguish among three patterns of liability, the patterns of manifest liability, of subjective liability, and of harmful consequences.[7] Even then, there might be some crimes that fall out-side these three patterns. Noonan's example of tax evasion could be treated as an example of subjective liability because the mens rea for the crime lies at the heart of the prosecution.

Much of my work pays careful attention to language—both our language and foreign usage. A few of the articles in this volume address these issues. Victoria Nourse writes an elegy for my 1985 article on the European concept of Right and the American concept of reasonableness. John Gardner adopts my linguistic approach in joining my early effort to understand the distinction between pun-ishment and compensation. He takes a slightly different approach from mine and puts into question some issues that I have taken to be sacred cows. For example, he thinks that when equally situated parties impose harm on each other with the intent to show disapproval, this should constitute punishment. In taking this line, he rejects one of Hart's five conditions of punishment,[8] as well as Kant's well-considered position holding that punishment between equally situated states is conceptually impossible.[9] Apparently, Gardner would extend the notion of war to include reprisals and military campaigns to teach the other side a lesson.

Douglas Husak pays me the compliment of addressing my favorite question on the theory of punishment: What is punishment imposed for? Husak essentially agrees with my analysis but shows that there might be some contexts in which the question elicits a range of replies. My purpose is to underscore the importance of wrongdoing as a distinct dimension of liability. The correct answer, in my view, is that punishment is imposed not for guilt, not for bad character, but solely for wrongdoing. In holding to this line I am influenced by Hart, who held that pun-ishment is imposed "for offenses against legal rules," and by Robert Nozick's bril-liant but generally ignored insight that the correct level of retributive punishment is determined by the formula $P = r \cdot W$, where P stands for deserved punishment, r for the degree of responsibility, and W for the gravity of the wrongdoing. R can vary only between 0 and 1, but W varies from 0 to infinity. Under this formula, assessing the gravity of the wrong is the critical first step in analyzing deserved punishment. For the full commission of the crime ($r = 1$), the liability is full. When reduced, say, on grounds of provocation or diminished capacity, the punishment is lower. When r effectively equals 0 as in the case of complete excuses, there is no punishment even for the gravest wrongs.

The distinction between wrongdoing and responsibility, as clarified so beau-tifully in Nozick's formula, parallels the distinction between justification and excuse. Many writers in this volume give me credit for elaborating the distinc-tion between justification and excuse as though these structural issues were par-ticularly original and insightful. In fact, they are quite trivial and well known in most civil law systems and indeed in the early common law, which distinguished between excusable and justifiable homicide. I deserve no credit for the conceptual apparatus of justification and excuse, even though many scholars in the common law still have trouble understanding the implications of the ideas expressed in the categories of wrongdoing, responsibility or culpability, justification, and excuse.

A good example is Alon Harel, who engages in serious reflection about the constructs of self-defense I developed many years ago.[10] One of these is based on a wrongful attack without culpability on the part of the attacker—the case of the so-called psychotic aggressor. The justification for self-defense against a psychotic aggressor is based exclusively on his wrongdoing, since in fact he is not culpable. Kant and the German tradition are clear that under principles of Right you are completely justified in repelling the attack by a psychotic aggressor—at whatever cost. This position has been tempered in recent jurisprudence by imposing limitations under the civilian doctrines of "abuse of rights." Harel thinks, however, that the psychotic aggressor is not the person who is appropriately considered the originator of the danger to the party who must act in self-defense. He says that the aggressor is equivalent to a bystander and therefore repelling the attack and causing him injury is wrong on Kantian grounds: the defender is said to be using the aggressor (bystander) as a means to an end. Like much of Harel's work, this is a very clever point. Unfortunately, it is wrong. It is critical to see that the psychotic aggressor must be acting (not just flailing his limbs in an epileptic fit). That he is acting contrary to the legal order and that he brings the danger onto the defender is sufficient to distinguish him from a bystander.

In her very thoughtful article, Susan Estrich also expresses doubts about the distinction between justification and excuse. Or at least she thinks that the need to classify particular issues one way or the other is overdone. I think this is a careless aside on her part. In fact, it has made a tremendous difference in the battered women's cases whether self-defense is conceptualized as an excuse or a justification. It is much easier to prevail by relying on a theory of excuse. This is what I argued as early as 1972, and many early feminists picked up the argument and ran with it. The later literature reverted to a version of self-defense that stressed either the desert of the evil man or the right of the abused woman. It is no surprise that the movement to provide a complete defense for these women has been notably unsuccessful.[11] The woman who kills her abuser in his sleep is lucky to get off with manslaughter. This is clearly an instance in which ideological commitments generate bad lawyering.

The surprise ending in Estrich's article is that she comes out against the individualization of excusing conditions. The rest of the society has the right that those who suffer peculiar sensitivities bring their conduct to the level that others expect. This is a problem of "trust," she says. Let me expand on this suggestive point. In torts cases involving contractual elements, we do draw a distinction between ordinary medical practitioners and specialists. Specialists are supposed to know more, their clients rely on the way they present themselves to the public, and therefore if something goes wrong, they are held to a higher standard. The reasonable person under the circumstances is the urban specialist who holds himself out as such. This is an appropriate case to invoke the trust of the clients to impose a higher standard of care.

Now suppose the issue is the one in *Decina*.[12] A driver on the road has a predictable blackout and crashes into another car. Is he to be judged against the standard of the reasonable person who occasionally has blackouts? The answer is no. His condition actually worsens his case. If the blackout that led to the accident was the first he ever had, he would possibly have a good excuse. But in light of his knowledge of his medical condition, he could have been expected to take precautions against the risk of his having a blackout.

On the other hand, if two people are in a relationship, one is a seven-foot athlete and the other is a ninety-eight-pound weakling, and if the larger person attacks the smaller, the law obviously considers their relative strengths in assessing the reasonable amount of force used under the circumstances. This is the point of the *Wanrow* case that became pivotal in feminist jurisprudence.[13]

Joshua Dressler realizes the importance of relying on a theory of excuses in battered women's cases. He is right. In his many-faceted essay in this volume, he also does a good job defending the imminence requirement in cases of justificatory self-defense. This is the central problem for abused women who kill their husbands or lovers while they are sleeping. They might be terrified of what the man will do when he wakes up, but this does not justify their killing him.

Preventive self-defense (prior to an imminent risk) is no more justifiable in domestic law than it is in international law. International lawyers are hopelessly confused when they discuss these issues because they use the phrase "preemptive self-defense" to cover the cases of self-defense against an imminent attack. One reason for their confused terminology is that the United Nations Charter Article 51 permits self-defense only in cases where "an armed attack occurs." The international lawyers start, therefore, from the opposite end of the spectrum. A strike against an imminent threat of force still appears to them as the first strike, and therefore they call it preemptive—even though it is justified. Nonetheless, good international lawyers do everything possible to interpret the charter to cover cases such as the Israeli defense of its borders in the Six-Day War as legitimate self-defense. In my opinion, if the fact is that the Israelis were resisting an imminent attack, that simple fact alone is sufficient to justify their action.

Dressler goes wrong, in my view, in his stand on putative self-defense. These are cases where the defender is mistaken about the nature and gravity of the threat. A good case would be Bernhard Goetz, who used deadly force against four black youths who surrounded him on the subway. The statute required that he use only reasonable force when he reasonably believed that a robbery was about to occur. But no one knows whether a robbery was about to occur. There are two ways to interpret Goetz's response—as real self-defense against a robbery in fact and as putative self-defense against an imagined robbery. The common law does not recognize this distinction, and therefore at trial in the jury instructions the two issues got jumbled together. Both forms of self-defense were treated as claims of justification. The problem would be critical only if, hypothetically, the blacks who were being shot at used defensive force to subdue Goetz. If the use of force is justified, the response is not—on the theory that if the defender is exercising a right, then the opposing party cannot, as a matter of principle, have a right to resist.

Most people intuitively agree that if I have a right to do A, you cannot have an inconsistent right that I not do A. If someone has a right to smoke in class, you cannot have a right that no one smokes in class. This is part of the logic of rights. The same logic holds in the analysis of self-defense, so far as it treated as a right to use force. If Israel had a right to use defensive force against Egypt in the beginning of the Six-Day War, it cannot be the case that Egypt also had a right to attack Israel.[14]

Many theorists are willing to accept the idea of inconsistent claims of justification. Their trick is to reduce the moral significance of a justification to a "warrant" or a "permission."[15] Of course, there might be inconsistent permissions. You are permitted to smoke, I am permitted to insist that you not. The exact logical content of a warrant or permission remains hazy. The better view is that self-defense consists in a right[16] to ward off the attack (not to kill or inflict injury as an end in itself).

Apart from this point about the logic of rights, the proper analysis of putative justification is to recognize that it represents a purely subjective claim of a right to use force. It is not grounded in reality. The question is whether personal beliefs alone can generate rights that others must respect. I find it hard to understand how this could happen.

In international law, it would be very dangerous to recognize a purely subjective conception of dangers as a basis for legitimately going to war. In the international arena, it is important that the claim of self-defense under the UN Charter be based on some objective event or evidence that the world can see. Think of the photographs of Soviet missiles installed in Cuba that Adlai Stevenson displayed so effectively in the UN General Assembly in 1962. More recently, President George W. Bush made claims that Saddam Hussein had weapons of mass destruction, but he never produced any evidence that would have been taken seriously. Without objective evidence there can be no serious claim of a right to use force in international self-defense.

On the other hand, a subjective belief in the conditions of self-defense can generate the excuse known as putative self-defense. This is not a right. It is compatible with a justification on the other side.

It is not clear to me why Dressler takes the view he does on putative self-defense. This is the way he puts it:

> Fletcher's rejection of "putative justifications"—a claim of justification
> based on a mistaken, albeit reasonable, belief that justifying conditions

exist—has in turn been rejected by most scholars (including me) and by virtually all courts and penal codes. (226) (internal citation omitted).

This is a noteworthy comment. It illustrates the point I made earlier that common-law scholars think of their own law as the entire relevant world of law. Perhaps it is the case that the majority of common-law scholars reject the doctrine that putative justifications are excuses (this is the correct way to put the point), but this is certainly not true on a worldwide basis. The standard view in Germany, Spain, Latin America, Japan, Taiwan (perhaps Russia and China), and all the other states in the school influenced by German law is that putative justification must be treated as an excuse bearing exclusively on culpability.[17]

In making this argument from "the way the law is," Dressler engages in a form of argument that I often invoke myself. In fact, I am inclined to make the argument in an even radical form. "None of the leading legal systems recognizes X or Y." Is this a legitimate way of using comparative law—as a hammer for winning arguments? I am of mixed minds on the point. The Rome Statute recognizes the comparative synthesis of general principles as a source of law.[18] On the other hand, when someone argues the way the law ought to be, it is not much of a claim to say, yes, but the law is not that way.

I admit that a good part of my scholarship consists in defending the way the criminal law actually has taken shape—in the foreign as well as the common-law system. You might want to call this: arguments from a descriptive theory of law. Relying upon this descriptive theory, I should like to identify three arguments that I regard as fallacious but nonetheless of persistent appeal. For short, I will refer to these as the "objective thesis" (Paul Robinson's theory of objective self-defense), the choice thesis (you can only be culpable for what you choose), and the control thesis (you can only be culpable for matters under your control). All three of these arguments are to be found in the commentary of this volume.

Peter Westen defends the objective theory under the label "unity thesis." By unity he means that there is no important difference between elements of the definition of the offense (called *Tatbestand* or *tipo* in other languages) and the elements of justification. In German this is called the theory of justification as negative element of the *Tatbestand*. Robinson first came upon this thesis when he was my student in the early 1970s.[19] It was a glorious moment. In his persistent faith in the view that self-defense and necessity did not require a subjective dimension, you could see an academic mind being born. Robinson has never changed his mind, and indeed he has attracted some followers, Westen and surely others.

I fail to understand the appeal of the argument. It is based on a confusion between social harm and the overriding value of the justificatory claim. There are two good ways to flesh out my objection to the unity thesis. The first requires attention to the theory of protected legal interests (*Rechtsgueter*). We do not talk about this very much in Anglo-American criminal law, but it is an important subject, especially in organizing codes of liability. The legal interest protected by the law of homicide is, we all assume, the right to life. If you follow Robinson, however, you have to say that the protected legal interest is the life of nonaggressors. Aggressors are no more protected than flies.

I think it is more plausible to describe killing in self-defense as an infringement of the right to life that is justified under the circumstances. John Gardner usefully described this view as the "remainder" thesis. In cases of justification, something of the wrong remains.[20]

There is another way of looking at the problem that is sufficient in itself to convince me that claims of justification are logically distinct from elements of the definition. Let us break down the elements of homicide: (1) causing (2) death of (3) another (4) human being. We could represent this as A + B + C + D. Now suppose we describe the elements of self-defense as (1) knowingly (2) using force that is (3) necessary and (4) proportional (5) to repel (6) an attack. We could represent these as E + F + G + H + I + J. If we the put the two together, the composite rule defining unlawful homicide would be A + B + C + D that is not justified, namely, that it is not the case that (E + F + G + H + I + J). The important thing to recognize about the elements A to D is that the prosecution must prove all of them. For there to be a case of no self-defense, it is sufficient to prove that one of the elements E through J is absent. If you carry the negative through the parentheses, the conjunctive becomes disjunctive. Thus the prosecution must prove A + B + C + D and –E or –F or –G or –H or –I or –J. This may not be convincing to people for whom this way of symbolizing rules is mysterious or foreign, but those who know something about symbolic representation should see immediately that the logic of justification differs totally from the logic of the crime or the definition itself.

The last essay to address is the argument by Larry Alexander and Kimberly Kessler Ferzan that negligence is not a proper basis for criminal liability. Following H.L.A. Hart,[21] I have defended the punishability of negligence from the very beginning of my scholarly career.[22] The argument to the contrary seems to pop up every twenty years or so. Jerome Hall took this line,[23] and so did Claire Finkelstein. I have never understood how anyone who actually works in or studies criminal law could hold this view. It is obvious that a morally sensitive criminal law could not survive without a principle of responsibility for negligence.

The clearest case is one that may not occur to common lawyers because of our general ignorance about mistake of law. No morally sound theory of criminal liability can totally ignore the issue of mistake of law. The Rome Statute purports to do this in Article 32(2). Take, for example, the ignorance by Israeli officials as to whether their policies in occupied territories constitute a "direct or indirect" transfer of the civilian population.[24] How can they fairly be punished for their "war crime" when no one knows precisely which conduct constitutes a violation (not to mention the even more egregious problem in the Rome Statute that the range of potential violators for war crimes and other offenses is not specified)?

I suppose you could take the view that every good faith mistake of fact should constitute a defense—if it could be established. But I am not sure how you could say that every good faith mistake of law should be a defense. If that were the law, ignorance would become a valuable commodity. The Germans toyed with this idea for a brief period after World War II when they sought to reestablish the morality of their system of criminal law. But in 1952, they gave in to the obvious moral truth. There are some cases in which you can fairly demand that people inquire about the law governing their transaction.[25] The particular case involved a lawyer who raised his fee in the middle of a trial. He was charged with extortion, and he claimed he did not know that what he was doing was unlawful.

Extortion is the kind of charge in German law where people can easily claim ignorance. The police chief in Frankfurt who recently threatened to use torture to force a suspect to reveal the location of a kidnapped child was also convicted under this theory. He was surely acting in good faith (unlike the lawyer in the 1952 case), but good faith is not enough. There are cases when we have to say— you should have known that your conduct was wrongful and illegal. That is to say, we have to punish on the basis of negligence.

Alexander and Ferzan argue that the essence of culpability is choice. There is no choice in cases of negligence; ergo, no culpability. This strikes me as an elementary confusion between the criteria for blaming and the subject's awareness of those criteria. It would be a wonderful world if I could never be blamed for forgetting appointments or ignoring my wife's birthday. It is obvious, however, that if we live in relationships, we bear the burden of finding out when the interests of others may be affected by what we do or do not do.

The wonderful thing about this field of criminal law is that old arguments neither die nor fade away. They remain on our agenda—to be taught and reargued in every generation.

NOTES

Chapter 1

1. Douglas Husak, *Crimes Outside the Core*, 39 TULSA L. REV. 755, 755 (2004).
2. Kent Greenawalt, *The Perplexing Borders of Justification and Excuse*, 84 COLUM. L. REV. 1897, 1897 (1984).

Chapter 2

1. *See* H.L.A. HART, *Prolegomenon to the Principles of Punishment*, *in* PUNISHMENT AND RESPONSIBILITY: ESSAYS IN THE PHILOSOPHY OF LAW 1 (1968); HERBERT MORRIS, *Persons and Punishment*, *in* ON GUILT AND INNOCENCE: ESSAYS IN LEGAL PHILOSOPHY AND MORAL PSYCHOLOGY 31 (1976).
2. *See* HART, *Legal Responsibility and Excuses*, *in* supra note 1, at 28; J.L. Austin, *A Plea for Excuses*, *in* 57 PROC. ARISTOTELIAN SOC'Y 1 (1957); George P. Fletcher, *The Individualization of Excusing Conditions*, 47 S. CAL. L. REV. 1269 (1974); George P. Fletcher, *Proportionality and the Psychotic Aggressor: A Vignette in Comparative Criminal Theory*, 8 ISRAEL L. REV. 367 (1973); Paul H. Robinson, *A Theory of Justification: Societal Harm as a Prerequisite for Criminal Liability*, 23 UCLA L. REV. 266 (1975).
3. *See* MODEL PENAL CODE § 5.05(1) (Proposed Official Draft 1962); JOEL FEINBERG, DOING AND DESERVING: ESSAYS IN THE THEORY OF RESPONSIBILITY 33 (1970); HART, *Intention and Punishment*, *in* supra note 1, at 113, 129–131; THOMAS NAGEL, *Moral Luck*, *in* MORTAL QUESTIONS 24 (1979); Sanford H. Kadish, *Foreword: The Criminal Law and the Luck of the Draw*, 84 J. CRIM. L. & CRIMINOLOGY 679 (1994); Stephen Schulhofer, *Harm and Punishment: A Critique of Emphasis on the Results of Conduct in the Criminal Law*, 122 U. PA. L. REV. 1497 (1974).
4. *See* JONATHAN GLOVER, CAUSING DEATH AND SAVING LIVES (1977); George P. Fletcher, *Prolonging Life*, 42 U. WASH. L. REV. 999 (1966–1967); Sanford H. Kadish, *Letting Patients Die: Legal and Moral Reflections*, *in* IN HARM'S WAY: ESSAYS IN HONOR OF JOEL FEINBERG 290 (1994); Sanford H. Kadish, *Respect for Life and Regard for Rights in the Criminal Law*, 64 CALIF. L. REV. 871 (1976); Judith Jarvis Thomson, *A Defense of Abortion*, 1 PHIL. & PUB. AFF. 47 (1971).
5. *See* SUSAN ESTRICH, REAL RAPE (1987); E.M. Curley, *Excusing Rape*, 5 PHIL. & PUB. AFF. 325 (1976); Susan Estrich, *Rape*, 95 YALE L.J. 1087 (1986).
6. *See* PATRICK DEVLIN, THE ENFORCEMENT OF MORALS (1965); H.L.A. HART, LAW, LIBERTY AND MORALITY (1963); Sanford H. Kadish, *More on Overcriminalization: A Reply to Professor Junker*, 19 UCLA L. REV. 719 (1972); Sanford H. Kadish, *The Crisis of Overcriminalization*, 374 ANNALS AM. ACAD. POL. & SOC. SCI. 157 (1967).

7. Herbert Wechsler & Jerome Michael, *A Rationale of the Law of Homicide: I*, 37 COLUM. L. REV. 701 (1937) [hereinafter Wechsler & Michael *I*]; Herbert Wechsler & Jerome Michael, *A Rationale of the Law of Homicide: II*, 37 COLUM. L. REV. 1261 (1937) [hereinafter Wechsler & Michael *II*].

8. *See* JEROME MICHAEL & HERBERT WECHSLER, CRIMINAL LAW AND ITS ADMINISTRATION (1940).

9. *See* MODEL PENAL CODE (Proposed Official Draft, 1962).

10. *See* MONRAD G. PAULSEN & SANFORD H. KADISH, CRIMINAL LAW AND ITS PROCESSES (1962).

11. *See* JAMES FITZJAMES STEPHEN, A HISTORY OF THE CRIMINAL LAW OF ENGLAND (1883).

12. *See* JOHN STUART MILL, ON LIBERTY 22 (Gertrude Himmelfarb ed., Penguin Books 1985) (1859).

13. *See* JEREMY BENTHAM, AN INTRODUCTION TO THE PRINCIPLES OF MORALS AND LEGISLATION (J.L. Burns & H.L.A. Hart eds., 1996) (1823).

14. *See* WILLIAM BLACKSTONE, COMMENTARIES ON THE LAW OF ENGLAND (1765).

15. Literally translated: "The act is not criminal unless the mind is criminal."

16. *See* EDWARD COKE, THE THIRD PART OF THE INSTITUTES OF THE LAW OF ENGLAND 107 (1644).

17. *See* MORRIS, *supra* note 1.

18. *See* FEINBERG, *supra* note 3; JOEL FEINBERG, THE MORAL LIMITS OF THE CRIMINAL LAW (1984) [hereinafter FEINBERG, MORAL LIMITS].

19. *See* ROBERT NOZICK, ANARCHY, STATE AND UTOPIA (1974) [hereinafter NOZICK, ANARCHY]; ROBERT NOZICK, PHILOSOPHICAL EXPLANATIONS (1981).

20. *See* JUDITH JARVIS THOMSON, RIGHTS, RESTITUTION, AND RISK: ESSAYS IN MORAL THEORY (William Parent ed., 1986).

21. For more in this vein, see George P. Fletcher, *What Law Is Like*, 50 SMU L. REV. 1599 (1997).

22. *See* SANFORD H. KADISH & STEPHEN J. SCHULHOFER, CRIMINAL LAW AND ITS PROCESSES (6th ed. 1995).

23. *See, e.g.*, sources cited *supra* note 3.

24. *See* FEINBERG, *supra* note 3; Kadish, *supra* note 3.

25. *See* PAUL H. ROBINSON & JOHN M. DARLEY, JUSTICE, LIABILITY AND BLAME: COMMUNITY VIEWS AND THE CRIMINAL LAW (1997).

26. *See* R. v. Martineau [1990] 2 S.C.R. 633.

27. *See* GÜNTHER JAKOBS, STRAFRECHT ALLGEMEINER TEIL 470–75 (2d ed. 1993); 1 CLAUS ROXIN, STRAFRECHT ALLGEMEINER TEIL § 19 (3d ed. 1997); Corte cost., 23–24 mar. 1988, *available in* 31 REVISTA ITALIANA DI DIRITTO E PROCEDURA PENALE 686 (1988).

28. *See* CODICE PENALE [C.P.] § 49(2) (Italy); *see also* SHIGEMITSU DANDO, THE CRIMINAL LAW OF JAPAN 202–08 (B.J. George trans., 1997); GIOVANNI FIANDACA & ENZO MUSCO, DIRITTO PENALE: PARTE GENERALE 430–31 (3d ed. 1995).

29. *See* CÓDIGO PENAL [C.P.] § 16(1) (Spain) (defining attempt to require action that "objetivamente deberían producir el resultado" [that would objectively produce the result]).

30. *See* IMMANUEL KANT, FUNDAMENTAL PRINCIPLES OF THE METAPHYSICS OF MORALS 17–18 (Thomas K. Abbott trans., 1949).

31. *See, e.g.*, Michael S. Moore, *The Independent Moral Significance of Wrongdoing*, 5 J. CONTEMP. LEGAL ISSUES 237, 240 (1994); Adrian W. Moore, *A Kantian View of Moral Luck*, 65 PHIL. 297, 304 (1990).

32. KANT, *supra* note 30, at 11.

33. *See* IMMANUEL KANT, FOUNDATIONS OF THE METAPHYSICS OF MORALS 11 (Lewis White Beck trans., 1959) (1785); *see also* George P. Fletcher, *Law and Morality: A Kantian Perspective*, 87 COLUM. L. REV. 533 (1987).

34. *See* Fletcher, *supra* note 33, at 537.

35. *See* IMMANUEL KANT, THE METAPHYSICAL ELEMENTS OF JUSTICE (John Ladd trans., 1985).
36. For a critical assessment of my views on *der Wille and die Willkür,* see Peter Benson, *External Freedom According to Kant,* 87 COLUM. L. REV. 559, 561–62 (1987).
37. *See, e.g.,* CHARLES FRIED, RIGHT AND WRONG 48 (1978); Joshua Dressler, *New Thoughts About the Concept of Justification in the Criminal Law: A Critique of Fletcher's Thinking and Rethinking,* 32 UCLA L. REV. 61, 80 (1984).
38. *See* Michael Corrado, *Automatism and the Theory of Action,* 39 EMORY L.J. 1191 (1990); John Gardner, *The Gist of Excuses,* 1 BUFF. CRIM. L. REV. 575 (1998); Kyron Huigens, *Virtue and Inculpation,* 108 HARV. L. REV. 1423 (1995).
39. *See* MICHAEL MOORE, PLACING BLAME: A GENERAL THEORY OF THE CRIMINAL LAW (1997).
40. *See* Russell L. Christopher, *Self-Defense and Defense of Others,* 27 PHIL. & PUB. AFF. 123 (1998); Russell L. Christopher, *Self-Defense and Objectivity: A Reply to Judith Jarvis Thomson,* 1 BUFF. CRIM. L. REV. 537 (1998); Russell L. Christopher, *Unknowing Justification and the Logical Necessity of the* Dadson *Principle in Private Defence,* 15 OXF. J. LEG. STUD. 229 (1995); Russell L. Christopher, *Mistake of Fact in the Objective Theory of Justification: Do Two Rights Make Two Wrongs Make Two Rights...?* 85 J. CRIM. L. & CRIMINOLOGY 295 (1994).
41. *See* FEINBERG, MORAL LIMITS, *supra* note 18.
42. *See* JOHN RAWLS, A THEORY OF JUSTICE (1971).
43. *See* RONALD DWORKIN, LAW'S EMPIRE (1986).
44. *See* BRUCE A. ACKERMAN, SOCIAL JUSTICE IN THE LIBERAL STATE (1980).
45. *See* NOZICK, ANARCHY, *supra* note 19, at 106–07, 135, 137–40.
46. The movement to educate a new person suitable for life under socialism made the Soviets particularly hostile to the theory of excuses. *See generally* HAROLD J. BERMAN, JUSTICE IN THE U.S.S.R. (1963).
47. *See* MILL, *supra* note 12.
48. *See* Rome Statute of the International Criminal Court, Preamble, *in* 37 INT. LEGAL MATERIALS 999 (1998).
49. *See* Robinson v. California, 370 U.S. 660 (1962).
50. *See* Theodor Lenckner, Commentary, *in* ADOLF SCHÖNKE & HORST SCHRÖDER, STRAFGESETZBUCH: KOMMENTAR § 13 preliminary remarks, at 173–74 (25th ed. 1997).
51. *See, e.g.,* Wechsler & Michael *I, supra* note 7, at 757; Wechsler & Michael *II, supra* note 7, at 1272.
52. *See* STRAFGETSETZBUCH [StGB] § 22 (F.R.G.). This legislated acceptance of the subjective theory of attempts finds general endorsement in the literature. *See, e.g.,* Albin Eser, Commentary, *in* ADOLF SCHÖNKE & HORST SCHRÖDER, STRAFGESETZBUCH: KOMMENTAR § 22, at 340–57 (25th ed. 1997).
53. *See* MOORE, *supra* note 39, at 154.
54. *See* discussion *supra* notes 15–16 and accompanying text.
55. *See* COKE, *supra* note 16, at 107.
56. *See id.* at 54.
57. This point is further explained in GEORGE P. FLETCHER, RETHINKING CRIMINAL LAW 27 n.59 (1978).
58. Ronald M. Dworkin, *The Model of Rules,* 35 U. CHI. L. REV. 14 (1967).

Chapter 3

1. R.A. Duff, *In Defense of One Type of Liberalism: A Reply to Begaric and Amarasekara,* 24 MELB. U. L. REV. 411, 415 (2000).
2. Ernest W. Weinrib, *Law as a Kantian Idea of Reason,* 87 COLUM. L. REV. 472, 474 (1987).

3. *Id.* at 500.
4. *Id.* at 482–83.
5. *Id.* at 483–84.
6. *Id.* at 486–88.
7. *Id.* at 490.
8. *Id.* at 485–86.
9. *Id.* at 485.
10. *Id.* at 505.
11. *Id.* at 488–89.
12. *Id.* at 489.

Chapter 4

1. *See* GEORGE P. FLETCHER, RETHINKING CRIMINAL LAW 410–414 (1978).
2. *See* George P. Fletcher, *Blackmail: The Paradigmatic Crime,* 141 U. PA. L. REV. 1617 (1993).
3. I am indebted to Russell Christopher for this suggestion.
4. THE NICOMACHEAN ETHICS OF ARISTOTLE § 1131a. (David Ross trans., 1925) (on distributive justice).
5. *Id.* at § 1131b (on rectificatory or corrective justice).
6. On the principle *kimle bdraba mina,* see George P. Fletcher, *Punishment and Self-Defense,* 8 LAW AND PHILOSOPHY 201, 203 (1989).
7. Vosburg v. Putney, 50 N.W. 403 (Wis. 1891); RESTATEMENT (SECOND) OF TORTS 461 (1965).
8. Sindell v. Abbott Laboratories, 26 Cal.3d 588, 6–7 P.2d 924, 163 Cal. Rptr. 132 (1980), *cert. den.* 449 U.S. 912 (1980).
9. *See generally* MICHEL FOUCAULT, DISCIPLINE AND PUNISH (1979).
10. IMMANUEL KANT, THE METAPHYSICS OF MORALS 169 (Mary Gregor trans., 1991).
11. *Id.* at 142.
12. H.L.A. HART, *Prolegomenon to the Principles of Punishment, in* PUNISHMENT AND RESPONSIBILITY 4–5 (1968).
13. Michael S. Moore, *The Independent Moral Significance of Wrongdoing,* 5 J. CONTEMP. LEGAL ISSUES 237, 240 (1994).
14. On the two concepts of law, see George P. Fletcher, *Two Modes of Legal Thought,* 90 YALE L.J. 970, 980–84 (1981).
15. JAMES B. JACOBS, DRUNK DRIVING: AN AMERICAN DILEMMA 83–85 (1989).
16. The notable exception is the Model Penal Code § 5.05(1), which recognizes as its default rule that "attempt, solicitation and conspiracy are crimes of the same grade and degree as the most serious offense that is attempted or solicited or is an object of the conspiracy." According to the commentaries to the Code, only a few states have adopted this principle. *See* MODEL PENAL CODE § 5.05 at 486 (Revised Code and Commentaries, 1985). Even the reformist Model Penal Code concedes, however, an exception for the most serious offenses. *See id.* at § 5.05(1) (sentence 2).
17. *See, e.g.,* Stephen Schulhofer, *Harm and Punishment: A Critique of Emphasis on the Result of Conduct in the Criminal Law,* 122 U. PA. L. REV. 1497 (1974).
18. BRUCE ACKERMAN, PRIVATE PROPERTY AND THE CONSTITUTION 10–22 (1977).
19. *See* Russell L. Christopher, *Control and Desert: A Comment on Moore's View of Attempts,* 5 J. CONTEMP. LEGAL ISSUES 111 (1994).
20. *See* Michael Moore, *Choice, Character, and Excuse,* 7 SOCIAL PHILOSOPHY AND POLICY 29, 58 (1990) ("perhaps negligence by itself does not merit any moral blame").
21. Jerome Hall, *Negligent Behavior Should Be Excluded from Penal Liability,* 63 COLUM. L. REV. 632 (1963).
22. *See supra* note 2.

23. Homicide seems to be a special case. We could treat the decedent's loved ones as secondary victims, but they do not suffer from the same fear of recurrence that characterizes other forms of violent crime.

Chapter 5

1. H.L.A. HART, *Prolegomenon to the Principles of Punishment, in* PUNISHMENT AND RESPONSIBILITY 4–5 (1968).
2. Fletcher himself seems to claim that a proper understanding of the question about the justification of punishment commits us to a retributive solution. He claims that "the preposition 'for' demands not a goal but an untoward state of affairs" (43).
3. *See* Michael S. Moore, *The Independent Moral Significance of Wrongdoing,* 5 J. CONTEMP. LEGAL ISSUES 237 (1994). Moore contends that "between the two, wrongdoing and culpability, wrongdoing thus is something of the poor relation." *Id.* at 238.
4. *See, e.g.,* A.P. Simester, *Is Strict Liability Always Wrong? in* APPRAISING STRICT LIABILITY 21 (A.P. Simester ed., 2005).
5. *See* Douglas Husak, *Malum Prohibitum and Retributivism, in* DEFINING CRIMES: ESSAYS ON THE SPECIAL PART OF CRIMINAL LAW 65 (R.A. Duff and Stuart Green eds., 2005).
6. *See* DOUGLAS HUSAK, OVERCRIMINALIZATION (2008).
7. *See* R.A. DUFF, PUNISHMENT, COMMUNICATION, AND COMMUNITY (2001).
8. I address some of these questions in Douglas Husak, *Retributivism In Extremis,* LAW AND PHILOSOPHY (forthcoming, 2012).
9. *See* MICHAEL S. MOORE, PLACING BLAME (1997); and Larry Alexander and Kimberly Kessler Ferzan with Stephen Morse, CRIME AND CULPABILITY: A THEORY OF CRIMINAL LAW (2009).
10. *See* VICTOR TADROS, CRIMINAL RESPONSIBILITY (2005).
11. For a discussion of grand theorizing and those commentators who aspire to it, see R.A. Duff, *Theorising Criminal Law: A 25th Anniversary Essay,* 25 OXF. J. LEG. STUD. 353 (2005).
12. GEORGE FLETCHER, RETHINKING CRIMINAL LAW (1978).
13. *See* Douglas Husak, *Crimes Outside the Core,* 39 TULSA LAW REV. 755 (2004).

Chapter 6

1. The classic text is IMMANUEL KANT, METAPHYSICHE ANGANGSGRÜNDE DER RECHTSLEHRE § 49E at 452–459 (1797). *See also* HERBERT MORRIS, *Persons and Punishment, in* ON GUILT AND INNOCENCE 32 (1976); C.S. Lewis, *The Humanitarian Theory of Punishment,* 6 RES. JUDICATAE 224 (1953).
2. JEREMY BENTHAM, THE PRINCIPLES OF MORALS AND LEGISLATION 170 (1823 ed.).
3. Fong Yue Ting v. United States, 149 U.S. 698, 730 (1893) (deportation determined not to constitute "punishment").
4. Hugh Evander Willis, *Measure of Damages When Property Is Wrongfully Taken by a Private Individual,* 22 HARV. L. REV. 419, 420–421 (1909).
5. *See generally* Comment, *The Concept of Punitive Legislation and the Sixth Amendment: A New Look at Kennedy v. Mendoza-Martinez,* 32 U. CHI. L. REV. 290 (1965).
6. Tax lawyers do debate whether funds paid to an employee are deductible from company income as "a reasonable allowance for salaries or other compensation." I.R.C. § 162(a). *Cf.* Patton v. Commissioner, 168 F.2d 28, 31 (6th Cir. 1948) (deduction disallowed).
7. A.M. Quinton, *On Punishment, in* GERTRUDE EZORSKY, PHILOSOPHICAL PERSPECTIVES ON PUNISHMENT 12–13 (1972). *See* Richard Wasserstrom, *Some Problems with Theories of Punishment, in* JUSTICE AND PUNISHMENT 180–81 (J. Cederblom & W. Blizek eds. 1977).

8. GUIDO CALABRESI, THE COSTS OF ACCIDENTS (1970).

9. RICHARD POSNER, ECONOMIC ANALYSIS OF LAW (1972).

10. *See* CALABRESI, *supra* note 8, at 357–74; POSNER, *supra* note 9, at 24–33.

11. ROBERT NOZICK, ANARCHY, STATE AND UTOPIA 149–231 (1974).

12. *See, e.g.,* CALABRESI, *supra* note 8, at 73; POSNER, *supra* note 9, at 320–332.

13. U.S. CONST. amend. V.

14. Frank Michelman, *Property, Utility, and Fairness: Comments on the Ethical Foundations of "Just Compensation" Law,* 80 HARV. L. REV. 1165 (1967).

15. BRUCE ACKERMAN, PRIVATE PROPERTY AND THE CONSTITUTION 72–76 (1977).

16. *See, e.g.,* Michelman, *supra* note 14, at 1193.

17. JOHN RAWLS, A THEORY OF JUSTICE 62 (1971).

18. *Id.* at 8, 244–45 (responding to injustice in "the conduct of individuals" excluded from the ideal conception of justice).

19. NOZICK, *supra* note 11, at 169.

20. *Id.* at 150–53.

21. *Id.* at 26.

22. *Id.* at 101–02.

23. *Id.* at 108.

24. *Id.* at 78–79 (epileptic must be compensated); *id.* at 110 (those deprived of self-enforcement must be compensated).

25. *Id.* at 110–13.

26. Nozick has been criticized for simply assuming that individuals have rights and not offering any argument or rationale for these rights. *See* Thomas Nagel, *Book Review,* 85 YALE L.J. 136, 137–38 (1975). This assumption does not trouble me. The logic of Nozick's derivation of the minimal state depends, however, on the assumption that independents are entitled to compensation for the loss of their right of self-enforcement. NOZICK, *supra* note 11, at 110. The principle that harmful activities may be prohibited only if compensation is paid runs against the common law as well as other legal traditions. Defending this principle, critical to Nozick's argument, would be the place to begin the shoring up.

27. For agreement on this point, see H.L.A. HART, *Prolegomenon to the Principles of Punishment, in* PUNISHMENT AND RESPONSIBILITY 1, 4–5 (1968) (listing five elements in a definition of punishment).

28. *Id.* at 4 (the first element of punishment).

29. U.S. CONST. art. II, § 4.

30. U.S. CONST. art. II, § 2, cl. 1.

31. For further elaboration of this argument, see GEORGE FLETCHER, RETHINKING CRIMINAL LAW 408–13 (1978).

32. *Compare* Perez v. Brownell, 356 U.S. 44, 60 (1958) (expatriation of citizens who vote in foreign elections upheld on the ground that expatriation terminated the American involvement in foreign elections) *with* Trop v. Dulles, 356 U.S. 86, 103 (1958) (expatriation of wartime deserters invalidated as cruel and unusual punishment, no constitutionally valid end achieved by sanctioning wrongdoing with the deprivation of citizenship).

33. Vosburg v. Putney, 80 Wis. 523, 530, 50 N.W 403, 404 (1891) (defendant liable for unexpected consequences of kick); Thompson v. Lupone, 135 Conn. 236, 239, 62 A. 2d 861, 863 (1948) (defendants held liable for complications due to victim's being overweight; "The defendants took her as they found her.").

Chapter 7

1. For example: JULES COLEMAN, RISKS AND WRONGS (1992); ERNEST WEINRIB, THE IDEA OF PRIVATE LAW (1995); DORI KIMEL, FROM PROMISE TO CONTRACT (2003).

2. Two very different versions of this thesis: Richard Epstein, *A Theory of Strict Liability*, 2 J. LEG. STUD. 151 (1973); Tony Honoré, *Responsibility and Luck*, 104 LAW Q. REV. 530 (1988).

3. They have tried to switch attention from the defendant's wrongful action to the activity of which it forms part. Observing that the plaintiff is also (typically) engaging in an activity when she suffers her loss, and that the loss comes of the interplay of the two activities, many economists conclude that both plaintiff and defendant are agents of the loss. This is fallacious. When A and B are fighting, both are engaged in the activity of fighting. Nevertheless, A's punching B in the face is an action by A of which B is the patient, and B's using his head to ram A is an action of B of which A is the patient. One can make an infantile joke out of the difference by saying, after punching someone: "Next thing I knew, his head rammed into my fist." This is the infantile joke that the economists are a bit too clever to get. They elevate it to a serious proposal. I am thinking particularly of Ronald Coase, *The Problem of Social Cost*, 3 J. L. & ECON. 1 (1960), which has had widespread influence on economistic thinking about law. It has also influenced the work of some philosophers, such as Jules Coleman and Arthur Ripstein in *Mischief and Misfortune*, 41 MCGILL L.J. 91 (1995).

4. Arguably this is a case of restitution rather than a case of reparation. The intrinsic aim of restitution is to restore things to the way they were, not to the way they would have been in the absence of the theft.

5. This was Coleman's old view, defended or illuminated in several of the essays collected in his MARKETS, MORALS AND THE LAW (1988).

6. See my OFFENCES AND DEFENCES (2007), chs. 10–12.

7. For further discussion, see Joseph Raz, *Personal Practical Conflicts*, in PRACTICAL CONFLICTS: NEW PHILOSOPHICAL ESSAYS 172 (P. Baumann and M. Betzler eds., 2004). Much the same idea is briefly floated by Weinrib in THE IDEA OF PRIVATE LAW, *supra* note 1, at 135. It points to one possible interpretation of his more famous thesis that the tortfeasor always enjoys a "normative gain" corresponding to the victim's "normative loss."

8. I have done some but not all of that work in *What Is Tort Law For? Part 1: The Place of Corrective Justice*, 30 LAW AND PHILOSOPHY 1 (2011).

Chapter 8

1. Louis Kaplow & Steven Shavell, *Fairness Versus Welfare*, 114 HARV. L. REV. 961 (2001).

2. The leading formulation of the distinction is in MODEL PENAL CODE §§ 2.02(2)(c), (d) (1962) [hereinafter MPC].

3. I argue against this way of grading culpability in GEORGE P. FLETCHER, BASIC CONCEPTS OF CRIMINAL LAW 115–116 (1996).

4. GLANVILLE WILLIAMS, CRIMINAL LAW: THE GENERAL PART 262 (1961).

5. MPC § 2.02(3).

6. Jerome Hall, *Negligent Behavior Should Be Excluded from Penal Liability*, 63 COLUM. L. REV. 632 (1963).

7. OLIVER WENDELL HOLMES, JR., THE COMMON LAW 80 (1881).

8. *Id.*

9. *Id.* at 82.

10. The Thorns' Case, Y.B. 6 Edw. 4, 7, pl. 18 (1466).

11. HOLMES, *supra* note 7, at 82.

12. *Id.* at 116–17.

13. *Id.* at 108.

14. *Id.*

15. *Id.* at 48 ("Public policy sacrifices the individual to the general good."). In my earlier work, I took this and other references to the general welfare to be sufficient to classify Holmes' theory as utilitarian. GEORGE P. FLETCHER, RETHINKING CRIMINAL LAW 507 (1978). Today I would be more inclined to regard this language as surplusage.

16. HOLMES, *supra* note 7, at 108.
17. *Id.*
18. *Id.*
19. *Id.*
20. *Id.* at 86–87.
21. *Id.*
22. *Id.* at 87.
23. *See, e.g.,* FLETCHER, *supra* note 15, at 504–515.
24. GEORGE P. FLETCHER, OUR SECRET CONSTITUTION: HOW LINCOLN REDEFINED AMERICAN DEMOCRACY 225–29 (2001).
25. HOLMES, *supra* note 7, at 109.
26. *Id.*
27. *Id.*
28. *Id.*
29. *Id.*
30. *Id.*
31. *Id.* at 108.
32. JULES COLEMAN, RISKS AND WRONGS 219 (1992).
33. *Id.*
34. Ernest Weinrib, *Law as a Kantian Idea of Reason,* 87 COLUM. L. REV. 472, 475 n.10 (1987).
35. HOLMES, *supra* note 7, at 98–103.
36. Foucha v. Louisiana, 504 U.S. 71 (1992).
37. 132 Eng. Rep. 490 (C.P. 1837).
38. *Id.* at 493.
39. Commonwealth v. Pierce, 138 Mass. 165 (1884).
40. These factors recently received renewed theoretical interest. *See* John Goldberg & Benjamin Zipursky, *The Restatement (Third) and the Place of Duty in Negligence Law,* 54 VAND. L. REV. 657 (2001).
41. Note that MPC § 2.02(2)(d), reproduced above in the text, does not mention duty or breach as elements of negligence.
42. Parrot v. Wells-Fargo Co., 82 U.S. 425 (1872).
43. Judgment of July 26, 1994, BGHSt 40, 219.
44. Art. 34 StGB.
45. Genesis 19:32–33.
46. Art. 17 StGB.
47. For the impact of the case in analyzing the criminal liability of East German officials for the criminal conduct of border guards who shot at fleeing citizens, see FLETCHER, *supra* note 3, at 199–200.

Chapter 9

1. The occurrence of harm is immaterial to the actor's culpability (and, we would argue, to the actor's blameworthiness and punishability).
2. H.L.A. HART, PUNISHMENT AND RESPONSIBILITY 148 (1968); Brenda M. Baker, *Mens Rea, Negligence, and Criminal Law Reform,* 6 LAW AND PHILOSOPHY 53, 83–85 (1987); George P. Fletcher, *The Theory of Criminal Negligence: A Comparative Analysis,* 119 U. PA. L. REV. 401, 417 (1971).
3. *See* Ishtiyaque Haji, *An Epistemic Dimension of Blameworthiness,* 57 PHILOSOPHY & PHENOMENOLOGICAL RESEARCH 523 (1997); Michael J. Zimmerman, *Moral Responsibility and Ignorance,* 107 ETHICS 410 (1997). For an attempt to rebut Zimmerman, see James Montmarquet, *Zimmerman on Culpable Ignorance,* 109 ETHICS 842 (1999).

See also Peter B.M. Vranas, *I Ought, Therefore I Can*, 136 Philosophical Studies 167 (2007).
4. It also does not help to say the actor should have gotten more information before he acted. Sometimes, when there is time to wait, the actor will be *reckless* for acting rather than waiting and inquiring further.

Chapter 10

1. *See, e.g.,* Brainerd Currie, *Married Women's Contracts: A Study in Conflict-of-Laws Method*, 25 U. Chi. L. Rev. 227 (1958); Brainerd Currie, *Survival of Actions: Adjudication Versus Automation in the Conflict of Laws*, 10 Stan. L. Rev. 205 (1958).
2. [1975] 2 W.L.R. 913.
3. *Id.* at 926–960.
4. People v. Hernandez, 61 Cal. 2d 529, 393 P.2d 673, 39 Cal. Rptr. 361 (1964).
5. *Id.* at 536, 393 P.2d at 677–78, 39 Cal. Rptr. at 365–66.
6. People v. Goetz, 68 N.Y.2d 96, 497 N.E.2d 41, 506 N.Y.S.2d 18 (1986).
7. *Id.* at 114–15, 497 N.E.2d at 52, 506 N.Y.S.2d at 29–30.
8. People v. Brown, 105 Cal. 66, 38 P. 518 (1894); Larceny Act 1916, 6 & 7 Geo. 5, c. 50, § 1.
9. *See* Morissette v. United States, 342 U.S. 246, 276 (1952).
10. *Morgan*, 2 W.L.R. at 927–31.
11. *Goetz*, 68 N.Y.2d at 114–15, 497 N.E.2d at 52, 506 N.Y.S.2d at 29–30.
12. MPC § 2.02(1) (1985).
13. Virtually all recent legislative revisions and proposals follow the MPC in setting up general standards of culpability. *Id.* § 2.02 commentary at 283.
14. MPC § 2.02(2)(c) defines "recklessly" as requiring that the actor's disregard of "a substantial and unjustifiable risk…involves a gross deviation from the standard of conduct that a law-abiding person would observe in the actor's situation."
15. MPC § 2.02(2)(d) defines "negligently" as requiring that the actor's "failure to perceive [a substantial and unjustifiable risk]…involves a gross deviation from the standard of care that a reasonable person would observe in the actor's situation."
16. I Model Penal Code and Commentaries (Official Draft and Revised Comments) 264 (1985) [hereinafter cited as Commentaries].
17. MPC § 2.02(3). Literally, this provision specifies that purpose, knowledge or recklessness is required unless the legislature clearly imposes liability for negligence or strict liability. But note MPC § 2.02(5), which ranks the four kinds of culpability in the following transitive order: purpose, knowledge, recklessness and negligence. When any one of these is required, every form of culpability to the left will suffice for liability. It follows that we can interpret § 2.02(3) as requiring at least recklessness.
18. MPC § 2.05(2)(a).
19. *See* 1 Commentaries, *supra* note 16, at 282–83.
20. MPC § 2.03.
21. *Id.* §§ 2.05(1)(b), 2.05(2)(a) & (b).
22. *Id.* § 2.02(3).
23. *Id.* § 1.13(9) which provides:
    (9) "element of an offense" means (i) such conduct or (ii) such attendant circumstances or (iii) such a result of conduct as
    (a) is included in the description of the forbidden conduct in the definition of the offense; or
    (b) establishes the required kind of culpability; or
    (c) negatives an excuse or justification for such conduct; or
    (d) negatives a defense under the statute of limitations; or
    (e) establishes jurisdiction or venue….

24. *Id.* § 1.13 (10).
25. The commentators to the MPC do not have much to say about these definitions and their implications. *See* 1 COMMENTARIES, *supra* note 16, 210–11.
26. MPC § 1.13(10).
27. MPC § 2.02(2) (a), (b). Note that the definitions of recklessness and negligence require value judgments, respectively, about "the standard of conduct that a law-abiding person would observe in the actor's situation," *id.* § 2.02(2)(c), and the "standard of care that a reasonable person would observe in the actor's situation." *Id.* § 2.02(2)(d).
28. *Id.* § 1.13(10).
29. In some exceptional situations, the defendant must also bear the burden of persuasion on self-defense. *See* Martin v. Ohio, 107 S. Ct. 1098, 1103 (1987).
30. On the common-law definition of murder, see 4 WILLIAM BLACKSTONE, COMMENTARIES ON THE LAWS OF ENGLAND 194–95 (1769).
31. *See* MPC § 2.04(1).
32. *See id.* §§ 210.0–4.
33. *Id.* § 211.1.
34. *Id.* § 212.3.
35. *Id.* § 2.02(4).
36. *Id.* §§ 210.1, 210.29(1)(a).
37. *See id.* § 3.04(1).
38. The logic of this conclusion may need clarification. Self-defense requires the proof of two conditions, A + B. The prosecution disproves (A + B) by showing either not-A or not-B. If knowledge extends to the material elements not-A or not-B, then the actor must know either not-A (he is not being aggressed against) or not-B (it is not necessary to use the degree of force in question to repel the attack).
39. MPC § 2.02(3).
40. *Id.* § 2.02(4).
41. *Id.* § 210.2.
42. *See* 1 COMMENTARIES, *supra* note 16, at 245–46.
43. *Id.* at 246 n.38.
44. N.Y. PENAL LAW § 15.20(1)(a), (b), (c) (McKinney 1987).
45. The implication of the New York position in the analysis of mistake in cases of justification proceeds independently of the culpability required for the core elements. All mistakes must be reasonable (those that a reasonable person would have made) under the circumstances. *See* People v. Goetz, 68 N.Y.2d 96, 497 N.E.2d 41, 506 N.Y.S.2d 18 (1986).
46. MPC § 1.13(10).
47. *Id.* § 2.04(1).
48. *See id.* §§ 3.02–.08.
49. *See* DRAFT CRIMINAL CODE BILL § 47 (referring in "circumstances which exist or which [the actor] believes to exist"), *in* THE LAW COMMISSION, CODIFICATION OF THE CRIMINAL LAW 195 (1985).
50. See the opinion by the majority of the appellate division, People v. Goetz, 116 A.D.2d 316, 329, 501 N.Y.S.2d 326, 334–35 (1986).
51. Although the Commentaries claim that numerous states have adopted provisions analogous to § 3.09(2), 2 COMMENTARIES, *supra* note 16, at 153, Singer's research reveals that no state has both adopted this provision and applied it in an appellate case. Richard Singer, *The Resurgence of Mens Rea: II—Honest but Unreasonable Mistake of Fact in Self Defense*, 28 B.C. L. REV. 459, 505–506 (1987).
52. MPC § 3.02.
53. *Id.*
54. *Id.* § 3.09.
55. *Id.* § 3.09(2).
56. *Id.* § 2.04(1).
57. *Id.*

58. This follows from the definition of knowledge in § 2.02(2)(b).
59. *Id.* § 2.04(1).
60. *Id.* §§ 3.04, 3.09(2).
61. George Fletcher, *The Right and the Reasonable,* 98 HARV. L. REV. 949 (1985).
62. MPC § 2.04(1).
63. *Id.* § 2.10. If the actor knows the order to be unlawful, he has no defense. If he mistakenly believes that the order is lawful, he has a good defense.
64. *See* StGB § 32 (self-defense), § 34 (necessity) (22d ed. 1985).
65. *See id.* § 32 at 393–94.
66. The difference might be more easily grasped in symbolic form. Self-defense consists of the elements A and B. For a good claim of self-defense, the defendant must know both A and B. To be guilty of knowingly committing homicide (in the absence of self-defense) he must know either not-A or not-B.
67. MPC § 2.04(1).
68. *See id.* § 220.3 (criminal mischief).
69. *Id.* § 2.02(9).
70. *Id.* § 2.04(1).
71. *Id.* § 1.13(10)(ii).
72. For an older German case recognizing the mistake, see 19 RGST. 209 (1889) (hunter kills dog who strayed onto his property).
73. For recent work, see JOSHUA DRESSLER, UNDERSTANDING CRIMINAL LAW (1987); DOUGLAS HUSAK, THEORY OF CRIMINAL JUSTICE (1986); PAUL ROBINSON, CRIMINAL LAW DEFENSES (1984).
74. The MPC treats insanity, generally recognized as an excuse, as sufficiently complex to warrant a separate chapter. *See* MPC art. 4. Also, the drafter made one obvious blunder. There is no warrant for including consent in Article 2. *See id.* § 2.11. The whole point of consent is to render nominally invasive conduct an expression of a joint will and therefore right.
75. *Id.* § 2.10.
76. *Id.* § 2.04(3).
77. *Id.* § 2.13.
78. *Id.* § 2.09(1).
79. *Id.*
80. *Id.* § 2.09(2) (note that defense is forfeited for negligence as to crimes that can be committed negligently).
81. *Id.* § 2.04(1).
82. *See supra* text accompanying notes 73–74.
83. MPC § 2.02(9).
84. Note § 3.11(1) which defines "unlawful force" for purposes of self-defense so that conduct under duress is nonetheless unlawful. Therefore, so far as "unlawful" and "illegal" are interchangeable, a good claim of duress does not negate the illegality of conduct.
85. MPC § 2.04(3).
86. *Id.*
87. *See* Meir Dan-Cohen, *Decision Rules and Conduct Rules: On Acoustic Separation in Criminal Law,* 97 HARV. L. REV. 625 (1984).
88. MPC § 2.04(3)(b) commentary at 277–80.
89. *Id.* § 3.11(1).

Chapter 12

1. Blackstone perceived the essence of excuses to be the "want or defect of *will.*" 4 WILLIAM BLACKSTONE, COMMENTARIES *20. The subject of excuses has received little attention in the contemporary literature of the common law, but it has been of interest to

philosophers. *See* John L. Austin, *A Plea for Excuses, in* PROC. ARISTOTELIAN SOC'Y 1 (1956–1957), *reprinted in* FREEDOM AND RESPONSIBILITY 6 (Herbert Morris ed. 1961); H.L.A. Hart, *Prolegomenon to the Principles of Punishment,* 60 PROC. ARISTOTELIAN SOC'Y 1, 13, 17–24 (n.s. 1959), *reprinted as the first chapter in* H.L.A. HART, PUNISHMENT AND RESPONSIBILITY (1968) [hereinafter cited as HART].

2. This is a good rule-of-thumb (*see* W. LAFAVE & A. SCOTT, CRIMINAL LAW 381 (1972)), but it admits of exceptions. The German Penal Code of 1871 § 54 [hereinafter cited as STGB] regulates the defense of necessity (*Notstand*); STGB § 52 regulates duress (*Nötigungsstand*). Yet § 54 does not by its terms exclude threats emanating from human beings; and the courts have held the provision applicable to cases of human threats falling below the threshold required for self-defense under STGB § 53. *See* Judgment of July 12, 1966, 1966 NEUE JURISTISCHE WOCHENSCHRIFT 1823 (Bundesgerichtshof, Germany); Judgment of July 12, 1926, 60 Entscheidungen des Reichsgerichts in Strafsachen 318 [hereinafter cited as RGSt.]. In the new Criminal Code, effective January 1, 1975 [hereinafter cited as STGB 1975], the legislature consolidated necessity and duress under one provision, thus rendering irrelevant the distinction between responses to human threats and responses to natural pressure. STGB 1975 § 35. *Cf.* FRENCH PENAL CODE § 64 [hereinafter cited as C. PÉN.] (covering cases both of necessity and duress).

3. 4 BLACKSTONE, COMMENTARIES *30 (considering *duress per minas as a* species of necessity); STGB § 52; MODEL PENAL CODE § 2.09 (Proposed Official Draft 1962) [hereinafter MPC]. The French Penal Code has only one provision, C. PÉN. § 64, which regulates both necessity and duress (excusing anyone "compelled to act by a force that he could not resist."). The Soviet Criminal Code does not provide for either duress or necessity as excuses. It provides only for the justification of lesser evils which covers a subset of the cases of necessity and duress. R.S.F.S.R. 1960 UGOL. KOD. [CRIM. CODE] § 14. *See* text accompanying notes 51–56 *infra*.

4. M'Naghten's Case, 8 Eng. Rep. 718 (H.L. 1843). The test is whether

at the time of the committing of the act, the party accused was laboring under such a defect of reason, from disease of the mind, as not to know the nature and quality of the act he was doing, or if he did know it that he did not know he was doing what was wrong.

Id. at 722.

5. Durham v. United States, 214 F.2d 862 (D.C. Cir. 1954), holding that an accused should not be held "criminally responsible if his unlawful act was the product of mental disease or defect." *Id.* at 874–75. This test was rejected in United States v. Brawner, 471 F.2d 969 (D.C. Cir. 1972), and replaced by the standard proposed in MPC § 4.01.

6. ARISTOTLE, ETHICA NICOMACHEA 1110ª (W.D. Ross transl. 1925) [hereinafter cited as ARISTOTLE].

7. With regard to the rationale of punishment and its just distribution, the text follows H.L.A. Hart's position in HART, *supra* note 1. As adapted in the text, the chain of reasoning is: (1) Punishment is just only if its distribution is just; (2) the just distribution of sanctions presupposes an allocation of burdens according to the desert of the offenders; (3) the desert of offenders is a function of their character, as manifested in committing a legally prohibited act; (4) in a case of excused conduct, one cannot determine the character of the offender; and (5) it is unjust, therefore, to punish excused offenders.

8. This distinction is explored in Fletcher, *Fairness and Utility in Tort Theory,* 85 HARV. L. REV. 537, 558–60 (1972) [hereinafter *Fairness and Utility*].

9. The close connection between excusing and the personal position of the actor has caused some confusion in common law thinking. It induced Blackstone to treat excuses as questions pertaining to the specification of the "persons capable of committing crimes." 4 BLACKSTONE, COMMENTARIES *20 (title to chapter treating excuses). *See also* CAL. PENAL CODE § 26 (West 1971).

10. MPC § 2.09.

11. MPC § 3.02. The commentaries to the code suggest that the problem of necessity as an excuse should be faced in drafting a provision on duress. *See* MPC § 3.02, Comment at 8 (Tent. Draft No. 8, 1958). But the provision on duress, § 2.09, is limited to "threats." *See* text accompanying notes 52–54 *infra*.

12. *See* R.S.F.S.R. 1960 Ugol. Kod. [Crim. Code] § 14; 2 Kurs Sovetskogo Uogolnogo Prava [Course in Soviet Criminal Law] 380–92 (A. Piontovskij, C. Romashkin, V. Chkhikvadze, eds. 1970) [hereinafter cited as Kurs].

13. This is a recurrent problem in the theory of necessity. *See* M. Hale, Pleas of the Crown 53–54 (1680) (denying the defense in cases of starvation); *cf.* Judgment of the Court of Appeals in Amiens, France, April 22, 1898, [1899] S. Jur. II. 1 (affirming an acquittal of a starving woman who stole bread to feed herself and her starving child).

14. *See, e.g.,* Judgment of the Reichsgericht, Mar. 11, 1927, 61 RGSt. 242; The King v. Bourne, [1939] 1 K.B. 687.

15. *See, e.g.,* Surocco v. Geary, 3 Cal. 69, 58 Am. Dec. 385 (1853).

16. There is some dispute whether this type of case should be considered one of necessity or self-defense. *See* George P. Fletcher, *Proportionality and the Psychotic Aggressor: A Vignette in Comparative Criminal Theory,* 8 Israel L. Rev. 367, 373–74 (1973) [hereinafter cited as *Psychotic Aggressor*] (discussing common law and French tendencies to regard the danger posed by a psychotic as a problem of necessity).

17. This is the classic situation posed in Regina v. Dudley & Stevens, 14 Q.B.D. 273 (1884).

18. Kant refers to this case as one in which the act is not punishable though culpable (or at least not free from culpability). Immanuel Kant, The Metaphysical Elements of Justice 41–42 (J. Ladd transl. 1965).

19. Indeed the fact of furthering the greater good is likely to make the actor's choice appear to be responsive to rational and balanced reflection, rather than the pressure of circumstances. Therefore the range of involuntary, excused conduct is limited at both ends: (1) the harm cannot unduly exceed the cost (if it does, the actor is subject to blame for yielding to the pressure of the situation), and (2) the benefit should not exceed the harm (if it does, the conduct is more likely to appear voluntary, and the appropriate rationale for acquittal is justification, rather than excuse). But note cases like *Ménard,* Judgment of the Court of Appeals, Amiens, France, Apr. 22, 1898, [1899] S. Jur. II. 1 (starving mother stealing loaf of bread), where the benefit clearly exceeded the cost, yet the conduct also seemed to be patently reflexive and involuntary.

20. This is the problem posed in Cross v. State, 370 P.2d 371 (Wyo. 1962).

21. It is important to recall the difference between physical involuntariness and the evaluative dimension of involuntariness discussed in the text. English usage on this point is not clear. In discussing excuses, including duress, H.L.A. Hart notes, "most people would say of them that they were not 'voluntary' or 'not wholly voluntary.'" Hart, *supra* note 1, at 14. In contrast, Glanville Williams insists that cases of coerced and necessitated conduct are voluntary so long as there is any choice at all to yield to the pressure of circumstances. Glanville Williams, *The Defense of Necessity,* 6 Current Legal Problems 216, 223 (1953). Aristotle notes that cases of this class are voluntary in one sense, "but in the abstract perhaps involuntary." Aristotle, *supra* note 6, at 1110a. The distinction between the two dimensions of involuntariness is captured neatly by the French differentiation between *la contrainte physique* and *la contrainte morale. See, e.g.,* 1 P. Bouzat & J. Pinatel, Traité De Droit Pénal Et De Criminologie 343, 348 (2d ed. 1970).

22. The theory is obviously that a close personal tie with the victim is one factor tending to render the intervention involuntary. Limiting the scope of a defense to dependents and relatives is a sign that the theory of the defense is one of excuse, rather than justification.

23. 14 Q.B.D. 273 (1884).

24. *Id.* at 286.

25. Immanuel Kant, Grundlegung zur Metaphysik der Sitten § 2 (1785).

26. In cases excluding homicide from the scope of the defense of duress, the courts frequently stress the impermissibility of killing an innocent person. *See, e.g.,* Watson v. State, 212 Miss. 788, 55 So. 2d 441 (1951); State v. Nargashian, 26 R.I. 299, 58 A. 953 (1904).
27. S. KADISH & M. PAULSEN, CRIMINAL LAW AND ITS PROCESSES 544 (2d ed. 1969).
28. James Goldschmidt, *Der Notstand, ein Schuldproblem,* 1913 OESTERREICHISCHE ZEITSCHRIFT FÜR STRAFRECHT 129, 224.
29. *Id.* at 134–35.
30. *See* BGB §§ 228 & 904.
31. Judgment of Mar. 11, 1927, 61 RGSt. 242.
32. Law of July 4, 1969 (Zweites Gesetz zur Reform des Strafgesetz), § 34–35, [1969] BGBl. I 717.
33. The Queen's Bench did not even discuss the possibility of excusing, as opposed to justifying the homicide. It identified the issue of yielding to pressure with "temptation to murder" (14 Q.B.D. at 287) and held that "temptation" could not be "an excuse for crime." *Id.* at 288.
34. *Id.* at 286.
35. A more charitable reading of the opinion is that the court regarded any chosen form of conduct, however limited the options of choice, as fully voluntary and therefore unexcused.
36. 14 Q.B.D. at 287. It is not clear what the "fatal consequence" would be; presumably the public would confuse the acquittal with approbation, and thus others would be encouraged to kill and cannibalize innocent persons.
37. The court defines the "real question in the case" to be whether the killing "be or be not murder." *Id.* at 281.
38. *Id.* at 286.
39. *Id.* at 288.
40. As noted by the reporter "A.P.S." *Id.*
41. Yet it is important to note, as the court concedes, *id.* at 288, that clemency is an expression of mercy; excusing, in contrast, is an expression of compassion.
42. GLANVILLE WILLIAMS, CRIMINAL LAW: THE GENERAL PART 741–45 (2d ed. 1961); Glazebrook, *The Necessity Plea in English Criminal Law,* 30 CAMB. L.J. 87, 112–17 (1972); MPC § 3.02, Comment at 9–10 (Tent. Draft No. 8, 1958) [hereinafter cited as Comment].
43. Comment, *supra* note 42, at 10.
44. Charles Fried once argued, interestingly, that the killing of the two drunks could be justified on a theory akin to self-defense. One would have to picture the driving on the highway as the normal state of affairs; the two drunks, lying in the roadway, might then appear as aggressors against the driver. Some views of self-defense permit the causing of unlimited harm in the interest of protecting the defender's autonomy. *See* Fletcher, *Psychotic Aggressor, supra* note 16, at 378–80 (discussing Self-Defense III). The argument is interesting, for it illustrates how much turns on picturing the running over the two drunks as defensive or passive conduct as opposed to assertive killing. For a similar effort to generate an image of abortion as defensive conduct, see Judith Jarvis Thomson, *A Defense of Abortion,* 1 PHIL. & PUB. AFF. 47 (1971).
45. State v. Green, 470 S.W.2d 565 (Mo. 1971), *cert. denied,* 405 U.S. 1073 (1972).
46. The majority defined the defendant's claim to be that "the conditions of his confinement justified his escape." *Id.* at 568. Further, it defined the relevant defense of justification to require a determination that the conduct optimized utility. *Id.* In contrast, Judge Seiler, dissenting, stressed the analogy between coercion or duress as a defense and the necessity of Green's escape. The issue for the dissent is not whether Green chose the greater good, but whether his conduct was blameless. *Id.* at 570.
47. The record of appellate decisions hardly gives one cause to believe that balancing interests might lead to an acquittal or a reversal. Dempsey v. United States, 283 F.2d 934 (5th Cir. 1960) (defense rejected on behalf of escapee who was a diabetic and claimed that

he escaped to get a needed shot of insulin); State v. Palmer, 45 Del. 308, 72 A.2d 442 (Ct. Gen. Sess. 1950) (defense of necessity rejected in escape case, the court stressing "[s]ound reasons of public policy," *id.* at 310, 72 A.2d at 444); Hinkle v. Commonwealth, 23 Ky. L. Rptr. 1988, 66 S.W. 816 (1902) (possibility of defense rejected even though defendant argued that he escaped for fear of being shot); People v. Noble, 18 Mich. App. 300, 170 N.W.2d 916 (1969) (defense rejected on facts comparable to *Green;* the court feared a "rash of escapes, all rationalized by unverifiable tales of sexual assault," *id. at* 303, 170 N.W. 2d at 918).

48. There is some evidence that focusing on the issue of compulsion rather than lesser evils aids the defendant. Note the acquittal of defendants Terry and Cooper in the case of People v. Cooper, No. 38602 (Sacramento County Super. Ct., Aug. 11, 1971), *discussed in* Note, *Duress and the Prison Escape: A New Use for an Old Defense,* 45 S. CAL. L. REV. 1062 (1972). According to the latter report, defense counsel argued at trial that because the inmates feared for their lives, the case should be treated as one of duress under CAL. PENAL CODE § 26(8) (West 1970). Note, *supra,* at 1062–63. *See also* State v. Green, 470 S.W.2d 565, 568 (Mo. 1971) (Seiler, J., dissenting) (arguing that the theory of duress should encompass prison escapes where the defendant's conduct is blameless).

49. The text writers maintain that necessity is a defense recognized in the Anglo-American legal tradition. MPC § 3.02, Comment at 6 (Tent. Draft No. 8, 1958); LAFAVE & SCOTT, *supra* note 2, at 382; WILLIAMS, *supra* note 42, at 724. But one is hard pressed to find criminal cases where a court actually reverses for mistake by the trial judge in instructing or excluding evidence on the issue of necessity. When common law courts discuss the defense of necessity, it is typically by way of holding the defense inapplicable. *E.g.,* United States v. Kroncke, 459 F.2d 697 (8th Cir. 1972); *cf.* People v. Brown, 70 Misc. 2d 224, 333 N.Y.S.2d 342 (1972) (N.Y. PENAL LAWS § 35.05 (McKinney 1967) held to be applicable only to "technically criminal behavior that no one would consider improper.").

50. *See* cases cited note 47 *supra.*

51. D'Aquino v. United States, 192 F.2d 338 (9th Cir. 1951); State v. St. Clair, 262 S.W.2d 25 (Mo. 1953); Regina v. Hudson, [1971] 2 W.L.R. 1047, [1971] 2 All E.R. 244 (Ct. of Appeal, Crim. Div.).

52. *See generally* Neiman & Weizer, *Duress, Free Will and the Criminal Law,* 30 S. CAL. L. REV. 313 (1957).

53. *E.g.,* CAL. PENAL CODE § 26(8) (West 1970); MINN. STAT. ANN. § 609.08 (1964).

54. A long line of cases rejects the applicability of duress in homicide cases: Arp v. State, 97 Ala. 5, 12 So. 301 (1893); Taylor v. State, 158 Miss. 505, 130 So. 502 (1930); State v. Nargashian, 26 R.I. 299, 58 A. 953 (1904). *See also* 1 E. EAST, PLEAS OF THE CROWN 225 (1806); 4 BLACKSTONE, COMMENTARIES *30. *But cf.* Jones v. State, 207 Ga. 379, 62 S.E.2d 187 (1950) (homicide conviction reversed, duress recognized as a defense). In 1968, the Georgia legislature intervened to bring Georgia law back in line with the dominant common law position. *See* GA. CODE ANN. § 26–906 (1972) (expressly exempting murder from the scope of coercion as a defense).

55. Judgment of Jan. 14, 1964, 1964 NEUE JURISTISCHE WOCHENSCHRIFT 730 (Bundesgerichtshof, Germany) (recognizing the applicability of necessity and duress as defenses in prosecutions arising out of the mass murder of Jews in White Russia in 1941).

56. MPC § 2.09, Comment at 8 (Tent. Draft No. 10, 1960).

57. In fact, however, common law courts are disinclined to consider the defendant's psychiatric condition in assessing the defenses of duress and necessity. People v. Goldman, 245 Cal. App. 2d 376, 53 Cal. Rptr. 810 (1966) (defendant's "psychiatric assertions" irrelevant in considering whether prison escape was excused); Ross v. State, 169 Ind. 388, 82 N.E. 781 (1907) (court rejected defendant's mental disability in analyzing defense of duress). *But cf.* State v. St. Clair, 262 S.W.2d 25 (Mo. 1953) (conviction reversed for failure to instruct adequately on the issue of duress; the court suggests that it would be relevant in

assessing the defense that the defendant suffered food poisoning as a child and was "mentally impaired").

58. This concession is implicit in the test of insanity under MPC § 4.01(1), which provides in part that the actor is not responsible if "he lacks substantial capacity to appreciate the criminality [wrongfulness] of his conduct." The draftsmen left open the choice between the terms "criminality" and "wrongfulness." In United States v. Brawner, 471 F.2d 969 (D.C. Cir. 1972), the District of Columbia adopted this test and opted for the word "wrongfulness." *Id.* at 971. If the insane actor does not appreciate the wrongfulness of his act, it follows that his act is regarded, objectively, as wrongful.

59. *See, e.g.,* JEROME HALL, GENERAL PRINCIPLES OF CRIMINAL LAW 436 n.85 (2d ed. 1960) ("[A]n insane person is not bound by duties of the penal law.").

60. CAL. PENAL CODE § 26 (West 1970).

61. HERBERT PACKER, THE LIMITS OF THE CRIMINAL SANCTION 134 (1968).

62. ABRAHAM GOLDSTEIN, THE INSANITY DEFENSE 161–167 (1967); Goldstein & Katz, *Abolish the "Insanity Defense"—Why Not?,* 72 YALE L.J. 853, 866–869 (1963).

63. *E.g.,* Satterfield v. State, 172 Neb. 275, 280, 109 N.W.2d 415, 418 (1961); State v. Woods, 107 Vt. 354, 356–57, 179 A. 1, 2 (1935).

64. Judgment of Sept. 25, 1880, 2 RGSt. 268.

65. Judgment of Mar. 18, 1952, 2 BGHSt. 194.

66. The test as formulated by the German Supreme Court is whether the mistake is unavoidable *(unülberwindlich). Id. at* 209. If it is, it provides a complete defense. If it is avoidable *(liberwindlich),* it functions merely to mitigate guilt.

67. This judgment may be overly harsh, for there are some path-breaking cases that seem to acknowledge reasonable mistake of law as a defense. People v. Vogel, 46 Cal. 798, 299 P.2d 850 (1956); Long v. State, 44 Del. 262, 65 A.2d 489 (1949). The reasoning typically is that a reasonable mistake of law negates the "wrongful intent" or "general criminal intent"—terms that invoke the prestige of the word "intent" to introduce criteria of culpability into the analysis of liability.

68. 276 N.Y. 384, 12 N.E.2d 514 (1938).

69. *Id.* at 386, 12 N.E.2d at 514 (emphasis omitted).

70. *Id.* at 389–90, 12 N.E.2d at 515–16.

71. The common law seems destined to fluctuate between rejecting all mistakes, *see, e.g.,* Regina v. Prince, 2 Cr. Cas. Res. 154 (1875), and acknowledging even unreasonable mistakes as a defense on the ground that they negate the requisite intent, *see, e.g.,* Morissette v. United States, 342 U.S. 246 (1952); People v. Weiss, 276 N.Y. 384, 12 N.E.2d 514 (1938). There seems to be no clearly received rationale for both recognizing a mistake and requiring that it be reasonable. To explain why the mistake must be reasonable, the courts sometimes confuse the evidentiary requirement that the defense be reasonably raised with the substantive question of whether the mistake must be reasonable, *see, e.g.,* United States v. Short, 4 U.S.C.M.A. 437, 16 C.M.R. 11 (1954). Or sometimes the courts hold that the mistake must be reasonable if it is to negate "criminal intent" or "wrongful intent," *see, e.g.,* People v. Hernandez, 61 Cal. 2d 529, 393 P.2d 673, 39 Cal. Rptr. 361 (1964). It becomes clear why only reasonable mistakes should negate "criminal intent" if one reads the latter to refer generally to culpability or fault and one takes a reasonable mistake to be one that is free from fault.

72. MPC § 2.04(3). That the draftsmen perceive mistake of law to be different is reflected (1) in the specification of the kinds of situations in which the mistake would constitute a defense without adverting to a principle for including these situations and excluding others, and (2) shifting the burden of persuasion to defendant. *Id.* § 2.04(4). *Cf. id.* § 2.09 (defense of duress based on a broad general principle, with the burden of persuasion on the prosecution to disprove a properly raised claim).

73. HALL, *supra* note 59, at 383; Hopkins v. State, 193 Md. 489, 498, 69 A.2d 456, 460, *appeal dismissed,* 339 U.S. 940 (1950) ("If an accused could be exempted from punishment for

crime by reason of the advice of counsel, such advice would become paramount to the law."). For thoughtful replies to this argument, see LA FAVE & SCOTT, *supra* note 2, at 368 (but the authors also respectfully repeat Hall's statement of the argument, *id. at* 364); Houlgate, Ignorantia Juris: *A Plea for Justice*, 78 ETHICS 32, 39 (1967).

74. See text accompanying notes 58–62 *supra*.

75. Payne v. Arkansas, 356 U.S. 560, 567 (1958); Fikes v. Alabama, 352 U.S. 191, 197 (1957). *See generally* Comment, *The Coerced Confession Cases in Search of a Rationale*, 31 U. CHI. L. REV. 313, 318 (1964).

76. One response has been that of the rule skeptics who take their cue from Holmes' famous aphorism, "General propositions do not decide concrete cases," Lochner v. New York, 198 U.S. 45, 76 (1905) (Holmes, J., dissenting). Much of contemporary jurisprudence is devoted to the pursuit of alternatives to Holmes' nihilistic view of the role of rules in legal decision-making. See H.L.A. HART, THE CONCEPT OF LAW 132–37 (1961); Ronald Dworkin, *The Model of Rules*, 35 U. CHI. L. REV. 14 (1967).

77. For a good example of this empiricist frame of mind, see Glazebrook, *supra* note 42, at 108, in which the author defines a criminal offense to be "the total effect of the judicial decisions determining the extent of criminal liability in respect of a particular type of conduct."

78. As Holmes originally put it: "The prophecies of what the courts will do in fact, and nothing more pretentious, are what I mean by the law." Oliver Wendell Holmes, *The Path of the Law*, 10 HARV. L. REV. 457, 460–61 (1897). *Cf.* KARL LLEWELLYN, BRAMBLE BUSH 12 (1930) (defining the law as what "officials do about disputes").

79. Southern Pacific Co. v. Jensen, 244 U.S. 205, 222 (1917) (Holmes, J., dissenting).

80. At least in Powell v. Alabama, 287 U.S. 45, 68 (1932), the Court based its analysis of a right to a hearing on what it perceived to be an "immutable principle of justice," rather than on the contingent predicted benefits of allowing defendants to be heard. From its perception of the right to a hearing the court inferred the now well developed right to counsel in state criminal trials.

Chapter 13

1. See, *e.g.*, Larry Alexander, *Justification and Innocent Aggressors*, 33 WAYNE L. REV. 1177 (1987); Mitchell Berman, *Justification and Excuse: Law and Morality*, 53 DUKE L.J. 1 (2003); Alan Brudner, *A Theory of Necessity*, 7 OXF. J. LEG. STUD. 39 (1987); Joshua Dressler, *New Thoughts About the Concept of Justification in the Criminal Law*, 32 UCLA L. REV. 1 (1984); Heidi Hurd, *Justification and Excuse: Wrongdoing and Culpability*, 74 NOTRE DAME L. REV. 1551 (1999); Mordechai Kremnitzer, *Proportionality and the Aggressor's Culpability in Self-Defense*, 39 TULSA L. REV. 875 (2004).

2. H.M. HART & A.M. SACKS, THE LEGAL PROCESS: BASIC PROBLEMS IN THE MAKING AND APPLICATION OF LAW (1994).

3. Duncan Kennedy, *Form and Substance in Private Law Adjudication*, 89 HARV. L. REV. 1685 (1976).

4. See, *e.g.*, Elizabeth M. Schneider, *Describing and Changing: Women's Self-Defense Work and the Problems of Expert Testimony on Battering*, 9 WOMEN'S RIGHTS LEGAL REPORT 195 (1986); Holly Maguigan, *Battered Women and Self-Defense: Myths and Misconceptions in Current Reform Proposals*, 140 U. PA. L. REV. 379 (1991); E. BOCHNAK, WOMEN'S SELF-DEFENSE CASES (1981).

5. See SUSAN ESTRICH, REAL RAPE (1987); SUSAN ESTRICH, GETTING AWAY WITH MURDER: HOW POLITICS IS DESTROYING THE CRIMINAL JUSTICE SYSTEM (1998); MARTHA MINOW, MAKING ALL THE DIFFERENCE: INCLUSION, EXCLUSION AND AMERICAN LAW (1990); CATHARINE MACKINNON, FEMINISM UNMODIFIED, DISCOURSES ON LIFE AND LAW (1987).

6. *See* State v. Green, 470 S.W.2d 565 (Mo. 1971), *cert. denied,* 405 U.S. 1073 (1972).
7. R.A. Duff, *Rethinking Justifications,* 39 Tulsa L. Rev. 829, 829 (2004). *See also* Kent Greenawalt, *The Perplexing Borders of Justification and Excuse,* 84 Colum. L. Rev. 1897 (1984); Robert Schopp, Justification Defenses and Just Convictions 2–11 (1998).
8. *See, e.g.,* C. Littleton, *Reconstructing Sexual Equality,* 75 Cal. L. Rev. 1279 (1987); K.T. Bartlett, *Feminist Legal Methods,* 103 Harv. L. Rev. 829 (1990); W. Williams, *The Equality Crisis: Some Reflections on Culture, Courts, and Feminism,* 7 Women's Rights L. Rep. 175 (1982).
9. *See, e.g.,* R. Kennedy, *The State, Criminal Law and Racial Discrimination: A Comment,* 107 Harv. L. Rev. 1255 (1994); R. Austin, *The Black Community, Its Law Breakers, and a Politics of Identification,* 65 S. Cal. L. Rev. 1769 (1992); D. Bell, Race, Racism, and American Law (1992).
10. Alan Dershowitz, The Abuse Excuse and Other Cop-outs, Sob Stories, and Evasions of Responsibility (1994). *See also* James Q. Wilson, Moral Judgment: Does the Abuse Excuse Threaten Our Legal System? (1997).

Chapter 14

1. The Uniform Commercial Code, the Model Penal Code, and the various restatements couple the adjective "reasonable" and the adverb "reasonably" with over 100 different words. One example of this is the phrase "reasonable force," which appears in Restatement (Second) of Torts §§ 63(1), 77, 97, 101, 147(2), 150 (1965).
2. On the distinction between *Recht* and *Gesetz* and its significance, see 4 W. Fikentscher, Methoden des Rechts 328 (1977), and George Fletcher, *Two Modes of Legal Thought,* 90 Yale L.J. 970, 980–984 (1981).
3. The term "flat" may strike some readers as pejorative. It is hard to find a neutral term. Professor Albin Eser of Freiburg, West Germany, has usefully suggested to me the term "holistic" to capture the self-contained quality of flat legal reasoning. Yet "holistic" seems too mystical and thus, for some, too approving.
4. StGB § 32.
5. StGB § 53 (repealed in 1975).
6. *See, e.g.,* Judgment of Sept. 20, 1920, Reichsgericht, Ger., 55 Reichsgericht in Strafsachen [RGSt] 82. The defendant shot and wounded fruit thieves. The Supreme Court affirmed the acquittal, reasoning that Right should prevail "in the struggle against anti-Right." *Id.* at 85.
7. *See, e.g.,* Himmelreich, *Nothilfe und Notwehr: insbesondere zur sog. Interessenabwägung,* 21 Monatsschrift für Deutsches Recht 361, 363–64 (1967); Stratenwerth, *Prinzipien der Rechtfertigung,* 68 Zeitschrift für die gesamte Strafrechtswissenschaft 41, 60 (1956) (noting that the dominant scholarly opinion in Germany rejected balancing the interests of the victim against those of the aggressor).
8. *See, e.g.,* Baumann, *Rechtsmissbrauch bei Notwehr,* 16 Monatsschrift für Deutsches Recht 349 (1962); Schaffstein, *Notwehr und Güterabwägungsprinzip,* 6 Monatsschrift für Deutsches Recht 132, 135 (1952). Some current treatises and textbooks are noncommittal about the grounds for limiting the right of self-defense. *See, e.g.,* H. Jeschek, Lehrbuch des Strafrechts 279 (3d ed. 1978); K. Lackner, Strafgezetzbuch 175 (15th ed. 1983).
9. *See* Judgment of Jan. 22, 1963, Oberlandesgericht, Bavaria, 16 Neue Juristische Wochenschrift [NJW] 824. The defendant attempted to frighten a woman out of a parking spot by driving toward her. On the defendant's plea of self-defense, the court found that although the driver had a right to the parking spot, he had used a degree of force that was excessive and therefore an "abuse of right." This doctrine was invoked more recently in Judgment of Nov. 24, 1976, Oberlandesgericht, Hamm, 30 NJW 590, 592.

10. Some writers favor a limitation on self-defense without utilizing a two-stage analysis. They derive such a limitation directly from the statutory condition in StGB § 32 that self-defense be required (*geboten*) under the circumstances. *See* Lenckner, *"Gebotensein" und "Erforderlichkeit" der Notwehr,* 1968 GOLTDAMMER's ARCHIV FÜR STRAFRECHT 1; Roxin, *Die "sozialethischen Einschränkungen" des Notwehrrechts,* 93 ZEITSCHRIFT FÜR DIE GESAMTE STRAFRECHTSWISSENSCHAFT 68, 79 (1981).

11. *See, e.g.,* RESTATEMENT (SECOND) OF TORTS § 63(1) (1965) (an actor may use "reasonable force" to defend himself when he "reasonably believes" that another intends to attack him); W. LAFAVE & A. SCOTT, HANDBOOK ON CRIMINAL LAW 391 (1972).

12. Blackstone defined murder as "all homicide..., unless where *justified* by the command or permission of the law; *excused* on a principle of accident or self-preservation; or *alleviated* into manslaughter." 4 W. BLACKSTONE, COMMENTARIES * 201. The reliance on these common law categories survives in criminal codes enacted in the nineteenth century, such as CAL. PENAL CODE §§ 197–99 (West Supp. 1985).

13. For a thoughtful discussion of the question whether "justification" means "rightful" or "tolerable," see Joshua Dressler, *New Thoughts About the Concept of Justification in the Criminal Law: A Critique of Fletcher's Thinking and Rethinking,* 32 UCLA L. REV. 61, 93–91 (1984).

14. In an important recent article, Kent Greenawalt challenges the notion that one may infer from society's approval of an act the rights of other parties either to resist or to assist the act. *See* Greenawalt, *The Perplexing Borders of Justification and Excuse,* 84 COLUM. L. REV. 1897, 1919–21 (1984).

15. This conceptual precondition of excusing is apparent in the American Law Institute's increasingly influential definition of insanity as an actor's lack of "substantial capacity...to appreciate the criminality [wrongfulness] of his conduct." MODEL PENAL CODE § 4.01(1) (Proposed Official Draft 1962) [hereinafter MPC]. The issue of capacity arises only if it is first determined that the act is "wrongful" or "criminal."

16. The finding of "not guilty by reason of insanity" implicitly affirms the "wrongfulness" or "criminality" of the act. *See supra* note 15. Unless the act is wrongful, it would be incoherent to say that the actor lacked capacity to appreciate the wrongfulness of his act.

17. The MPC does distinguish between claims of justification and other defenses, *see* MPC art. 3; but these "other" defenses are dispersed between article 2 (duress, mistake) and article 4 (insanity).

18. *See, e.g.,* LAFAVE & SCOTT, *supra* note 11, at 356–413 (using "justification" and "excuse" interchangeably); JOHN C. SMITH & BRIAN HOGAN, CRIMINAL LAW 155–211 (4th ed. 1978) (ignoring distinction in discussion of "general defenses").

19. ENCYCLOPEDIA OF CRIME AND JUSTICE (S. Kadish ed. 1983) [hereinafter cited as ENCYCLOPEDIA].

20. *See e.g.,* John L. Austin, *A Plea for Excuses,* 57 PROC. ARISTOTELIAN SOC'Y 1 (1956); Fingarette & Hasse, *Excuse: Intoxication, in* 2 ENCYCLOPEDIA, *supra* note 19, at 942; Morawetz, *Justification: Necessity, in* 3 ENCYCLOPEDIA, *supra* note 19, at 957.

21. CAL. PENAL CODE § 26 (West Supp. 1985).

22. The adjudication of strict liability claims might appear to entail an R/W ordering, but this is because strict liability dispenses with the question of wrongdoing altogether.

23. This point is well expressed in the formula devised by Robert Nozick, in which the amount of punishment is determined by r x H. H represents the wrong and r the degree of responsibility or blameworthiness. H is, in principle, unlimited, but r varies only between 0 and 1. In a case of excused conduct, r equals 0. *See* ROBERT NOZICK, PHILOSOPHICAL EXPLANATIONS 363–66 (1981).

24. For further elaboration of the theory of excuses, see George Fletcher, *Rights and Excuses,* CRIM. JUST. ETHICS, Summer–Fall 1984, at 17.

25. *See* MPC § 1.13(10) (1962).

26. According to § 2.09(1) of the MPC, the defense of duress applies only if a person of "reasonable firmness" is unable to resist the threat. *Id.* § 2.09(1).

27. *See* People v. Lovercamp, 43 Cal. App. 3d 823, 827, 118 Cal. Rptr. 110, 112 (1974) (holding that escape was "the only viable and reasonable choice available").

28. Herbert Fingarette, *Victimization: A Legalist Analysis of Coercion, Deception, Undue Influence, and Excusable Prison Escape*, 42 WASH. & LEE L. REV. 65 (1985).

29. *See* George Fletcher, *Fairness and Utility in Tort Theory*, 85 HARV. L. REV. 537, 560 (1972).

30. *See* JEREMY BENTHAM, AN INTRODUCTION TO THE PRINCIPLES OF MORALS AND LEGISLATION 170–203 (1823 & photo. reprint 1973) (1st ed. Oxford 1789).

31. *See* CESARE B. BECCARIA, ON CRIMES AND PUNISHMENTS (2d ed. London 1769) (1st ed. London 1767).

32. *See* IMMANUEL KANT, THE METAPHYSICAL ELEMENTS OF JUSTICE 102 (J. Ladd trans., 1965).

33. The most popular version of this view is the thesis that criteria of desert and retribution function as a desirable limitation on the pursuit of utilitarian goals. *See* FRANCIS ALLEN, THE DECLINE OF THE REHABILITATIVE IDEAL 71–72 (1981); HERBERT PACKER, THE LIMITS OF THE CRIMINAL SANCTION 58–62 (1968).

34. *See* BRUCE ACKERMAN, PRIVATE PROPERTY AND THE CONSTITUTION 41–87 (1977) (discussing both Kantian and utilitarian theories as examples of comprehensive views). Unfortunately, the view that a sound proposal must satisfy opposed standards (for instance, those of Kant and Bentham) has gained increasing currency. *See, e.g.*, Dressler, *supra* note 13, at 81–83.

35. *See, e.g.*, MPC § 1.02(1)(c) (one purpose of the Code, among others, is "to safeguard conduct that is without fault from condemnation as criminal"); H.L.A. Hart, *The Aims of the Criminal Law*, 23 LAW & CONTEMP. PROBS. 401 (1958).

36. THOMAS HOBBES, A DIALOGUE BETWEEN A PHILOSOPHER AND A STUDENT OF THE COMMON LAWS OF ENGLAND 55 (J. Cropsey ed. 1971).

37. *See* RONALD DWORKIN, TAKING RIGHTS SERIOUSLY 107–110 (1977) (arguing that principles supplement but do not displace statutory law); Lon Fuller, *Positivism and Fidelity to Law—A Reply to Professor Hart*, 71 HARV. L. REV. 630, 647–651 (1958) (expressing the view that legislative commands must be just in order to constitute law).

38. *See* KANT, *supra* note 32, at 34. Unfortunately, Professor Ladd's translation of Kant mistakenly renders *Recht* as "justice." *See id.*

39. *See* IMMANUEL KANT, FOUNDATIONS OF THE METAPHYSICS OF MORALS 53–54 (L. Beck trans. 1959).

40. By virtue of this guarantee, individuals are obligated to enter into civil society and may be compelled to do so. *See* KANT, *supra* note 32, at 65–66.

41. *See* JOHN RAWLS, A THEORY OF JUSTICE 60 (1971) ("[E]ach person is to have an equal right to the most extensive basic liberty compatible with a similar liberty for others.").

42. Rawls regards these issues as beyond the scope of his book. *Id.* at 315.

43. StGB § 32 (author's translation).

44. The literal translation of the German term *Notwehr* would be "necessary defense."

45. *See* MPC § 3.04(1). The Code makes an inept effort to define "unlawful" in § 3.11(1). The definition is prolix primarily because the drafters could not formulate a concept (like excuse) to describe defenses that even if successfully asserted by an aggressor, would leave the unlawfulness of the attack unaffected.

46. *See* StGB § 34 (if the provision applies, the act is "not wrongful").

47. The dominant view in German law is that self-defense is allowed against excused aggression. *See* JESCHECK, *supra* note 8, at 273. The MPC concurs, but without a concept of excuse. *See* MPC § 3.11(1); *supra* note 45. Some German scholars, however, have concluded that the right of self-defense does not apply against excused aggression. *See, e.g.*, E. SCHMIDHÄUSER, STRAFRECHT: ALLGEMEINER TEIL 151–52 (2d ed. 1975).

48. *See* sources cited *supra* notes 8–9.

49. The maxim dates back at least to Berner, *Die Notwehrtheorie*, 1848 ARCHIV DES CRIMINALRECHTS 547, 557, 562.
50. *Cf.* KANT, *supra* note 32, at 36 (the Right entails the authorization to use coercion against anyone who violates the Right).
51. *Id.* at 36–37.
52. This is the standard line of the textbooks and treatises. *See, e.g.,* JESCHECK, *supra* note 8, at 277; A. SCHÖNKE, H. SCHRÖDER & T. LENCKNER, STRAFGESETZBUCH § 32, at 457 (20th ed. 1980). As to attacks occurring within the family, see the supportive language in the Judgment of Sept. 25, 1974, Bundesgerichtshof, W. Ger., 28 NJW 62.
53. *See* cases cited *supra* note 9.
54. *See* Judgment of Jan. 22, 1963, Oberlandesgericht, Bavaria, 16 NJW 824.
55. *See* 4 BLACKSTONE, *supra* note 12, at *181–82.
56. The treatment of this mistake is controversial under German law. The code recognizes only two types of mistake: those that concern the factual elements of the offense and those that concern the prohibited nature of the act. A faultless or negligent mistake about the elements of the offense negates the intent required for intentional liability; such a negligent mistake will support liability for negligence if a specific provision so stipulates. *See* STGB § 16. An unavoidable mistake about the legal status of an act negates the culpability required for conviction; if the mistake is avoidable, it can only mitigate punishment. *See* STGB § 17. A mistake about the factual presuppositions of self-defense falls between these statutory stools. It is neither a mistake about the definition of the offense nor a mistake about the legal characterization of the act. The tendency today is to extend § 16 by analogy to cover mistakes about the factual presuppositions of self-defense. *See* Judgment of June 6, 1952, Bundesgerichtshof in Strafsachen, 3 BGHSt 105; JESCHECK, *supra* note 8, at 375; G. STRATENWERTH, STRAFRECHT: ALLGEMEINER TEIL I, at 152–53 (3d ed. 1981). *But see* H. WELZEL, DAS DEUTSCHE STRAFRECHT 168 (11th ed. 1969) (classifying putative self-defense as a mistake about the wrongfulness of the aggression). For a totally different approach to the problem, see E. SCHMIDHÄUSER, *supra* note 47, at 151 (arguing that the mistaken defender does not act wrongfully unless he sticks to his action after being advised of the mistake).
57. *See* MPC §§ 3.04(1), 3.09(2).
58. *See e.g.,* ARIZ. REV. STAT. ANN. § 13–404(A) (1978); ILL. ANN. STAT. ch. 38, § 7–1 (Smith-Hurd 1972).
59. *See* KANT, *supra* note 39, at 9.
60. *See* CHARLES FRIED, RIGHT AND WRONG 48 (1978); *see also* Dressler, *supra* note 13, at 80 (relying on Kant).
61. *See* KANT, *supra* note 39, at 19–20.
62. *See* KANT, *supra* note 32, at 36.
63. Acting out of duty alone (that is, the will's being good) requires that no other motives inform the action. The will cannot be good if self-interest or other sentiments motivate the action, even in part. *See* KANT, *supra* note 39, at 17. Good intentions, by contrast, are perfectly compatible with conscious self-interest or a feeling of fear in resisting the supposed attack.
64. "The mere agreement or disagreement of an action with the Right, without regard to the incentive of the action, is called [legality]; but, when the Idea of duty arising from the law is at the same time the incentive of the action, then the agreement is called the [morality] of the action."

    KANT, *supra* note 32, at 19 (translation amended by the author).
65. A great deal of confusion about Kant derives from the natural assumption that his use of "morality" coincides with our use of the term today. One can never be moral in the Kantian sense simply by conforming to a rule, even if that rule expresses deontological values. For Kant, morality requires that the will be pure, which means that the act be free and that the

exclusive motive for acting be duty (reverence for the moral law). Kant concedes that a moral act in this highly restricted sense may never have occurred. *See* KANT, *supra* note 39, at 23–24.

66. Perhaps one could argue that a killing in self-defense would be moral if the actor executed the killing solely because it was his legal duty to do so. *See supra* note 65. But self-defense is not regarded as a legal duty today (there are no legal consequences of choosing to suffer the invasion), and I am reluctant to attribute this view to Kant. One might argue, however, that there is a duty to defend the Right against aggression, precisely as there is a duty to punish. *See* KANT, *supra* note 32, at 36.

67. MPC § 3.04(1). Generating a defense from this provision is, in fact, not so easy. In order to invoke the privilege of self-defense, the actor must (1) believe that defensive force is immediately necessary (2) to protect himself against (3) unlawful force. If Allan knows that Dan is mistaken, it is hard to see how he could believe that Dan's attack is unlawful, for Dan's force would not be unlawful under § 3.04, coupled with § 3.11(1).

68. *See* FRIED, *supra* note 60, at 48 (in the case supposed, in which Allan defends against Dan's mistaken attack, Fried concludes "we will have a fight between two persons, both acting justifiably. This is unfortunate but in no sense a contradiction....").

69. *See generally* Meir Dan-Cohen, *Decision Rules and Conduct Rules: On Acoustic Separation in Criminal Law*, 97 HARV. L. REV. 625, 637–48 (1984) (exploring the distinction between ex ante conduct rules and ex post decisional rules).

70. *See* StGB §§ 32, 34.

71. *See, e.g.,* WELZEL, *supra* note 56, at 81.

72. Judith Jarvis Thomson, *Some Ruminations on Rights*, 19 ARIZ. L. REV. 45, 47–49 (1977).

73. This point holds only for the traditional conception of Right. The modern conception, *see supra* text following note 42, treats rights as relative rather than absolute.

74. This conclusion receives some support in JOEL FEINBERG, SOCIAL PHILOSOPHY 72 (1973).

75. *See, e.g.,* DWORKIN, *supra* note 37, at xi.

76. *See* Gertrude Ezorsky, *The Ethics of Punishment, in* PHILOSOPHICAL PERSPECTIVES ON PUNISHMENT xi, xvii (G. Ezorsky ed. 1972).

77. The doctrine of "prima facie" duties originated, apparently, in W. ROSS, THE RIGHT AND THE GOOD 55–56 (1930). That rights could be "prima facie" in the sense that when infringed, they no longer exist, is criticized in A. MELDEN, RIGHTS AND PERSONS 15 (1977).

78. *See* HERBERT MORRIS, *Persons and Punishment, in* ON GUILT AND INNOCENCE 31, 55–56 (1976) (stressing that when a person is not accorded a right, the right is nonetheless infringed); *cf.* H.L.A. HART, PUNISHMENT AND RESPONSIBILITY 20 (1968) (in cases of strict liability, where fault is not an issue, we have "the sense that an important principle has been sacrificed").

Chapter 15

1. Victoria F. Nourse, *After the Reasonable Man: Getting Over the Objectivity/Subjectivity Question*, 11 NEW CRIM. L. REV. 1 (2008).

2. Fletcher illustrates this with a long discussion of the "putative" self-defender (162–65), arguing that a claim of self-defense cannot be justified or "right" simply because the person who asserts self-defense "believes" the claim to be right. I note for those interested in self-defense that one can accept such an argument and still contend that it does nothing to resolve the problem of the battered woman because the question is not one of subjectivity or objectivity, belief in right or justification, but in applying standards of justification or excuse in cases created by the state's failure to protect. *See, e.g.,* V.F. Nourse, *Reconceptualizing Criminal Law Defenses*, 151 U. PA. L. REV. 1691, 1707 (2003); Nourse, *supra* note 1.

3. *See also* CYNTHIA LEE, MURDER AND THE REASONABLE MAN (2003).

4. 2 John Kaplan et al. Criminal Law: Cases and Materials 630–48 (3d ed. 1996); Sanford H. Kadish et al., Criminal Law and Its Processes: Cases and Materials 801–26 (6th ed. 1995).
5. *See* Director of Public Prosecutions v. Camplin, 2 All E.R. 168 (1978); State v. Wanrow, 559 P.2d 548 (Wa. 1977); People v. Wu, 286 Cal. Rptr. 868, 884 (Cal. App. 1991).
6. Nourse, *supra* note 1.
7. Meir Dan-Cohen, *Decision Rules and Conduct Rules: Acoustic Separation in Criminal Law,* 97 Harv. L. Rev. 625 (1984).
8. The baseline problem can be illustrated with the question: "How can reasonable provocation be a partial defense to homicide if reasonable people do not kill?" The baseline implied (reasonable people do not kill) is that of law-abiding citizens, rather than the much smaller universe of those committing murder (the Holmesian bad actor). Taken to its logical conclusion, a reasonableness standard that applied a descriptive, statistical view of law-abiding behavior as baseline could wreak havoc with the criminal law: crime is statistically an anomalous affair and successful defenses potentially even more anomalous. If statistical normalcy is the implied standard, then most criminal law defenses should fail automatically, as the question about provocation implies.

Chapter 16

1. This generalization about Italian opinions is based on extensive discussions with Italian scholars in Turin, Milan, Bologna, Florence, and Trento in April 1992.
2. For more on this point, see my discussion in A Crime of Self-Defense: Bernhard Goetz and the Law on Trial 54–55 (1988).
3. The reader will forgive me if I do not repeat here my oft-made comments about the difference between the two terms for law in other languages and their absence in English. For a summary, see George Fletcher, *Two Modes of Legal Thought,* 90 Yale L.J. 970 (1981).
4. Judith Jarvis Thomson, Rights, Restitution and Risk 40–42 (1986).
5. This is the line taken by Paul Robinson in one of the significant early articles in this area. *See* Paul Robinson, *A Theory of Justification: Societal Harm as a Prerequisite of Criminal Liability,* 23 UCLA L. Rev. 266 (1975).
6. Judgment of the Reichsgericht, 11 March 1927, 61 RGSt 242.
7. One is tempted to call this a "precedent." According to the conventional wisdom, however, German courts do not recognize precedents. This decision had its impact, in fact, not directly, but indirectly, as a stimulus to the leading commentators to pick up the theory of "extra-statutory" justification and to incorporate it into the law as they presented it in their textbooks.
8. This thesis is by no means obvious. Excusing conditions function more clearly as decision rules rather than conduct rules. Claims of justification do enter into debates between individuals about whether their conduct is right or wrong. The question is whether it is the legislative language as such, or rather the general principles of justification, that enter into these debates. On the distinction between decision rules and conduct rules, see Meir Dan-Cohen, *Decision Rules and Conduct Rules: On Acoustic Separation in Criminal Law,* 97 Harv. L. Rev. 625 (1984).
9. *E.g.* Papachristou v. City of Jacksonville, 405 U.S. 156 (1972) (vagrancy ordinance unconstitutionally vague); International Harvester Co v. Kentucky, 234 U.S. 216 (1914) (price and trade regulation unconstitutional).
10. People v. Belous, 71 Cal. 2d 954, 458 P 2d 194, 80 Cal. Rptr. 354 (1969), *cert. denied* 397 U.S. 915 (1970).
11. On the details of "more or less" resemblance, see my paper *The Right and the Reasonable,* 98 Harv. L. Rev. 949 (1985).

12. *See* SCHÖNKE-SCHRÖDER, STRAFGESETZBUCH KOMMENTAR (23rd ed., Munich 1988), s. 23 at 177 (citing aphorism and commenting on the debate).
13. People v. Snipe, 25 Cal. App. 3d 742, 102 Cal. Rptr. 6 (1972).

Chapter 17

1. H.L.A. Hart, *Analytical Jurisprudence in Mid-Twentieth Century*, 105 U. PA. L. REV. 953, 964 (1957).
2. GEORGE FLETCHER, RETHINKING CRIMINAL LAW 759–817 (2000) (originally published 1978) [hereinafter RETHINKING].
3. *See* Joshua Dressler, *New Thoughts About the Concept of Justification in the Criminal Law*, 21 UCLA L. REV. 61 (1984); PAUL ROBINSON, STRUCTURE AND FUNCTION IN CRIMINAL LAW 95–123 (1997) [hereinafter STRUCTURE AND FUNCTION]. Kent Greenawalt famously questions the distinction between justification and excuse. For criticism of Greenawalt's analysis, see Peter Westen, *An Attitudinal Theory of Excuse*, 25 LAW AND PHILOSOPHY 289, 311–24 (2006).
4. *See* GEORGE FLETCHER, BASIC CONCEPTS OF CRIMINAL LAW 93–110 (1998) [hereinafter BASIC CONCEPTS]; FLETCHER, RETHINKING, *supra* note 2, at 552–79.
5. *See* ROBINSON, STRUCTURE AND FUNCTION, *supra* note 3, at 101. This is not to say that justification negates the harm or evil *as stated* in the elements of an offense, for most elements overstate the harms and evils the state seeks to prevent. *See* Westen, *supra* note 3, at 298–304.
6. Robinson argues that in addition to the normative advantages discussed below, his view of what renders *A*'s conduct justified vis-à-vis *B* has the further normative benefit of correlating with what renders *A*'s conduct such that *B may not* lawfully resist it and that third persons, *C, may* lawfully assist it. ROBINSON, STRUCTURE AND FUNCTION, *supra* note 3, at 105–08. However, this claim of Robinson's is true only if *B*'s disability to resist *A* and *C*'s right to assist *A* are *solely a function* of *A*'s right to act. For the argument to the contrary, see Peter Westen & James Mangiafico, *The Defense of Duress in Criminal Law*, 6 BUFF. CRIM. L. REV. 833, 839–42, 866–72, 917–24 (2003).
7. It can be further argued that if culpability consists of a lack of appropriate regard for persons whom the state seeks to protect from such wrongdoing, then "excuse" merely negates culpability—thus reducing the two elements of "culpability" and "lack of excuse" to culpability alone. *See* Westen, *supra* note 3, at 309–10, 353–71.
8. For the argument that any justification can be stated in the negative as an element, see Glanville Williams, *Offences and Defences*, 2 LEGAL STUDIES 233 (1982).
9. *See* FLETCHER, BASIC CONCEPTS, *supra* note 4, at 162–63; FLETCHER, RETHINKING, *supra* note 2, at 697, 707–13.
10. *See* authorities cited in Anthony Dillof, *Unraveling Unknowing Justification*, 77 NOTRE DAME L. REV. 1547, 1550 n.4 (2002).
11. *See* ROBINSON, STRUCTURE AND FUNCTION, *supra* note 3, at 111–12; FLETCHER, RETHINKING, *supra* note 2, at 459.
12. *See* FLETCHER, BASIC CONCEPTS, *supra* note 4, at 102–06; FLETCHER, RETHINKING, *supra* note 2, at 768.
13. FLETCHER, BASIC CONCEPTS, *supra* note 4, at 85; FLETCHER, RETHINKING, *supra* note 2, at 458–59.
14. *See supra* note 12.
15. *See supra* note 9. Fletcher treats mistaken justification as "excuse."
16. Fletcher defines wrongdoing to consist of the "elements" (or "definition") of an offense plus the absence of "justification." *See* FLETCHER, BASIC CONCEPTS, *supra* note 4, at 101; FLETCHER, RETHINKING, *supra* note 2, at 553–54. The elements (or definition) of an offense consist not only of the presumptive harms and evils the state seeks to prevent by

means of a statute, but also some mens rea elements, such as "malice" in murder statutes. *See* FLETCHER, RETHINKING, *supra* note 2, at 554. Justification, in turn, consists not only of circumstances that negate the aforementioned harms and evils but also belief on an actor's part that the circumstances exist. *See id.* at 556–57.

17. *See* FLETCHER, RETHINKING, *supra* note 2, at 454–59, 562–66.
18. *Id.* at 515.
19. FLETCHER, BASIC CONCEPTS, *supra* note 4, at 106.
20. *Id.* at 96. Fletcher argues that justification must not only defeat a presumptive harm or evil but also be empirically and/or culturally regarded as unusual. *See* FLETCHER, RETHINKING, *supra* note 2, at 556–68. However, if that is so, then contrary to what Fletcher says, the relationship of justifications to elements is not a matter of "principle" (173–74) but rather something that varies from place to place, and from year to year.
21. Fletcher presents one direct defense (175–76), that he expands upon in a subsequent work. The argument is this: (1) "[s]aving oneself... from an aggressive attack is a good reason for using force"; (2) "good reasons do not exist in the abstract"; (3) therefore, "they must be reasons that those who use force... actually possess." FLETCHER, BASIC CONCEPTS, *supra* note 4, at 106. Even if premises 1 and 2 are valid, however, the conclusion 3 does not necessarily follow. The "good" reasons in favor of allowing a person to act in self-defense are not "abstract" if they are embraced by the *state*, regardless of whether they are also subjectively motivated the actor.
    Fletcher further relies on an argument by Russell Christopher to the effect that the law cannot provide a defense to an actor who lethally shoots a rival without realizing that the latter was about to kill him, without falling into a contradictory logical loop. *See* FLETCHER, BASIC CONCEPTS, *supra* note 4, at 105–06. For criticism of this and other ingenious arguments of Christopher's to the same effect, see Westen & Mangiafico, *supra* note 6, at 877 n.92.
22. *See supra* notes 9–12.
23. ROBINSON, STRUCTURE AND FUNCTION, supra note 3, at 95, 111.
24. *See* Peter Westen, *Why Criminal Harms Matter*, 1 CRIMINAL LAW AND PHILOSOPHY 307–16 (2007).
25. Indeed, Robinson himself prefers that justifications continue to be framed as defenses rather than in the negative as elements. *See* ROBINSON, FUNCTION AND STRUCTURE, *supra* note 3, at 111. On the economies of drafting, see FLETCHER, BASIC CONCEPTS, *supra* note 4, at 97.
26. For the argument that the principle of legality does not require that legislatures enact offenses, see Peter Westen, *Two Rules of Legality in Criminal Law*, 26 LAW AND PHILOSOPHY 229, 286–92 (2007) [hereinafter *Two Rules*]. However, if Fletcher is correct that legality requires that legislatures enact "elements," it does not follow that everything unity theory regards as an element is also an "element" for purposes of legality.
27. *See, e.g.,* ROBINSON, FUNCTION AND STRUCTURE, *supra* note 3, at 118–21.
28. Stated differently, what unity theory regards as an element is not necessarily an "element" for purposes of the rule that actors must possess fair warning of "elements."
29. For an analysis of "reasonableness" in criminal law, see Peter Westen, *Individualizing the Reasonable Person in Criminal Law*, 2 CRIMINAL LAW AND PHILOSOPHY 137 (2008).
30. For the argument that statutes ought never to be invalidated for "vagueness," see Westen, *Two Rules*, *supra* note 26, at 292–302.

Chapter 18

1. *Proportionality and the Psychotic Aggressor. A Vignette in Comparative Criminal Theory*, 8 ISRAEL L. REV. 367 (1973).
2. For a sampling of the literature, see generally the essays in the two-volume reader, GEORGE FLETCHER AND ALBIN ESER, JUSTIFICATION AND EXCUSE (1987); 2 PAUL ROBINSON,

DEFENSES TO CRIME 1–468 (1984); J.C. SMITH, JUSTIFICATION AND EXCUSE IN THE CRIMINAL LAW (1989); Barbara Sharon Byrd, *Wrongdoing and Attribution: Implications Beyond the Justification-Excuse Distinction* 33 WAYNE L. REV. 1289 (1987); Kent Greenawalt, *The Perplexing Borders of Justification and Excuse,* 84 COLUM. L. REV. 1897 (1984); Miriam Gur-Arye, *Should the Criminal Law Distinguish Between Necessity as a Justification and Necessity as an Excuse?,* 102 L. Q. R. 71 (1986); Mordechai Kremnitzer, *Proportionality and the Psychotic Aggressor: Another View,* 18 ISRAEL L. REV. 178 (1983); Paul Robinson, *Criminal Law Defenses: A Systematic Analysis,* 82 COLUM. L. REV. 199 (1982); Glanville Williams, *The Theory of Excuses* [1982] CRIM. L. REV. 732; Albin Eser, *Justification and Excuse,* 24 AM. J. COMP. L. 621 (1976).

3. The other categories are object of the offense, subjective side and objective side of the act.

4. Fletcher, *supra* note 1, at 375.

5. IMMANUEL KANT, *The Doctrine of Right* 235, *in* THE METAPHYSICS OF MORALS 60 (Mary Gregor trans., 1991).

6. For some of the literature on this problem, see Peter Arenella, *Convincing the Morally Blameless: Reassessing the Relationship Between Legal and Moral Accountability,* 39 UCLA L. REV. 1511 (1992); NICOLA LACEY, STATE PUNISHMENT, POLITICAL PRINCIPLES, AND COMMUNITY VALUES (1988).

7. *See* Meir Dan-Cohen, *Boundaries of the Self,* 105 HARV. L. REV. 959 (1992); Michael S. Moore, *Causation and the Excuses,* 73 CALIF. L. REV. 1091 (1985).

8. KANT, *supra* note 5, at 60 [235]: "For the issue here [referring to the case of the ship-wrecked sailor] is not that of a *wrongful assailant* upon *my* life whom I forstall by depriving him of his life...."

9. 14 Q. B. D. 273 (1884).

10. A third sailor, Brooks, participated in the cannibalism, but was not indicted for murder. Apparently he did not aid or abet the killing. *See* BRIAN SIMPSON, CANNIBALISM AND THE COMMON LAW (1984).

11. KANT, *supra* note 5, at 60 [235].

12. Greenawalt, *supra* note 2, at 1903.

13. Admittedly, not all defenses represent "warranted action." Presumably, the psychotic aggressor has neither a "warrant" nor a "reason" for his act.

14. MARTHA NUSSBAUM, THE FRAGILITY OF GOODNESS 63–79 (1986).

15. This point is captured in the apt title by LAURENCE TRIBE, ABORTION: THE CLASH OF ABSOLUTES.

16. *See generally* GEORGE FLETCHER, A CRIME OF SELF-DEFENSE: BERNHARD GOETZ AND THE LAW ON TRIAL (1988).

17. ARISTOTLE, NICHOMACHEAN ETHICS 1135a–1136a.

18. Greenawalt, *supra* note. 2.

19. *Id.* at 1908.

20. *Id.* at 1908–09.

21. People v. Young, 11 N.Y. 2d 274, 183 N.E. 2d 319, 229 N.Y.S. 2d 1 (1962).

22. Greenawalt, *supra* note 2, at 1919.

23. *Id.* at 1904.

24. *Id.* at 1909.

25. *Id.*

26. *Id.* at 1910.

27. *Id.*

28. *Id.* at 1911.

Chapter 20

1. For my criticisms of the economic thinking in criminal law, see George P. Fletcher, *A Transaction Theory of Crime?,* 85 COLUM. L. REV. 921 (1985).

2. Mark Kelman, *Interpretive Construction in the Substantive Criminal Law*, 33 STAN. L. REV. 591 (1988).

3. SUSAN BROWNMILLER, AGAINST OUR WILL: MEN, WOMEN AND RAPE (1975).

4. *See infra* notes 6 and 7.

5. For the more significant recent writing in the field, see Sharon Byrd, *Till Death Do Us Part: A Comparative Law Approach to Justifying Lethal Self-Defense by Battered Women*, 1991 DUKE J. COMP. & INT'L L. 169; Anne Coughlin, *Excusing Women*, 82 CALIF. L. REV. 1 (1994); Holly Maguigan, *Battered Women and Self-Defense: Myths and Misconceptions in Current Reform Proposals*, 140 U. PA. L. REV. 379, 391–397 (1991); Richard Rosen, *On Self-Defense, Imminence, and Women Who Kill Their Batterers*, 71 N.C. L. REV. 371 (1993); Elizabeth M. Schneider, *Describing and Changing: Women's Self-Defense Work and the Problem of Expert Testimony on Battering*, 9 WOMEN'S RTS. L. REP. 195 (1986); Robert F. Schopp et al., *Battered Woman Syndrome, Expert Testimony, and the Distinction between Justification and Excuse*, 1994 U. ILL. L. REV. 45.

6. Susan Estrich, *Rape*, 95 YALE L.J. 1087, 1137–39 (1986).

7. Susan Estrich, *Palm Beach Stories*, 11 LAW & PHIL. 5, 12–13 (1992).

8. For a critique of this ruling, see GEORGE P. FLETCHER, WITH JUSTICE FOR SOME: VICTIMS' RIGHTS IN CRIMINAL TRIALS 120–25 (1995).

9. State v. Norman, 378 S.E.2d 8 (N.C. 1989).

10. *See* JOEL FEINBERG, DOING AND DESERVING (1970).

11. It seems that some writers use the term "preemptive strike" more broadly to refer to defensive attacks prior to the actual initiation of hostilities by the aggressor. *See* MICHAEL WALZER, JUST AND UNJUST WARS 80–85 (1977).

12. For an analysis of the extent to which this principle is recognized in American law, see George P. Fletcher, *The Right and the Reasonable*, 98 HARV. L. REV. 949 (1985).

13. *See* GLANVILLE WILLIAMS, TEXTBOOK OF CRIMINAL LAW 504 (2d ed. 1983) ("The law would be oppressive if it said: It is true that you took this action because you felt it in your bones that you were in peril, and it is true that you were right, but you cannot now assign reasonable grounds for your belief, so you were only right by a fluke and will be convicted."); 2 PAUL H. ROBINSON, CRIMINAL LAW DEFENSES § 122 (1984).

14. Russell Christopher has developed a more sophisticated argument for the intent requirement. He claims, convincingly, that not requiring intent would lead to an irreconcilable contradiction in conjunction with the rule permitting defensive force only against unlawful, unjustified attacks. *See* Russell Christopher, *Unknowing Justification and the Logical Necessity of the Dadson Principle in Self-Defence*, 15 OXFORD J. LEGAL STUD. 229 (1995).

15. *See* THOMAS AQUINAS, SUMMA THEOLOGIAE pt. II-II, q. 64, a.7.

16. MODEL PENAL CODE § 3.04(1) (1962).

17. State v. Wanrow, 559 P.2d 548, 555 n.7 (Wash. 1977) (quoting Jury Instruction No. 10).

18. IMMANUEL KANT, FOUNDATIONS OF THE METAPHYSICS OF MORALS (Lewis W. Beck trans. & Robert P. Wolff ed., 1969) (1785).

19. Kent Greenawalt, *The Perplexing Borders of Justification and Excuse*, 84 COLUM. L. REV. 1897, 1908 (1984).

20. *Id.*

21. *Id.* at 1908–09.

22. *Id.* at 1908.

23. People v. Young, 183 N.E.2d 319 (N.Y. 1962).

24. *Id.* at 319–20.

25. Greenawalt, *supra* note 19, at 1919.

26. On the relationship between emulable behavior and the theory of excuses, see Claire Finkelstein, *Duress: A Philosophical Account of the Defense in Law*, 37 ARIZ. L. REV. 251 (1995).

27. State v. Norman, 378 S.E.2d 8, 11, 13, 16 (N.C. 1989).

28. Consider this hypothetical case presented in Schopp et al., *supra* note 5, at 66–67:

[T]he hikers X and Y...engage in a ten-day race across the desert. The only source of water in the desert is a single water hole approximately half way to the finish line. Each hiker must carry a five to six day supply of water and replenish the supply at the water hole in order to survive the race. During the first few days, X catches Y attempting to sabotage X by changing trail markers and attempting to steal X's compass and water. If successful, each of these efforts would have caused X to die in the desert.

As day five begins, both hikers are almost out of water and must replenish their supplies the next day at the water hole. As Y passes X on the trail on the morning of the fifth day, Y holds up a box of rat poison and says to X, "I'll get you this time; I'll beat you to the water hole, get my water, and poison the rest; You'll never get out of here alive." Both hikers walk all day, but due to a sprained ankle, X can barely keep up with Y. That evening, as X is forced to stop due to the sprained ankle and exhaustion, Y says "I'll walk all night and get to the water hole before morning." As Y begins to walk away, X, who is unable to continue that night, says "wait," but Y walks in the direction of the water hole. X shoots Y, convinced by Y's prior threats and sabotage that this is the only way to prevent Y from poisoning the water hole the next morning.

29. *See supra* note 17 and accompanying text.

30. For an original defense of the subjectivist bias, see Russell L. Christopher, *Mistake of Fact in the Objective Theory of Justification: Do Two Rights Make Two Wrongs Make Two Rights...?*, 85 J. CRIM. L. & CRIMINOLOGY 295 (1994).

31. MODEL PENAL CODE § 3.04(1) (1962).

32. At least this objective requirement was assumed, without much argument, in the trial of Bernhard Goetz. *See* GEORGE P. FLETCHER, A CRIME OF SELF-DEFENSE: BERNHARD GOETZ AND THE LAW ON TRIAL 39–62 (1988).

33. *See* DEL. CODE ANN. tit. 11, § 463 (1987) ("to avoid an imminent...injury which is about to occur"); COLO. REV. STAT. § 18-1-702 (1986) (same language as Delaware); KY. REV. STAT. ANN. § 503.030 (Baldwin 1995) ("imminent...injury"); *see also* United States v. Kroncke, 459 F.2d 697, 701 (8th Cir. 1972) (necessity available to justify the stealing of draft cards during the Vietnam War only if the action was undertaken to avoid a "direct and immediate peril").

34. State v. Norman, 378 S.E.2d 8, 10 (N.C. 1989).

35. California Jury Instructions, Criminal No. 5.12 (Arnold Levin ed., 5th ed. 1988) [hereinafter CALJIC].

36. The guiding jury instruction, *id.* at No. 5.17, reads as follows: "A person, who kills another person in the honest but unreasonable belief in the necessity to defend against imminent peril to life or great bodily injury, kills unlawfully, but does not harbor malice aforethought and is not guilty of murder."

37. Elizabeth Gleick, *Blood Brothers*, PEOPLE, Sept. 27, 1993, at 32.

38. Seth Mydans, *The Other Menendez Trial, Too, Ends with the Jury Deadlocked*, N.Y. TIMES, Jan. 29, 1994, at A1.

39. Nothing in the language of the jury instructions, *supra* note 36, suggests the defendants' perceptions should be controlling on the question of imminence. The leading case is People v. Flannel, 603 P.2d 1 (Cal. 1979). This opinion is also ambiguous on the same question. Judge Weisberg ruled for purposes of the second trial that the evidence of child abuse was inadmissible. *See* Alan Abrahamson, *Judge Moves to Block Menendez Abuse Experts*, L.A. TIMES, Apr. 18, 1995, at A1.

40. State v. Norman, 378 S.E.2d 8, 18 (1989) (Martin, J., dissenting).

41. See the way the argument that self-defense is punishment functioned in the *Goetz* case. FLETCHER, *supra* note 32, at 27–29.

42. 559 P.2d 548 (Wash. 1977).

43. *Id.* at 551.

44. *Id.*

45. *Id.* at 550.

46. *Id.*
47. *See supra* note 17 and accompanying text.
48. 559 P.2d at 555.
49. *Id.* at 557 (quoting State v. Dunning, 506 P.2d 321, 322 (Wash. Ct. App. 1973)).
50. *Id.* at 558.
51. *Id.* at 559 (quoting Frontiero v. Richardson, 411 U.S. 677, 684 (1973)).
52. *See* George P. Fletcher, *The Individualization of Excusing Conditions*, 47 S. CAL. L. REV. 1269 (1974).

Chapter 21

1. George P. Fletcher, *Prolonging Life*, 42 U. WASH. L. REV. 999 (1967).
2. *See* R.A. Duff, *Twenty-Five Years of George P. Fletcher's* Rethinking Criminal Law, 39 TULSA L. REV. 829, 829 (2004) (Fletcher "deserves much of the credit for persuading Anglo-American criminal law theorists to think seriously about justifications and excuses as two quite different ways... [to] ward off conviction for a criminal offense").
3. Fletcher has generally argued that "justifications" imply that the actor's conduct is morally right and not merely permissible or tolerable. I disagree. *See* Joshua Dressler, *New Thoughts About the Concept of Justification in the Criminal Law: A Critique of Fletcher's Thinking and* Rethinking, 32 UCLA L. REV. 61 (1984).
4. *Id.*
5. I am willing to see the common-law imminency rule expanded to the extent seen in the Model Penal Code, which justifies deadly force when it is "immediately necessary... on the present occasion." MODEL PENAL CODE §3.04. This standard focuses on the immediacy of the need to use defensive force rather than on the temporal proximity of the attack itself. This test, however, would very likely still bar Judy Norman from killing her husband, John, while he sleeps.
6. Ironically, Fletcher's political theory approach buttresses my claim. In a Rawlsian "veil of ignorance"—in which any one of us might be the person who fears attack or might be the person who mistakenly is believed to be the attacker—we would likely devise a rule of law that neither requires an objective threat to life nor justifies a mere subjective belief, but which is based on reasonable (albeit perhaps inaccurate) belief. That is one reason why Fletcher's rejection of putative justifications strikes me as unacceptable.
7. Joshua Dressler, *Battered Women and Sleeping Abusers: Some Reflections*, 3 OHIO ST. J. CRIM. L. 457 (2006); *see also* Joshua Dressler, *Battered Women Who Kill Their Sleeping Tormenters: Reflections on Maintaining Respect for Human Life While Killing Moral Monsters, in* CRIMINAL LAW THEORY: DOCTRINES OF THE GENERAL PART (Stephen Shute & A.P. Simester eds., 2002).

Chapter 22

1. On the methodology of reflective equilibrium, see JOHN RAWLS, A THEORY OF JUSTICE 48–51 (1971). Rawls explains the process of reflective equilibrium as follows: "When a person is presented with an intuitively appealing account of [a problem]... he may well revise his judgments to conform to its principles.... He is especially likely to do this if he can find an explanation for the deviations which undermines his confidence in his original judgments...." *Id.* at 48.
2. For example, negligently causing personal injury and property damage is inefficient, but as a rule it is not subject to criminal punishment. *See* George Fletcher, *The Theory of Criminal Negligence: A Comparative Analysis*, 119 U. PA. L. REV. 401, 402 (1971).

3. *See* MODEL PENAL CODE § 223.4 (1962) (theft by extortion) ("A person is guilty of theft if he purposely obtains property of another by threatening to... (2) accuse anyone of a criminal offense....").

4. The Model Penal Code states:

It is an affirmative defense to prosecution based on paragraph[ ] (2)... that the property obtained by threat of accusation, exposure, lawsuit or other invocation of official action was honestly claimed as restitution or indemnification for harm done in the circumstances to which such accusation, exposure, lawsuit or other official action relates, or a compensation for property or lawful services.

Id. This provision seems to suggest that there would no criminal blackmail even in case 1, if the threat to complain to the local prosecutor was motivated by an "honest claim" for "restitution or indemnification."

5. *See id.* ("A person is guilty of theft if he purposely obtains property of another by threatening to... (3) expose any secret tending to subject any person to hatred, contempt or ridicule....").

6. MPC § 223.4 is limited to the acquisition of property. *See id.* Nonetheless, extortion of the lascivious-employer variety is typically considered a form of criminal blackmail. *See* 4 JOEL FEINBERG, THE MORAL LIMITS OF THE CRIMINAL LAW: HARMLESS WRONGDOING 239 (1988) (proposing the exploitation principle as a rationale for blackmail's criminalization).

7. Cases 9 and 10 are based on then-candidate David Dinkins's reportedly paying $9500 to a controversial group headed by Sonny Carson. Roger Ailes, the opposition's campaign manager, charged that the money was "a payoff for... keeping [Carson] quiet until after the election." Howard Kurtz, *With Ailes's Aid, Convict Becomes "Willie Horton" of N.Y. Campaign*, WASH. POST, Oct. 20, 1989, at A14. I use this example in the text without implying that Roger Ailes was right or that Mayor Dinkins did anything improper during his 1989 campaign.

8. *See* STRAFGESETZBUCH [StGB] §§ 240 Nötingung (Coercion), 253 Erpressung (Blackmail).

9. Scott Altman, for example, relies heavily on this criterion in developing his account of coercion and exploitation as the basic wrongs of blackmail. *See* Scott Altman, *A Patchwork Theory of Blackmail*, 141 U. PA. L. REV. 1639, 1640–45 (1993).

10. *See* FEINBERG, *supra* note 6, at 241.

11. One can imagine a variation of the *baseball* case (no. 6) in which setting the price at $6000 constitutes a threat. Suppose that *D* sells sports memorabilia and the normal asking price for the ball autographed by Babe Ruth is $600. If *V* has an expectation and a right to buy at $600, then *D*'s setting the price ten times higher constitutes a threat to withhold the ball unless *V* pays the exploitative price. It is as though *D* threatened to take the ball away from *V* if *V* did not pay an additional $5400.

12. *See* ROBERT NOZICK, ANARCHY, STATE, AND UTOPIA 84–87 (1974) (defining a productive activity as one that makes the purchaser better off than if the seller had never existed, and an unproductive activity, like blackmail, as one that leaves the purchaser no better off than she was before the sanction).

13. *Id.* at 85.

14. *See* James Lindgren, *Unraveling the Paradox of Blackmail*, 84 COLUM. L. REV. 670 (1984).

15. *Id.* at 702.

16. *Id.*

17. *Id.*

18. *See* Altman, *supra* note 9, at 1648.

19. *See id.*

20. *Id.* at n.34.

21. *See* CESARE B. BECCARIA, ON CRIMES AND PUNISHMENTS 17–19 (David Young trans., 1986) (1764).

22. *See* JEREMY BENTHAM, AN INTRODUCTION TO THE PRINCIPLES OF MORALS AND LEGISLATION 165–74 (J.H. Burns & H.L.A. Hart eds., 1970) (1789).

23. IMMANUEL KANT, THE METAPHYSICS OF MORALS 183 (Mary Gregor trans., 1991) (1797).
24. *Id.* at 141.
25. *Id.*
26. *See* GEORG W.F. HEGEL, THE PHILOSOPHY OF RIGHT § 99 (T.M. Knox trans., 1952) (1821).
27. *See infra* text accompanying notes 39–41.
28. *See supra* text accompanying note 24.
29. For example, one could benefit society by voluntarily submitting to medical experiments. *See id.* at 141.
30. *See infra* text accompanying note 33.
31. *See* KANT, *supra* note 23, at 141.
32. *See id.*
33. *See id.* at 51.
34. For the background to this analysis in Kant's legal and moral theory, see generally George Fletcher, *Law and Morality: A Kantian Perspective*, 87 COLUM. L. REV. 533 (1987).
35. *See* KANT, *supra* note 23, at 142.
36. *See id.*
37. *See id.* at 169.
38. *See id.*
39. *See* MICHEL FOUCAULT, DISCIPLINE AND PUNISH: THE BIRTH OF THE PRISON 3–16 (Alan Sheridan trans., Pantheon Books 1977) (1975).
40. KANT, *supra* note 23, at 142.
41. *See* DAVID DAUBE, STUDIES IN BIBLICAL LAW 122–24 (1947) (noting how, in ancient times, the victor in a battle drank the blood of the vanquished).
42. *See* Richard A. Serrano & Tracy Wilkinson, *All 4 Acquitted in King Beating: Violence Follows Verdicts; Guard Called Out*, L.A. TIMES, Apr. 30, 1992, at A1.
43. As a technical matter, of course, the jury in the Rodney King case only concluded that they had a reasonable doubt about whether the four indicted officers used excessive force. I am speaking here of the popular understanding of the verdict, not its technical meaning. For more on this point, see GEORGE P. FLETCHER, A CRIME OF SELF DEFENSE: BERNHARD GOETZ AND THE LAW ON TRIAL 199–217 (1988) (analyzing how many unfortunately interpreted the Goetz verdict in racial, rather than legal, terms).
44. *See supra* part IV.
45. Homicide seems to be a special case. We could treat the decedent's loved ones as secondary victims, but they do not suffer from the same fear of recurrence that characterizes other forms of violent crime.
46. *See* HEGEL, *supra* note 26, § 99.
47. *See* FLETCHER, *supra* note 43, at 199–200.
48. *See* Altman, *supra* note 9, at 1641–43.
49. *See id.* at 1644–45.
50. *See* Lindgren, *supra* note 14, at 70.
51. *See* Richard A. Posner, *Blackmail, Privacy, and Freedom of Contract*, 141 U. PA. L. REV. 1817, 1823–26 (1993).
52. *See* Douglas H. Ginsburg & Paul Shechtman, *Blackmail: An Economic Analysis of the Law*, 141 U. PA. L. REV. 1849, 1859–65 (1993).

Chapter 24

1. *See* ALAN WERTHEIMER, COERCION (1987).
2. *See* Richard Arneson, *Review of Joel Feinberg, Harmless Wrongdoing*, 100 ETHICS 368 (1990).

3. *See* H.L.A. Hart, *Prolegomenon to the Principles of Punishment, in* H.L.A. HART, PUNISHMENT AND RESPONSIBILITY: ESSAYS IN THE PHILOSOPHY OF LAW 1 (1968); John Rawls, *Justice as Fairness*, 67(2) PHILOSOPHICAL REVIEW 164 (April 1958).

Chapter 25

1. One of the first instances of this slogan occurred when Hasidic Jews began to protest the killing of Yankel Rosenbaum on August 19, 1991. *See* GEORGE P. FLETCHER, WITH JUSTICE FOR SOME: PROTECTING VICTIMS' RIGHTS IN CRIMINAL TRIALS 1 (1995).
2. *See No Justice No Peace*, at http://nojusticenopeace.blogspot.com/ (devoted specifically to issues of violence and injustice in Haiti).
3. See my exploration of the issue in FLETCHER, *supra* note 1, at 149–176.
4. For a systematic consideration of the differences between the position of the defendant in common law and civil law trials, see GEORGE P. FLETCHER & STEVE SHEPPARD, AMERICAN LAW IN A GLOBAL CONTEXT: THE BASICS 531 (2005).
5. This is the way the Bible speaks of the victim of the first homicide. *See* Genesis 4:10 (Cain and Abel).
6. Lord Campbell's Act, 1846, 9 & 10 VICT. c. (Eng.) (entitled, "An [a]ct for compensating the [f]amilies of [p]ersons killed by [a]ccidents"), soon served as the model for similar legislation in most of the American states as well as Canada. The first U.S. variation was passed in New York in 1847. *See generally* FRANCIS B. TIFFANY, DEATH BY WRONGFUL ACT: A TREATISE ON THE LAW PECULIAR TO ACTIONS FOR INJURIES RESULTING IN DEATH (1893).
7. Someone might refer to persons condemned and executed as the "victims of our system of criminal justice." It is clear that this usage would be metaphorical.
8. There is now a vast literature on the distinction. *See* Russell L. Christopher, *Symposium Foreword*, 39 TULSA L. REV. 737, 744, 751 (2004).
9. I do not address in this Article the profound phenomenon that in virtually all languages tied to Abrahamic religions (Judaism, Christianity, and Islam) the word for the victim of crime is the same as the victim of religious sacrifice. This topic is examined in detail in GEORGE P. FLETCHER, THE GRAMMAR OF CRIMINAL LAW: AMERICAN, EUROPEAN AND INTERNATIONAL: VOLUME ONE: FOUNDATIONS (2007).
10. I have argued this line in FLETCHER, *supra* note 1, at 247–48.
11. *See, e.g.,* Payne v. Tennessee, 501 U.S. 808, 828 (1991).
12. For a discussion of the case, see FLETCHER, *supra* note 1, at 141–48.
13. This is one point in which I part company with the conventional victims' rights movement, which apparently endorses victims' impact statements at sentencing. *See id.* at 247–48.
14. U.N. International Criminal Court, Rome Statute, art. 1, U.N. Doc. A/CONF.183/9* (1999).
15. U.N. International Criminal Court, Rome Statute, Preamble, U.N. Doc. A/CONF.183/9* (1999).
16. *See* Convention for the Protection of Human Rights and Fundamental Freedoms, Nov. 4, 1950.
17. X. & Y. v. The Netherlands, App. No. 8978/80 (Feb. 28, 1985), *available at* http://www. echr.coe.int/Eng/Judgments.htm.
18. *Id.*
19. *Id.* at para. 23.
20. Convention for the Protection of Human Rights and Fundamental Freedoms, *supra* note 16, at art. 3.
21. A. v. U.K., App. No. 25599/94 (Sept. 23, 1998), *available at* http://www.echr.coe.int/ Eng/Judgments.htm.

22. *Id.*
23. *Id.* at para. 22.
24. M.C. v. Bulg., App. No. 39272/98 (Dec. 4, 2003, final judgment Mar. 4, 2004), *available at* http://www.echr.coe.int/Eng/Judgments.htm.
25. *Id.*
26. *Id.* at para. 149.
27. *Id.* (concurring opinion).
28. DeShaney v. Winnebago County Dep't of Soc. Servs., 489 U.S. 189 (1989).
29. *See* George P. Fletcher & Jens D. Ohlin, *Reclaiming Fundamental Principles of Criminal Law in the Darfur Case*, 3 J. INT'L CRIM. JUST. 539 (2005).
30. U.N. International Criminal Court, Rome Statute, Preamble, U.N. Doc. A/CONF.183/9* (1999).
31. U.N. International Criminal Court, Rome Statute, art. 63, U.N. Doc. A/CONF.183/9* (1999).
32. U.N. International Criminal Court, Rome Statute, art. 67, U.N. Doc. A/CONF.183/9* (1999).
33. Rome Statute, Preamble, *supra* note 15.
34. *Id.*
35. *See* FLETCHER, *supra* note 1, at 6–7.
36. U.N. International Criminal Court, Rome Statute, art. 17(1)(a), U.N. Doc. A/CONF.183/9* (1999).
37. Rome Statute, Preamble, *supra* note 15.
38. The leading text on retributive punishment is IMMANUEL KANT, THE METAPHYSICS OF MORALS (Mary Gregor trans. 1996) (1797).
39. For a debate on whether the advocacy of victims' rights in fact endorses retributive thinking, see George P. Fletcher, *The Place of Victims in the Theory of Retribution*, 3 BUFF. CRIM. L. REV. 51 (1999), and Michael S. Moore, *Victims and Retribution: A Reply to Professor Fletcher*, 3 BUFF. CRIM. L. REV. 65 (1999).
40. NUNCA MÁS: THE REPORT OF THE ARGENTINE NATIONAL COMMISSION ON THE DISAPPEARED (1986).
41. The immediate legacy of the Argentine trials is the recognition of the systematic or widespread "enforced disappearance of persons" as a crime against humanity. *See* U.N. International Criminal Court, Rome Statute, Art. 7(1)(i), U.N. Doc. A/CONF.183/9* (1999).
42. *See generally* JAIME MALAMUD-GOTI, GAME WITHOUT END: STATE TERROR AND THE POLITICS OF JUSTICE (1996).

Chapter 26

1. DeShaney v. Winnebago County Dep't of Social Services, 489 U.S. 189 (1989).
2. *See* Stephen J. Schulhofer, *The Trouble with Trials; the Trouble with Us*, 105 YALE L. J. 825, 825–26 (1995).
3. *See* SANFORD H. KADISH, STEPHEN J. SCHULHOFER & CAROL S. STEIKER, CRIMINAL LAW AND ITS PROCESSES 1014, 1016–18 (8th ed., 2007); Carsten Stahn, Héctor Olásolo & Kate Gibson, *Participation of Victims in Pre-trial Proceedings of the ICC*, 4 J. INTL. CRIM. JUST. 219, 220 (2006). Domestic violence has to some degree been an area of distinctive developments; in most American jurisdictions, domestic violence victims now have the right to insist that prosecutors press charges. *See* KADISH, SCHULHOFER & STEIKER, *supra*, at 1015–16.
4. *See id.* at 1014.
5. 410 U.S. 614 (1973).
6. App. No. 8978/80 (Eur. Ct. Hum. Rts. 1985).
7. [2003] ECHR 39272/98 (Eur. Ct. Hum. Rts. 2003).

8. *See* STEPHEN J. SCHULHOFER, UNWANTED SEX (1998).
9. IMMANUEL KANT, THE PHILOSOPHY OF LAW (W. Hastie trans. 1887), *quoted in* KADISH, SCHULHOFER & STEIKER, *supra* note 3, at 80.

Chapter 27

1. The only candidate I have heard is United States v. Falcone, 311 U.S. 205 (1940). Some might like the opinion in the English case Regina v. Dudley & Stephens, 14 Q.B.D. 273 (1884), but I think that it is a disaster for failing to recognize the possibility of excusing the cannibalists.
2. See the symposium in the TULSA LAW REVIEW, *Twenty-Five Years of George P. Fletcher's Rethinking Criminal Law*, Volume 39, Number 4 (2004), and the two symposia on my penultimate book, THE GRAMMAR OF CRIMINAL LAW: AMERICAN, COMPARATIVE, AND INTERNATIONAL (Oxford University Press 2007). CARDOZO LAW REVIEW, Volume 28, Number 6 (2007) and 27 CRIMINAL JUSTICE ETHICS 3–103 (2008). These three symposia alone contain more than thirty articles by serious scholars of the theory of criminal law. For examples of common law criminal theorists engaging with their civil law counterparts, see the essays in JUSTIFICATION AND EXCUSE: COMPARATIVE PERSPECTIVES (Albin Eser & George P. Fletcher eds., 1987).
3. One self-conscious exception is HANS HEINRICH JESCHECK & THOMAS WEIGEND, LEHRBUCH DES STRAFRECHTS (5th ed. 1996), in which each chapter is followed by cursory references to foreign sources.
4. LUDWIG WITTGENSTEIN, TRACTATUS LOGICO-PHILOSOPHICUS (C.K. Ogden trans., 1922).
5. LUDWIG WITTGENSTEIN, PHILOSOPHICAL INVESTIGATIONS (G.E.M. Anscombe trans., 1953).
6. GEORGE P. FLETCHER, RETHINKING CRIMINAL LAW 388–90 (1978, 2000).
7. *Id.*
8. H.L.A. HART, PUNISHMENT AND RESPONSIBILITY: ESSAYS IN THE PHILOSOPHY OF LAW 4–5 (1968).
9. IMMANUEL KANT, THE METAPHYSICS OF MORALS 140 (Mary Gregor trans. 1991).
10. George P. Fletcher, *Proportionality and the Psychotic Aggressor: A Vignette in Comparative Criminal Theory*, 8 ISRAEL L. REV. 367 (1973).
11. *See, e.g.,* State v. Norman, 378 S.E.2d 8 (N.C. 1989); GEORGE P. FLETCHER, WITH JUSTICE FOR SOME: VICTIMS' RIGHTS IN CRIMINAL TRIALS (1995).
12. *See* People v. Decina, 138 N.E.2d 799 (1956).
13. State v. Wanrow, 559 P.2d 548 (Wash. 1977).
14. The logic of war is, however, different from the logic of self-defense in domestic law. In the preceding example, Egypt would have the right to use force against Israel even if Egypt was the aggressor. The reason is that the initial blow is governed by the principles of jus ad bellum. Once hostility begins, the focus shifts to jus in bello, which treats both sides and their rights equally. There is no comparable distinction in domestic self-defense. *See generally* GEORGE P. FLETCHER & JENS OHLIN, DEFENDING HUMANITY: WHEN FORCE IS JUSTIFIED AND WHY (2008) [hereinafter DEFENDING HUMANITY].
15. *See* Joshua Dressler, *New Thoughts About the Concept of Justification in the Criminal Law: A Critique of Fletcher's Thinking and Rethinking*, 32 UCLA L. REV. 61 (1984); Kent Greenawalt, *The Perplexing Borders of Justification and Excuse*, 84 COLUM. L. REV. 1897 (1984).
16. *See* U.N. Charter art. 31 (inherent right). The French version of the charter refers to a "natural right." On the critical difference between the French and English versions of the Charter, see FLETCHER & OHLIN, DEFENDING HUMANITY, *supra* note 14, at 63–85.

17. I know of one exception. My friend Francisco Munoz Conde has sided with the common-law view. *See* Francisco Munoz Conde, *"Rethinking" the Universal Structure of Criminal Law*, 39 TULSA L. REV. 941, 952–53 (2004). I think, however, that he misunderstands the idea of a reasonable mistake and equates it with a mistake that any sensible person might make. In these cases, where there is no way to find out the truth of the matter about, say, the timing of a hurricane, the defendant may treat the best available scientific view as equivalent to reality.

18. Rome Statute Article 21(3).

19. Paul H. Robinson, *A Theory of Justification: Societal Harm as a Prerequisite for Criminal Liability*, 23 UCLA L. REV. 266 (1975).

20. John Gardner, *Fletcher on Offences and Defences*, 39 TULSA L. REV. 817, 820 (2004).

21. HART, *supra* note 8, at 136–57. The Canadian Supreme Court also follows Hart. On the history of their shifting from Glanville Williams, who was skeptical about punishing negligence, to Hart, see my *The Meaning of Innocence*, 48 U. TORONTO L. REV. 157 (1998).

22. *See* my *The Individualization of Excusing Conditions* herein at Ch. 12; *see also* my *The Theory of Criminal Negligence: A Comparative Analysis*, 119 U. PA. L. REV. 401 (1971).

23. *See* Jerome Hall, *Negligent Behavior Should Be Excluded from Penal Liability*, 63 COLUM. L. REV. 632 (1963).

24. Rome Statute Art. 8(2)(b)(viii).

25. *E.g.*, Resolution of March 18, 1952, 2 BGHSt. 194.

BIBLIOGRAPHY OF FLETCHER'S ADDITIONAL ESSAYS ON CRIMINAL LAW

Major Articles

2006 *The Indefinable Concept of Terrorism*, JOURNAL OF INTERNATIONAL CRIMINAL JUSTICE 4 5(894) (November)

2005 *Parochial Versus Universal Criminal Law*, JOURNAL OF INTERNATIONAL CRIMINAL JUSTICE 3 1(20) (March)

2004 *Ambivalence About Treason*, 82 NORTH CAROLINA LAW REVIEW 1611

2004 *Punishment, Guilt, and Shame in Biblical Thought*, 18 NOTRE DAME JOURNAL OF LAW, ETHICS, AND PUBLIC POLICY 343

2002 *The Storrs Lectures: Liberals and Romantics at War: The Problem of Collective Guilt*, 111 YALE LAW JOURNAL 1499

2002 *What Common Lawyers Can Learn from European Theorists of Criminal Law*, 17 BAR-ILAN STUDIES IN LAW 91

2001 *Criminal Theory in the Twentieth Century*, 2 THEORETICAL INQUIRIES IN LAW 265

2000 *The Place of Victims in the Theory of Retribution*, 3 BUFFALO CRIMINAL LAW REVIEW 51

2000 *Strafrechtsdogmatik in ausländischer Sicht, in* DIE DEUTSCHE STRAFRECHTWISSENSCHAFT VOR JAHRTAUSENDWENDE. RÜCKBESINNUNG UND AUSBLICK (Munich: A. Eser, W. Hassemer, & B. Burkhardt eds.) [*guest lecture in Germany: German Criminal Theory from a Comparative Perspective*]

1999 *Disenfranchisement as Punishment: Reflections on the Racial Uses of Infamia*, 46 UCLA LAW REVIEW 1895

1999 *A Trial in Germany*, 18 CRIMINAL JUSTICE ETHICS 3

1998 *Dogmas of the Model Penal Code*, 2 BUFFALO CRIMINAL LAW REVIEW 3

1998 *The Fall and Rise of Criminal Theory*, 1 BUFFALO CRIMINAL LAW REVIEW 275

1998 *The Meaning of Innocence*, 48 UNIVERSITY OF TORONTO LAW JOURNAL 157

1998 *New Voices in Criminal Law Theory*, 1 BUFFALO CRIMINAL LAW REVIEW (Guest Editor for Issue No. 2)

1997 *The Case for Linguistic Self-Defense, in* THE MORALITY OF NATIONALISM 324 (Robert McKim & Jeff McMahon eds.)

1997 *Self-Defense of Battered Women*, [in Hebrew], 6 ISRAEL JOURNAL OF CRIMINAL JUSTICE 65

1996 *Complicity*, 30 ISRAEL LAW REVIEW 140

1996 *Domination in Wrongdoing*, 76 BOSTON UNIVERSITY LAW REVIEW 347

1996   *Punishment and Responsibility, in* A COMPANION TO PHILOSOPHY OF LAW AND LEGAL THEORY 514 (Dennis Patterson ed.)

1995   *Democracy in Jury Selection,* 3 JAHRBUCH FÜR RECHT UND ETHIK 135

1995   *Is Conspiracy Unique to the Common Law?* (Review of Elisabetta Grande, Accordo Criminoso E Conspiracy), 43 AMERICAN JOURNAL OF COMPARATIVE LAW 171

1995   *Political Correctness in Jury Selection,* 29 SUFFOLK LAW REVIEW 1

1994   *On the Moral Irrelevance of Bodily Movements,* 142 UNIVERSITY OF PENNSYLVANIA LAW REVIEW 1443

1993   *The Adventures of Eric Blair* (Review of Norval Morris, *The Brothel Boy and Other Parables of the Law*), 91 MICHIGAN LAW REVIEW 1422

1993   *Is It Better to Be Tried for a Crime in a Common Law or Civilian System? in* TRANSITION TO DEMOCRACY IN LATIN AMERICA: THE ROLE OF THE JUDICIARY (I. Stotzky ed.)

1993   *Punishment and Human Rights,* THE WORLD AND I, 413 (November)

1992   *After Los Angeles: Reforming the Jury System,* 2 RIGHTS & RESPONSIBILITIES 6

1991   *Self-Defense as a Justification for Punishment,* 12 CARDOZO LAW REVIEW 859

1991   *Talmudic Reflections on Self-Defense, in* CRIME, PUNISHMENT, AND DETERRENCE: AN AMERICAN JEWISH EXPLORATION 61 (Los Angeles: Wilstein Institute, D. Gordis ed.)

1990   *Defensive Force as an Act of Rescue,* 7(2) SOCIAL PHILOSOPHY AND POLICY 170, *and in* CRIME, CULPABILITY, & REMEDY (Basil Blackwell Ltd. (UK) ed., Ellen Frankel Paul, Fred D. Miller Jr., & Jeffrey Paul eds.)

1989   *Introduction from a Common Law Scholar's Point of View, in* JUSTIFICATION AND EXCUSE: COMPARATIVE PERSPECTIVES (Albin Eser & George P. Fletcher eds.).

1989   *Prezumptsia nevinovnosti* [Presumption of Innocence, in Russian], 1989(11) SOVETSKOE GOSURDARSTVO U PRAVO [Soviet State and Law] 132

1989   *Punishment and Self-Defense,* 8 LAW AND PHILOSOPHY 201

1987   *The Unmet Challenge of Criminal Theory,* 33 WAYNE LAW REVIEW 1439

1986   *Constructing a Theory of Impossible Attempts,* 4(1) CRIMINAL JUSTICE ETHICS 53, *reprinted in* CRIME, JUSTICE AND CODIFICATION (P. Fitzgerald ed.)

1985   *Criminal Theory as an International Discipline: Reflections on the 1984 Freiburg Workshop,* 4(1) CRIMINAL JUSTICE ETHICS 60

1985   *Paradoxes in Legal Thought,* 85 COLUMBIA LAW REVIEW 601

1985   *A Transaction Theory of Crime?* 85 COLUMBIA LAW REVIEW 921

1984   *The Ongoing Soviet Debate About the Presumption of Innocence,* 3(1) CRIMINAL JUSTICE ETHICS 69

1984   *Rights and Excuses,* 3(2) CRIMINAL JUSTICE ETHICS 17

1983   *Excuse: Theory and Justification: Theory,* articles appearing *in* ENCYCLOPEDIA OF CRIME AND JUSTICE (Sanford Kadish ed.)

1982   *The Case for Treason,* 41 MARYLAND LAW REVIEW 193

1981   *The Recidivist Premium,* 1(2) CRIMINAL JUSTICE ETHICS 54

1981   *Reflections on Felony Murder,* 12 SOUTHWESTERN UNIVERSITY LAW REVIEW 413

1981   *Two Modes of Legal Thought,* 90 YALE LAW JOURNAL 970

1980   *Manifest Criminality, Criminality, Criminal Intent and the Metamorphosis of Lloyd Weinreb,* 90 YALE LAW JOURNAL 319

1980   *Ordinary Language Philosophy und die Neubegründung der Strafrechtsdogmatik, in* ABWEICHENDES VERHALTEN IV (edited by Lüderssen & Sack) (written in German). [Ordinary Language Philosophy and a New Foundation for the Theory of Criminal Law]

1980   *The Right to Life,* 13 GEORGIA LAW REVIEW 1371 (1979) *and in* 63 THE MONIST 1

1979   *Should Intolerable Prison Conditions Generate a Justification or an Excuse for Escape?* 26 UCLA LAW REVIEW 1355

1978   *Criminal Omissions: Some Perspectives,* 24 AMERICAN JOURNAL OF COMPARATIVE LAW 203

1976   *The Metamorphosis of Larceny,* 89 HARVARD LAW REVIEW 269

1975   *Proportionality and the Psychotic Aggressor: A Vignette in Comparative Criminal Theory*, 8 ISRAEL LAW REVIEW 367 (1973); *reprinted in* STUDIES IN COMPARATIVE CRIMINAL LAW 123 (E. Wise & G. Mueller eds., 1975)

1975   *The Right Deed for the Wrong Reason: A Reply to Mr. Robinson*, 23 UCLA LAW REVIEW 293

1971   *The Theory of Criminal Negligence: A Comparative Study*, 119 UNIVERSITY OF PENNSYLVANIA LAW REVIEW 401

1968   *Two Kinds of Legal Rules: A Comparative Study of Burden-of-Persuasion Practices in Criminal Cases*, 77 YALE LAW JOURNAL 880

1968   *The Presumption of Innocence in the Soviet Union*, 15 UCLA LAW REVIEW 1203

1967   *Prolonging Life*, 42 UNIVERSITY OF WASHINGTON LAW REVIEW 999

1965   *The Concept of Punitive Legislation and the Sixth Amendment: A New Look at Kennedy v. Mendoza Martinez*, 32 UNIVERSITY OF CHICAGO LAW REVIEW 290

Op-Ed and Shorter Articles for the General Public

The End of Treason (or the Beginning), January 2, 2002, published online www.project-syndicate, and then in translation in several newspapers around the world

Let Victims Attend Bombing Trial and Testify, THE NEW YORK TIMES, July 23, 1996

Justice for All, Twice, THE NEW YORK TIMES, April 24, 1996

Prayer Wasn't Issue in Child's Wrongful Death, THE NEW YORK TIMES, February 4, 1996

Rodney, Yankel, and the Jury, JERUSALEM REPORT, March 25, 1993, p. 54

On Trial in Gorbachev's Courts, 36(8) NEW YORK REVIEW OF BOOKS 13 (1989)

Small Steps Toward Reform, NEWSDAY MAGAZINE, July 16, 1989

Blasting Houses on the West Bank: Israeli Soldiers as Police and Jurors, LOS ANGELES TIMES, January 29, 1989

Breaking the Law for Larger Social Interest, LOS ANGELES TIMES, May 22, 1988

A Guide to the Goetz Case, 34(7) NEW YORK REVIEW OF BOOKS 22 (1987)

INDEX